CU00796976

THE EUROPEAN UNION SERIES
General Editors: Neill Nugent, William E. Paterson

The European Union series provides an authoritative general introductory texts to definitive assessments and policy processes, and the role of member states.

Books in the series are written by leading scholars in their fields and reflect the most up-to-date research and debate. Particular attention is paid to accessibility and clear presentation for a wide audience of students, practitioners and interested general readers.

The series editors are **Neill Nugent**, Emeritus Professor of Politics at Manchester Metropolitan University, UK, and **William E. Paterson**, Honorary Professor in German and European Studies, University of Aston. Their co-editor until his death in July 1999, **Vincent Wright**, was a Fellow of Nuffield College, Oxford University.

Feedback on the series and book proposals are always welcome and should be sent to Stephen Wenham, Palgrave, 4 Crinan Street, London N1 9XW, or by e-mail to **s.wenham@palgrave.com**.

General textbooks

Published

Visit Palgrave's EU Resource area at www.palgrave.com/politics/eu/

The European Union and Global Capitalism

Origins, Development, Crisis

J. Magnus Ryner
and
Alan W. Cafruny

First published 2017 by
PALGRAVE

Palgrave in the UK is an imprint of Macmillan Publishers Limited,
registered in England, company number 785998, of 4 Crinan Street,
London, N1 9XW.

Palgrave® and Macmillan® are registered trademarks in the United States,
the United Kingdom, Europe and other countries.

ISBN 978-1-4039-9752-4 hardback

ISBN 978-1-4039-9753-1   ISBN 978-1-137-60891-8 (eBook)
DOI 10.1007/978-1-137-60891-8

A catalogue record for this book is available from the British Library.

A catalog record for this book is available from the Library of Congress.

Contents

Preface and Acknowledgements

This is a book that has had a long gestation period, and the idea of writing it has an even longer history.

The question of 'Europe' has always been important to the field of international political economy that we entered into as scholars in the 1980s and 1990s. It became even more salient with the 'relaunching' or what we have termed elsewhere the 'second project of integration' that was spearheaded by the Single European Act (SEA) of 1986. At the present time, of course, the question has become nothing less than paramount as the EU confronts a set of existential crises whose origins and implications are the subject of this book.

Critical political economy flourished during the 1960s and 1970s amid the political turbulence and intellectual ferment of what could be seen in retrospect as a transitional era. Indeed, such scholarship played a key role in the development of the field of international political economy. By the end of the 1980s, however, critical political economy was becoming marginalised. The result of this for the study of the EU was unfortunate. Critical scholars entered a field already occupied by an established discipline of European integration scholarship, with its own narrative and canon. Critical political economists recognised many of the assumptions, concepts, and empirical modes of argumentation in this discipline, but they found the debates surrounding them limiting. Liberal pluralism certainly remained a leading and respected perspective in international political economy, but its previous debates with other perspectives were never openly and sufficiently replicated with respect to European integration scholarship. Consequently, misrecognition and miscommunication arose at different levels of scholarly conduct. While the number of critical political economists working on the EU gradually increased, they remained marginalised. The problem became increasingly obvious after the 2008 financial crisis and then the crisis of the Eurozone, both of which clearly demonstrated the merits of critical scholarship. Not the least among problems, there was a lack of synthetic critical political economy statements that could be used for pedagogical purposes.

When Steven Kennedy responded enthusiastically to the idea of publishing such a book in the leading Palgrave European Union Series, this was therefore an opportunity that was too important to miss. We would like to record here our enormous gratitude to Steven as well as the general series editors for giving us this opportunity. Steven's unique combination of subject knowledge, incisive (and ruthless!) reviewer's eye, good humour, and patience, makes him a truly exceptional editor, and it has been a privilege to work with him. Patience has indeed been an important virtue given the length of time it has taken us to complete this book. While we did not manage to finish it before Steven's retirement, we nevertheless hope he believes that it has been worth the wait.

We would also like to record our appreciation of Otto Holman. Otto was originally going to be a co-author of this book, but his many other commitments came in the way. The book would no doubt have looked different had Otto been a co-author, and therefore he bears no responsibility for its shortcomings. Nevertheless, Otto played a very significant part in the original conception of the book, from which we have benefitted enormously, and we would therefore like to take this opportunity to thank him.

Apart from this, we have benefited from discussions and interactions with too many colleagues and friends over the years to be able to mention everyone by name. We therefore extend our thanks to all, no one mentioned and no one forgotten. The chief forums where such discussions have taken place have been the annual or semi-annual meetings of the Critical Political Economy Research Network of the European Sociological Association, the European International Studies Association (formerly the Standing Group on International Relations of the European Consortium of Political Research), the British International Studies Association (especially the International Political Economy Group), and the International Studies Association. Magnus Ryner would like to thank his former employer, Oxford Brookes University, and his current employer, King's College London, for granting him study leave to work on the manuscript. He would also like to thank the Department of Business and Politics of the Copenhagen Business School for hosting him during a crucial phase in the development of the argument. Alan Cafruny benefited greatly from a Fulbright scholarship that enabled him to spend an academic year teaching and writing in the Faculty of World Economy and International Affairs at the Higher School of Economics (Moscow). He also received generous support from the Henry Platt Bristol endowment at Hamilton College.

We thank the anonymous reviewers for excellent feedback and hope that we have taken at least some of the opportunities thus afforded to improve our argument. On the production side, we thank Palgrave for their efficiency and professionalism. On that score, we are grateful to Stephen Wenham and Tuur Driesser for their patience and sage advice. Many thanks to Tina Schivatcheva for her copyediting work at the end of the process.

Finally, no work of this sort can easily be completed without support from home. Despite their own very busy careers, Mari Assaid and Sushuma Chandrasekhar have provided that in abundance over the years, and we remain as always immensely grateful for that.

Acronyms

ABM Treaty	Anti-Ballistic Missile Treaty
ACP-States	African, Caribbean and Pacific States
ACUE	American Committee on United Europe
AGFA	Aktiengesellschaft für Anilinfabrikation
BRICS	Brazil, Russia, India, China, South Africa
CAP	Common Agricultural Policy
CDU	Christian Democratic Union
CETA	Comprehensive Economic Trade Agreement
CFSP	Common Foreign and Security Policy
COMECON	Council for Mutual Economic Assistance
CSDP	Common Security and Defence Policy
DCFTA	Deep and Comprehensive Free Trade Area
DG	(European Commission) Directorate General
EAGF	European Agriculture Guarantee Fund
EBRD	European Bank of Reconstruction and Development
EC	European Communities
ECB	European Central Bank
ECJ	European Court of Justice
ECLA	(United Nations') Economic Commission for Latin America
ECOFIN	Economic and Financial Affairs Council
ECSC	European Coal and Steel Community
ECU	European Currency Unit
EDA	European Defence Agency
EDC	European Defence Community
EDP	Excessive Deficit Procedure
EEA	European Economic Area
EEAS	European External Action Service
EEC	European Economic Community
EES	European Employment Strategy
EMCF	European Monetary Cooperation Fund
EMS	European Monetary System
EMU	Economic and Monetary Union
ENEL	Ente Nazionale per l'Energia Elettrica
ENP	European Neighbourhood Policy
EP	European Parliament
EPC	European Political Cooperation
EPU	European Payments Union
ERDF	European Regional Development Fund

ERM	Exchange Rate Mechanism
ERT	European Roundtable of Industrialists
ESF	European Social Fund
ESM	European Stability Mechanism
ETUC	European Trade Union Confederation
EU	European Union
EUBAM	European Union Border Assistance Mission
EUFOR	European Union Force
EURATOM	European Atomic Energy Community
EZ	Eurozone
FRG	Federal Republic of Germany
FSAP	Financial Services Action Plan
GATT	General Agreement on Tariffs and Trade
GDR	German Democratic Republic
GNI	Gross National Income
IAR	International Authority for the Ruhr
IBM	International Business Machines
IEA	International Energy Agency
IMF	International Monetary Fund
IOCs	International Oil companies
IPE	International Political Economy
ISAF	International Security Assistance Force
ISDS	Investor-State Dispute Settlement
JHA	Justice and Home Affairs
LTROs	Long Term Refinancing Operations
MENA	Middle East and North Africa
MERCOSUR	Mercado Común del Sur
MNCs	Multinational corporations
NATO	North Atlantic Treaty Organisation
NIEO	New International Economic Order
NTBs	Nontariff Barriers
OECD	Organisation for Economic Co-operation and Development
OEEC	Organisation of European Economic Cooperation
OMC	Open Method of Coordination
OMT	Outright Monetary Transactions
OPEC	Organization of the Petroleum Exporting Countries
PHARE	Poland and Hungary: Assistance for Restructuring the Economies
PIIGS	Portugal, Italy, Ireland, Greece, Spain
PPP	Purchase Power Parity
QMV	Qualified Majority Voting
R2P	Responsibility to Protect
SCO	Shanghai Cooperation Organization
SEA	Single European Act
SEM	Single European Market

SGP	Stability and Growth Pact
SPD	Social Democratic Party of Germany (Sozialdemokratische Partei Deutschlands)
SSM	Single Supervisory Mechanism
STABEX	Système de Stabilisation des Recettes d'Exportation
TEU	Treaty of the European Union
TFEU	Treaty on the Functioning of the European Union
TISA	Trade in Services Agreement
TPP	Trans-Pacific Partnership
TTIP	Transatlantic Trade and Investment Partnership
TUC	British Trades Union Congress
UN	United Nations
UNICE	Union of Industrial and Employers Organizations in Europe
VSTF	Very Short Term Financing
WEU	Western European Union
WTO	World Trade Organization

Introduction

For something that is often described as a faceless Brussels bureaucracy, the European Union (EU) surprises in its ability to provoke contradictory public emotions, ranging from euphoria and hubris to disappointment and revulsion. In Bournemouth in 1988, French élite civil servant and Commission President Jacques Delors (1988) earned an unlikely standing ovation from rank and file representatives of British workers by calling for a European 'social dimension'. The speech provoked immediate and equally emblematic rebukes from Prime Minister Margaret Thatcher (1988) and, more prosaically, the British tabloid *The Sun* ('Up Yours, Delors'). This pithy formulation captured a sentiment that subsequently grew in strength, and ultimately, with the 'Brexit' referendum of 23 June 2016, the British electorate voted to leave the EU.

The intensity and frequency of such emblematic instances have not waned in recent times. Quite the contrary. In Ukraine on 25 May 2014, the 'Euromaidan' uprising – the first time blood was spilt in the EU's name – culminated in Petro Poroshenko's presidential election victory. Intending to 'return Ukraine to its natural European state', Poroshenko then signed the Association Agreement previously rejected by the ousted President Viktor Yanukovich. Meanwhile, farther west on the same day, an entirely different verdict was rendered in the European parliamentary (EP) elections. After five years of crippling austerity, anti-EU parties made massive gains, prompting European Council President Herman van Rompuy to concede that 'the difference between the Parliament and those who take the real decisions is very clear to the citizens' (*Financial Times*, 2014). This 'clarity' of insight compelled the traditionally pro-EU Dutch electorate in March 2016 to indeed reject ratification of the very Association Agreement that President Poroshenko had signed.

In the case of Greek Prime Minister Alexis Tsipras, the contradictions are even contained in one and the same person. Having successfully campaigned in the 5 July 2015 referendum for a resounding rejection of what he described as a draconian EU bailout package, he proceeded to sign an even tougher one. Despite 61 per cent of the Greek electorate having agreed with his original advice, signing the tougher package was seen as the only way to satisfy the preference of most Greeks to retain the Euro as their currency.

Finally, three years after the EU was awarded a Nobel Peace Prize for 'the advancement of peace and reconciliation, democracy and human rights', Germany and Denmark's response to the 'refugee crisis' included authorizing the confiscation of the personal jewellery of North African

1

and Middle Eastern migrants and refugees. While Europe's own role is in question in generating this exodus, which in 2015 alone compelled 1.2 million people to cross the Mediterranean with more than 3500 perishing in the attempt, walls and fences were being erected across the European continent. This culminated in a sordid deal with Turkey's authoritarian president, Recep Tayyip Erdogan. The EU capped the number of refugees that it would accept, and Turkey agreed to prevent them from crossing the Aegean, even though both moves were widely condemned by human rights organizations and the UN High Commission for Refugees as a blatant violation of the Refugee Convention. In exchange, the EU agreed not only to pay Turkey three billion euros and establish visa-free entry for Turkish citizens but also to reopen negotiations over Turkish accession to the EU even as Erdogan proclaimed 'Democracy, freedom and the rule of law....For us, these words have absolutely no value any longer' (*Financial Times*, 2016).

If we are to make sense of these contradictory emotions and – more to the point – the developments that generate them, two central and related sets of questions need to be addressed. The first concerns the response of the EU to globalization. During the first three decades after World War II, a period labelled '*les trentes glorieuses*' in French and simply 'the Golden Age' in English, Western Europe's 'social market economies' managed to achieve rapid economic development along with increased social security and entitlements. Combining civil and political rights via social rights (Flora and Alber, 1981), there are strong reasons to suppose that this post-war project was central to making capitalism and democracy compatible. Since then, though, Europe's social model has been put under severe pressure from the development of a hyper-mobile, neoliberal, 'finance-led' capitalism, intensifying market competition and facilitating the entry of more than two billion largely unprotected workers into global labour markets. Is the EU part of the solution to the challenges posed by globalization, as Jacques Delors proclaimed in Bournemouth, or is it part of the problem, as an increasing portion of Europeans clearly believe? Can the achievements of the social market economies be defended, indeed perhaps further developed and democratized through a concerted EU-wide response to globalization? Or, does the EU actually expose the 'social market' more fully to the imperatives of neoliberal globalization as the aftermath of the Greek referendum seems to confirm? In Britain, a curious electoral alliance emerged between losers from globalization who blamed the EU for their situation and right-wing Conservatives who thought that too many of Delors' promises had been delivered. A second, but clearly related, set of questions concern the EU's global role. This is illustrated by the crisis in Ukraine and the Refugee Crisis, but they have deeper roots, which go back to the protests against the Vietnam War in 1968, the Anglo-French invasion of Egypt in the Suez Crisis in 1956, and perhaps even the 1916 Sykes-Picot Treaty. Can the EU project a 'soft' power such that it behaves differently from the great powers of the past? In that regard, is the EU serving as a counterweight to American – or Russian – power?

The salience of these questions is hardly diminished by the global financial crisis that started in 2007, which has exposed profound institutional weaknesses in the Economic and Monetary Union (EMU) and put paid to the dreams of the euro challenging the dollar as a global currency (e.g. Kupchan, 2002), as well as generated deep and as-of-yet unresolved distributive conflicts among regions (e.g. North vs South; East vs West), social classes (e.g. financial capitalists vs public sector workers) and states (e.g. Germany vs the so-called PIIGS – or Portugal, Ireland, Italy, Greece, and Spain – and perhaps even France). Opinions may diverge on what the answers to these questions might be. But there can be no doubt that the questions are vitally important. Should one be interested in investigating these questions through the study of mainstream European integration scholarship, though, one would find that it has so surprisingly little to say about them.

Drawing on what one might broadly call the critical-theoretical tradition in political economy (or, in short, critical political economy), this book offers a critique of what one might call *traditional* European integration scholarship. This scholarship, we believe, has succumbed to a sanitized, idealized, and teleological understanding of the EU. In doing so, it has overstated the rationality of the constitutive properties of European 'integration' and understated its limitations, contradictions, and crisis tendencies. Despite its sheer volume of research and the complex ecosystem of analytical models that it offers, traditional integration scholarship addresses a narrow set of questions within a limited and inadequate conceptual range (Rosamond, 2007; Ryner, 2012). While these questions are by no means unimportant, their restricted range has been one-sided. This book offers the first synthetic introduction to perspectives on the EU from a critical political economy viewpoint, which we believe are more adequate for answering the questions formulated above and consequently for understanding the present travails of the EU.

Argument and structure of the book

Historical narratives and theory

Chapters 1, 2, and 3 introduce key concepts and theories and show how they are used to interpret the origins and evolution of the EU. Readers should be aware that especially the first two chapters are the most technical in the book. They are foundational to what follows, but also likely to be more challenging to those unfamiliar with the source material. Readers should bear in mind that the analysis becomes more applied from the third chapter on, and they may in some cases even wish to skip forward to these chapters and then return to these early chapters once they have seen how the theory helps make sense of the practice. We start out in Chapter 1 by introducing some basic *narratives* of integration and relate these to traditional liberal and realist theories. Each of these narratives contributes to understanding the EU, animated as they are by the key concepts of the competing theories and their different claims about the drivers behind European integration. Awareness of how the narratives are thus informed by competing concepts serves a dual purpose. First, it introduces 'basic facts' about EU developments for the uninitiated. Second, it serves as an entry point to investigate the strengths and weaknesses of different theories about the EU, a subject that is pursued more fully in the second part of each of these chapters.

Basic codes, teleology, and blind spots

In Chapter 1 we argue that, despite their differences, liberal and realist theories of European integration share specific foundational assumptions or, as Thomas Kuhn (1962) put it in his seminal sociology of knowledge, 'basic codes' that define not the nature of scientific theories *but the terms of scientific debate among different theories*. It is here that we begin to develop our argument: these foundational assumptions set overly restrictive limits on the terms of debate and produce blind spots that prevent integration scholarship from adequately addressing the questions about the EU that we posed above. We argue that the sanitized, idealized, and teleological assumptions in no little measure are the result of the dominant role played by international trade theory and the conception of social relations as a 'density of interactions' derived from sociological systems theory. These lead to an understanding of 'integration' as a largely self-stabilizing benevolent process of increasing transactions that can be equated with the general good and rationality. The specific power relations and the attendant arbitrariness that inhere in the integration process itself and the interests that this process serves are not addressed. Integration is rather assumed to express the unfolding realization of potentials inherent in human nature (Cox, 1976: pp. 177–81). Arbitrariness and power are instead treated as exogenous to integration and are exclusively associated with nationalism and the old European interstate system, which integration is supposed to overcome and replace. The debate between liberals and realists is therefore all about whether one should be 'optimistic' or 'pessimistic' about integration, managing to do so by keeping nationalist 'dramatic-political actors' (Haas, 1968: p. xxiv) at bay. Traditional theories that subsequently have been developed, and accounted for in Chapter 3, merely occupy 'middle positions' in this one-dimensional register.

We develop the argument in Chapter 1, with special reference to the foundational works on European integration in the 1950s and 1960s. Our emphasis on foundational works is warranted because, as Kuhn (1962: p. 10) notes, such works 'implicitly define the legitimate problems and methods of a research field for succeeding generations'. In other words, it was here that the basic code was formulated, and parameters of subsequent theoretical developments set, in the debates between trade-theorists, neo-functionalists, and intergovernmentalists. We bring this point home in subsequent chapters, above all in Chapter 3, on the nature and significance of the single market project, where the focus is on the more recent supranationalist, liberal intergovernmentalist, multi-level governance, constructivist, and various neo-institutionalist theories. This theoretical critique is then revisited and concretized in different ways in each of the subsequent chapters of the book. Empirically, we point to how blind spots resulted in the dual misdiagnosis of what is called the 'empty chair crisis' and the run-up to Germany's Ostpolitik in the 1960s (Chapter 1); a massive over-estimation of the benefits of single market competition and the stability of the emergent Euro-polity (Chapters 3 and 4); the failure to identify the emergent properties of the Eurozone crisis (Chapter 4); unwarranted optimism about the 'social dimension' (Chapter 5); neglect of problems associated with the geographically uneven nature of European capitalist development (Chapter 6); and a fundamental misconception of 'normative power Europe' as post-imperialist (Chapters 7 and 8).

Instrumental purposes, traditional theory, and critical theory

Thomas Kuhn (1962) contended that the basic codes of scientific debate are successful in large measure for instrumental reasons. They provide answers to questions that are considered 'acute'. But who decides what might be an acute question? We will argue that the specific codes and assumptions of traditional integration scholarship, commensurate with a managerial ethos, successfully addressed a central question in the 1940s and the 1950s that concerned the American foreign policy community and the nascent Commission of the European Communities. That was the question of how one might reconstruct Western Europe according to the template of American modernization after the end of World War II, and hence consolidate an enduring organic alliance between the United States and the states of Western Europe (Milward and Sørensen, 1993; see also van der Pijl, 1996). The European Commission, especially, has continued to champion these terms of intellectual reference (Klinke, 2015).

The problem with traditional integration scholarship is neither that it is inadequate in offering answers to this question nor that this might be a worthy question to address. The problem is rather that it tends to represent this particular instrumental concern in universal terms. It is at least implicitly assumed by traditional integration scholarship that the questions it asks and the answers it provides constitute *the* way to study and research the EU. There is, however, an emerging body of work in the field of political economy that has begun to more directly address the questions posed here and therefore challenge traditional scholarship. Apart from introducing this emerging body of critical work, this book also contributes to it by formulating a distinct interpretation of Europe's contemporary predicament.

This task begins in Chapter 2. Building on an alternative narrative of socioeconomic phases, the historical roots of this way of understanding the EU are traced to Europe's indigenous mercantilist, post-Keynesian, and neo-Marxist traditions, as well as a number of foundational works written in the 1960s and 1970s that have informed subsequent research. One of these works was produced by French industrialist intellectual Jean-Jacques Servan-Schreiber, and two others were produced by two leading neo-Marxist thinkers, Ernest Mandel and Nicos Poulantzas. Concerned with further democratization of the social market and the transcendence of imperialism, which were engendered by the crisis of the late 1960s, these works assume a different standpoint from traditional theory that we share and that we argue provide the basis of an analytically more adequate response to our two sets of key questions.

Traditional theory develops in response to particular and instrumental purposes. Yet, in search of a scientific aura, it generalizes arbitrarily from these purposes through idealization and hence obscures the conditions of its own historical specificity (Horkheimer, 1937: p. 198). Herein lie the sources of its blind spots. Critical theory, by contrast, starts by interrogating the social conventions of what is considered 'reasonable' that serve as the foundations of traditional theory. It thereby negates the universal claims of traditional theory and reveals these as part of the reality that traditional theory seeks to rationalize. Hence, critical theory seeks a more historically grounded account of the social contexts that shape the character of agents and structures. That means rethinking the question of the EU with reference to the structures of European capitalism as embedded in global capitalism as these have developed at least since the 18th century.

An analysis that seeks to understand the EU in terms of its relation to capitalism as a mode of production requires a different approach to that of traditional European integration scholarship. Indeed, in some respects critical and traditional scholarship are mirror images of one another. Rather than assuming an inherent self-stabilizing rationality, which turns crises into surprising puzzles, the starting point for critical theory is the inherent crisis tendencies of capitalism. That means that the periods of stability and the limits of their demarcated conditions of existence between crisis periods are what need to be explained – in Horkheimer's (1937: p. 225) words, they are the 'regulatory effects' that ensured that 'bourgeois society did not immediately fall apart under the pressure of its own anarchic principle but managed to survive'. More concretely, an analysis based in critical theory requires an *epochal* reading of EU developments.

The Fordist and neoliberal finance-led epochs

In Chapter 2, we introduce the distinction between Fordist and neoliberal finance-led epochs or phases of post-war European integration. In the Fordist epoch of the 1950s and the 1960s, the common market and the EC, together with the transatlantic Bretton Woods System, were integral to the development of welfare states and a productive system based on the integration of mass production and mass consumption through social wage and were underwritten by productivity growth. As this system succumbed to its internal contradictions in the 1970s, the (re)launching of the single market and the EMU spearheaded the neoliberal restructuring of capitalism in the 1980s and the 1990s. The EU helped to institutionalize a finance-led epoch of capitalism characterized by the gradual return to a more classical form of labour market and in which the financial system came to integrate production and consumption by the extension of debt that was underwritten by increased asset values. The financial crisis is understood as the outcome of the internal contradictions of this phase of capitalism, as growth became dependent on expanding financial operations into ever riskier segments of the market, including, as it turned out, real estate in Eastern Europe and Southern Europe. The Eurozone crisis is an important aspect of this development. We consider this to be the central thread that connects the multiple dimensions of Europe's contemporary crisis. While all these dimensions cannot be reduced to money and finance (though many of them can), the capacity of the EU to deal with them is significantly conditioned by them.

Limits and possibilities in neo-institutionalism

Subsequent chapters explore these developments in concrete detail in particular areas. Together, they account for contemporary developments that have established what might be called the *asymmetrical regulation* of the EU (Holman, 2004). Chapter 3 addresses the project of the Single European Market (SEM), which originated in the mid 1980s and was formally established in 1992. Retrieving and further elaborating on arguments concerning the strengths and weaknesses of different approaches introduced in Chapters 1 and 2, Chapter 3 reviews competing theoretical interpretations of the nature, causes, and implications of the completion of the SEM. Liberal and realist scholarship served, not surprisingly, as the point of departure of theoretical debate. The chapter also discusses critically a number of more finely grained perspectives (such as multi-level governance and constructivism) that were developed in the wake of the launch of the single market. In particular, the chapter underlines the extent to which European integration scholarship has embraced the neo-institutionalist turn in social science. It is argued that the effects of neo-institutionalism on EU scholarship have been contradictory. On the one hand, they have facilitated a synthesis of mainstream approaches, which in some ways has further entrenched the normalization of mainstream research and the resultant lack of attention to the limitations of the foundational assumptions and basic codes as discussed in Chapter 1. Much integration scholarship remains as trapped as ever in these assumptions and codes. On the other hand, neo-institutionalism opens up fruitful avenues of development and synthesis with critical political economy. Therefore, it holds the promise to overcome the limitations of mainstream scholarship as well as neo-Marxism. Connecting with Chapter 2, we argue that French regulation theory and neo-Gramscian theory provide a promising avenue forward in that regard. The latter point is worth emphasizing because it means that when de-coupled from its teleological assumptions, traditional theoretical analysis can be recast and can contribute to a critical analysis. Hence, the main point is not primarily to point out how traditional analysis is wrong. Rather, it is to seek constructive ways for integrating such analysis in order to inform a critical-theoretical interpretation.

Asymmetrical regulation

Chapters 3, 4, and 5 elucidate in detail the asymmetrical regulation of the EU. Supranational regulation in the spheres of competition and corporate governance (Chapter 3) and finance and money (Chapter 4) is combined with intergovernmental regulation in the areas of fiscal policy (also discussed in Chapter 4) and social affairs (Chapter 5). Rather than seeing this mix of supranationalism and intergovernmentalism as a stage on the route to an end point of union or a pluralist system, as much integration scholarship does, we view this as a broadly coherent yet contradictory structural configuration that underpins a form and substance of neoliberal rule, which has been central in shaping European capitalism since the 1980s. We offer a critique of this configuration by pointing to the specific social interests that have advanced this development, most notably transnational business connected to transatlantic circuits of capital accumulation. Furthermore, in each chapter we expand on different dimensions of the limits and contradictions of finance-led growth and the attendant crisis-tendencies that have been generated. Contrary to promises, the single market has not resulted in increased growth and prosperity, but rather in austerity based on disciplinary fiscal and social policies that make it increasingly difficult for European states to mediate conflict and reproduce broader socio-political legitimacy. A basic problem in this regard has emerged after attempts to institutionally graft an Anglo-American economic model onto a continental European social setting. As such, Europe's asymmetrical regulation can be seen as a self-limiting accommodation to an American hegemony that became increasingly predatory in this period – an argument that we expand on in Chapter 7. We must emphasize that, due to lack of space, our account of asymmetrical regulation is not exhaustive. Notably, the book lacks chapters on environmental regulation and migration. However, we suggest that the idea of asymmetrical regulation could also fruitfully be applied to other policy fields than only the ones that we cover here.

Our account of asymmetrical regulation continues in Chapters 6 to 8. In Chapter 6 we pay specific attention to the geography of Europe and to how what one might call the 'deepening' problematic relates to the 'widening' problematic. The most recent enlargement of the EU into Central Europe and Eastern Europe and the signing of association and partnership agreements with countries of the former Soviet Union have not eliminated fault lines between the north-western, central, and southern parts of Europe. Indeed, these fault lines were acutely exposed in the wake of the financial and Eurozone crisis, which demonstrated that uneven development and core-periphery divides continue to characterize capitalist development in Europe and that these may ultimately be too difficult to manage within the framework of asymmetrical regulation.

American hegemony, German power, and capitalist geopolitics

The question of capitalist geopolitics, which was introduced in Chapter 6, is extended in Chapter 7. A central theme throughout the book is that EU developments must be seen in the context of broader transatlantic relations with the United States. This chapter addresses the question of transatlantic capitalist geopolitics directly and explicitly. It expands on the argument that, far from ushering in a 'European challenge', the second project of European integration was constructed within the framework of an increasingly predatory American hegemony, based on preponderance in the financial and security fields. The chapter concludes by posing the question, does the financial crisis signal the end of US hegemony and a shift of power towards emerging markets in the 'BRICS' (Brazil, Russia, India, China, and South Africa)? If so, what are the implications for a Europe that is also experiencing geopolitical turbulence and the growth of German economic power? These questions are further addressed in Chapter 8, which considers the EU's relationship to the Global South in the context of the conditions of transatlantic hegemony. The chapter also concludes that, the rise of China notwithstanding, it is still premature to write off America as a hegemonic power and that there is most certainly no end in sight to Europe's subordination to the United States.

Conclusions: an ordoliberal iron cage

The book ends with a recapitulation of the main arguments of the previous chapters and integrates them into a concluding statement. We draw on the concluding statement to address explicitly the question of the Eurozone crisis, which we believe is the central problem for contemporary European politics and whose resolution we believe is necessary – if not sufficient – for the long-term survival of the EU. We recapitulate our central argument that traditional theory not only failed to anticipate the crisis but has also had very little to say about Europe's inability to resolve it. We conclude by mobilizing our own critical political economy approach for an explicit engagement with the works of Europe's arguably most distinguished leading critical thinkers, Jürgen Habermas and Yanis Varoufakis. We explain why the 'Habermas' vision of an emancipatory post-national constellation of European 'constitutional patriotism' has been frustrated in favour of what we, drawing on Max Weber, call an ordoliberal iron cage – a deeply troubled situation from which it is impossible to escape, despite the disenchanted realization that the Celestial City will never be reached (Baehr, 2001). The conditions of this metaphorical iron cage explain why, in our view, the Eurozone endures despite its mounting social costs and conflicts.

Chapter 1

Traditional Narratives, Traditional Theory

Since its origins in the immediate post-World War II period, the EU has experienced changes of both an evolutionary and transformative nature. Scholars have proposed a variety of historical narratives to make sense of these changes and, as we shall see, these narratives in turn can be related to theories of integration. Precisely because of this, historical narratives – and the theories to which they are linked – are never straightforward, neutral, or objective. This is because it is never entirely clear which events and facts are more important than others. In the words of the distinguished historian and international relations scholar E.H. Carr, 'When we attempt to answer the question, what is history?, our answer, consciously or unconsciously, reflects our own position in time, and forms part of our answer to the broader question, what view we take of the society in which we live' (1961: p. 5). Hence, even though historians have a moral and intellectual obligation to seek the truth, their narratives cannot but reflect different judgements or their 'view' of society.

History can always be written from a variety of perspectives, and different perspectives illuminate different aspects or 'facts' of history. The history of the EU illustrates this point. The first part of this chapter introduces three narratives of the EU: widening, deepening, and interstate bargaining. By juxtaposing them, it is possible to highlight what each reveals and conceals. Moreover, because the narratives of deepening and interstate bargaining correspond to the traditional theoretical perspectives on European integration, we also begin to introduce in this part the mainstream theories of the EU. This is followed by a more sustained critical review of these theoretical perspectives, focusing on what from a Kuhnian perspective can be understood as foundational works that were produced to make sense of the European integration in the 1950s and 1960s. As we noted in the Introduction, the main purpose is not merely to record what theorists thought of European integration half a century ago. The more important objective is to highlight the enduring and contemporary significance of these works in establishing the foundational assumptions and basic codes of traditional integration theory. We will pursue this objective throughout the book, and we will expand on it especially in Chapter 3. It is by going back to

11

the foundational works that we can identify their enduring blind spots, because it is here that these codes are most transparently and explicitly formulated.

The widening perspective

The most straightforward story of the EU is what one might call the 'widening perspective'. This perspective chronicles the growth of the EU from six to 28 states. It starts with 'the original six': the founding members of France, the Federal Republic of Germany, the Netherlands, Belgium, Luxembourg, and Italy. These were the original signatories of the Treaty of Paris in 1950, constituting the European Coal and Steel Community (ECSC) and the Treaty of Rome in 1957, constituting the European Communities (the EC) (apart from the ECSC, including the European Economic Community (EEC) and Euratom). In 1973 the United Kingdom, Denmark, and the Republic of Ireland became member states. The so-called southern enlargements took place in the 1980s, with Greece becoming a member in 1981 and Spain and Portugal joining in 1986. The end of the Cold War in 1989 removed a massive obstacle to EU widening. The Western neutral states of Austria, Finland, and Sweden joined in 1995, paving the way for the major eastern enlargements of the 2000s. Poland, Hungary, the Czech Republic, Slovakia, Slovenia, Cyprus, Malta, as well as the former Soviet republics of Estonia, Latvia, and Lithuania, joined in 2004. Romania and Bulgaria joined the EU in 2007 and Croatia in 2013. In the future, the EU may well expand farther into former Yugoslavia, as well as perhaps into other former Soviet republics. Turkey's fraught accession negotiations with the EU have been long and remain unresolved. The Lisbon Treaty of 2009 also made it possible for countries to leave the EU, a prospect that has progressively become more palatable as Europe's multiple and deepening crises unfold, and indeed one that seems to have become a reality with the UK 'Brexit' referendum in 2016.

The widening perspective is certainly essential for any understanding of the EU. If nothing else, it points to the important issues of geopolitics and the boundaries of the EU. More generally, eastern enlargement looms large over the contemporary dynamics of the EU, and fault lines from the southern enlargement remain. In the 2000s, debate on EU policy was dominated by the question whether EU rules that were really designed for an organization consisting of a small number of similar states were adequate in a radically expanded EU, comprising different kinds of states with very different histories. Indeed, this question sparked a series of constitutional changes and referenda throughout the 2000s, which demonstrated growing nationalism and dissatisfaction with the EU. Furthermore, eastern enlargement rendered more important the question of 'flexible' integration, or 'variable geometry', where some members forge ahead with deeper (in formal-legal EU language 'enhanced') cooperation in some areas while others opt out (such as the UK opting out of the common currency, the euro, and some members not qualifying). As the Eurozone (EZ) crisis deepened throughout 2011, it became apparent that the Eurozone itself comprised a 'two-tier' system of 'Nordics' and 'PIIGs' (Portugal, Italy, Ireland, and Greece), with France located somewhere in the middle. The 'variable geometry' notion could be expanded to include states that are not formal members but that have association agreements with the EU – for instance, through the European Economic Area (EEA) and the European Neighbourhood Policy (ENP) – and therefore have certain rights and responsibilities in relation to EU treaties and agreements. As discussed in the Introduction, Ukraine's association agreement has been especially contentious and arguably marks a geopolitical turning point in the relationship between Russia and the West. In a similar vein to association agreements are the strategic partnerships that the EU has forged with many of the BRICS states, as we will discuss in Chapter 8.

The widening story has obvious limitations. For one, it is essentially descriptive: it tells us very little about what kind of organization the EU is. The widening perspective cannot tell us whether the EU is in any meaningful way different from, say, the United Nations (UN) or the World Trade Organization (WTO). For this reason, the widening narrative has not led to the construction of comprehensive theories of the EU, although its imperial dimensions have been recognized ever since the first enlargement (e.g. Galtung, 1973). In Chapter 6 we will also show how widening can be integrated into a critical political economy perspective. However, on its own, the widening perspective is not theoretical but simply descriptive. This is in sharp contrast to the 'deepening perspective', which is quintessentially all about constructing theories about the qualitative organizational developments of the EU.

The deepening perspective

The deepening perspective is closely associated with the liberal tradition in economics and political sociology and with its normative and analytical concerns for 'integration'. Liberalism gives rise to what are essentially *transactionist* theories. According to these theories, transactions between rational individual actors provide the basis for mutually advantageous aggregate social outcomes that provide the foundation of prosperity and peace. Deepening is understood in terms of the increased 'density' of such transactions, including trade and investment flows in the economic sphere, communication in the social sphere, and policy deliberation among international organizations in the political sphere.

Drawing at least implicitly on a metaphor from sociology, the density of such social relations is seen as the antidote against antisocial behaviour. The deepening perspective considers traditional Realpolitik as a sort of antisocial behaviour that twice brought European civilization to the brink of collapse during the world wars of the 20th century. Increased density goes hand in hand with mutually beneficial trade and with the substitution of traditional diplomacy and security policy with rational administration.

The deepening perspective tells a story of evolution from a low density of integration immediately at the end of World War II in 1945 to a high density today. In this story, there are two periods of rapid integration (1945–1965 and 1979–1999) punctuated by two periods of stagnation (1966–1979 and 2000–present). The story typically begins with what Winston Churchill (1946) called 'the tragedy of Europe'. This was the tragedy of a sophisticated European culture and civilization having been torn asunder by nationalism, interstate rivalry and wars. This tragedy is related to economic protectionism, as manifested in the collapse of the gold standard, the beggar-thy-neighbour devaluations, and increased tariffs in the late 1920s and 1930s that formed part of the build-up to World War II (1939–1945). From its 'low point' in 1945, integration progressively picked up, first under American leadership with the 1947 Marshall Plan. The Marshall Plan provided massive financial aid for the reconstruction and development of a war-torn Western Europe. Marshall Aid was given on the condition that Western European states would commit themselves to free trade, restore currency convertibility, and reduce tariffs. These conditions were achieved progressively through the formation and work of the Council of Europe, the Organisation of European Economic Cooperation (OEEC), and the European Payments Union (EPU). These early US-led initiatives are generally seen as part of a broader Atlanticist grand design that also included the formation of the North Atlantic Treaty Organization (NATO) in the security field, the so-called Bretton Woods system in the monetary field, and the General Agreement on Tariffs and Trade (GATT) in the area of trade (Deudney and Ikenberry, 1999). Bretton Woods instituted a system of multilateral fixed exchange rates anchored in the US dollar, aimed at preventing unilateral competitive devaluations that had contributed to the world economic collapse in the 1930s. This exchange rate system was supported by the International Monetary Fund (IMF), mediating the transfer of payments between surplus and deficit countries.

The establishment of multilateral institutions under US tutelage served as the foundation for European regional integration. But the process of integration that is unique for Europe really took off in the 1950s with the formation of the ECSC and the EC through the Treaty of Paris and the Treaty of Rome. This is the story of 'the original six' members, guided by the intellectual leadership of visionaries such as Jean Monnet,

Robert Schuman, Paul-Henri Spaak, Altierio Spinelli, and Walter Hall-stein, concluding that US-led intergovernmental cooperation would not be sufficient to ensure peace and prosperity on the European continent. The Treaty of Rome was a free trade agreement. Through the common market, member states eliminated tariffs internal to the community by 1968. However, according to the deepening perspective, the Treaty of Paris and the Treaty of Rome entailed much more, most notably a common organization of governance with significant supranational elements and the explicit aim to work towards an 'ever closer union'. The common market was not only a customs union with a common external tariff. It also entailed common policies, harmonization, and common policy coordination, notably in the steel sector (through the ECSC) and the Common Agricultural Policy (CAP), the latter financed through a common community budget.

Even more important for the deepening account than increased cooperative density in these substantive policy areas was the supranational organizational framework of the EC. It went well beyond the run-of-the-mill secretariats of other international organizations. The right to propose legislation – Directives and Regulations – would not reside with member states in the Council of Ministers but rather with the supranational administrative branch, the European Commission (in the ECSC, the High Authority). At the apex of the Commission was a president who headed the College of Commissioners, and all the people at the College directed their own specialist administrative branch of the Directorate General (DG). While they were nominated and appointed by the member states, they were not representatives. They were rather oath-bound to represent the EC and its treaties as a whole. Furthermore, it would not be left to the member states to interpret their obligations under the treaties. Rather, the European Court of Justice (ECJ) was to form the juridical branch, with the Commission having a role as chief prosecutor. In this arrangement, to be sure, the member states still held the legislative authority as it was the Council of Ministers that decided whether directives and regulations would be adopted. But also there, according to the deepening narrative, state sovereignty was in the process of attenuation as qualified majority voting (QMV) loomed on the horizon. In addition, while originally having only consultative rights, the treaties had also formed the European Parliament (in the ECSC, the Common Assembly), which as of 1979 was directly elected and could claim to be a general representative assembly of the European electorate as a whole. A complex system of committees of experts ('comitology') links the deliberation of these bodies, as national administrators and administrators employed in Brussels meet to deliberate in the preparation of policy.

A more nuanced version of the deepening perspective also draws attention to a set of precedent-setting rulings in 1963 and 1964 in the

ECJ, which established important supranational principles through precedent-making case-law decisions. The precedent-setting cases were, first, van Gend en Loos vs the Dutch Tax Authorities, which established that EU directives and regulations had direct effect and did not need to be ratified by national legislation in order to take effect. Second, Costa vs ENEL (Ente Nazionale per l'Energia Elettrica) established that EU law had supremacy over national law within its remits. These rulings made European law an entity with a distinct quality that is different from international law, which does not have direct effect or supremacy over the sovereignty of national law.

If the deepening narrative has its heroes, it also has its villains, who are seen as having put spanners in the works of integration. The arch villain in this story must surely be French President Charles de Gaulle, who is seen as having stopped the first integration phase through the empty chair crisis of 1965. The empty chair crisis is called this because France – at that time by far the most powerful member state – removed its ministers from the Council, hence effectively grinding deliberations to a halt. The immediate cause was the Commission's quest to obtain independent budgetary resources by allocating the proceeds of the Customs Union directly to itself, rather than to the member states. To prevent a vote on the matter, France withdrew its representatives, and the issue was not resolved until the Luxembourg Compromise of 1966. To call this a 'compromise' is something of a misnomer because the French government obtained exactly what it sought: a national veto on matters deemed (by the states themselves) to be of 'vital national interest'.

In the 'deepening' narrative, many view the empty chair crisis and the subsequent Luxembourg Compromise as having punctuated integration and started the first phase of stagnation, lasting until the 'relaunch' of integration in the 1980s. The relaunch started with the Fontainbleau Summit of 1984, the Milan Summit of 1985, and the Luxembourg Intergovernmental Conference (IGC) in 1986, resulting in the Single European Act (SEA). Ratified in 1987, the SEA served as a mechanism to institute a single European market by 31 December 1992 (what was called the 'Europe 1992' project). Apart from addressing non-tariff barriers (NTBs) through the principle of 'mutual recognition' (a principle that articulated the 1979 Cassis de Dijon case – another milestone ECJ ruling), by embracing QMV in areas pertaining to the implementation of the SEM, these events and actions effectively repealed the Luxembourg Compromise. This phase of integration, which is described in further detail especially in Chapters 3 and 4, reached its culmination at the 1991 Treaty of Maastricht (or Treaty of European Union – TEU), which formally instituted the European Union and committed the European Union to an Economic and Monetary Union (EMU) and the single currency, which was achieved in 1999 with the launching of the euro. As part of this process, the Stability and Growth Pact (SGP) was forged in 1997, setting out common macroeconomic norms. When mutual recognition was seen as insufficient for liberalization of labour and financial markets, the so-called Lisbon Agenda was pursued through 'soft law', the non-binding instrument of the Open Method of Coordination (OMC). Its success was uneven, and from then on the EU entered another period of stagnation. This is indicated by the 2000 Treaty of Nice, which was generally seen as inadequate as a framework for post-eastern EU enlargement, and the failure to ratify a new Constitutional Treaty, which instead resulted in an incremental amendment of the Treaty of Nice in the form of the Treaty of Lisbon (not to be confused with the Lisbon Agenda). The divisions that characterized the EU during the Iraq War and the financial crisis can be seen as further indications of stagnation, at least from a 'deepening' perspective. However, some argue that the new fiscal regime set in place to deal with the Eurozone crisis (the so-called New Economic Governance, consisting of the Fiscal Compact, Six Pack, and the Two Pack – see Chapter 4), whereby 'hard' supranational law applies in the field of fiscal policy discipline and structural reform, is indicative of further deepening (Niemann and Ioannou, 2015).

The interstate bargain perspective

Whereas the 'deepening' narrative assumes that a higher density of integration serves gradually to transcend the national state, a third perspective, that of *intergovernmentalism*, challenges this central assumption. Intergovernmentalism understands the history of the EU in terms of a series of interstate bargains that reflect the regional and global balance of power and attendant state interests. Despite – or indeed because of – modest steps towards supranational governance, nation states remain the most important actors and determinants of European politics. From this perspective, the balance of power among states and their interests remains the most important determinants of world and European politics. As such, this narrative is closely associated with the realist theoretical tradition.

The narrative of interstate bargains agrees that the events highlighted by the deepening narrative are among the essential ones in the formation of the EU. But this narrative understands their causes and significance differently. The interstate bargaining perspective explains the nascent movement towards integration in the 1940s in terms of the US grand design and strategy in an emergent Western alliance during the Cold War. In this alliance, the balance of power was so concentrated in favour of the United States that it exercised unchallenged leadership, or hegemony, and hence was able to suppress any remaining interstate rivalry among its junior partners (e.g. Gilpin, 1987). Indeed, hegemonic stability theory sees such a concentration of power as benevolent since it temporarily suspended the 'European tragedy' of interstate rivalry and created the political conditions for a liberal order. The Treaty of Paris and the Treaty of Rome are thus expressions of a distinctly European dimension of this US-led Western alliance. The most important aspect of this is Franco-German reconciliation (e.g. McCarthy, 1998). Placing German strategic industries under supranational control through the ECSC secured French acquiescence to German reindustrialization and rearmament, which in turn was seen by the United States as essential to the Cold War effort. Failure to ratify the European Defence Community (EDC) in 1954 affirmed the central role of nation states, as did the Luxembourg Compromise, at a time when the Commission was losing a sense of its place in the order of things.

For the intergovernmentalists, the central dynamic was not an inexorable process of 'deepening' but rather the Franco-German relationship conditioned by US hegemony. The Élysée Treaty of 1963 consolidated reconciliation among these rivals and formal antagonists. Henceforth, Franco-German cooperation would be the 'motor' of European integration. No important decisions would take place without Franco-German leadership, and no initiatives would pass without Franco-German agreement. The forward movement of the EU has been driven by these partnerships: Adenauer and de Gaulle, Schmidt and Giscard d'Estaing, Kohl and Mitterrand, Schröder and Chirac, and Merkel and Sarkozy (indeed, Merkozy). The health of the Franco-German axis has been questioned many times in history, and this has certainly been the case during the current Hollande presidency. Be that as it may, given the growing weakness of the French economy Germany is increasingly emerging as *the* central power on the European continent.

The liberal tradition and European integration

If the widening perspective has not generally lent itself to theoretical exposition, the same is not the case for the perspectives of deepening and interstate bargaining. As noted above, each of these narratives corresponds to prominent theoretical perspectives. With special reference to foundational works in the Kuhnian sense, the remainder of this chapter deals with the theoretical underpinnings of deepening and interstate bargaining, which constitute the traditional or 'mainstream' approaches towards the analysis of European integration. The former is underpinned by liberalism and has been extraordinarily influential in both normative and policy terms, serving to rally support for the institutions of the EU and the concept of supranational governance. More than any other theoretical tradition, liberalism is based on a strict delineation of the social science disciplines. Hence, in the case of liberalism, we need to make a distinction between the 'economics' and the 'political science' of European integration. Neoclassical economic theory rationalizes moral doctrines of liberalism and transforms these into axiomatic propositions about a supposedly essential economic human nature (Myrdal, 1954). It was highly influential during the formative years of the EEC, and it prescribes the elimination of tariffs, quotas, and other restrictions on trans-border economic activity. In the words of Walter Hallstein, the first president of the European Commission, 'Since Adam Smith, the arguments in favour of free trade have been refined and qualified by a very considerable body of economic doctrine, but the core of the theory still stands' (Hallstein, 1962: p. 31, cited in Holland, 1980: p. 4). If liberal trade theory served as an important guide to community policy during the 1950s and 1960s, it is even more important to the contemporary EU as a result of the enthusiastic – if not messianic – embrace of market competition.

Typically invoking a passage in Adam Smith's *The Wealth of Nations* (1776) – which argues that trade, truck, exchange, and barter are the essential human propensities – economic liberalism subscribes to a universal and trans-historical view of human nature. The free market – in which commodity exchange and price formation operate freely and ensure that quantities supplied and demanded are matched in a 'clearing' process – constitutes the realm of inner rationality and freedom. The free market ensures prosperity by spontaneously optimizing the division of labour; it ensures social harmony by generating absolute gains where everyone is better off than they otherwise would have been (what is called 'Pareto-optimality'). Extended into the sphere of international relations, free trade provides the basis for political harmony as the web of mutually beneficial interdependencies makes conflict and war increasingly costly. David Ricardo's concept of comparative advantage (1817), albeit sanitized from his class theory concerning the relationship between industrialists and landowners, is the key concept of the international dimension of neoclassical economic liberalism. The market mechanism, then, holds the key to the unfolding of what Immanuel Kant (1795) called the 'eternal logos' that would result in 'perpetual peace.' From a sociological perspective, Joseph Schumpeter argued that imperialist wars were caused by residual pre-capitalist sentiments that would eventually die out: 'the more completely capitalist the structure and attitude of the nation, the more pacifist ... the idea that glorifies the ideology of fighting ... withers in the office among all the columns of figures .... [T]he industrial and commercial bourgeoisie is fundamentally pacifist' (1942: p. 333). Thus the liberal tradition considers capitalism and geopolitics as distinct and even mutually exclusive.

Ricardo was not the first to make a sustained case for free trade. However, he was the first to specify in a systematic and theoretically rigorous way the argument that it was beneficial to trade in commodities not only where a country (due, for example, to natural endowments) had an absolute advantage of production but also where it had a 'comparative' advantage. Ricardo asserted that not only would it be possible to consume commodities that were not producible at home (such as bananas in Western Europe). Free trade would also result in the most efficient use of the factors of production (land, labour, and capital) in each country as it would compel states to specialize in what they were comparatively productive, hence maximizing utility and minimizing opportunity costs at an international level. Ricardo's optimal state of affairs would arise spontaneously from free price setting at an international level, a process that required the elimination of tariffs and other restrictions to trade.

Jacob Viner's *The Customs Union Issue* (1950) is the foundational application of the concept of comparative advantage to European integration. Viner's verdict was ambiguous. While he endorsed the trade creation that results from European integration, he simultaneously warned against trade diversion. The problem of trade diversion arises from the fact that the ECSC, the EEC, and later the Single European Market (SEM) were preferential trade agreements exclusive to its members and embedded in a customs union. This preferential treatment was likely to result in imports being diverted from comparatively advantageous producers located outside the preferential trade area and customs union. Such trade diversion would also require that production factors within the common (or single) market now had to be used to make up for the loss of import opportunities, hence preventing their comparatively most advantageous use. The result of this would be higher production costs and price levels and lower production quantities (for a contemporary application, see Bhagwati, 2008). Hence, according to Viner, the merits of European integration depended on whether the trade-creating effects were larger than the trade-diverting ones. This in turn depended on the size of the tariff levied on those outside the customs union and the size of the efficiency gap between the producers outside and inside the common (single) market.

Bela Belassa (1961) offered a more unambiguously positive assessment of European integration than did Viner. According to Balassa, Viner's traditional Ricardian approach was too *static* and did not fully account for the beneficial *dynamic* effects of European integration. For example, European integration encourages the realization of economies of scale: The most efficient producers within the common market would be able to treat the entire area as their home market. This would enable the most efficient and modern producers of complex industrial products (such as cars), which had to invest in expensive fixed overheads (such as large-scale factories, and research and development) irrespective of how much of the final product is produced, to increase their quantity of production in a way that was – in contrast to the United States – not possible within only a nation state of the relatively modest West European size. This increase in the number of units produced within their factories would result in a significant reduction of cost per unit, which could be passed on to consumers in the form of lower unit prices. Further dynamic economies may derive from organizational learning (economies of experience) as well as the discipline of competition as such ('x-efficiency'): as units within the common (single) market adapt to the new conditions, costs may be reduced at any given quantity of output. These dynamic economies are associated with technological developments (for an overview, see Healy, 1995: pp. 33–40). In addition, Balassa pointed to the advantages that the common market actually or potentially had in promoting common or coordinated policies to address regional and social inequality, and macroeconomic problems such as asymmetries in the balance of payments between surplus and deficit countries.

Balassa's endorsement of the common market and customs union, which assigned importance to an activist macroeconomic policy, reflected the particular Keynesian turn that economics took after the 1930s that was informed by the 'neoclassical synthesis' (Hicks, 1937), which dominated that discipline during the first three decades after World War II. Keynesianism in this variant remained true to liberalism in the sense that it accepted that the collapse of free trade in the 1930s had been a problem for economic prosperity and had contributed to the outbreak of World War II. However, Keynesianism was also critical of a one-sided concern of economic policy with price stability (as expressed, for instance, in the 19th-century gold standard) and the assumption that unemployment problems are merely about obstacles to flexible wage formation on the labour market. Keynes and others famously argued that the Great Depression demonstrated that the free market itself was not adequate as an institutional framework for modern industrial societies. State intervention was required to solve problems such as mass unemployment and attendant social and political fallouts in order to save liberalism from itself (e.g. Keynes, 1936). In contrast to more radical 'post-Keynesians' that have strong affinities with Marxism (see Chapter 2), neoclassical Keynesians do not view these problems as fundamental. Rather, they have to do with market imperfections in modern industrial society, such as 'sticky' price adjustments to market signals in oligopolistic markets and imperfect information, which are perfectly manageable through prudent macroeconomic policies. Hence, liberal intellectuals sought to develop a modified 'political liberalism' suitable to such management. This is further discussed in the next section.

Balassa's work has been highly influential on, indeed foundational to, the economic analysis of European integration (Ryner, 2012: pp. 656–9). His influence can above all be seen in what are called the 'High Level' Expert Reports that have been concomitant with each major policy initiative to develop the single market: the Cecchini Report for the single market (European Commission, 1988); the Padoa-Schioppa

Report for the EMU (Padoa-Schioppa et al., 1987); and the Sapir
Report for the Lisbon Agenda (Sapir et al., 2003; see also Sapir, 2007).
Crucially, it is the trade-theoretical aspects of Balassa's work on static
and dynamic economies that these reports, as well as the vast body of
economic studies that have been driven by the research agenda on the
economics of European integration, have followed. His macroeconomic
policy prescriptions have, on the other hand, been severely discounted,
because in the neoliberal zeitgeist in which these reports were written,
a more sanguine attitude developed with regard to market imperfections. In Chapters 4 and 9, we will see how this played a crucial role
in ignoring warnings about the design of the monetary union that even
a conventional Keynesian analysis might have issued – and indeed in a
few exceptional cases did in fact issue – with reference to what is called
the 'optimum currency area problem'.

Modified political liberalism

The problems of classical liberalism and the solutions offered by modified political liberalism were brilliantly summarized by Theodore Lowi
(1979: pp. 15–21). Lowi asserted that while the self-regulating market
may very well tend towards a general equilibrium, it does not spontaneously generate solutions to its own externalities, of which mass unemployment was only one, albeit important, aspect. Therefore, general
economic equilibrium is unlikely to produce social stability. In particular, market forces generate alienation and conflict alongside growth: this
is the Janus-faced nature of social differentiation caused by the market,
a phenomenon observed not only by Marx but also by the founding
fathers of sociology, Weber and Durkheim, and indeed by Adam Smith
himself. The multiplication of dependencies generated by the division of
labour, the proliferation of social roles, and the attendant fragmentation
of the perceptions of the external world reduce the chances for people
to develop 'whole' personalities. Consequently, they become alienated
from themselves (anomie) and from other people (their family, friends,
and community). Work becomes a mere compulsion as opposed to a
meaningful life-activity. From this process of social estrangement, it is
not a major leap to anticipate an increasing propensity towards social
conflict, especially in the contexts of diminishing economic returns,
spatial differentiation, and scarcity of urban land (expressed in increasing property prices and rent), generated by the concentration of populations, the inability to realize economics of scale, and the incapacity to
deal with increased life risks that industrial society unleashes even as
it undermines levels of informal subsistence-economy support that are
held to be characteristic of traditional agrarian society.

    Modified political liberalism proposes to resolve these problems.
In contrast to classical liberalism, and with Keynesian economic

management as an excellent case in point, modified political liberalism endorses deliberate public intervention designed to restore social equilibrium at optimal levels. It thereby embraces the reformist ethos of sociological and systems theories. Such intervention is to be based on the distinctly liberal principle of rationality, which is defined as 'conscious and systematic application of legitimate controls on conduct' (ibid.: p. 21) in production, technology, exchange, commerce, social control, and administration. At the outset, however, questions are raised about whether such a 'visible hand' in the service of the state can be maintained within the strict confines of administration understood as 'formal adaptation of means to ends' without degenerating into the arbitrary exercise of power. For liberals, the solution lies in the very social differentiation that had been a problem during the crisis of laissez faire. A rationally organized society generates a complex set of checks and balances that prevent any particular ideologies, special interests, and protracted social conflicts from dominating public life. The multiplication of roles and complex differentiation give rise to a multidimensional, open, and decentralized civil society of interest groups with roughly equal and countervailing access to the administrative state, which is checked by a complex and pluralistic political system.

Neo-functionalism

It was precisely this type of modified liberalism, as 'interest group' (ibid.), 'corporate' (van der Pijl, 1984), or 'embedded' liberalism (Ruggie, 1982), and its pluralist conception of modernization, that informed the extraordinarily popular and influential neo-functionalist theorizing during the early years of European integration (Rosamond, 1999: pp. 50–73; Hansen & Williams, 1999). The prior functionalist variant implied a deterministic and more or less automatic process. Observing the development of international organizations, such as the Universal Postal Union and the International Civil Aviation Organization, functionalists believed that an administrative-rational transformation process on the international level was immanent in the commercial relationships that developed as a result of industrialization. In order to realize Pareto-optimal outcomes in international trade among complex industrial societies, common infrastructural problems must be managed through international organizations based on universal administrative standards and expertise rather than on narrow national interests, resulting in increased density of social relations at the international level. As individuals in industrial society came to enjoy the benefits of these international utilities, their loyalties would progressively shift towards a nascent transnational, pluralist system, thereby displacing the old power politics of interstate relations (Mitrany, 1943).

Yet, World War II made it abundantly clear that, notwithstanding the utility of the Universal Postal Union, the transfer or loyalties from nation states to such organizations was by no means automatic (to put it mildly). Neo-functionalists acknowledged that the transition from power politics to pluralist political community was not straightforward but rather dependent on a set of contingent political conditions interacting with infrastructural developments that improve communications and financial transactions (Deutsch et al., 1957; Haas, 1964: pp. 47–50). It was against this backdrop that Ernst Haas (1968) conducted his seminal analysis of European integration and the key concept of spillover. The theory is not, perhaps, as deterministic as subsequent caricatures and simplifications might suggest (Rosamond, 2005). Integration required a degree of agency: it was likely to evolve only if, as in the case of the High Authority of the ECSC under Jean Monnet's leadership, central agents and organizations were 'willing to follow policies giving rise to expectations and demands for more – or fewer – federal measures' (ibid.: p. xxxiii). Haas was, moreover, open to the possibility that integrative transition in strategic sectors such as coal and steel was dependent on

> an overwhelmingly powerful external economic centre. Economic integration might have been much slower if the government had been compelled to come to grips with investment, currency and trade questions – decisions which were in effect spared them by the direct and indirect role of United States economic policy'. (ibid.: p. xxxvi)

Nevertheless, for Haas, once these conditions had been satisfied, it would be impossible to confine supranational rational management within the specific sectors of coal and steel. Given the central importance of these industries, there would be strong pressures for the formation of a more general common market ('functional spillover').

Even more important for Haas, and following the basic premise of modified liberalism, was the impossibility of maintaining a common market without the establishment of a corresponding regulatory framework. The absence of such a framework would generate negative expectations among a broad range of interest groups, with regard to social welfare provision and adequate regulatory standards. Under conditions of pluralism, the outcome of short-term 'muddling through' would be a convergence of interests and demand for further supranational integration. Haas thus anticipated that the need for regulation would provide the political basis for the High Authorities and European Commission to push the integration agenda forward. Modified political liberalism and pluralism would then engender political spillover (ibid.: pp. 301, 283–6, 299–301).

The early experience of integration seemed to support neo-functionalism. The Treaty of Rome (1957) was widely viewed as a product of spillover from coal and steel to the manufacturing economy in general. The common market was also achieved within the time frame set out in the Treaty of Rome. However, the empty chair crisis brought this seemingly evolutionary process to a halt. Indeed, the crisis was so abrupt and far-reaching that it was hard not to interpret it as a falsification of neo-functionalism as a general theory. As we shall see, especially in Chapter 3 but also throughout the book, neo-functionalism has never recovered its dominant position. Its share of followers has diminished, and it is generally conceived as somewhat anachronistic. A crucial problem with (neo-)functionalism is that it raises the question, functional for what (Runciman, 1963: pp. 112–13)? That is not so much of a problem when one works within timescales where social purpose is constant, but it becomes a problem when social purpose is in flux, as it arguably was in Europe after 1966.

At the same time, the demise of neo-functionalism can be exaggerated. Although the approach does not help to explain the end of deepening phases, it has continued to attract scholars to make sense of dynamics within such phases (e.g. Tranholm-Mikkelsen, 1991). As we shall see throughout the book, there is no shortage of neo-functionalist accounts of various contemporary issue-area dynamics. Especially in circles close to the European Commission, neo-functionalist explanations are prized. For instance, applying the formula Balassa + Haas, the Padoa-Schioppa Report used the concept of spillover to argue that the European monetary union is an inexorable consequence of the single market (Padoa-Schioppa et al., 1987; see also Padoa-Schioppa, 1994). Notably though, the neo-functionalists have moved the goalposts for what counts as functional spillover. Haas painted the rather attractive vision that the common market would compel the development of a common European social policy. By contrast, the neo-functionalists of the 1980s and 1990s slimmed down the definition of successful spillover to include the transition to a federal monetary policy. This is notwithstanding that the MacDougall Report in its time had argued that a common fiscal policy would be a functional necessity for monetary union (see Chapter 6).

As will be elaborated upon in Chapter 3, the more profound enduring legacy of neo-functionalism on traditional theory resides in the way in which its critics have chosen to disagree with neo-functionalism – that is, in ways that accept the terms of debate and foundational assumptions as defined by neo-functionalism (Ryner, 2012: pp. 651–5, 659). As Schmitter (2003: p. 45) points out in an extensive review of literature since the 1970s, alleged 'novelties' are not theoretical novelties at all and 'neofunctionalist thinking ... [is] very much alive, even if it [is] usually being re-branded as a different animal'. Indeed, as we will see in the next section, the acceptance of neo-functionalist terms of the debate originated with the foundational intergovernmentalist critique of neo-functionalism by Stanley Hoffman: he couched the argument as a 'pessimistic' response to neo-functionalist 'optimism'.

Realism and the intergovernmentalist critique

If the empty chair crisis was devastating to the dominant position of neo-functionalism as a general theory, it initially seemed to vindicate the realist perspective on international relations. Realists subscribe to a Hobbesian conception of politics under which liberal notions of Pareto-optimal transactions, peace, rule of law, cooperation, and international organization presuppose a monopoly of violence concentrated in sovereign state power. Hobbes (1651) famously and metaphorically sought to capture this benevolent conception of sovereign state power in a biblical reference to the sea-giant Leviathan. Absent this power, politics degenerates into a violent 'state of nature' characterized by a war of 'all against all' as individual passions and wills collide. The liberal commonwealth is based on the monopoly of violence institutionalized in the nation state. But world politics is anarchical: a state of nature based on mutual fear. Peace and order can be secured only when states mutually deter the potential aggression of one another – that is, when power relations 'cancel each other out' in a balance of interstate power (e.g. Waltz, 1986).

Seen from this perspective, the integration that neo-functionalists attributed to qualitative transformation of the international system was for realists made possible by a series of interstate bargains that express a particular European and global balance of power at a particular period in time, of which hegemony was a particular sort. The post-World War II balance depended, according to this interpretation, on three factors (Calleo, 2001). First, the bipolar balance of power between the superpowers of the United States and the Soviet Union. The common threat from the east provided the impetus for Western European states – former great powers now reduced to second-rank – to forge alliances under American tutelage. Second, within the Western sphere, the United States possessed in effect a Leviathan-like monopoly of violence. The fact that the United States had become hegemonic enabled the Western alliance to become something more than simply a tactical alliance. It allowed the United States to shape Western Europe according to its own interests and, in important respects, its own image. Hence, with the Marshall Plan, the United States reshaped the Western European economies and societies along liberal lines, greatly expanding US export markets and material capabilities. These liberal economic relations also contributed to prosperity in Western Europe, thereby serving to stabilize Western European societies and rendering them less vulnerable to communist and Soviet influence.

Realists also pointed to a third dimension of the post-World War II balance of power. This was the transformation of the Franco-West German relationship from rivalry and suspicion to reconciliation and bilateral partnership. Franco-German harmony was crucial for the EEC. The importance of this dimension is illustrated by the tensions between the United States and France – the most important ally of the United States on the European continent – over West German rearmament in 1949. The United States considered this crucial to the Cold War effort. Having been invaded by Germany three times in 70 years, France strongly opposed it. From the realist perspective, the ECSC should be understood precisely against this backdrop. By placing Germany's strategic coal and steel sectors in a supranational authority over which France exercised considerable influence, French and US interests could be reconciled. For West Germany, the ECSC represented a means to return progressively to the international stage as a respected and recognized partner.

Coming broadly from such a 'pessimistic' and sceptical perspective, Stanley Hoffman (1966) referred to the empty chair crisis to challenge neo-functionalist optimism. Hoffman did not deny that the processes that neo-functionalists had identified were real. For him, they were a tendency towards pluralist state-formation on a broader Western European scale that had been made possible by the weakening of nationalism and the decline of the European colonial empires after World War II. However, with regret, he also argued that there were counter-tendencies at work that the neo-functionalists had ignored; they were growing stronger and not weaker. They accounted for the abrupt halt to the integration process which the empty chair crisis signified. Europe was returning to its old antisocial history of state nationalism.

Hoffman identified a number of causes of growing fragmentation. First, the nuclear stalemate of 'mutual assured destruction' between the superpowers paradoxically created a wider scope for nationalist politics in Europe. While the Soviet threat had initially compelled Western European states to cooperate under the aegis of American leadership, the stalemate generated some room for manoeuvring. Indeed, it served in some ways to reinforce the current configuration of states since invasions and annexations were no longer – at least with respect to Europe – on the agenda. In addition, the stalemate created doubts in some quarters about the American commitment to use its 'second strike capability' to protect Europe. In this context, did it make sense for the larger European states, such as France, to create its own independent nuclear capability, which would to some extent restore its status as a great power? This is where Hoffman identified his second chief source of fragmentation, which he called the 'national situation' (ibid.: pp. 866–9). From this, Hoffman derived the 'national interest' which was co-determined by the global balance of power as viewed from the particularities of individual nation states as well as from the dynamics within states themselves. By the late 1960s, Hoffman believed that the convergence of state interests that underpinned the Treaty of Paris and the Treaty of Rome had been seriously weakened. Especially in France the changing power dynamic had engendered a more nationalistic stance. Even West Germany was increasingly prone to articulate policies in terms of the national interest, a tendency that was clearly evident after Ludwig Erhard, who was much less prone to seeking compromises with France, succeeded Konrad Adenauer as Chancellor. As a result, Hoffman predicted increasing tensions between France and West Germany, especially in their respective relations with the USSR, with France seeking somewhat closer cooperation and Germany maintaining a hard-line Cold War stance. Hoffman considered Germany to be the closer ally of the United States, but in the context of a nuclear stalemate, he did not rule out the eventual reassertion of a German Sonderweg and nationalism.

Drawing on systems-theoretical concept of 'density' of social relations, neo-functionalist accounts of integration tended to overlook the role played by underlying power relations. Perhaps the chief merit of Hoffman's analysis – and of the realists more generally – was to resurrect state power as a central factor in European integration. As we will see in Chapter 3, his understanding of 'the national situation' as co-determined by the global balance of power and domestic politics has subsequently been analytically refined by the highly influential liberal intergovernmentalist theory that was developed by Andrew Moravscik. Furthermore, Hoffman's article has proven foundational in the sense that it defines a theoretical polar opposite to the neo-functionalism of Haas, in which more recent theories locate themselves as middle positions. However, if the empirical evidence of the 1960s casts doubt on key premises of neo-functionalism, then it was also awkward for realists. Soon after the publication of Hoffman's seminal 1966 article, the Erhard Administration in West Germany collapsed. It was replaced by a grand coalition between Christian and Social Democrats that was in turn quickly succeeded by a Social Democrat/Liberal government. Under Willy Brandt, the new government ushered in the policy of detente with the Eastern Bloc, known as Ostpolitik. In addition, Franco-German relations remained sufficiently warm to maintain and eventually refine their bilateral 'engine' of EC cooperation under a new generation of political leaders, not least in the monetary field. This anomaly would seem to suggest that there was something about the developments within European states and societies themselves that Hoffman's analysis missed, despite his reference to 'the national situation'.

The analyses of both Hoffman and the neo-functionalists ultimately reflected the limited horizons of a distinctively American problematic, albeit in very different ways. While Hoffman begrudgingly accepted de Gaulle's use of the term 'double hegemony' (which he considered insulting) to refer to the dominance of the superpowers in their respective spheres, he departed from dispassionate realist analysis in asserting that this hegemony was exercised as a matter of necessity and not self-interest. By contrast, the assertion of French 'nationalism' was characterized in negative terms. Both Haas and Hoffman lamented the prospects of a resurrection of European state power (ibid.: pp. 862–3, 872–901; Haas, 1968: pp. xv–xxii). This is quite in line with Milward and Sørensen's (1993) assertion, as noted in the Introduction, of an unacknowledged subjective and instrumental dimension in the way in which social scientific theories were 'imported' from American academia to make sense of the EC and the EU. The a priori anti-statism of these theories ultimately produced a limited and one-sided analysis. As we shall see in Chapter 3, this common denominator becomes ever more apparent when we consider theoretical developments geared towards explaining the single market that stake out middle positions between Haas and Hoffman.

Conclusion

This chapter has reviewed traditional theories of European integration, with particular reference to foundational works and attendant narratives. We rehearsed the famous anomaly that the empty chair crisis posed for neo-functionalism but also the anomaly that Willy Brandt's Ostpolitik and the enduring Franco-German axis posed for Hoffman's realist account. The common denominator is a failure to reflect on the significance of social context and its possible transformation – in the case of realist approaches that such changes are relevant and in the neo-functionalist case that they may result in changes of the social purpose for which systems should be functional. In other words, these anomalies point to the limitations of a teleological account of European developments on the basis of supposed universal axioms about 'human nature', whether this reading is 'optimistic' or 'pessimistic'. Social contexts are not captured by liberal foundational myths but must be historicized. In subsequent chapters, we will see how integration theory continues to be trapped by this teleological conception of the foundational works and how this continues to generate blind spots.

Chapter 2

Critical Political Economy

Chapter 1 concluded that it is important to be sensitive to social and historical context when analysing the EU. This is not only about taking history seriously. More profoundly, it concerns the philosophical issue of what should be the starting point of analysis. According to critical theory, that cannot be some ahistorical myth about universal human 'nature', whether Smithian or Hobbesian. Social developments are not adequately captured when we see history merely in 'whiggish' terms as movement (or lack thereof) towards the ideals of this or that myth. What human nature is and might become is itself inseparable from history and particular social relations as emerged through real historical developments. As Marx put it, 'man [*sic*] is not an abstract being squatted outside the world. Man [*sic*] is the human world, the state, society' (1843: p. 131).

This does not mean that social development should be reduced to a random flow of events. History is not just, as Arnold Toynbee (1957) put it, one damned thing happening after another. It is because human practices (ranging from mundane everyday routines, to business cycles, to foreign policy in hegemonic epochs) tend to repeat themselves within certain time frames that social science is possible in the first place. It is these repetitions that create the regularities that social science can study. But repetitions and regularities do not last forever. Sometimes big events become decisive in social developments – think of the significance of the storming of the Bastille or the Winter Palace as turning points in the French Revolution and Russian Revolution, respectively. Or, for that matter, think of the momentous events in Eastern Europe in 1989, such as the decision of the East German authorities to open the Berlin Wall. Those events are momentous exactly because they engender new historical structures that lend new regularity to the 'flow' of history, whether they act as conjunctural rhythms or – if they are truly revolutionary – they define for centuries what Fernand Braudel (1958) called the *longue durée*.

From such a starting point, critical political economy develops an altogether different narrative from those presented previously. Here European 'integration' is not primarily about ever denser, deeper webs of transaction realizing underlying pluralist-liberal human essence. Nor is the history of the EU merely a series of iterative interactions between states pursuing inherent interests. Rather, it must be understood with reference to socioeconomic epochs (phases) of transnational capitalism.

This chapter introduces the key concepts of a critical political economy of the EU that are applied, expanded on, and further elaborated in the remainder of the book. We start by discussing concepts about the most general mechanisms and properties that obtain in all epochs of capitalism and show how these relate to the EU. We discuss The Red Queen Syndrome and attendant contradictions and crisis tendencies whereby capitalism needs to run in order to stand still. Drawing on 'open Marxism', we will then identify essential functions that capitalist governance must serve and depoliticized forms that it must take. We will suggest that EU competition and monetary governance is crucial in that regard. Having discussed matters at a general level of abstraction, we will then begin to disaggregate capitalism and consider the EU, capitalist competition, and rivalry. Here we will review the response of foundational neo-Marxist works by Mandel and Poulantzas to the social mercantilist writings of Servan-Shreiber. We point to the centrality of cross-national mergers and capitalist 'amalgamation' as drivers of European integration. We also show how the transatlantic economy has been structured to subordinate the EU to American society. Finally, we will describe and explain the qualitative transformations involved in the transition from Fordism to finance-led accumulation and the repression of distinct European alternatives, engaging with the work of French regulation theory and the neo-Gramscian 'Amsterdam School'.

An alternative narrative: socioeconomic epochs

When the EU is understood as part of broader transnational capitalist developments, events must be considered that happened much earlier than the Treaty of Rome. One must start with the great bourgeois revolutions of 1789 and above all 1688. The English Glorious Revolution established and consolidated a constitutional state, private property rights, and competitive markets. Importantly, abolishing peasant land rights on the commons helped form a 'free' labour market, wherein workers had nothing to sell but labour power. From then on the profit motive became essential for the survival of economic units, and capitalist dynamics were established as a global driving force (Gill, 2003; p. 54; Corrigan & Sayer, 1985). This transformed international political relations because this historically unprecedented dynamism greatly enhanced the material capabilities of states within which capitalist social relations were established. From the Seven Years' War (1754–63) on, contender states had to accept social transformations to keep up with leading capitalist states (e.g. van der Pijl, 1998; Teschke, 2003).

The foundation of capitalism as the dominant mode of production thus established what, following Alice in Wonderland, might be called The Red Queen Syndrome, whereby one must run in order to stand still:

> Think of the Red Queen's garden as capitalism. The relentless search for markets and profits brings about faster and faster changes in production and space, industry and commerce, occupation and locale, with profound effects on the organization of classes and states. It is through this ferocious process of extension and change that capitalism preserves itself, remains capitalism, stays the same system. This paradox can only be grasped if we understand that [in Marx's and Engels' words] the 'bourgeoisie cannot exist without revolutionizing the instruments of production, and thereby the relations of production, and with them the whole relations of society'. (Panitch, 1994: p. 60)

Once capitalism has been established as the dominant mode of production, it has an in-built expansionary impulse. But herein lies a contradiction: this expansion tends to outgrow the social relations – technological, social, political, and cultural conditions – that supported capitalism within a certain epoch in the first place. The history of capitalism, including European integration, is about managing the crisis tendencies that emerge from this contradiction – that is, Horkheimer's 'regulatory effects' as discussed in the Introduction. This is a history about how certain sociopolitical arrangements enabled capitalism to work in a certain way in a certain period, but how the confrontation between the expansionary impulse and the limitations of these arrangements already contained the seeds of the next crisis. It is also the history about how transitions from one epoch to another were managed without capitalism collapsing and how this provided conditions for expanding the horizons of economic, social, and political development. It bears repeating what was already stated in the Introduction: The starting point in critical political economy is the mirror image to that of traditional theory. Rather than attributing inherently rational properties to the EU and being surprised by crises, the problem is about understanding how capitalism as a contradictory, neurotic, and crisis-prone – but simultaneously highly productive and innovative – system can, within limits, establish order in the first place.

In this narrative, the formation of the EU was closely related to socioeconomic innovations in the United States. The liberal view is not entirely off the mark, then, when it suggests that the US superintended novel developments in Europe after World War II through the Marshall Plan, Bretton Woods, the EPU, the OEEC, and NATO. But this did not put Europe on the course of universal rationality. Rather, EU developments are bound up with a historically unique and specifically American capacity of 'integrating all the other capitalist powers into an effective system of coordination under its aegis' (Panitch & Gindin, 2012: p. 8). In previous capitalist phases, the expansionary impulse of capitalism came up against the limits of nation states and interstate relations, wherein bourgeois class power and capitalist social relations were established and organized (Rosenberg, 1994). After the depression of the 1870s, the territorial scale of nation states was insufficient to profitably invest the stock of accumulated capital. This made the major capitalist powers 'scramble' for colonies and other dependencies. Territorial expansion, in turn, led to imperialist rivalries and conflicts that put the entire system in peril in the two world wars. Post-World War II American hegemony addressed this fundamental contradiction. Thus, Churchill's 'tragedy of Europe' speech was internally related to capitalist dynamics that American hegemony addressed after 1945 (Harvey, 2003: pp. 26–61).

Clearly, there are affinities with the realist narrative here, as our detailed review of transatlantic relations in Chapter 7 makes clear. 'Coordination under American aegis' after 1945 would not have been possible without overwhelming American capabilities. All the events that the realist narrative invokes, including the Franco-German bargain, are accepted as central (Anderson, 2009: pp. 4–15). But from the standpoint of critical political economy, realism profoundly underestimates the importance of qualitative changes in social relations that American hegemony and the formation of the EC presupposed and cultivated. Neither liberalism nor realism develops a satisfactory understanding of the co-determination of capitalism and geopolitics.

Realism discounts the salience of these social transformations while liberalism idealizes them. Critical political economy, by contrast, follows Marx beyond the sphere of transactions and exchange – the 'very Eden of the innate rights of man [*sic*] ... the exclusive realm of Freedom, Equality, Property and Bentham' (Marx, 1867: p. 280) – to consider power relations that inhere in production. The production process is essential for unlocking the secrets to US hegemony and the formation of the EC. No doubt this process was, as Lowi's modified pluralist liberalism suggested, about 'modernization'. But modernization has a particular substantive kernel, to which liberalism not so much offers an analysis as legitimating scientific aura. No doubt, as realism suggests, the process was also about America's superior capabilities. But to refer to capabilities is not to go deep enough into understanding their social foundations, which reside in the novel ways in which productive life and the relationship between classes were being reorganized first in the US in the 1930s and 1940s and then in Western Europe after World War II (Maier, 1991; Rupert, 1995). This novel way of organizing the production has, following Gramsci (1971: pp. 279–318), been called 'Fordism'.

Named after famous automobile magnate Henry Ford, Fordism refers to socioeconomic organization that became paradigmatic in the transatlantic area during the post-war period but whose elements were already present 15 years before World War II. Fordism was based on heavy mechanical engineering, product-specific conveyor-belt technology and 'scientific management', which rationalized intensity of the labour effort. This facilitated economies of scale and continuous productivity growth. Fordism produced core consumer products (automobiles, whiteware) and allied industry input products on a mass scale.

Fordism unleashed new and unprecedented productive capabilities but was vulnerable to market fluctuations, as was amply demonstrated by the Great Depression. Beyond the production process then, the regulation and organization of market competition was another major Fordist social innovation. Fordist mass production required high, stable, and expanding consumer demand. To facilitate this, public institutions and the state intervened to stabilize markets, ensuring the integration of mass consumption with mass production ex ante. This idea was contained in Henry Ford's '5 dollar wage' (whereby Ford paid salaries above marginal productivity so that his workers could eventually buy his cars). But it was only with Keynesian macroeconomic policy and welfare-state expansion – Roosevelt's New Deal, so-called – that mass consumption was adequately integrated with mass production (Bowles, Gordon, & Weisskopf, 1983: pp. 77–8). Hence, market power encountered definite limits in Fordism.

Fordism was actively promoted in Europe after World War II, with similar economic and social reforms: the Beveridge Reforms in Britain; the 'social state' enshrined in West Germany's Basic Law; and the social security programme formulated by the French National Council of Resistance. The 1947 Italian Constitution, proclaiming a 'democratic republic founded on labour', made similar commitments. These developments ended the overtly antagonistic class conflict of the interwar period, described by one eminent Marxist sociologist as a European 'civil war' (Therborn, 1995: pp. 21–4). They reflected not only economic imperatives but also the strength of socialism, communism, and organized labour.

Innovations in international organization were integral to transatlantic Fordism (van der Pijl, 1984; Ruggie, 1982). Bretton Woods, GATT, OEEC, the ECSC, and the EC were part of the embedded liberal compromise, balancing economic openness, trade, and market discipline with protectionism and state autonomy required for macroeconomic and social policy. Mutual recognition on capital controls on short-term financial flows, and publicly regulated financial intermediation through the IMF, were essential (Helleiner, 1994).

Fordism in Europe was not a simple copy of an American template. Within certain limits, distinct forms were permitted and developed according to particular circumstances in different societies. Furthermore,

American leadership was not simply imposition but rather 'empire by invitation' (Lundestad, 1991). Working in tandem with American leadership, Fordist possibilities were seized actively by indigenous European actors to reconstruct European states through welfare-state accords, facilitating a steady 'rise of earnings ... against the background of long pent-up unsatisfied demand' (Anderson, 2009: p. 4; cf. Milward, 1984). The ensuing convergence of domestic preferences made the Treaty of Paris and the Treaty of Rome possible (Milward, 1992).

When seen as parts of Fordism, the Treaty of Rome on the common market and the Luxembourg Compromise were not antinomies but rather two sides of the 'embedded liberal' coin. The latter confirmed requisite state autonomy. The former facilitated the scale expansion of markets. The ECSC and CAP played important roles in pricing commodities and organizing production in input industries according to Fordist rationality (van der Pijl, 1978, 2006: pp. 40–1, 75; cf. Monnet, 1976: p. 51). The ECSC structured supply agreements between steel producers and the emergent consumer industries, compelling the former to retool away from military production.

Much was achieved in the Fordist epoch, such as unprecedented affluence, social mobility, and security for mass populations in the US and Western Europe (Aglietta, 1979; Armstrong, Glyn, & Harrison, 1991: pp. 117–50). Integrating mass production and mass consumption within states also greatly reduced the geopolitical lateral pressure for territorial expansion that had driven imperialist rivalry. Hence, Lowi's and Haas' accounts of modified liberalism are not without substance, and there was no return to interstate anarchy as feared by Hoffman. But though capitalist contradictions were managed for a while, they were not transcended. For critical political economy, the subsequent period of 'Eurosclerosis' in the 1960s and 1970s had less to do with nationalism as such than with such contradictions and attendant crisis tendencies (Armstrong, Glyn, & Harrison, 1991: pp. 192–230).

First, conveyor-belt mechanization and scientific management came up against their sociotechnological limits and could not sustain prevailing rates of capital accumulation. Productivity growth decreased with diminishing returns to further rationalization of production. Here it is important to appreciate that, contrary to what was promised by the remedial measures of Lowi's 'modified liberalism', Fordism was Janus-faced for workers. Wage increases through productivity growth went hand in hand with deskilling and intensified alienation at work (Braverman, 1974); meanwhile full employment and mass consumption increased aspirations about quality of life. When mixed with student politics reacting against wars and proxy wars in (former) colonies and Cold War confrontations, this generated an explosive and potentially revolutionary cocktail. The May 1968 events in France were the most striking. The great philosophical mentor of the student movement,

Herbert Marcuse (1964), had made the case that psychological repression and the unfulfilled promise to combat anomie and alienation were by no means confined to production but rather permeated all aspects of social life (see also Adorno & Horkheimer, 1944).

Contradictions between domestic and international aspects of embedded liberalism reduced the capacity to manage growing antagonisms, not least because nascent, trade-driven capital mobility and international wage competition from East Asia reduced the policy space for reform. There was also a tendency to renew inter-capitalist conflict as different Fordist experiences in the US and Europe challenged the boundaries of the transatlantic 'tandem' (Lundestad, 1991: p. 143) and generated competing ideas on how to address the Fordist crisis. These challenges were issued variously in the form of Gaullism, German social democracy under Willy Brandt, and Italy's 'historic compromise' between the Communist Party (PCI) and left Christian democrats. These took on a special edge when they involved a particularly strategic input commodity: oil. For critical political economy, these are underlying drivers of the anxieties over the post-war transatlantic settlement that Hoffman registered at an early stage but ultimately misdiagnosed.

But the Fordist crisis did not end American hegemony. American structural strengths could not be matched, based as they were on a 'judicial system disembedding markets as far as possible from ties of custom, tradition and solidarity, whose very abstraction from them ... proved – American firms like American films – exportable and producible across the world, in a way that no other competitor could quite match' (Anderson, 2002: pp. 24–25, cited in Panitch & Gindin, 2012: p. 25). This provided the basis for a neoliberal reorganization of American hegemony based on purer market principles. After the collapse of Bretton Woods, American domestic- and foreign-policy decisions (and non-decision) were central for constituting finance-led accumulation. But so were the 'bonfire of controls' of the Single European Market; the 'new constitutional' and 'disciplinary neo-liberal' arrangements of the EMS, the EMU, and the Stability and Growth Pact, locking in macroeconomic commitments to price stability even at the price of mass unemployment (Gill, 1992, 1998); labour market flexibility reforms and financial liberalization pursued in the Lisbon Agenda (Bieling, 2003; Bieling & Schulten, 2003); and rapid eastern enlargement that provided finance-led accumulation with large pools of cheap labour and assets. Hence, for critical political economy, the European 'relaunch' of the 1980s and 1990s was not so much about returning to more vigorous deepening. It was rather part of the constitution of a new capitalist socioeconomic epoch based on principles quite different from those of Fordism, and which the New Economic Governance seeks to extend. Democratic socialist aspirations had their swan-song in the early days in Mitterrand's presidency, but were defeated.

Apart from liberalizing and globalizing financial markets, neoliberalism has delinked wage increases and employment from growth through the return to a more classical labour market where unemployment serves a disciplinary function. Crucially, technological change and trade and investment liberalization have increased the scope for corporations to organize production on a transnational scale in complex commodity chains and to take advantage of low wage pools of labour, for instance through outsourcing. Neoliberal transformation has also been facilitated by a reorientation of macroeconomic policy towards price stability (in product markets, but not asset markets).

The major reason why traditional theories, as mentioned in the Introduction, failed to identify the factors generating the financial and Eurozone crisis was that they failed to appreciate the specific way finance-led growth was caught up in capitalism's Red Queen Syndrome. Finance-led growth could draw on computer, cybernetic, and information technology and on financial innovation (securitization and derivatives) to restore profit rates. For this, the redistribution of value added from wages to especially financial profits was crucial (Bengtsson & Ryner, 2015). Nonetheless, this system never returned output and productivity growth to the levels which had been achieved during the Fordist period, and certainly not in Europe. It did restore socioeconomic stability in the transatlantic area for 20 years. But as the 2008 crisis revealed, within the system there was a fundamental contradiction.

While Fordism had maintained economic growth by integrating mass consumption and mass production through negotiated wages and the welfare state, this was an anathema to neoliberalism. Rather, the system was based on financial markets extending and managing debt, underwritten not by productivity growth but by increasing asset values ('leveraging'). Since capitalism is a system that needs to run in order to stand still, debt had to be extended into ever riskier segments of the market – segments that became riskier because of increased inequality (Ivanova, 2013; Soederberg, 2014). In 2008 the extent of defaults in the American sub-prime mortgage market spread, through interdependencies between different financial markets, and generated a global financial crisis. As revealed by the Eurozone crisis that broke out in 2009, some of the major problems proved to be in the European market in the form of 'toxic' assets in failed real estate investments in Eastern and Southern Europe. The failure of traditional theory to understand this and yet the ability to use critical political economy to provide a comprehensive, coherent and empirically verifiable account underlines the importance of the latter perspective.

The Red Queen Syndrome

Why does critical political economy suppose that capitalism suffers from The Red Queen Syndrome? According to Marx, the underlying reason is the contradictions that are inherent in generalized commodity production. The liberal concept of market equilibrium treats market exchange as if it were merely a means to an end. It is as if capitalists sell in order to buy something of use to them. But this is not at all what motivates capitalists, whose object rather is to make profit and for whom the particular products involved are coincidental and merely the means to an end. Capitalists do not sell in order to buy. They buy in order to sell, to make more money out of money. As Marx famously wrote in the first volume of *Capital*, 'Accumulate, accumulate! This is Moses and the Prophets.' It is this that engenders capitalism with 'moving substance' and 'immanent force' (Marx, 1867: p. 256). Assets are invested into a value-added process, which when commodities are sold on the market generate profit. If there is no profit to be had, investment and production will not take place (Marx, 1867: pp. 247–57). The liberal conception falsely gives the impression that production takes place in capitalism even when the total quantity of value is constant (it is merely seen as a matter of allocating it so as to maximize utility). However, the total quantity of value must actually continually increase if capitalists at the aggregate (or as Marx put it, 'social') level are going to be able to make more money out of money and continue to invest and produce. Anyone who doubts this should consider the impact of sustained zero growth for a capitalist economy.

Capitalist profits can be made in several ways. Merchants buy cheaply at one end (wholesale) and sell more expensively elsewhere (retail). Financiers invest money in exchange for interest, dividends, or capital gains. But in a highly integrated market system, the value of exchanges are equal, and the surplus upon which profitability is based depends in the last instance on the very special character of the labour market. In the labour market, workers are rewarded according to the cost for reproducing their livelihood, not according to how much value is produced when they are employed at work. Here resides an essential power relation in the very inner core of the market system that liberal economics does not acknowledge. It is this power relation that ensures that workers are paid less than the value they produce – the formal Marxist definition of exploitation (Marx, 1867: pp. 270–80). Normative questions of 'fair shares' aside, this system suffers from a fundamental systemic contradiction. In order to ensure that more money can be made out of money at the aggregate/social level, markets must continually expand to sustain the profitable deployment of accumulated capital. But this presupposes in the last instance the continuous expansion of final consumption though the incomes of the vast body of consumers – the workers – by the very nature of surplus extraction cannot easily expand at the same rate. Hence, there is a built-in tendency towards over-accumulation and crisis in capitalism.

Marx's *Capital* is a fundamental source for understanding entropic tendencies in capitalism that require Horkheimer's 'regulatory effects'.

Another source is Keynes, whose legacy is ambiguous as two distinct competing Keynesian schools emerged. Neo-Keynesianism emerged through the 'neoclassical synthesis' and, as discussed in Chapter 1, plays a central role in traditional integration theory. But there is also a more radical 'post-Keynesianism', which derived a general theory of growth from Keynes' analysis of the short term that ultimately rests on class analysis (Stockhammer, 2016). In the so-called Cambridge Capital Controversy over the determination of the returns to capital which clarified the lines of disagreement between the two Keynesian schools, Joan Robinson and Piero Sraffa argued that the very measurement of capital cannot be abstracted from power relations with labour.

As a theory on general properties and mechanisms of capitalism, post-Keynesianism sometimes overlaps and sometimes diverges from Marxism. Though grounded in an analysis of capital and labour as factors of production, aggregate demand is the fundamental post-Keynesian unit of analysis because it is held to determine the level of output and growth under conditions of involuntary unemployment. Income distribution is a critical variable as capitalists have a lower marginal propensity to consume than workers do. Hence, market-determined inequality tends to generate inadequate levels of aggregate demand ('under-consumption'). By stressing the importance of future expectations under conditions of fundamental uncertainty (which among other things mean that capitalists need not necessarily invest all their profits because of competitive pressure), finance, and credit as creating money rather than the other way around, post-Keynesians in many respects depart further from assumptions about perfect markets than Marxists do. Nevertheless, as we shall see, many critical political economists in their concrete analysis find it constructive to draw on both Marxism and post-Keynesianism.

At this general level of abstraction, it is possible to identify different ways in which surplus value can be extracted and potentially provide ways for ensuring that, for a while, capitalism can 'run in order to stand still'. Marx's distinction between 'absolute' and 'relative' surplus value is crucial here. Marx conceived of surplus value extraction in terms of the working day. It is divided between the time required for workers to produce the value required for reproducing their livelihood – 'socially necessary labour time' – and the time when the substance of profit, surplus value, is produced. In the extraction of absolute surplus value, socially necessary labour time is fixed and can be increased only through the extension of the working day. Relative surplus value extraction is, however, crucial for modern capitalism and for unlocking the secrets of its staying power. It is relative surplus value extraction that makes it possible to reduce socially necessary labour time.

The two epochs of capitalism that form the socioeconomic context in which the EU has developed are principally based on two different ways of extracting surplus value. The amount of time required to produce the means of workers' livelihood was reduced in Fordism, because more widgets could be produced per hour as the production process was *intensified* through the conveyor belt and scientific management. That created negotiating space between employers and trade unions, because it was possible to maintain high profit rates while real wages increased. This possibility was especially so when wage increases helped sustain effective aggregate demand (Aglietta, 1979). In neoliberal finance-led accumulation, relative surplus value is augmented in a different way. Disciplinary 'labour market flexibility' has reduced workers' negotiating space, and productivity growth has become anaemic. Instead, the costs for securing workers' livelihoods in the capitalist core have been reduced through an unequal exchange with workers in the periphery. Cheap clothing, consumer durables and even holiday travel have been made possible because of low wage rates in the periphery, secured through commodity chains of transnational corporations (Millberg & Winkler, 2013). Finance-led accumulation is an *extensive* system based aligning relative surplus value in the core and absolute surplus value in the periphery.

Open Marxism: basic functions and form of capitalist governance and the EU

Having explained the essential reasons for the entropic tendencies that require Horkheimer's 'regulatory effects', it is time to consider more directly how these 'effects' are produced through governance. Contrary to the pluralist idea that no particular ideology or interests dominate political life, critical political economy asserts that capitalist governance – including EU governance – has a definite, a priori, substantive kernel that stands above negotiation and democratic deliberation. This is something that is usually elided in the formalities of liberal democratic politics. But the Eurozone crisis has, given the sanctity of the New Economic Governance, sometimes made this overly obvious. When as central an institution as the labour market depends on power, and when The Red Queen Syndrome requires management, administration must not be seen as merely a formal adaptation of means to ends. There are structurally predefined ends. The Euro-polity is not part of a nebulous entity where diffuse interest groups check and balance each other. By the necessity of serving core regulatory functions for capitalism, it forms part of a stratified system of political domination, which systematically privileges certain social groups and classes over others (Jessop, 1990: p. 28). It shapes agendas and preferences by delineating what is seen as the limits of the possible of 'normal' politics and policy. It disciplines individuals and collective entities and makes them 'do what they otherwise would not do'.

When it comes to addressing how the EU contributes to securing basic forms and functions of European capitalism, the 'Open Marxist' school is second to none. It focuses on functions that maintain inter alia capitalist discipline in the labour market and basic structures of capitalist competition (including contract and property law and money as institutions) and that deal with over-accumulation problems. Capitalism requires state structures to secure these functions, because it is beyond the capacity of private market actors to do so. Despite its *substantive* artificiality (politics and economics cannot in reality be kept apart), the separation between the economic and political spheres must as much as possible be *formally* maintained. Private property, competition, discipline on the labour market, and keeping economic policy within acceptable bounds require '*depoliticization*' of economic relations. Here, extraterritorial, legal, and monetary provisions are important. They are important because they prevent territorially based political units from operating in certain – say socialist or mercantilist – ways, whilst at the same time engendering operational capacity to operate in other – say capitalist – ways. For 'Open Marxists', the EC and the EU have played a crucial role in this regard in post-war Europe (Holloway & Picciotto, 1978; Bonefeld, 2002).

Werner Bonefeld (2002, 2012a) offers the most sustained account of the EU from an 'Open Marxist' perspective. He stresses the policy of the market-liberal character of competition, enshrined already in the Treaty of Rome, and the monetarist character of the EMS and the EMU. Competition and monetary policy created a constitution-like framework and autonomous agents – DG Competition, the ECJ, and the ECB (and in the EMS, the German Bundesbank, operating in effect as a European central bank) – that depoliticized these policy areas located at the inner sanctum of capitalist social relations and took them out of the purview of representative democratic politics (see Chapters 3 and 4). This constitution-like framework ensured that state intervention and the welfare state would remain within the essential parameters of capitalism and closed off possible avenues towards socialism. This should not be understood as a weakening of the nation state. On the contrary, this constitutional delimitation of the political enables the capitalist state to serve its basic functions. For Bonefeld, the German doctrine of ordoliberalism, whose main objective was to clarify how capitalist markets can be politically constituted, provided the main ideological framework for these arrangements.

Bonefeld offers one of the most insightful accounts of the origins, nature, rationale, and effects of ordoliberalism and is peerless in elucidating its ideological role for the co-constitutive and enabling relationship between the EU and Europe's states as capitalist states. His argument about the role of competition policy for neutralizing latent mercantilist and socialist tendencies in member states accords with and

updates Peter Cocks' (1980) panoramic and more comparative historical analysis. Yet questions can be raised about the overall coherence
that Bonefeld attributes to capital as a social force both in space and
time.

Bonefeld and Open Marxists give us the sense of policy being a direct
response to a collective capitalist: a 'capital in general' whose concrete
existence can be taken for granted. This underestimates the degree to
which capitalism changes over time. While Bonefeld rightly points to
the importance of ordoliberal figures such as Müller-Armack in the
shaping of competition policy, he understates countervailing forces. In
the Fordist period, EC market competition regulation was constrained
by many exemptions. There were few restrictions on mergers to create 'national champions'. There was plenty of scope for inter-company
agreements, cartels, state aids, and national industrial policy operating in ways that contravened rather than conformed to market logic
(Buch-Hansen & Wigger, 2010b: pp. 57–72; see also Ziltener, 1999).
Furthermore, though the common market coincided with the return of
full currency convertibility, Bretton Woods allowed for capital controls
that were frequently used by member states to modify market outcomes
(Chapter 4). As Perry Anderson puts it, in the first decades, ordoliberalism was 'a somewhat recessive gene in the makeup of the Community,
latent but never the most salient in its development' (2009: p. 65).

This would certainly change with the EMS and the relaunch in the
1980s. But change itself needs to be explained. Arguably, EU monetary
and competition policy have gone through three phases: from embedded
liberalism to disciplinary neoliberalism to an increasingly authoritarian neoliberal form in the post-Eurozone crisis. The latter increasingly
dispenses with even formal-constitutional niceties, where the 'specific defined generality' of legal regulation is increasingly replaced by
blanket 'general clauses' (cf. Neumann, 1937) that increasingly enable
arbitrary executive power. Cases in point include the inclusion of the
vague category of 'structural policy' in the 'Economic Partnership Programmes' of countries in the Excessive Deficit Procedure (EDP); reverse
majority voting, where such Procedures instigated by the Commission
are held to carry the day unless it is explicitly voted against by QMV in
the Council; and infringements on constitutional procedure (as laid out
in TEU Article 121 and TFEU Article 136) in the adoption of the New
Economic Governance. Legal scholar Christian Joerges (2012: p. 377)
suggests that this gives Carl Schmitt (the lawyer and political theorist
who put legal form to the transition from the Weimar Republic to the
Nazi regime in Germany) 'alarming topicality' (cited in Oberndorfer,
2015: p. 188; see also Menéndez, 2014). Bonefeld's stress on basic functions that capitalist governance must serve is helpful in this context and
is certainly consistent with the content of the two later phases. But his
framework is less helpful in understanding the change itself.

Bonefeld also understates the importance for EC/EU developments of divisions among individual capitalist groupings that after all are in competition with one another. In concrete reality, different capitalist sectors cannot be assumed to automatically have the same interests. Conflicts of interest among various sectors and groupings, and the different balance of power between them in different social formations, condition interstate competition and rivalry. Bonefeld states, not unlike Schumpeter, that 'capital is not interested in war. It is interested in profits' (2002: pp. 76–7). This raises the question of how and why could the interest be satisfied when, according to Marxists, contradictions generated by national capitalist amalgamations and rivalry had resulted in two world wars. With these, according to Lening, capitalism had entered its highest, final and terminal stage.

The EU and inter-capitalist rivalry: the legacies of Servan-Shreiber, Mandel, and Poulantzas

Capitalist competition was the major focus of the foundational Marxist works on the EC by Ernest Mandel and Nicos Poulantzas in the late 1960s and early 1970s. They wrote in response, not to academic European integration scholarship with implicit transatlanticist commitments, but rather to the bestselling *The American Challenge* (*le defi americain*) by Jean-Jacques Servan-Shreiber (1969). Servan-Shreiber gave voice to the alternative 'indigenous' European perspective that Milward (1992; Milward & Sørensen, 1993) identified as prevalent in member state policy practice. Here, the purpose of the EC was not *transcending* nation states but *rescuing* them after the war by pooling resources in certain strategic areas to secure governing capacity and redirecting these to new social purposes. Contrary to assumptions of traditional integration theory, this resulted in the unprecedented increase of state capacities to intervene in socioeconomic developments through Keynesian macroeconomic management, social policy, and industrial policy. In the first decades after World War II, there was congruence between European actors working within this indigenous state tradition and transatlanticism. The learning from Fordist techniques and the international help to reconstitute European states as functional units were actively embraced. However, disagreements emerged in the late 1960s on how to address the Fordist crisis. Serven-Shreiber's book resonated with this standpoint. By critiquing Servan-Shreiber, both Mandel and Poulantzas were in part captured by this standpoint and represented the radical left in this indigenous European tradition. A similar intellectual development took place in West Germany, where Helmut Schmidt's electoral concept of 'Modell Deutschland' animated a critical response in the form of a neo-Marxist research programme (Esser et al., 1979;

Ziebura, 1982; Graf, 1992: pp. 1–2 Deppe, 1975), which – although it lost organizational coherence quite quickly – has cross-fertilized with the French works reviewed here and inspired subsequent generations of critical scholarship.

Servan-Shreiber: The American Challenge and the European social model

A close associate of former French Premier Pierre Mendes-France, Servan-Shreiber wrote from a social mercantilist perspective. Against liberal trade theorists, mercantilists argue that a state should not be indifferent to the composition of its trade as generated by comparative advantage. Comparative advantage theory not only ignores geopolitical vulnerability but is also criticized for ignoring prospects of mark-up pricing and productivity growth that determine terms of trade, which vary significantly with trade-composition. States must not be indifferent to their competitive position in strategic sectors (List, 1856; Weber, 1895). This is a salient issue in capitalism, based on social bargains between capital, labour, and other social groups, where terms of trade determine the scope for social compromises. From this perspective, *The American Challenge* warned that it was American multinationals that took advantage of the common market through foreign direct investments, strengthening a transatlantic division of labour, where the US was dominant in future strategic sectors. For Servan-Shreiber, the antidote was the formation of 'European champion' MNCs and federal-European structures in research and development and industrial policy. These would make possible *les grandes operationes* required to challenge US dominance in strategic sectors and would take full advantage of the promises of computer technology. This would facilitate national corporatist bargaining, which, by mobilizing new technology, could integrate the aspirations of the social movements concerned with alienation and Europe's imperialist legacy perpetuated by complicity in American imperialism. Here, Servan-Shreiber saw the German SPD under Willy Brandt as a role model.

Servan-Shreiber's intervention has one important merit. It begins to make the institutional logic of European capitalism – the social model – analytically visible on its own terms as something that has its own positive existence and modernizing logic. Together with other industrialist intellectuals from the French 'statist' traditions (Stoffäes, 1978; Albert, 1993), Servan-Shreiber's work became a central point of reference for a comparative political economy on varieties of capitalism (for an overview, see Clift, 2014). While there are varieties within this body of scholarship itself, it is united in arguing that actually existing capitalism depends on a whole host of 'necessary impurities', which are mediated within market logic in different ways through institutions

(Hodgson, 1996). The 'necessary impurities' include information asymmetries and dependence on informal social relations such as the family. Indeed, productive organization itself cannot be organized through market exchange alone, as manifested by the corporation as an institution. Also, modus vivendi between capital and labour is held to be beyond the market as such.

To the varieties of capitalism literature, there is no a priori reason why one type of institutional arrangement is more rational or competitive. But European, sometimes called 'Rhineland', varieties are generally thought to reduce trade-offs between efficiency, equality, and extra-economic values. Typically, European varieties of capitalism are as open to trade competition as 'Anglo-American ones', if not more so. But as 'stakeholder' rather than 'shareholder' models, they are based on non-market state intervention, cartels, or collective bargaining in finance, in corporate governance, and on the labour market. Any costs that these arrangements incur in terms of lack of flexibility are said to be compensated for by higher levels of dedicated capital, longer time horizons in investments, and social consensus on the implementation of progressive technological change. A major question to which we will return concerns the implications of the EU and single market for these varieties of capitalism.

To caution against 'postulates of homogeneity' is salutary. Institutional analysis is crucial in addressing the question of the constraints of and possibility for relative surplus value augmentation and intensive accumulation upon which the terms of social bargains rest (Aglietta, 1998: pp. 42–3). However, focusing too narrowly on the specifics of institutions can also be problematic, and the varieties of capitalism literature arguably bend the stick too far the other way. There are functionalist dangers entailed in the normative and analytical fascination with tripartite agreements between capital, labour, and the state on one hand and the attendant more general concept of 'institutional complementarity' on the other. The danger is that 'institutions' as containers of national social partnership come to be seen as foundational to social relations rather than the other way around (Bruff, 2011). Capitalism manifests itself in a variety of ways, but they are still varieties *in capitalism*. Certain structural properties, such as the basic power relation entailed in capitalist ownership and The Red Queen Syndrome, are still foundational and shape the conditions of institutional settlements and social partnership. These structural properties are institutionally refracted in various ways, but they are not transcended (Bohle & Greskovits, 2009; Bruff, 2011; Kannankulam & Georgi, 2014).

This relates to a weakness in concrete analysis. Given its comparative vocation, varieties of capitalism scholarship tends to treat all advanced capitalist states and varieties as equal units of analysis. This ignores the power relations between them and how they have asymmetrically interpenetrated one another (Panitch & Gindin, 2003; Brenner, Peck, & Theodore, 2010; Jessop, 2012, 2014). The latter is admittedly more a problem in recent works than in Servan-Shreiber's, for whom the interpenetration in question was the central theme. But his faith in European federalism and social partnership as an antidote was voluntarist and was contradicted by the multinational social forces that concerned him. Given such interpenetration, how could concerted European action be mobilized in the first place? These issues featured already in Mandel's critique of Servan-Shreiber.

Mandel: over-accumulation and capitalist rivalry

Mandel's critique of Servan-Shreiber was partly empirical. As subsequent developments have proven, Servan-Shreiber exaggerated the dominant position of American MNCs (e.g. Junne & van Tulder, 1988; Dicken, 2010: pp. 13–48, 109–66). But more fundamentally, Mandel critiqued *The American Challenge* theoretically as 'an adroit popularization of the views of capitalist circles in favour of "European companies"'. Mandel considered Servan-Shreiber as a spokesman for an emergent European capitalist class with imperialist aspirations of its own at a particular stage of development. However, he saw Servan-Shreiber as less successful in elucidating whether these aspirations could be realized (Mandel, 1969: pp. 36–9). Mandel's own attempt to do so addressed a question that Bonefeld and much scholarship on critical political economy takes for granted: Had European capitalism reached a stage conducive to transcending European rivalry?

Mandel's answer was affirmative. Post-World War II 'absolute dominance' of US capital, facilitating trade and investment on transatlantic and European levels, had reorganized the operative sphere of national capitalists. As American dominance waned, Mandel anticipated growing inter-imperialist competition between 'amalgamated European capital' and American capital. Although the common market was central to the US's grand design, it had contradictory qualities as it was facilitating European capital accumulation on a continental scale.

Mandel's work is firmly situated within the classical Marxist theory of imperialism as developed by Rudolf Hilferding, Nikolai Bukharin, and Lenin (for an excellent overview, see Brewer, 1980). Focusing on developments from the 1870s to World War I, these authors tried to show links among the growing maturity of capitalism, the direct penetration of monopoly groupings in the state, the fusion of capitalism and militarism, and acute international rivalry. When rates of technological change and lowering reproduction costs of labour (cheaper consumption goods) no longer maintain relative surplus value augmentation, over-accumulation problems emerge and profit rates fall, which in turn generate ever fiercer competition for market shares. Indeed, attempts by individual capitalist units to compete by reducing wage costs exacerbate the problem since this inhibits market expansion. The consequence is that only some units survive while others succumb and are subsumed in takeovers, leading to a concentration of capital. The increased centrality of money and finance is a related consequence, caused by 'latent hoarding' (Marx, 1893: pp. 76–8) when productive and commercial capital lack adequate sales outlets. This relates to increased concentration because monetary and financial mechanisms are central to mergers and acquisitions (Hilferding, 1910).

At the economic 'base', Mandel saw direct parallels between the developments in the late 19th century and developments in the 1960s. But because of the more unified spaces created in Europe after World War II under American hegemony, national capitalist rivalry within Europe was no longer the dominant tendency, and the scope of operation had outgrown the scale of European national units (Mandel, 1967: pp. 28–9, 1969: pp. 20–7). Though national mergers were still viable strategies in the short run, European amalgamation was ultimately the only route for European capital to escape subordinate interpenetration with American capital. At the time of writing, comparisons were made between the merger of German AGFA and Belgian Gevaert and IBM's takeover of French Machine Bulls (which had so exercised Servan-Shreiber). Supranationalism was seen by Mandel as the logical superstructural political consequence of amalgamation. De Gaulle's triggering the empty chair crisis was self-defeating because it would only prepare the ground for European capital being swallowed up by the Americans.

Mandel's account is certainly consistent with subsequent developments in French political economy. Contrary to de Gaulle, Mitterrand would endorse the single market project at Fontainebleau in 1984, and his erstwhile finance minister, Jacques Delors, presided over the European 'relaunch' in the Commission. Mandel's analysis serves as a cue for some contemporary analyses, arguing that within transatlantic neoliberalism and under conditions of over-accumulation (growth rates never returned to the level of the mid 1960s) (Brenner, 2006), a distinct amalgamated European capital has emerged. Geopolitically, it competes with American capital for control over transport routes, commodity and capital-flows, and access to raw materials and energy (Altvater & Mahnkopf, 2007, cited in Bieling, 2010: p. 229). Most of these accounts do not consider amalgamation to have gone as far as eliminating national divisions, and hence they are seen as taking place under German dominance. They point to increasingly coherent European networks of strategic ownership and interlocking directorships that are no longer as subordinate to American groupings as they were in the past. German insurance company Allianz, and to a lesser extent Deutsche Bank, are seen to form the centre of this amalgamation. Since the 2000s these groupings have started to make inroads into the Russian energy sector and into the transatlantic arena from a position of strength (van der Pijl, Holman, & Raviv, 2011). Inferences are made that this forms the context for Germany's stubbornly 'neo-mercantilist' commitment to securing export surpluses and spaces for capital outflows (e.g. Lapavitsas et al., 2012; Flassbeck & Lapavitsas, 2015).

But Mandel's analysis is marred by a major inconsistency. He insists on continuity in inter-imperialist rivalry in the transatlantic sphere while arguing that it has been transcended within Europe. He never explains, if it endures in one sphere, then why is it transcended in the other? Poulantzas addresses this question more satisfactorily – indeed presciently – in his account of a more universal but uneven transatlantic process of transformation, or *interiorization*, whereby European integration forms part of a structural subordination to the American social formation. From this vantage point he is more sceptical about European integration rising to 'The American Challenge'.

Poulantzas: transatlantic 'interiorization' and Europe's structural subordination to the US

Poulantzas' verdict was in a sense closer to Servan-Schreiber's (1974: pp. 161–9). Poulantzas agreed with Mandel that European capitalists could retain competitive autonomy through amalgamation. But they would nevertheless become increasingly dependent on the US, because of US dominance in sectors that were strategic not only in competition but in *structuring* the transatlantic and global economy. This included the growing significance of US-centred money capital, which at the time was beginning to affect access to credit. For Poulantzas, this particular sort of prominence of US capital in Europe determined a whole series of corporate 'practices, know-how, modes and rituals to do with the economic sphere' – in short, 'ideology' in a broad and materialist sense (Poulantzas, 1974: p. 164). He proposed the concept 'interior bourgeoisie' to describe a European bourgeoisie that was not wholly dependent on the United States (as the Third World 'comprador' bourgeoisie) but was nevertheless increasingly interconnected with American capital and its distinct social formation on subordinate terms (Poultantzas, 1974: pp. 164–7). This argument forms the basis of a major recent study by Leo Panitch and Sam Gindin (2012). In particular, Panitch and Gindin point to the removal of capital controls in the early 1990s and the leading role that Wall Street investment banks (Goldman Sachs, Morgan Stanley, Citigroup, and Merrill Lynch) played as underwriters of Initial Public Offerings (IPOs) of privatizations (such as that of Deutsche Telekom) and in European mergers and acquisitions in the single market. Indeed, 65 per cent of German mergers and acquisitions were handled by US financial advisers in the 1990s. In addition, by the 1990s, American IT companies (Apple, Hewlett Packard, IBM, and Microsoft) supplied 80 per cent of Europe's software and computer market. The emulation of American business models (including the principle of 'shareholder value') must be seen in this context (Panitch & Gindin, 2012: pp. 199–203).

Such 'interiorization' has resulted in a relative dislocation of Europe's transnational capital from the particularities of Europe's social formations and social bargains. This dislocation has made it harder for European states – including Germany (Bonder, Röttger, & Ziebura, 1992) – to act as 'factors of social cohesion' – that is, to mediate Europe's distinct class compromises and maintain attendant constructions of political subjectivity that distance politics from overt class rule (Cafruny & Ryner, 2007: pp. 73–104). Poulantzas (1975, 1978) argued that herein lay a profound danger of increasingly authoritarian tendencies that, as has already been suggested (see pp. 18–19), seem to be confirmed not the least in the New Economic Governance.

Poulantzas' analysis is based on two distinctive theoretical contributions that he made to Marxist theory. First, he developed a theory that conceived of class subjects in disaggregated and composite terms. Drawing especially on Volumes 2 and 3 of Marx's *Capital* (1893, 1894), Poulantzas stressed the importance of taking into account the different forms that capital takes at different moments in the circuit of expanded reproduction – as commercial, money, and productive capital. In concrete capitalist society this has given rise to different functional *'fractions' of capital*. Bankers, traders, industrialists, and commercial farmers do not 'automatically' experience their economic reality and interests in the same way. This fragmentation can most certainly be reconciled. But this reconciliation is really part of the process of capitalist subject formation and can take place in many different ways. Affirming a point already made by Gramsci (1971: p. 181), Poulantzas held such subject formation to be political and ideological at its very core. This resort to politics and ideology gives capitalism more flexibility and resilience in reproducing its own legitimacy beyond a narrow class base. It may indeed be that non-capitalist groupings, such as remnants of ruling classes from previous modes of production (landowners) or certain working class groupings (for example, highly skilled workers) can be brought into this political process of reconciliation, osmosis, or 'interpellation'. Poulantzas (1975) calls the coalition that is produced by this composite process the 'power bloc'. The concept of power bloc resonates with the social settlement between landed interests and the bourgeoisie in British capitalism and with the liberal orientation of crafts-based unionism (Anderson, 1964; Leys, 1983: p. 48). Power blocs of landed interests, industrial capitalists, and the working class were central characteristics of European corporatist societies (Lehmbruch & Schmitter, 1979). The interiorization of European capital with American capital reduces flexibility in maintaining inclusive power blocs in European societies.

This brings us to an even more important contribution of Poultanzas': his theory of the capitalist state. Classical Marxists such as Mandel saw the relationship between the capitalist class and the capitalist state as a straightforward one, and they followed some of the more 'instrumentalist' passages in Marx and Engels which suggested that the state was 'the executive committee for the common affairs of the bourgeoisie'. But Poulantzas' complex structuralist views on subject formation and the relationship between economics, ideology, and politics drew him to other parts of their work, especially a passage by Engels on the 'relatively autonomous' nature of the capitalist state.

> [The state] is a product of society at a certain stage of development; it is the admission that this society has become entangled in an insoluble contradiction with itself, that it has split into irreconcilable antagonisms which it is powerless to dispel. But in order that these antagonisms and classes with conflicting economic interests might not consume themselves and society in a fruitless struggle, it became necessary to have a power seemingly standing above society that would alleviate the conflict, and keep it within the bounds of 'order'; and this power, arisen out of society but placing itself above it, and alienating itself more and more from it, is the state. (Engels, 1884: p. 576, cited in Poulantzas, 1973: p. 48)

Here the state is not understood as a mere instrument of the ruling class. It is a structure that has been produced – one of Horkheimer's 'regulatory effects' – to ensure social cohesion. It does so as the site where collectively binding decisions are made that mediate contradictions and antagonisms of capitalism (Jessop, 1990: p. 341). To do so, it has to facilitate the general conditions for capital accumulation. On this score, there is common ground between Poulantzas and the Open Marxists. But the state also has to ensure societal legitimacy by mediating between the interests of dominant and subordinate classes according to the ideological terms set by the power bloc. Although Poulantzas showed how and why capitalist states had been much more successful in doing so than the classical Marxists had anticipated, his prediction that the interiorization process would increase contradictions and tensions in European societies and decrease the mediating capacities of states was prescient.

'Ensemble of state apparatuses' is a key concept of Poulantzas' state theory, to which we will have occasion to return. In this conceptualization, the state cannot be assumed to be a unitary entity. Rather, unity must be shaped and reproduced. In partial agreement with pluralists, Poulantzas sees the state as a social relation between interrelated agencies. But rather than being a horizontal and decentred network as suggested by pluralists, for Poulantzas the state has a potentially contradictory internal hierarchy which reflects the social balance of power, dominant ideologies, and priorities of interest within society. This enables some actors and constrains others. The different branches that constitute the state have different roles in the sociopolitical division of labour, with different mixes of different accumulation, legitimation, and repressive functions. These are related to one another in a complex and potentially contradictory matrix of authority, which obeys its own logic (Poulantzas, 1969). Above all, those state apparatuses that serve the function of reproducing the general conditions of capital accumulation most directly (for example, ministries of finance and central banks) have certain veto powers over more specialized agencies with functions of representing subordinate interests for legitimation purposes (for example, ministries of social affairs). This power is exercised through different media of social steering: law, money, and the budget process. As will be expanded on in subsequent chapters, the spatially asymmetrical configuration of the EU, with the division between supranational functions (in the fields of monetary policy, financial regulation, and competition), and intergovernmental functions (in fiscal, social and taxation policy) (Holman, 2004) play a crucial role in locking in preferences for Europe's interiorized neoliberal power bloc and in structurally constraining power mobilization for alternatives (Ziltener, 1999; Bailey, 2006; Kannankulam & Georgi, 2014).

Regulation theory: Fordism, finance-led accumulation, and the repression of social democratic alternatives

Marxist analyses help to explain social power relations that are constitutive of European integration. The one-dimensional teleological debate between liberal 'optimists' and realist 'pessimists' is avoided, and it becomes possible to reject idealizations while still appreciating the transformative powers of the EU as a key component of contemporary European, transatlantic, and global capitalism. But questions can be raised about the extent to which this possibility is realized. Works following the trails of Mandel and Poulantzas on capitalist competition, class fractions, and the state may address problems of assuming a unitary 'collective capitalist', as Open Marxism does. But there is a problematic tendency either to assume that crisis tendencies will result in systemic crisis (Mandel) or to overstate the extent of structural continuity and homogeneity over time (Poulantzas). These problems became evident in the 1980s, when it became clear that capitalism was *not* collapsing but was *instead* undergoing profound qualitative transformations. Regulation theory responded to this problem, conceiving of a variety of capitalist configurations in time and space, with different social implications. As such, regulation theory makes up the quintessential perspective on socioeconomic epochs.

Regulation theorists see themselves as 'rebel sons' of structuralist Marxist Louis Althusser and the first post-war president of the French Commissariat général du Plan, Pierre Massé (Lipietz, 1987). The Marxist legacy is manifest in their insistence that 'the economy' is not analytically abstracted from other social relations but rather is part of a broader and contradictory social totality with multiple economic, ideological, and political determinations (Lipietz, 1988). However, regulation theorists rejected the structuralist overemphasis on reproductive coherence in capitalism. Like Horkheimer, they asked how, given the contradictions of capitalism, it was possible to maintain coherence and order in the first place. Answering this question required understanding how regulation in a broad sense is actually achieved and reflected their experience (not unlike Servan-Shreiber) as civil servants involved in agencies connected to the Commissariat général du Plan. They were concerned with formal models and institutions required to counteract capitalist contradictions and to direct economic development to defined social and political goals. A historical perspective combined the two legacies. The efficacy of a 'mode of regulation' depends on the particular conditions of particular epochs. The crisis of the 1970s made it clear to them that there were periods when certain regulations worked and other periods when they did not. Hence, the particular conditions of different epochs need to be identified.

Regulation theory emerged in the specific intellectual context of the 1970s (Aglietta, 1979). The theory emerged in economics and stood in sharp opposition to neoclassical theory, which was rejected because of its methodological individualism and lack of conception of sociohistorical time (Braudel, 1958). Empirically, the focus was on the crisis of the 1970s. Contrary to mainstream economic theory, the crisis was not seen by regulation theorists as an anomaly. Rather, it was the decades of stability preceding the crisis of the 1970s that had to be explained. Hence, investigating the reasons which had allowed for the long-term, stable growth of the post-war period in Europe and the United States became the central concern. At a 'middle range' or 'intermediate level of abstraction' regulation theorists searched for the social and institutional factors that had facilitated high levels of economic growth based on stable and dynamic economic accumulation, and their findings inform our analysis of Fordism. Based on this, regulation theorists tried to understand why this accumulation regime had come to an end and why the Fordist regulation modes now fell short of ensuring the reproduction of the accumulation regime (Bieling, Jäger & Ryner, 2016).

Regulation was understood not in functionalist terms but as resulting from contingent social processes. The 'wage relation' is essential for the regulation of capitalism and for ensuring its stability and dynamic development in a given historical period and territory. This concept refers to the capital–labour relationship, in particular the technological transformation of the production (labour) process, wage determination, and their impacts on productivity. In addition, the form of competition (the relationship between different capitalist firms) and the 'monetary constraint' (the institutional configuration of money as 'universal equivalent' – that is, the lifeblood of capitalist exchange) are considered central elements of modes of regulation (Aglietta, 1982). A successful mode of regulation consisting of all the above elements reproduces and regulates capital accumulation. Specific types of accumulation, defined by the particular content of core technologies, the wage relation, the form of competitions, and the monetary constraint and also specific to particular epochs, are called 'regimes of accumulation'.

Initially, regulation theorists mainly focused on the Fordist regime of accumulation. This regime was predominantly based on intensive relative surplus value augmentation. Its wage relation was based on oligopolistic competition, state-regulated money, and the establishment of national collective bargaining regimes and welfare benefits predicated on the acquiescence of workers to scientific management. Stable expansion of domestic consumption ensured increased productivity growth through the progressive rationalization of conveyor-belt technology and vice versa. Regulation theorists subsequently became more interested in the possibilities and conditions of a post-Fordist regime of accumulation (Boyer & Saillard, 2002). This included the search for viable alternatives and active support of social democratic policies. Already very early, regulationist scholars recognized that neoliberal post-Fordism and financialized regimes of accumulation were unstable, and the internal contradictions were expected to lead rather sooner than later to a crisis (Boyer, 2000b).

The crisis of Fordism brought about a certain widening of options. Given the upswing of progressive social forces – the students' movement, the peace movement, and the labour movement – the 1970s were marked by both an increasing engagement for extended democracy, social participation, and more comprehensive macroeconomic management. Leading regulationist scholars contributed to these debates by identifying alternative post-Fordist scenarios. They focused on three areas (Bieling, Jäger & Ryner, 2016):

- The first area pertained to the wage relation and the organization of work in which they compared the productive and democratic potentials of different options (Bertrand, 2002: 84ff.). They identified work relations mainly based on 'external' or 'numerical' flexibility, on one hand, and on 'internal' or 'negotiated' flexibility and involvement of workers, on the other. While the first type represents neo-Taylorist patterns of work organization – focused on cutting labour costs and therefore without the social security and the benefits of the Fordist period – the second type, with a particular eye to the Volvo production site in Kalmar, sometimes called 'Kalmarism' (but also experiments in 'Third Italy' and diversified quality production influenced by co-determination in Germany), tried to generate productivity increases and relative surplus value through the occupational qualification, involvement, and active support of the employees (Leborgne & Lipietz, 1988; Boyer, 1991; Freyssenet, 1998).

- A regime of accumulation is determined not only by the wage relation and work but also by the form of competition and the monetary constraint – the broader macroeconomic arrangements. This second area concerns the sectorial composition of the economy and the corresponding forms of (re)distribution via goods, capital, credit markets, and public households. Next to the wage relation, therefore, the organization of all kinds of markets and the flows of money (taxes, public services, or welfare expenses) has an important impact on the production–consumption nexus. And given the changed priorities of supply-side politics – more competition due to liberalization, deregulation, and privatization; less progressive tax systems; consolidation of public households; and low inflation – domestic demand and a mid- to long-term improved competitiveness became less relevant.
- This overall shift indicates that the third area of analysis, namely the mode of regulation, is a constitutive element of capitalist development. Regulation theory has a wide understanding of regulation, including the manifold institutions and practices in everyday life – from the workplace to family, to school and education, to different parts of civil society, and up to the official state apparatuses – which contribute to (de)stabilizing capitalist relations. In that context, some scholars focus on the role of an 'extended' or 'integral' state (Jessop, 1993); and they point out that emerging post-Fordist types of states are certainly more competition-oriented but pursue these aims in still different – neoliberal, neocorporatist, or neostatist – institutional and strategic settings.

Against the backdrop of alternative post-Fordist trajectories, regulationist theorists offered a rather prescient critical analysis of the 'Europe 1992' single market project and issued warnings that would be confirmed by the EMU agreement at Maastricht. Both Boyer (1990) and Leborgne & Lipietz (1990) saw potentials in the then still quite open-ended 'Europe 1992' project for providing the broader macroeconomic and institutional arrangements that might enable a post-Fordist trajectory based on negotiated involvement, thus realizing Servan-Shreiber's synthesis of the aspirations of the New Left generation of 1968 with pragmatic social democracy. They stressed the potential in the economies of scale of the single market, 'les grandes operationes' of a Europe-wide industrial policy identifying and promoting market shares in the vanguard core products, potential post-Keynesian Kaldor-Verdoorn effects (virtuous circles between aggregate demand and productivity growth) of supranational macroeconomic governance, harmonized regulatory standards, and coordinated wage bargaining on a European scale as a means to diffuse intensive accumulation in the periphery while preventing unemployment through worktime reduction in the core. But especially Boyer warned that 'economies of learning' (learning by doing) and returns to scale could not simply be derived from Balassan assumptions about competition as assumed by the Cecchini Report. These were not likely to be realized through a mode of regulation exclusively based on negative integration and mutual recognition and a monetary union that simply continued the status quo ante of the EMS (see also Lipietz, 1989). Indeed, such a configuration had the danger of producing a 'worst of all worlds', where neither negotiated involvement nor an all-out neoliberal 'Californian' variant of post-Fordism would be realized (Boyer, 1990, pp. 128–36), and with deep regional divisions with growth dependent on the capacity to capture rents (Leborgne & Lipietz, 1990: p. 193). It is not difficult to reconcile Europe's subsequent malaise with this analysis.

The Amsterdam School: accumulation strategies and hegemonic projects

Regulation theory thus enriches an understanding of European political economy and the EU. However, it is not without its own weaknesses. Because it sees modes of regulation as responses to the requirements of regimes of accumulation, a residual functionalism arguably remains. What exactly are the practices, and who are the actors that determine what the objects of regulation should be? Like regulation theory, the 'Amsterdam School' offers a concrete analysis of distinctive regimes of accumulation. But in contrast to regulation theory, the constitution and strategies of agents that form modes of regulation are at the centre of its analysis. Kees van der Pijl, its leading proponent (1984, 1998, 2006), explains why it was possible for European capitalists strategically to coordinate Fordist regulation on an Atlantic scale and, later, the measures that instituted transnational neoliberalism (see also Overbeek, 1993). Macroeconomic management is only part of the story. It is also essential to account for how subjects themselves are formed in pursuit of winning 'accumulation strategies'. In this respect, van der Pijl gives concrete substance to the structural bones of Poulantzas' 'interiorization' concept.

Frankly, critical political economy has lacked something equivalent to the functionalist hypothesis, seeking to explain how anarchic rivalry is replaced or at least moderated. This entails explaining how military inter-imperialist geopolitical struggle is replaced by international collaboration. Van der Pijl offers exactly this. He suggests that American hegemony produced not only Fordism as a profound social innovation that qualitatively transformed capitalism but also Woodrow Wilson's 'universalism', which after World War II was instituted in formal and informal international organization (1984). With a lineage that goes back to informal networks such as the Freemasons, this created forums in which the interpersonal relationships between transnationally mobile capitalists and state managers were transformed in the course of seeking solutions to common socioeconomic problems (1998). Hence, through informal organizations such the International Chamber of Commerce, the Bilderberg Group, and later the Trilateral Commission, patterns of socialization among different national bourgeoisies changed. Rather than treating one another as part of external nature, they started to treat each other as part of the internal nature of common humanity. Hence, one can conceive of the formation of transnational power blocs as conditioning European integration. From a Marxist perspective, of course, this type of socialization is a highly one-sided representation of humanity, forged in exclusive circles of extreme privilege. The diffusion of Fordism as a concrete project not only produced regularities in capital accumulation that facilitated national class compromises but also enabled capitalist elites to resocialize themselves and their societies. If this story has something in common with both neo-functionalism and constructivism, it nevertheless provides a different analysis where capitalist power relations and interests – not institutions and ideas – are central to the story. Moreover, because capitalism is dynamic and contradictory, profound social and ecological dislocation and conflict continue to provide the main plot line (van der Pijl, 1997).

In the next chapter, we will show how the aforementioned transnational power blocs 'relaunched' European integration in a neoliberal direction. Here Bastiaan van Apeldoorn's (2002; see also Holman, 1992) study of the European Round Table of Industrialists (ERT) is exemplary. Taking his cues from Gramsci's 'relations of force' analysis (1971: p. 181) and van der Pijl's (1984) analysis of Atlantic Fordism, van Apeldoorn shows how the inner workings of the ERT unified European transnational capital around a neoliberal project that was successfully transmitted to policymakers. Van Apeldoorn highlights the inherently political and ideological nature of the process as mercantilist, and social democratic alternative conceptions were ultimately displaced in a process that assigned leadership to transnational, financial, and export-oriented capital fractions. Still, elements of mercantilism and social democracy remained at the margins as compensatory elements, providing for a broader-based power bloc. We view van Apeldoorn's analysis as a compelling account of how an elite accumulation strategy is formed. But we suggest that it overstates the supranational dimensions in the formation of broader inter-class hegemonic projects and understates the continued importance in that regard of nation states and interstate relations. Hence, while recognizing regulation-theoretical accounts of different regimes of accumulation and the contribution of the Amsterdam School in elucidating transnational agency in the power-laden transition from one regime of accumulation to another, we propose that these contributions are posed in an interstate conception that is closer to Poulantzas' original formulation (Cafruny & Ryner, 2007: pp. 18–21).

Conclusion

This chapter has introduced key concepts of critical political economy that will be applied and elaborated on in subsequent chapters. These concepts have been introduced through an epochal reading of EU history, a sociology of knowledge account of foundational works, and an account of how these inform contemporary critical scholarship.

We have underlined the central contribution of regulation theory – a synthesis of Marxist, post-Keynesian, and institutionalist insights – and its twin concepts of *mode of regulation* and *regime of accumulation*. The epochal narrative outlined in the first part of the chapter is above all a regulation-theoretical narrative. The two distinct epochs of EU developments are understood as aspects of a transnational mode of regulation, facilitating two distinct (Fordist and finance-led) regimes of accumulation.

However, the transition from one regime of accumulation to another is not a predetermined affair. Different developmental trajectories can be envisaged. Indeed, the main contribution of regulation theory to critical scholarship is its analysis of how the EU facilitated a neoliberal and finance-led regime of accumulation in Europe and repressed an alternative social democratic trajectory in the spirit of Servan-Shreiber. Understanding how one alternative is selected over another requires analysis of *accumulation strategies* and *hegemonic projects*. This has been the main contribution of the Amsterdam School, though debates can be had about whether hegemonic projects are undertaken by class and elite forces operating beyond the nation state or whether they reflect the balance of power between states.

The strength of concepts such as modes of regulation, regimes of accumulation, accumulation strategies, and hegemonic projects is their ability to show how and why capitalism avoids collapse but nevertheless changes over time. In short, they are useful for a conjunctural 'mid-range' analysis. As such, a direct line can be drawn between the epochal narrative in the introductory part of the chapter and the later sections. However, mid-range analysis makes sense only when grounded in an understanding of the underlying general generative structures of capitalism. This is offered in the intervening sections of the chapter in the discussion of The Red Queen Syndrome, Open Marxism, and works that have developed in the wake of the debate between Mandel and Poulantzas.

The Red Queen Syndrome refers to the basic structural necessity of capitalism to 'run in order to stand still' – that is, it must grow in order to avoid crisis. In marked contrast to liberal ideas of markets tending towards equilibrium, classical Marxism and post-Keynesianism have in different ways shown how this syndrome inherently generates the crisis tendencies of capitalism. The contradictory nature of the wage relation is crucial in this regard. Fordism and finance-led accumulation offered different ways of addressing these tendencies in different periods.

The contradictory nature and crisis tendencies of capitalism generate a substantive regulatory agenda that cannot be reduced, as liberals suggest, to a formal adaptation of means to ends. Rather, Marxist theories of the state suggest that this agenda constrains and confines democracy as major policy areas are formally *depoliticized*. Open Marxists have elucidated some of the key mechanisms of depoliticization and have illustrated the importance of EU competition and monetary policy. At a general level of abstraction, Open Marxists make a crucial contribution to the nature of EU governance and the nature of the capitalist state. However, when the assumption of a 'collective capitalist' is relaxed and the nature of capitalist competition is taken into account, insights derived from the debate between Mandel and Poulantzas become crucial.

Amalgamation and mergers of capital on a European scale, undertaken as a response to *over-accumulation* problems, are essential drivers of European integration. This is the crucial and enduring insight of Mandel to a critical analysis of the EU. These drivers generate an imperialist agenda at the EU level as socioeconomic requirements of amalgamated capital must be served. The question is, however, whether this results in an all-out imperial rivalry with the US. Following Poulantzas, we show that this is not the case. Rather, because of the dominance of the US in structurally strategic sectors, European business undertakes competitiveness strategies on terms defined by the US. In other words, the structures through which European capital is integrated (*interiorized*) into the transnational and transatlantic economy are fundamentally shaped on American terms. This structural context set the biased terrain on which the transition from Fordism to finance-led accumulation took place and on which neoliberal hegemonic projects were forged in Europe. It has resulted in increasingly *asymmetric regulation* where the EU plays a crucial part, which sits increasingly uneasily with the terms of legitimacy of European societies and which is becoming increasingly authoritarian.

Chapter 3

The Single Market: Consolidating Neoliberalism

Chapters 1 and 2 explored the main concepts and theoretical debates concerning European integration. We argued that traditional integration theories contain important blind spots that account for their inability to explain key developments in the history of the EU and that critical political economy provides a more satisfactory framework for understanding these developments. The chapters that follow analyse in more detail the key institutional developments and initiatives of the last 30 years, beginning in this chapter with the Single European Market (SEM). The creation of the SEM spearheaded a period of major neoliberal transformation in Europe and established the preconditions for the development of the monetary union, which will be explored in the next chapter. Indeed, the period of the 1980s that gave rise to the SEM and then the EMU is often referred to as the 'extended relaunch', because it gave new impetus to European integration after the empty chair crisis and the ensuing period of 'eurosclerosis' and institutional paralysis that accompanied the collapse of Bretton Woods in 1971.

This chapter starts out with a descriptive overview of the key diplomatic and institutional events surrounding the relaunch. We then take note of the neo-institutional turn in political science that coincided with the relaunch. Traditional approaches were informed by the neo-institutionalist turn to produce a new generation of theoretical perspectives on the EU: regime-theory – intergovernmentalism, multilevel governance, and constructivism – which promised a way out of the supranationalist–realist impasse. We show that these new theoretical perspectives in fact remain tethered to the realist or liberal frameworks and, hence, reproduce many of the same blind spots. However, neo-institutionalism does provide concepts and perspectives that offer the possibility of a synthesis. We conclude by connecting up to the previous chapter and show how the various strands of critical political economy can be woven together to identify the underlying power relations and structural problems in European and transatlantic capitalism that led to the single market and the extended relaunch of European integration.

The single market project: 'Europe 1992'

While the end of the Cold War led to substantial 'widening' in which Western states that had been non-aligned during the Cold War joined the EU in 1995, followed by most Eastern European states of the former communist bloc in 2004 and 2007, the relaunch is conceived from a 'deepening' perspective. The Fontainebleau European Council Summit of 1984 was key to this process. It resolved the long-standing issues of Spanish and Portuguese membership and the terms of the British budgetary rebate resulting from perceived inequity of the Common Agricultural Policy (CAP). This set the stage for a significant measure of consensus – especially between the Conservative British government under Thatcher, the German Christian Democratic government under Helmut Kohl, and the French Socialist government of François Mitterrand – on longer-term developments. After Mitterrand's U-turn away from a socialist Keynesian strategy amid a massive speculation against the franc, the French president was willing to join European partners on a project of European integration based on market liberalization and deregulation. As discussed further in Chapter 4, the successful realignment of currencies in the Exchange Rate Mechanism (ERM) of the EMS in 1983 served to consolidate this project. This realignment was based on an emergent consensus around monetarism, the paramount importance of asserting price stability even at the price of higher unemployment, and it relied on the German mark and, hence, 'sound money' – as an anchoring currency. Hence, the Fontainebleau Summit consolidated the ascendancy of neoliberal forces. It also resulted in the appointment of a new energetic president of the Commission, former French Socialist Minister of Finance Jacques Delors.

One year later, at the Milan Summit, the Commission presented the White Paper, Completing the Internal Market (1985), for which the British Conservative Commissioner Lord Cockfield was mainly responsible. This White Paper, which was adopted by the Council, embraced the ECJ's Cassis de Dijon ruling of 1979 that established the principle of mutual recognition (see also Padoa-Schioppa, 1987). The ECJ had ruled against the technicalities that had prohibited a variety of French liqueur being sold in the Federal Republic of Germany by asserting the principle that membership in the common market meant that states mutually recognized as legal the commodities that had been legally produced in other member states. By affirming the ECJ's liberal interpretation, the Milan Summit swept away a wide range of their nontariff barriers and charged the European Commission with lighting a 'bonfire of controls' that would eliminate all nontariff barrier restrictions that violated mutual recognition by the end of 1992. Under the leadership of Jacques Delors, the Commission engendered an unprecedented degree of commitment and élan to the programme. The slogan 'Europe 1992' would assume near-mythical proportions.

The Milan Summit bestowed formidable authority on the supranational agencies of the European Commission Directorate General of Competition (or, at the time, DG IV) as well as the ECJ. Armed with what in the Treaty of European Union (TEU) would become Articles 84 and 85 on restrictive practices and monopoly, the Merger Control Regulation of 1989 (through which the DG for Competition had to approve any major mergers), and restriction on state aids (Article 107), the DG for Competition became, in effect, a prosecutor general empowered to take companies and states to the 'Court of First Instance' (CFI) and ultimately the ECJ when practices infringed on EU competition policy. To balance the interest of building up large European oligopolies capable of competing on the world market, however, competition was understood in a particular way. Dominant position as such was not seen as a problem, but rather 'the abuse of' dominant position. Notably, the 'block exemptions' of Article 81(3) allow dominant position when it can be seen as 'benefiting the EU as a whole', when a 'fair share of the benefits go to the consumer', when 'any restriction is indispensable to the benefit' and there is 'no substantial elimination of competition' (e.g. Cini & McGowan, 1998).

However, the White Paper not only established the principle of 'negative integration' based on mutual recognition. It also estimated that 280 directives and regulations would need to be passed to complete 'Europe 1992', and it proposed eliminating the national veto in the Council of Ministers and a European Parliament 'cooperation procedure' (later co-decision) on issues pertaining to the implementation of the single market – in other words, as discussed already in Chapter 1, a (partial) repeal of the Luxembourg Compromise (European Commission, 1985). This call dovetailed with proposals of the so-called Dooge Committee on institutional reform. This call was met with resistance by Margaret Thatcher, who protested that Cockfield had 'gone native' in the Commission. However, the Italian president of the Council (Prime Minister Craxi) outmanoeuvred the British on a procedural technicality, which resulted in the 1986 Intergovernmental Conference in Luxembourg that passed the Single European Act (ratified in 1987), which amended voting rules so as to institute the requested qualified majority voting in a defined range of fields. Hence, 'Europe 1992' was given additional impetus, and a significant, albeit ring-fenced, move towards supranational governance was achieved.

It was against the backdrop that preparations were made for the most significant revision of the treaty structure to date and which indeed formally constituted the EU: The Treaty of European Union (TEU), negotiated in 1991 and ratified in 1993, also known as the Maastricht Treaty. The negotiations revealed tensions between political forces concerning what the implications of this completion should be that have persisted until the present time. The most ardent of neoliberals (personified by

Margaret Thatcher, but also including ordoliberal hawks in the Bundesbank, who held on to what's called 'coronation theory' (Dyson & Featherstone, 1999) believed that the Maastricht Treaty was unnecessary: Europe should remain a large single market and nothing much else. Other neoliberals thought that the single market would work better if complemented with formal market-accommodating rules accompanied by Qualified Majority Voting (QMV) and a common currency (this was increasingly becoming the view of business representatives in continental Europe, at least). For others (such as veteran German Foreign Minister Hans-Dietrich Genscher), the single market was a means to a larger political end of creating a European federation, or at least much closer political cooperation that combines intergovernmental and supranational elements. From such a perspective, a Treaty on European Union was the logical next step. Some federalists, mainly social democratic and left Christian democratic ones, hoped that the common currency would lead to agreement on common social standards – a 'social dimension' that would reconstitute the European welfare state on a continental level, when the nation state was no longer seen as a viable unit for the still desirable ends of the European 'social model'. Commission President Jacques Delors, who as Mitterrand's finance minister had witnessed firsthand how financial markets compelled the 'U-turn' on economic policy, embodied the latter tendency as for instance exemplified in his 1988 Bournemouth Speech to the British Trades Union Congress (see the Introduction and Chapter 5). In no small measure, the hopes of the last two tendencies depended on the prospects of extending QMV to areas beyond single-market implementation.

The federalists achieved some impressive gains. Most notably, a commitment was made to a common single currency through the Economic and Monetary Union, and the final and third stage of this process was indeed achieved in 1999 (Dyson & Featherstone, 1999). Furthermore, following some gains towards cooperation already in the SEA, the European Parliament was given significant authority as a genuinely legislative body through the 'co-decision' procedure. Henceforth, the predominant procedure of decision making would be one where legislative power was shared between the Council and the Parliament. Finally, European Political Cooperation in foreign policy and defence was formally incorporated into the Treaty as was cooperation on justice and home affairs. In other words, the remit of the EU went well beyond that set by the Treaty of Rome. On the other hand, the outcome of Maastricht can be read as a victory for the vision of the EU as essentially a single market: Common Foreign and Security Policy (CFSP) and Justice and Home Affairs (JHA) were quarantined as 'pillars' that were distinct from the amended Treaty of Rome structure, wherein cooperation and decision making would be purely intergovernmental, where the national veto remained, and where the Commission would not even have the legislative initiative. Furthermore, with company law, corporate governance regulation, and a Second Banking Directive based on mutual recognition, the EMU would be founded on deregulated financial markets and highly disciplinary convergence criteria (see Chapter 4), and the new European Central Bank (ECB) would have its mandate and constraint set by impeccably monetarist principles. Ensuring price stability for the single market would be its overarching brief. In addition the United Kingdom (and later Denmark and de facto, if not de jure, Sweden) were given and exercised opt-outs from the single currency.

Explaining the relaunch

The relaunch revived interest in the EU as a novel development in international relations and inspired a great deal of new scholarship. The SEA and the EMU provided an ideal testing ground for theories of European integration, and a great deal of the financial support for this scholarship on both sides of the Atlantic came from the Commission's new academic outreach programmes (Klinke, 2014). Liberal economic theory provided the intellectual and normative underpinnings of this scholarship. The Cecchini Report by the European Commission (1988) itself was, as explained in Chapter 1, essentially a cost-benefit analysis in line with Bela Balassa's variant of trade theory, albeit with relaxed assumptions on market imperfections. This report estimated the opportunity costs for failing to remove the nontariff barriers as laid out by the single market to be 5 per cent of total annual GDP. The Commission's economists predicted that if the single market programme had been fully implemented, single market annual growth would be 7 per cent by 1992, with an inflation rate of 4.5 per cent, and 5 million new jobs would have been created (European Commission, 1988: pp. 175, 176, cited in Boyer, 1990: pp. 114–15). The huge economic gains that would result from the completion of the single market would come from, inter alia, the static effects of a more refined division of labour and comparative advantage, the dynamic effects resulting from economies of scale, the elimination of x-inefficiencies through more stringent competition, and economies of learning as national boundaries for communication were eliminated.

While the explanations emerging from political science and international relations did generate new insights, traditional discourse remained within the terms set by the disciplinary split from economics. This was reflected in the privileging of the political-sociological question of integration, understood in terms of the density of social relations and the question of what the determining 'level' was that explains why the relaunch took place (see Chapter 1). Indeed, the problem was compounded because of the turn of economics away from Keynesianism, which increased confidence in the 'naturalness' of markets and their spontaneous tendency towards efficiency and equilibrium. Since political science has deferred to economics on economic issues, this reinforced the tendency to consider the market-driven motor-force of integration as a rational quasi-force of nature.

The neo-institutionalist turn

The discipline of political science was originally about understanding formal institutions. However, recognizing that much politics happened beyond the surface of formal institutions such as parliaments and international organizations, political scientists were increasingly drawn away from the study of institutions (Peters, 2005: pp. 3–15). As we have seen in the previous chapters, realists and neo-functionalists either reduced politics to the individual level of analysis or found individual-like behavioural attributes in units such as states. By contrast, Marxists, as well as some realists, increasingly turned towards structural explanations, where contextual parameters (whether understood as the capitalist mode of production or interstate anarchy) were held to explain outcomes. The 1970s saw a movement back to institutions (e.g. March & Olsen, 1984). This was not a return to the descriptive and naïve-formal institutionalism of old that denied the causal power of underlying individual motives or structures. Rather, it understood institutions as intervening variables that refracted and lent variance to underlying forces. Modern bureaucracies and organizations were too complex and sturdy to be mere passive transmission belts between underlying social contexts and outcomes. Institutions were seen as feeding back and partially shaping social environments and individual motives, incentives, and perhaps even identities. This complex interplay of structure, individual motives, and institutions also warranted scepticism concerning the ultimate rationality or optimality of outcomes (March & Olsen, 1984: pp. 737, 742–4). Events do not necessarily unfold in accordance with the functional requirements of underlying structures or individual preferences.

Neo-institutionalism exerted a strong influence over EU studies. To be sure, the theoretical debates inspired by the relaunch represented an extension of the perennial debate between 'supranationalists' and 'integovernmentalists'. The former inherited neo-functionalist arguments, and the latter took up the baton from the realists. However, these debates were also informed by neo-institutionalist approaches. Indeed, having learned from the anomalies that neither the original neo-functionalists nor realists could explain, there was much that the two protagonists could agree on.

The most prominent of the anomalies in question was the following: While the empty chair crisis had discredited the evolutionary predictions of neo-functionalism and the concept of spillover, the increased European cooperation that started at Fontainebleau in 1984 took place at a time when the competing realist hypothesis predicted less cooperation as a result of declining US hegemony (Gilpin, 1987; Kennedy, 1988). The combination of the empty chair crisis and developments towards more cooperation in the EC, not less, despite perceived US hegemonic decline, seemed to an increasing number of scholars to lend support to Robert Keohane's variant of regime theory, which drew on a rational choice 'calculus' approach to neo-institutionalism in order to synthesize liberalism and realism (1984). This approach holds that events are not shaped by factors behind human control, but rather by institutional 'path dependence'. Institutions provide actors with more or less certainty about the manner in which other actors are likely to act, hence significantly shaping mutual strategic calculations and therefore the prospects of overcoming collective action problems (Hall & Taylor, 1996: p. 939). In other words, social relations at the national and European level are shaped by institutions, raising questions about possibilities of designing or at least 'gardening' institutions so as to shape incentives and outcomes. Given the rigorous and parsimonious, yet generalized, answers that rational choice institutionalism gives to these questions, the attractions of this theory for policy prescription are obvious.

Regimes and institutions

Keohane conceded that neo-realists had captured the essential operative forces of world politics. However, following a 'calculus' variant of neo-institutionalism, he argued that once a hegemonic configuration had created institutions of international cooperation, these institutions might in turn reshape the incentive structures of states to such an extent that they could survive and even flourish despite hegemonic decline. Once created, institutions such as GATT and the EC generated the favourable outcomes that liberals predicted. That means that the opportunity costs for abandoning them became sufficiently high for states not to do so. What is more, the institutions could increase the confidence that other states made the same calculation, reducing the fear that other states would defect from the regime. In other words, regimes produce organizational certainty, which ensures that, once created, they and the liberal system that they have produced may survive hegemonic decline. This is a theoretical position that is sufficiently statist to be consistent with the empty chair crisis, while also being consistent with the Fontainebleau Summit and its aftermath: States are alive and well as actors despite increased interdependence and are not necessarily willing to concede sovereign powers. However, by 1984 the benefits of the common market were sufficiently institutionally entrenched to ensure that the EC not only survived the decline of US hegemony but also motivated the member states to respond to the US hegemonic decline by pursuing an even more ambitious integration agenda in the form of the single market, the SEA, and eventually both the Maastricht Treaty and the EMU.

The influence of Keohane's synthesis of realism and liberalism on EU studies in the form of an institutionalist calculus – and especially the relaunch – can hardly be overestimated. A great deal of scholarship followed Keohane's lead by seeking to understand the interactions between the balance of power and interest, on the one hand, and the regime institutional dynamic, on the other hand. Debates about how to explain the single market, the SEA, the Maastricht Treaty, and their aftermath thus took place *within* regime theory, turning on the more fine-grained and pragmatic question about whether supranational actors exercise meaningful autonomous authority in the political process, whether states remain the 'masters of the treaties', or whether the EU has produced some sort of distinct polity characterized by multilevel governance.

One of the first attempts to explain the causes of the SEA within this general framework was the supranationalist interpretation of Wayne Sandholtz and John Zysman (1989). Their allegiance to Keohane's liberal-realist synthesis is evident. The realist elements are evident not only in their rejection of neo-functionalist evolutionism but perhaps more significantly in their acceptance of the salience of relative economic gains, which provided a crucial impetus for the decision to embark on the single-market project. Pursuing an argument that curiously inverted that of Servan-Shreiber, they suggested that European states had been able to rely on technological spinoffs from the US to sustain their high-value-added industries in the post-war period. However, as American hegemony declined, and as US dominance in the vanguard sectors in the world economy eroded, it was no longer possible for the Europeans to rely on this transatlantic transmission mechanism. Not being able to rely on this mechanism meant that the economic innovation increasingly had to be generated within Europe itself, and this required not only tariff-free trade but the creation of a completely free home market on a continental scale.

However, if the impetus for the single market can be explained with reference to realist concerns for relative gains, the process that ensured its success was best explained by the resilience of liberal institutions of cooperation internal to the European community itself. Sandholz and Zysman asserted that supranational agency was crucial for its success. Not only was the mechanism of mutual recognition devised through precedent-setting rulings by the supranational ECJ, but also the European Commission played a decisive role by acting as a policy entrepreneur and setting the policy agenda that ensured success, including the drafting of reports and treaties that led to a qualified-majority-voting system. The Commission also acted as an interlocutor with transnationalizing European business, especially through its deliberations with the European Roundtable of Industrialists (ERT).

Andrew Moravcsik's intergovernmentalist interpretation also accorded with Keohane's regime theory: EC institutions ensured that commitments that member states made to agreements were conceived as credible by the partner states, addressing fears of defections. A consequence of such institutional regime resilience is that classical realist 'geopolitical' explanations do not work. However, Moravcsik challenged Sandholtz and Zysman's argument that supranational agency was crucial in the agreements behind the relaunch. Through a careful empirical analysis, he reaffirmed the realist dictum that states are the principal actors: The single market and Maastricht agreements should be understood as produced by interstate bargains, reflecting the balance of power between the member states. Especially important in this regard was the lowest common denominator of interests of the largest member states: France, the UK, and Germany, where the exit option of the most Eurosceptic of these (the UK) was tempered by the threat of exclusion (by the others proceeding also with lowest common denominator agreements outside formal structures, excluding the UK). This was complemented by side payments to smaller states as required to facilitate the smooth passing of agreements (Lange, 1993).

For Moravcsik, intergovernmentalism could explain the grand bargains underpinning the major treaties and treaty revisions. But where do state preferences come from in the first place? Originally, Moravcsik derived these preferences abstractly and in straightforward neorealist terms from each state's position in the international system but refracted by the informational and confidence-ensuring functions served by international institutions (1991). However, in recognition of empirical problems and the lack of substantive specificity entailed in such analysis (cf. Ruggie, 1982), he subsequently complemented his intergovernmentalist bargaining model with a liberal-pluralist model of preference formation. Hence, the preferences are seen as determined in the first instance by electoral and interest-group politics internal to each state. In other words, Moravcsik (1998) ultimately ended up with a two-level-game (pace Putnam, 1988) explanation of the politics of the EU.

Moravcsik's careful process of tracing effectively refuted supranationalist arguments concerning Commission entrepreneurship, especially by contrasting what the Commission originally advocated with actual outcomes. Supranationalists, however, tend to stick to their guns when it comes to the independent role of the ECJ (Burley & Mattli, 1993; Mattli & Slaughter, 1995), and on this score, intergovernmentalists – even Moravcsik – are prepared to concede ground (Garrett, 1995; Garrett & Tsebelis, 1996; Moravcsik, 1995). Supranationalists have also drawn on neo-institutionalism in economics to argue that institutional developments in the political sphere also institute markets in particular ways, reducing transaction costs and instilling confidence in such a way that increasingly supranational outcomes ensue that in turn feed into the political sphere (Fligstein & Stone Sweet, 2002; see also Stone Sweet & Sandholtz, 1998: pp. 1–26). David R. Cameron (1997) made a similar argument on the transition from the EMS to the EMU. Still, Moravcsik's argument, that member states are the central actors in the grand bargains at the key summits and IGCs, seems to have stuck.

Multilevel governance

Neo-institutionalism has also been called upon to argue that we should not overestimate the importance of the grand bargains at the expense of the cumulative impact of what one observer called 'everyday' (Wincott, 1995) decisions and practices in entities such as the ECJ, the Commission, and even subnational units. While not denying the importance of intergovernmental bargaining, this literature has suggested that 'everyday' supranational and sub-national as well as national policymaking would, over time, constrain and shape intergovernmental bargaining because of the short-term time horizons that national politicians have when they conclude grand bargains that limit their perspective (Pierson, 1996). Consequently, other 'levels' co-constitute EU polity, generating 'multilevel governance' (Marks, Hooghe, & Blank, 1996).

Simon Hix (1994, 1999, 2005) was one of the first scholars to develop a theoretically explicit explanatory framework to account for multilevel governance. Rather controversially, he asserted that the study of the EU had relied too much on the sub-discipline of international relations, and the antidote should be to analyse the EU through the lens of comparative politics. Questions that one might raise about the EU as it exists now are questions that one might ask about any multileveled political system (such as federal ones), '[a]nd the discipline of political science has developed a vast array of theoretical tools and analytical methods to answer ... these questions' (Hix, 1999: pp. 1–2). At its most fundamental level, Hix aligned his approach with David Easton's (1953) conventional, and arguably idealized, analytical model of the functioning of the 'political system' in liberal democracies.

For Hix, a political system is said to exist when the following elements are present, and which Hix suggests is now the case in the EU (Hix, 1999: pp. 2, 2–5): first, a stable and clearly defined set of institutions for collective decision making and rules that govern relations between and within these institutions and citizens and social groups seek to achieve their political desires through the political system, either directly or through intermediary organizations like interest groups and political parties; second, collective decisions in the political system have a significant impact on the distribution of economic resources and the allocation of social and political values across the whole system; third, there is a continuous interaction ('feedback') between these political outputs, new demands on the system, new decisions, and so on. Based on these criteria, Hix concedes that the EU as a political system is weak. In the absence of a powerful European mass media and public sphere of collective deliberation, 'national elites' control how EU policy is deliberated upon within nationally segmented spheres. Nevertheless, 'EU outputs affect the "authoritative allocation of values" (Easton, 1957) and "who gets what, when and how"' (Lasswell, 1936) (Hix, 1999: p. 4). Moreover, because of factors such as EU jurisprudence (especially the Supremacy of European law and Direct Effect), the EU has managed to develop these representative systemic properties of generating collectively binding decisions in the name of the 'general will' despite the fact that sovereignty understood in the conventional sense of the monopoly on the legitimate use of coercion remains in the nation state. Conventional conceptions, such as those underpinning the intergovernmental–supranationalist debate, have underestimated the extent to which these aspects of sovereignty can be separated from each other (Hix, 1999: pp. 4–5). Therefore, the EU should not be understood simply as a conventional international organization, a point which Simon Bulmer (1993: p. 355) puts across with the rhetorical question:

> In what other international organisations do we find the involvement of over 500 transnational interest groups, interaction with local government lobbyists, and elected parliament seeking to play its part in international institutional decision making, and a law-based mode of regulating collective governance?

From calculus to culture: constructivism

Constructivism emerged in international relations as a result of what some scholars suggested to be impasses in regime theory. In a seminal review article, Kratochwil and Ruggie (1986) argued that there was a fundamental contradiction in regime theory: While research had indicated that it was ideational properties ('implicit or explicit principles, norms, rules, and decision-making procedures around which actors' expectations converge') (Krasner, 1983: p. 2), regime theory ultimately subscribed to a materialist-rationalist ontology. The obvious redress was a theoretical shift in assumptions towards constructivism and a cultural approach to institutions. Constructivists asserted that instrumental self-interests should not be seen as the fundamental determinants of EU institutions at all. Rather, inverting the presumed causal chain between interests and ideas, they adopted a 'cultural' approach to institutions and assign fundamental importance to ideas. They brought to the forefront aspects that originally had been secondary to Haas' own work (Haas, 2001). Haas had, for instance, pointed to the integrative force that *'engrenage'* among policy elites could have: the subjective sense of belonging to the same professional community and the sharing of scientific and policy paradigms as well as technical know-how that transcended national borders.

Thomas Risse's work is a prominent case in point. He suggested that the convergence of international relations and comparative public policy research around the concept of multilevel governance, challenging the conventional 'Westphalian' notion of the unitary, sovereign state underlined the significance of constructivism (1996). All institutionalist research on the EU, even its most austere rational choice variants, had concluded that ideas about the single market were important for its institutionalization (Garrett & Weingast, 1993, cited in Risse-Kappen, 1996: p. 69). But research had not established why a certain idea became institutionalized over another. Underlying this lacuna was also the faulty assumption that nominal subscription to an idea for merely tactical and instrumental reasons was sufficient for institutionalization. By contrast, Risse argued that the requisite consensus that successful international negotiations over institutions implies requires a genuine sharing and internalization of beliefs about the way that the world works ('causal beliefs') as well as principles (Risse-Kappen, 1996: pp. 68–70). Drawing on a Habermasian distinction, international negotiations show, according to Risse, that 'communicative-active' and 'deliberative' processes occurring outside formal and 'instrumental' bargaining situations are decisive (Risse-Kappen, 1996: p. 70). In post-Westphalian organizational configurations, characterized by increased informality and non-hierarchy, more space is opened for such communicative action. If we are to understand the nature of the multileveled EU, therefore, the primary focus of attention has to be on the content of shared ideologies, identities, and scientific paradigms of experts through which perceptions of interests are filtered and refracted and on the extent to which these intersubjective meanings are shared (Risse-Kappen, 1996: p. 70).

Subsequently, a large body of constructivist research on the EU has emerged, taking the cue from Haas' notion of *engrenage*. The object is to investigate the extent to which cooperation in EU-level deliberations re-socializes actors and hence their preferences, making them less 'national' and more 'European'. Martin Marcussen's (1999) work on the progress from the EMS and the EMU is a case in point. Jeffrey Checkel (2003) has done research on the issue of civic rights, focusing on a Europe-level organization formally outside the EU, the Council of Europe. Risse, however, suggests that this is at best a secondary dynamic. Socialization into European identities works less through supranational policy deliberation and more through processes at the national level (see also Zürn & Checkel, 2005) – that is, taking a cue from neo-institutionalism, path-dependent processes through which

European identities are forged and embedded work through the reconstitution of national identities. In other words, being German means being European and vice versa. However, this is an uneven development with national identities being more or less resistant to such Europeanization (Risse, 2005).

A critical assessment of traditional theoretical developments

As this chapter has shown, the neo-institutionalist turn exerted a great deal of influence over traditional European integration scholarship. First, overly polarized and reductionist debates between neo-functionalists and realists could, through neo-institutionalist language, be transformed into explorations of theoretical synthesis, or at least a common language of agreement on empirically testable propositions. For instance, Moravcsik (1995) welcomed supranationalist and multilevel governance critiques of his work and suggested that disagreements hinged on the empirical questions of whether the member states could control their agents in EU institutions. Others have suggested that neo-institutionalism also provides a common language through which debates between rationalist 'calculus' approaches and constructivist 'cultural' approaches can be arbitrated through empirical tests. Here the main issue concerns the extent to which empirical realities best conform to instrumental behaviour or deliberative learning and persuasion (Jupille, Caporaso, & Checkel, 2003). As a result, integration research has become a lot richer. This is not least the case because the concept of multilevel governance at least opens up the possibility of considering substantive policy matters, as opposed to merely formal questions pertaining to the 'level' at which the 'real' EU action takes place. This includes, most notably, questions about democracy. Furthermore, constructivism also suggests the need to investigate 'common sense' about European integration by making it more difficult to rest arguments on a priori assumptions.

However, these various strands of traditional theory remain, on the whole, trapped in the constraints identified in the previous two chapters. The 'integration' process itself remains idealized and conceived in teleological terms. Power relations that are constitutive of it are still overlooked. The relational aspects (the first face) of power and agenda-setting power (the second face) are studied, but the fundamental structural power (the third face) is ignored. In this respect, regime theory does not transcend the debate between the liberal 'optimists' and realist 'pessimists' as discussed in Chapter 2. On the whole, regimes such as the institutional ensemble that is the EU are conceived in benevolent terms. The power-laden motives of states may to a lesser or greater extent have played into their creation, but they are themselves seen as expressions of Pareto-optimality that transcend state powers and interest or at least appropriately shackle these within checks and balances. Despite the groundwork done in the field of international political economy (IPE) over a couple of decades, power relations remain conspicuously absent from 'the economy'. Neoclassical assumptions concerning the self-equilibrating virtues of trade are more than ever accepted at face value. Indeed, these deficiencies have become, if anything, even more pronounced and have become so despite the fact that uneven development (see Chapter 6) and anaemic rates of growth (see Table 3.1 below) have made a mockery out of the Cecchini Report and (as we shall see in the next chapter) equally unrealistic claims concerning the impact of the monetary union on growth and social welfare, not to mention the inability to even identify the factors generating the financial and Eurozone crisis (see Chapter 4).

In this respect, the extensions of EU research into the realms of comparative public policy in the form of multilevel governance and constructivism have provided no novel insights. Indeed, these approaches have had virtually nothing to say about the crisis of the Eurozone. Simon Hix's 'political system' account conforms to the idealized pluralism of modified liberalism as identified in Chapter 1. This markedly contrasts with neo-pluralists in the 1970s recognizing the salience of the special interest-group power of business elites as developed in debates with neo-Marxist state theory, as was discussed in Chapter 2 (Lindblom, 1977), which resulted in scaling back their claims about the extent to which the real world of liberal democracy corresponds to the idealized self-description. Neo-Marxist critiques of pluralism have given rise to more fruitful engagement on a neo-pluralist conceptual terrain (e.g. Lindberg, Alford, Crouch, & Offe, 1975; Gilens & Page, 2014). Such engagement, however, has been painfully absent in EU scholarship, thus raising questions about its status as a progressive research programme.

To be sure, Hix does address the problem of social 'feedback' in the EU – the extent to which a broader European public can feed their responses to policy outputs back into the system – which is a reasonably apt way to capture the 'democratic deficit'. Yet, when we search for the problem, the spotlight shines on the usual suspects: 'national elites'.

Table 3.1   *Average annual rate of real GDP growth EU–15*

	Percentage Growth
1961–1973	4.3
1974–1985	2.1
1986–1995	2.5
1996–2005	2.4
2006–2015	0.8

Source: European Commission (2015a: Table 110)

And when he does address the social basis of representative democracy in political sociology – the richly researched material on social cleavages that followed in the wake of Lipset and Rokkan's work (e.g. Mair, 1990) – he reduces this complex question of class, religion, and language, to a single 'national/territorial' and transnational/socioeconomic' cleavage. Hence, despite professing to break out of the liberal vs realist debate, in this fundamental respect Hix remains firmly within the terms of the integration telos of that debate, with transnational rationalists squaring up against emotional nationalists (see also Fligstein, 2009). Similarly, constructivists such as Risse pose their questions about ideas, epistemic frames, and identities in terms of the extent to which they aid or hinder the integration process. The potentially power-laden and ideologically specific construction of the EU institutions themselves does not concern them. Never is this more evident than when Risse equates the constitution of EU institutions with Habermasian communicative rationality, where it is not interests but rather the 'better argument' that wins. Whereas for Habermas (1975) this was originally merely a counterfactual construct, which provides us with an analytical standpoint from which we can analyse how reality diverts from this ideal, for Risse this is reality itself. Here Risse harks back to a pre-functionalist Wilsonian liberal idealism. In Hall and Taylor's (1996: pp. 950–5) terms, multilevel governance and constructivism fall into the trap of providing 'bloodless' accounts that are symptomatic of rational choice and constructivist 'sociological' institutionalism. The absence of blood is a result of their refusal to address the power relations that inhere in the institutional constitution of the SEM itself.

The relaunch and Europe's social model of capitalism? Possibility of synthesis?

Put simply, European integration theories continue to be marred by the fundamental blind spot that follows from the disciplinary split and the integration telos. That being said, there are some exceptional works on the fault line of neo-pluralist comparative public policy and EU studies that escape this trap. To invoke Milward's terminology, they do so because they focus more on questions of European state formation than the idealized transatlantic problematic. In other words, they are primarily concerned with the implication of the EU and its mode of integration for Europe's model of welfare capitalism. Important work that can provide useful building blocks also for a critical political economy perspective have thus been developed from modified neo-functionalist, rational-choice, and constructivist perspectives.

Philippe Schmitter occupies a fascinating position among neo-functionalist theorists. His distinguished scholarship on the progressive and redistributive aspects of the 'modified liberalism' of the US New Deal had drawn him towards political economy and engagement with the ECLA school, pioneers of dependency theory in Latin American studies (e.g. Schmitter, 1972). In a European context, Schmitter did pioneering work on corporatism (e.g. Lehmbruch & Schmitter, 1979), provoking a surprisingly non-ideological exchange between neo-pluralists and neo-Marxists. This work was, first, shaped by a number of iterations in the 1970s of theoretical exchanges on the nature of the state between neo-pluralists and neo-Marxists. Second, it was shaped by the empirical departure that European public policy, characterized by Rhineland capitalism, made from the pluralist ideal type, in terms of corporatist organized interest intermediation between a limited number of quasi-official interest groups rather transparently representing certain class interests.

From such a perspective, Schmitter has offered a remarkable fusion of neo-functionalism and corporatist research, where he seeks to address the implications of the single market for Rhineland capitalism (1997). He addresses the fear that the expansion to a single market on the basis of 'negative integration' comes at the price of the progressive undermining of the Rhineland mechanisms. He mentions in particular the integration into Anglo-American-dominated global financial markets (e.g. Story & Walter, 1997), or the effects of mutual recognition on voice-based networks. Schmitter asks if the problems posed by mutual recognition for what he calls the intermediary institutions of the Rhineland Model are likely to lead to spillover towards a pan-European Rhineland Model. While the prospect of a formal politics in that direction is slim (e.g. Steeck & Schmitter, 1991), he explores the prospects of an informal spillover in the field of standard setting. Ultimately, he concludes on a pessimistic note that the requisite element of 'politicization' is missing.

Fritz Scharpf (2002) has captured this logic through the more formalized rational-choice, neo-institutionalist model of the 'joint decision-making trap', originally formulated with reference to German federalism. In this model, he has offered some rather sobering verdicts about the effects of a system that has been built on the edifice of mutual recognition: Even though mutual recognition probably was required to achieve sufficient scale to rejuvenate the European economy, the cost has been a joint decision-making trap in salient policy issue areas, especially social policy (see chapter 5). Even though EU states require minimum standards and tax rates to protect adequate social policies, it is impossible to meet the threshold for effective common action when the constituent member states in the Council share decision-making powers with supranational entities such as the Commission and Parliament. After all, the threshold of decision (de facto unanimity) is too high to achieve agreement on what precisely should be done to address the common problem. Still, a federal solution is unlikely given the extent to which social policy traditions are nationally segmented and central to national sovereignty. At the same time, for reasons stated by regime theory and economists, exiting the single market to shore up national models of welfare is not an option either. In other words, even though most scholars and observers recognize the policy problems of joint decisions, they are trapped.

These pessimistic conclusions are far from uncontested. Drawing on the historical-institutionalist idea of path dependence and 'gaps' that lend autonomy to supranational arrangements, Martin Rhodes (2002) and Ronald Doré (2000) suggest that the EU's rhetoric of creating a modified European 'social model' fit for the age of globalization has more purchase than the pessimists conclude. Colin Hay (2000) agrees, but he argues from a constructivist perspective that it is important to differentiate between structural-functional and contingent-ideational forces. He categorizes Europe's restrictive macroeconomic stance as a contingent-ideational force, which has been more detrimental to Europe's 'social model' than the putatively objective structural forces associated with 'globalization'.

Colin Hay and Ben Rosamond (2002; also Rosamond, 1999) have, we would argue, better realized the potential constructivist contribution to a critical perspective than the other constructivist works reviewed here. Rather than merely deploying constructivism to reconnect liberalism with idealism, they use it to ask questions about the politico-ideological constitution and institutionalization of the economy, which is associated with the relaunch of the EU. They then proceed to ask questions about the way that this particular contingent and politico-ideological construct of the economy becomes normalized and taken for granted as if it were an objective reality in public policy circles and among mass publics. For Hay and Rosamond, 'globalization' – the idea that we are now living in a world where the breakdown of communication bottlenecks has made product and capital markets hyper-mobile – is a meta-discourse that has generated the requisite policy cohesion to realize the single market, the EMU, and the Lisbon Programme and to furnish it with the content and direction that it has. Despite the fact that evidence suggests that this structural mobility is overstated, the attendant sense that 'there is no alternative' has demobilized opposition and alternatives. Hence, in a sort of self-fulfilling prophecy, negative integration as constituted by mutual recognition – especially in financial services, Maastricht's growth and stability norms, and ECB independence – have politically and ideologically constituted the constraints in question.

Whether thus intended or not, each of these three sets of work contribute insights to the critical political economy analysis of the European Union. Schmitter has productively recast neo-functionalism to address concerns about European models of capitalism, with a lineage back to the social mercantilism of Servan-Schreiber. Importantly, he identifies central problems that negative integration poses for the maintenance of the intermediary institutions upon which Rhineland capitalism, corporatism, and the welfare-state class compromises between organized capital and labour, have been based. At the same time (and contra the evolutionary optimism of Haas), Schmitter provides good reasons to be cautious about the prospects of reconstituting the 'social model' at the federal European level. Fritz Scharpf cuts through idealized accounts of multilevel governance, and through the parsimonious and austere language of rational choice theory, he puts the matters raised by Schmitter in a nutshell through the concept of the 'joint decision-making trap'. Though these may not be the final words on the matter, these are weighty issues to which we will have reason to return in the course of this book (see especially Chapter 5). Hay and Rosamond make a singularly critical contribution through their analysis of globalization as discourse by asking whether alleged natural constraints that are corrosive of European welfare capitalism ('There is no alternative') are in fact social constructions, and they thereby allow for alternatives to neoliberalism.

But there are also limitations to these accounts that, we believe, a creative engagement with critical political economy can overcome. Perhaps paradoxically, Schmitter and Scharpf do not take sufficient account of either structure or agency. As we will seek to demonstrate, the joint decision-making trap is not an accidental configuration but rather an expression of the structural power of capital, configured according to a US-centred, finance-led model of growth. Furthermore, this configuration is at least in part the outcome of the strategic coordination of dominant fractions of capital and state managers – a coordination that can be aptly described as a hegemonic strategy with neoliberal content. Hay and Rosamond contribute to the substantiation of this argument. Notwithstanding their insistence on the co-constitution of the ideational and the material in the abstract (e.g. Hay, 2002b), the ideational features almost as an independent variable in their account. We believe that this greatly underestimates the extent to which ideational discourses are moulded and promoted – sometimes remarkably pragmatically – from the vantage point of particular material interests. While it is true that material interests are always conceived through discourses, it is important to remember that the opposite is equally true.

The single market, neoliberalism, and finance-led growth

Meanwhile, at the liminal realm of European integration research, researchers in the regulation-theoretical tradition offered an alternative analysis and assessment of the SEM. Reacting to the capitalist restructuring that was underway in the 1980s, as already documented in

Chapter 2, regulation theorists issued strong warnings against a 'Europe 1992' based on negative integration, mutual recognition, and competition in the absence of a substantially meaningful social dimension, industrial policy, and a Keynesian mechanism at the macroeconomic level (Leborgne & Lipietz, 1990). John Grahl and Paul Teague (1989, 1990), for example, argued that this type of restructuring would not be adequate to institute a new, progressive, mode of regulation. Rather than providing an institutional framework adequate for the realization of production possibilities inherent in new technology, the policy would serve the narrow interests of Europe's existing multinational corporations. An important detriment, in this context, is that Servan-Shreiber's vision of a Europe-wide high-technology policy remains elusive and is nationally fragmented, which is to the detriment of developing new vanguard industries and sectors (Soete, 2009).

We already saw in Chapter 2 how Boyer (1990) expanded on this argument in slightly more diplomatic language. In a detailed and critical review of the Cecchini Report, he presciently suggested that Europe might be on the way to a stalemated neo-Fordist scenario, where the institutional frame for negotiated involvement would be lacking but institutional path dependencies from Europe's welfare states would pre-empt an all-out adaptation of flexible neoliberalism. The result would be low growth and continued high unemployment. In particular, Boyer took the Cecchini Report to task for its overly optimistic projections on the dynamic effects arising from returns to scale and their interaction with the economies of learning (by doing), which 'brings into play the competence and motivations of wage earners' (1990: p. 110). This optimism was based on macroeconomic modelling of cumulative effects that 'at best permits variations around a reasonably balanced growth path, but cannot allow for the transition to a new rate of growth':

> To the extent that the unification of the European market may prove to have such structural ramifications as European Community economists predict, it is risky to base simulations on data from the 1960s and the 1970s .... (It is thus warranted to strike) a cautionary note as regards the use of macroeconomic models to define the viability of a potential new growth regime. (Boyer, 1990: p. 115)

Given that these models have a 'Keynesian bias' (Boyer, 1990: p. 115), it would seem reasonable to ensure that Keynesian mechanisms are put into place in the SEM to ensure that the buoyant predictions of the Cecchini Report are realized. However, apart from concerns about the realization of the social dimension, it is here that regulation theory issued its most ominous and prescient warning with regard to the working of the European Monetary System (EMS) and a one-sided focus on market competition financial services, which would be extended to the Maastricht design of the EMU (Grahl & Teague, 1989: pp. 42–9; Lipietz, 1989: pp. 47–8). Indeed, Chapter 6 will show how this has been borne out by subsequent developments as the dynamics of uneven development threaten the single-market project itself. Subsequent writings by regulation theorists have argued (and as expanded on in Chapters 4 through 6) that the defensive path of restructuring that SEM facilitated resulted in a set of European socioeconomic developments that ranged between flexible neoliberalism and neo-Fordism, with retrenchment of social rights, anaemic growth (Table 3.1), and uneven development. A central element of this has been the new way of securing the expanded reproduction of capital through finance-led accumulation as discussed in the previous chapter and further elaborated in the next chapter. As Chapter 5 shows, this dynamic puts immense pressure on the European social model.

The strategic agency of capitalist elites

As we argued in the previous chapter, however, regulation theory has very little to say about the social forces that have constituted such accumulation regimes. One central dimension of this is the strategic agency of capitalist elites. Bastiaan van Apeldoorn (2002; see also Holman, 1992) has shown in considerable detail how the European Round Table of Industrialists (ERT) as a multilateral 'private planning network', inter alia, facilitated class unity of Europe's transnational capitalist groupings and exercised leadership over the direction and content of the single-market project. The socioeconomic content of the project was entirely in accordance with the neoliberal norms emanating from Atlanticist restoration. The ERT played a key role in forging such unity and thereby resolving real and potential fractional conflicts between export-oriented, import-competing, and domestically oriented producers in consumer and investment sectors. The ERT also set the agenda and coordinated Commission policy and strongly influenced the policy of nation states in the Council of Ministers. Finally, concessions to a 'social dimension' formed part of a process of the necessary extension the social basis of this accumulation strategy beyond the strict confines of economic corporate interests to secure sufficient legitimacy. Hence, van Apeldoorn connects Grahl & Teague's assessment of the interests that the SEM served with a sustained political analysis that resonates with Poulantzas' concept of a 'power bloc'. However, given that van Apeldoorn focuses on concrete strategies of agents rather than structural effects, his analysis is much more in line with Gramsci's original understanding.

Van Apeldoorn's analysis has informed a number of careful studies on the institutionalization of the SEM, especially in the fields of competition policy (Buch-Hansen & Wigger, 2010a, 2010b) and corporate governance (Overbeek, van Apeldoorn, & Nölke, 2007; Horn, 2012). Buch-Hansen and Wigger point to the importance of a 'public-private alliance of transnational actors', consisting of the DG for Competition and transnational business, in asserting a neoliberal 'competition only' form of regulation. This contrasts with the exemptions that EC competition policy allowed in the Fordist period on mercantilist and social policy grounds, when there was an absence of merger control and where certain anti-competitive agreements were exempt from competition policy (Buch-Hansen & Wigger, 2010a: p. 10). For Horn, a similar alliance enabled EU governance to mediate between the global dynamics of finance-led accumulation and the structural pressures identified by Grahl and a recasting of national corporate governance regulation so as to facilitate access of institutional investors to corporate ownership and trading in corporate assets. Hence co-determination (industrial democracy) as opposed to shareholder democracy has been decisively curtailed. This has been done by curtailing any attempts towards company law harmonization to that effect and replacing it with a regime based on minimum standards and mutual recognition, most recently in the form of the Company Law Action Plan as an aspect of the FSAP. Notably, this Action Plan has resulted in the directive on fostering an appropriate regime for shareholders' rights on the principle of 'shareholder value' and far-reaching transparency and disclosure provisions as required to trade corporate assets on securities markets. Furthermore, the 2004 Takeover Directive, though all its provisions have not been implemented, has firmly established the European principle of 'corporate control as a commodity exchangeable on the market' (Horn, 2012: p. 118). Especially important in that regard are Article 9 on board neutrality and Article 11 on the break-through rule. The former restricts the ability of the executive board to avert a takeover bid without authorization of a general shareholder meeting. The latter curtails restrictions on incumbent voting rights against a takeover.

The strength of these neo-Gramscian analyses lies in their account of how economic corporate interests are ideologically translated into coherent class interests and how this in turn translates into potent pressures on public policy formation at national, EU, and even global levels. As we shall see in Chapter 5, this includes the direct reshaping of industrial relations with organized labour, characterized by 'asymmetrical regulation', where supranationalism in market-making and intergovernmentalism in social policy are two sides of the same coin (Holman, 2004; see also Ziltener, 1999). As such, this form of analysis identifies the essential material context and concrete actors to the contingencies of neoliberal ideology in the formation of the Europolity, identified by Rosamond and Hay's constructivist account. Less systematic attention, however, has been given to the forging of civil societal mass consent (though see Bieling & Steinhilber, 1999). Indeed, the Amsterdam School probably overstates the supranational dimensions in the formation of broader interclass social hegemony and understates the continued importance of national capitalist classes, the nation state, and interstate relations. As we have seen, not only in the case of Moravcsik but also in the state of the art of constructivist research, the nation state discourse remains central. As Horn points out with regard to corporate governance, the EU *mediates* between global structural pressures and national regulation, such as the 1992 UK Cadbury Code on voluntary self-regulation, the French Viénot Recommendations, and German capital market reforms after the decidedly national *Standortsdebatte* on German competitiveness. The nation state is thus not a transient configuration whose time in history is passing, nor is it simply an instrument for mercantilist catchup. In modern society, the welfare state continues to play a crucial reproductive role for society as a whole. There is no reason to revise Poulantzas' (and Marx's) propositions that the nation state remains central as a factor of social cohesion as it is the nation state that mediates between different class interests and national policies; as national discourses remain central in the creation of political subjectivities; and as it is the nation state that serves the interests of national capitalist classes. Hence, in our own analysis, we have proposed a synthesis of neo-Gramscian analysis with Poulantzas' work (itself inspired by Gramsci) as accounted for in the previous chapter (Cafruny & Ryner, 2007: 18–21; see also Jessop, 1990).

The single market in transatlantic neoliberal consolidation

From such a perspective, one can return to the question of the relationship between Europe and the US that we raised in the previous chapter. What are the implications of the SEM for this relationship? One school of thought suggests, à la Mandel, that the SEM spearheaded a European challenge within neoliberal finance-led capitalism to American preponderance. Such accounts emphasize increased amalgamation and internal coherence of a continental European bloc around the gravitational pull of German capital and the long-term unsustainability of US hegemony, which ultimately cannot sustain deficit financing (e.g. van der Pijl, Holman, & Raviv, 2010; Arrighi, 2005). We will consider this view in more detail further on in the book, especially in the next chapter and in Chapters 7 and 8.

Taking its cue from Poulantzas, another school of thought stresses the qualitative nature of transatlantic linkages and the structural power that they express. This school of thought offers an assessment of the 'interiorized' relation between American and European capitalism, emphasizing the dominance of American capital in the strategic sector of financial services and the increased dominance of the monetary circuit of capital over the productive circuit (see Chapter 2, pp. 38-41). This interpretation is consistent with the paradoxical coexistence of the revival of profitability of European capital and continued stagnation of European GDP as well as increased difficulties for European mass parties of the centre-left and centre-right to reproduce legitimacy under finance-led growth. The 1979 Volcker Shock, which effected a massive redistribution from social wages to profits as well as from the profit of productive capital to financial capital, also served to reinforce American power and privilege (Dumenil & Levy, 2004). As we will show in the next chapter, a number of works have explored aspects of this reinforcement of American power and privilege, such as the capacity of US-centred finance to draw on the abstract principles of market exchange on a staggering scale to exert power over productive resources, compared to the particularisms of Europe's 'Rhineland' models and the institutional incomplementarities of US-centred finance with Europe's systems of innovation and internal social settlements, which contrasts with their organic development with the American social formation (Seabrooke, 2001; Konings, 2008). Following such an analysis, ominous implications for European unity and the health of social legitimacy can be discerned (Cafruny & Ryner, 2007, 2007). Hence, transnational neoliberal hegemony as expressed by the SEM continues to reflect American hegemony, albeit one that is more contested.

The entire plethora of the EU's asymmetrical regulation serves to institutionalize finance-led accumulation that has a particular institutional complementarity, or in Seabrooke's (2001) terms 'interactive embeddedness', with US civil society and America's distinctive liberal and residual model of welfare and social accord. This is above all indicated in the way in which financialization and securitization as organizational principles of neoliberal capitalism are institutionally complementary with America's stock-market-based institutions of financial intermediation, corporate governance, and retail finance. This ensemble is in turn configured with a welfare model based on (albeit sometimes subsidized) private insurance and home ownership (Konings, 2008, 2011). Seabrooke (2001) has shown how the United States developed a new post-Bretton Woods hegemonic strategy on the basis of continued seigniorage in monetary relations and the global dominance of US financial institutions. This strategy enabled the United States to pursue expansionary policies by extending credit and debt and hence aggregate demand, thereby maintaining high growth rates on the basis of high levels of middle-class consumption. It is this, rather than inflexible and inefficient labour markets, that

accounts for differences in US and EU economic growth in the 1990s
– an output and productivity gap that also indicates the hegemonic
character of interiorized transnational social relations. The global
financial crisis that erupted in the US subprime market in 2007 has of
course exposed the underlying problems and contradictions of the US
model. Yet, given its subordinate status, the crisis hardly presented
Europe with an opportunity, but rather revealed the massive underlying problems of the Eurozone, as we will show in Chapter 4 and the
Conclusion.

Conclusion

This chapter has offered a comprehensive review of the theoretical
literature that emerged in order to make sense of the single market
that formed the centrepiece of the relaunch of European integration
in the 1980s and the 1990s. Coinciding with the relaunch, the neo-
institutionalist turn in political science seemed to offer a means of
transcending what had become an unhelpful neo-functionalist–realist polarity. EU studies correspondingly generated a proliferation of
new analytical models which sought to incorporate insights from
neo-institutionalism, including regime-theoretical perspectives, the
concept of a putative EU 'polity' as an appropriate subject for comparative politics, intergovernmentalism, and multi-level governance.
However, while these approaches facilitated rich descriptive accounts
of transformative developments in Europe, we argue that they nevertheless remain stuck within the terms of the neo-functionalist–realist
debate as set by systems theory, and they continue to accept uncriti-
cally the full range of liberal assumptions about markets that have
ultimately proven to be so deeply problematic. These new analytical models have not addressed transatlantic and European socioeconomic power relations. They have not identified the social forces and
key actors that have driven the relaunch. And, just as with the EMU,
they did not anticipate the contradictory and destabilizing tendencies
that were set in motion by such a radical project of liberalization.

Critical political economy, by contrast, supplies concepts and perspectives that provide a deep and comprehensive explanation for the
emergence of the SEA. It has also proven to be remarkably prescient.
The SEA was signed within the context of a specific conjuncture of
European and transatlantic capitalism. It expressed the interests of
European capital organized both nationally and transnationally, itself
embedded in a transatlantic system rapidly moving towards a new
post-Fordist regulatory phase of finance-led growth. Although the
relaunch would provide one way out of the crisis, in doing so it also

set in motion the forces that would eventually produce new problems and contradictions for Europe and the EU. A project based on 'negative integration' alone – absent macro-economic stabilizers, a robust regional-industrial policy, and a social dimension – was inherently unstable and bound to disintegrate.

Chapter 4

Origins and Development of the EMU: Money and Finance in the European Union

Money and finance are not like other commodities. As a unit of account, store of value, and medium of exchange, money serves critical social steering functions; thus it stands alongside the monopoly of coercion as a crucial element of sovereignty. The power of determining future production and consumption possibilities is also in no small measure exercised through finance. Monetary and financial relations are decisive to the nature of structural change in the EU and in world order more generally. In the words of David Calleo (2003: p. 1), international monetary relations serve 'as a metaphor for general political economic relations in the world system'.

The significance of forging a Single European Market in financial services SEMFS and the EMU is beyond dispute. However, the implications of these novel developments for European economic stability and well-being warrant serious reconsideration. The financial crisis that spread over the world in 2008 raises serious foundational questions about the validity of traditional accounts. In this chapter, we will argue that the anomalies that the financial crisis posed for understanding the nature of money and finance in the EU demand a more radical theoretical recasting. In the first section, we will review broader historical developments of money and finance in Europe and situate the institutionalization of the EMU and the SEMFS and the current crisis in this broader context. We will then compare favourably the work within the critical political economy tradition on these developments with variants of traditional theory which, having been seduced by the integration telos, failed to predict or explain the crisis. Granted, some traditional work has contributed to understanding the crisis, but only insofar as it has departed from such teleological thinking. By contrast, we will point to the contributions that heterodox economists in the post-Keynesian tradition made in identifying these mechanisms and by issuing salient warnings about the current course of crisis management. However, we will also point to the limitations of the post-Keynesian approach. Current crisis management is not usefully understood as a 'mistake' but should rather be understood as a form of rule. To make sense of this, we will synthesize different strands of Marxism. We will steer clear of over-simplifications that either reduce crisis management to German dominance or transnational class rule. By contrast, we will offer an account that integrates an interstate understanding of how German Eurozone leadership works as a common but variegated European response to predatory post-Bretton Woods American hegemony over finance-led transnational capitalism. This configuration, though far from optimal for Europe, is not easily changed.

Monetary and financial developments in Europe

Analyses of monetary and financial integration in Europe generally start with wartime autarky, for which disintegration in the 1930s prepared the ground. During the 19th century the gold standard facilitated international and European trade in a multi-currency system. It was based on arbitrage in internationally open money markets and central banks committing themselves to sell gold in their own currency at a fixed price. In stylized terms, gold outflows from deficit countries required a reduction of the money supply to maintain the fixed price of gold while inflows to surplus countries required the money supply to increase. This increased the price level in surplus countries, while decreasing it in deficit countries. Hence, the quantity demanded decreased in surplus countries and increased in deficit countries until payments were in balance. The gold standard thus offered a universal means of exchange and an elegantly simple mechanism for balancing international payments with a degree of automaticity. But as even Ricardo (1817: pp. 81–2) admitted, the gold standard was far from perfect and suffered from some major drawbacks as there were built-in risks of economic stagnation. Most important, deflation was the main adjustment mechanism in deficit countries. Moreover, there was no guarantee that overall gold supply would grow proportionally to output or international trade.

Deflationary tendencies were kept in check in the 19th century because of the predominant position of the British Empire and its capacity to credibly expand the supply of bills of exchange denominated by British Pounds, underwritten by trade-strength and imperial access to bullion, not least in India (e.g. Schwartz, 1994). But the relative economic position of Britain eroded in the late 19th century, and attempts to restore the gold standard through the imposition of massive austerity failed after World War I. Problems with the balance of payments prompted the British in 1931 to take the pound off the gold standard, generating a cascade of devaluations. This, the failure to manage German reparations from World War I, the international financial crisis triggered by the 1929 Wall Street Crash, and the Great

Depression contributed to the protectionism of the 1930s (Kindle-berger, 1973). When World War II hostilities ceased in 1945, curren-cies were not even convertible (Helleiner, 1994: pp. 67–72).

After World War II, the reconstruction of international monetary relations was undertaken under American leadership. As discussed in previous chapters, the Marshall Plan required European states to cooperate through the OEEC in order to remove trade barriers. This cooperation included returning to full currency convertibility through the EPU, which was completed in 1958 when the Treaty of Rome was ratified (Eichengreen, 2007: pp. 52–85). In the 1950s and '60s, West-ern European monetary cooperation within and outside the EC took place through the US-centred Bretton Woods system. Its Keynesian design sought to redress the deflationary bias of the gold standard while still facilitating fixed and predictable exchange rates for international trade. Contrary to the gold standard, not all currencies were tied to gold; only the American dollar was (what's called 'gold window'). The exchange rates of all other currencies were in turn fixed to the dollar, although long-term payment imbalances could be redressed through multilaterally agreed currency realignments. American surpluses and export preponderance at the time enabled the credible expansion of the money supply in an era of rapid growth. As already described in Chap-ters 1 and 2, as part of the 'embedded liberal compromise', national capital controls were permitted and mutually supported to ensure fis-cal and monetary policy autonomy required to secure full employment according to the Fordist formula. Such controls were seen as neces-sary to prevent current account deficits and potential capital outflows (whether motivated by speculative exchange gain, inflationary expec-tations, or tax avoidance) constraining or neutralizing macroeconomic stimuli (Helleiner, 1994: pp. 33–4, 37–8). Short-term payment imbal-ances were not to be financed through markets but rather through pub-lic reserves deposited in the IMF (Block, 1977: pp. 51–2. The Treaty of Rome carefully refrained from the topic of capital market liberali-zation. Directives designed to open up capital markets in 1960 and 1962 included numerous opt-outs and safeguards, frequently used by member states.

The commitment of the US to national capital controls is question-able, and it did not introduce them at home (Helleiner, 1994: pp. 48–9). They might have represented a temporary accommodation to European economies too weak to be integrated into fully developed financial mar-kets (Konings, 2011; Panitch & Gindin, 2012: pp. 67–110), requiring protectionism for industrial catchup and full employment promotion in geopolitical conditions of Cold War rivalry (Calleo, 2001). Be that as it may, Bretton Woods collapsed in 1971, when the US closed the 'gold window' and let the dollar float on foreign exchange markets. The end of American export dominance in the 1960s resulted in the

'Triffin Dilemma' whereby the expansion of the supply of dollars to accommodate growth in international trade simultaneously generated the destabilizing of US balance-of-payments deficits. This tempted the US to close the gold window and thereby threatened the credibility of the system. Its credibility was threatened especially when, in a context of increased transatlantic rivalry, some central banks such as Banque de France under Jacques Rueff bought gold with their dollars in response to what was seen as deficit-financed US unilateralism (van der Pijl, 2006: pp. 94–5). French-led attempts to revive Keynes' idea of an international currency through IMF 'Special Drawing Rights' (SDRs) were kept to a minimum by Americans keen to protect the dollar as the international reserve currency. Perhaps most important, though, emerging out of the need to finance international commerce, 'offshore' financial markets such as the 'euro-dollar market' were generating flows notwithstanding national capital market controls. These novel developments severely tested the resilience of the fixed exchange rate system (Block, 1977: pp. 209–11; Helleiner, 1994: pp. 81–100).

As a central aspect of neoliberal transition, the Americans favoured an all-out move to capital market liberalization and flexible exchange rates after the collapse of Bretton Woods in 1971, where hedge funds would manage exchange-rate risks in a system where the dollar was still the reserve currency (Strange, 1986; Helleiner, 1994). However, flexible exchange rates were viewed by most EC members (though not Britain) as a threat to predictable exchange in the common market, and it is questionable whether CAP would have been viable with them. Turbulence generated in the foreign exchange market by American unilateralism drove the process towards increased European monetary cooperation (Hennnig, 1998). Hence, EC member states tried to create a European 'island of stability' in the new flexible exchange-rate regime. The 'Snake in the Tunnel' failed during the 1973 oil crisis because member states approached Fordist stagflation in radically different ways, some discounting the problem of unemployment more than others. The initiative by the Franco-German duo of President Valery Giscard d'Estaing and Chancellor Helmut Schmidt to create the European Monetary System (EMS) fared better. However, it was not until after the realignment following Mitterrand's U-turn in 1983, signalling consensus to prioritize the fight against inflation over unemployment, that the EMS stabilized (Eichengreen, 2007: pp. 282–90).

The 1979 EMS agreement was established outside the Treaty of Rome structure through the purely intergovernmental European Political Cooperation (EPC) mechanism of the European Council. Membership was conditional, and not all EC member states participated. The EMS looked superficially like a mini-Bretton Woods. Like Bretton Woods, the EMS had fixed exchange rates (the Exchange Rate Mechanism, or ERM). Though not endowed with the same legal weight as the dollar in the Bretton Woods Articles of Agreement, for all intents and purposes the West German mark (DM) became the anchoring currency of the EMS. Maintaining fixed exchange rates was a primary central-bank objective of EMS members which, when necessary, would be backed up by coordinated interventions on foreign exchange markets. If Bretton Woods had the IMF, the EMS had the European Monetary Cooperation Fund (EMCF) that gave unlimited access to VSTF (Very Short Term Financing) to defend currencies when exchange-rate margins were being breached. The European Currency Unit (ECU) could be seen as an equivalent to the SDRs in Bretton Woods, and it was used for hedge financing in private transactions, but it played no significant monetary policy role before the 1987 Basle-Nyborg Agreement (Ungerer et al., 1990).

But the EMS worked very differently from how the Bretton Woods system worked. Indeed, the EMS and later the EMU have in many respects more in common with the gold standard (e.g. Eichengreen & Temin, 2010; Bordo & James, 2013). First, the EMS operated in an environment of internationally mobile foreign exchange markets, which meant that financial flows exerted discipline through interest-rate risk premiums on overly expansionary economic policy. In such situations, VSTF finance became accessible only when the horse had bolted and speculative attacks made exchange rates untenable without major deflationary adjustment. Indeed, the efficacy of VSTF was weakened by the veto power of the independent German central bank, the Bundesbank. It had agreed to the EMS only with caveats set out in the so-called Emminger Letter, which authorized the Bundesbank to opt out from the EMCF and VSTF when it perceived its commitment to price stability to be threatened. The Bundesbank had also succeeded in removing the original proposal for a 'trigger mechanism', whereby policy adjustments would be coordinated and undertaken symmetrically by strong as well as weak currency countries (Eichengreen, 2007: pp. 285–6). Second, the West German mark, managed by the Bundesbank, had price stability as its unequivocal primary objective, even when at the expense of economic growth and unemployment. Indeed, the ERM was based on credibility accumulated by the Bundesbank as guarantor of price stability. This is in contrast to Bretton Woods, which was based on US macroeconomic expansion underwritten by the role of the dollar as the global reserve currency (which the DM emphatically was not). ERM membership, in other words, implied prioritizing price stability over growth and employment, and this was indeed borne out in macroeconomic developments.

The question of an EMU arose first with the 1969 Hague Summit and the Werner Plan, at Willy Brandt's initiative with French President Pompidou's approval amid transatlantic tensions over Bretton Woods. The EMU was then motivated by the desire to deal with adjustment costs in Bretton Woods, which were seen as falling disproportionally on Japan and Europe. The resultant revaluation pressures on the Deutsche Mark and devaluation pressures on the Franc threatened to unravel Franco-German economic relations (Eichengreen, 2011: pp. 72–5). The lasting legacy of the Werner Plan was its proposed three-stage approach to monetary union. In contrast to the Maastricht Agreement, it envisaged substantial interregional transfer payments akin to the US Tax and Transfer System. Fatally, however (though no doubt reflecting contemporary nationalist realities), the Werner Plan was vague on where European monetary policy authority would reside. The plan was abandoned a year later in favour of less ambitious fixed exchange rate cooperation in relation to the floating exchange of the Dollar (the so-called Snake-In-the-Tunnel) and eventually the EMS after the collapse of Bretton Woods (Eichengreen, 2011: p. 75; Henning, 1998: pp. 552–3).

The question of monetary union reappeared with the SEA but was pursued in earnest only after the appointment of the Delors Committee in 1988. Comprised of member state central bank governors, two Commissioners (including the president as chair), and three independent experts, it outlined clear and practical steps to a monetary union. Responding to tensions posed by dollar turbulence and increasingly integrated global financial markets, there were already changes underway within the EMS. The Basle-Nyborg Agreement had expanded ECU usage and extended the time limit of VSTF access in exchange for intensified member-state surveillance. Questions arose, though, whether full capital market liberalization in the single market would not require monetary union. Indeed, complete capital liberalization put in question the very viability of the EMS (Ungerer et al., 1990: p. 9; Padoa-Schioppa et al., 1987; European Commission, 1990). In Eichengreen's words,

> [Residual] controls had given governments limited room to run different monetary policies. They had provided the insulation from market pressures necessary to arrange orderly realignments. Now, with the relaxation of controls, even discussing realignment was riskier. If investors got wind that such discussions were underway, they were free to buy or sell the currencies in question in advance of the fact. There were no limits on how they could and sell, and the costs of such transactions were minimal. A 10 per cent devaluation expected to occur within a month offered an annualized return on investment of more than 300 per cent. Since it was clear which countries had problems of chronic inflation and inadequate competitiveness, speculating in currencies was a one-way bet. (2007: p. 347)

The question of the viability of the EMS was given further impetus by trans-border foreign direct investments and the transnationalization of production, generated by the single market project (Eichengreen, 2007: pp. 346, 352; cf. Dunning 1997a, 1997b). Finally, as Chapter 7 explores in more detail, German reunification and concerns about German dominance in the EMS served as a crucial catalyst (Dyson & Featherstone, 1999: pp. 124–201, 306–69; Eichengreen, 2007: pp. 347–52). Contrary to contemporaneous estimations, the 1992–3 ERM crisis increased rather than decreased resolve to implement the EMU (though Britain exited from the project). Germany's unilateral increase of interest rates to fund reunification went beyond what most EMS states could endure and was seen as symptomatic of unbearable asymmetries that the EMU might partially redress (Eichengreen & Frieden, 2001: pp. 4–5).

After the Delors Report (1989) was delivered to the European Council, the 1990 Dublin Summit convened the Intergovernmental Conference that resulted in the Maastricht Treaty and the provisions required to implement the EMU (e.g. Hix, 2005: pp. 314–16):

- A three stage approach starting with completing capital market liberalization and all EU members joining ERM (stage I); completion and consolidation of central bank independence, creation of ECB-precursor the European Monetary Institute (EMI), and member states completing 'convergence criteria' (see below) (stage II); and irrevocably fixing of exchange rates in 1998 and introduction of the single currency in 1999 (stage III).
- Convergence criteria
  - *inflation rates* not to exceed 1.5 per cent of that of the three countries with the lowest inflation rate;
  - average nominal long-term *interest rates* not to be more than 2 per cent above the three countries with the lowest rates;
  - member state *budget deficits* not to exceed 3 per cent of GDP;
  - *national debt* not to exceed 60 per cent of GDP;
  - *exchange rates* to remain within the narrow ERM-band (2.5 per cent around the central rate) for at least two years.
- A Bundesbank *writ large* central banking system consisting of an independent European central bank (the ECB) and a European system of independent national central banks (ESCB) (Article 107). The ECB is run by an executive board and a governing council. The six executive board members, headed by the President, are appointed by the European Council for eight-year, staggered, non-renewable terms. Together with national central-bank governors, executive board members form the Governing Council. While striving towards consensus, the Governing Council can make decisions by simple majority voting.
- A set of substantive monetary policy provisions: The primary goal of the ECB is to achieve price stability. 'Without prejudice' in this objective, the ECB shall 'support the economic policies of the Community' (Articles

3a and 105[1]). The ECB has the power to define this goal itself and has defined it to be an annual increase 'below 2 per cent in the harmonized index of consumer prices'. The ECB is explicitly forbidden from lending directly to EU institutions and member states (Article 104[1]).

The asymmetry between supranational monetary policy and intergovernmental fiscal policy is a major institutional feature of the EMU (Dyson, 2000: pp. 11–21). Interest-rate setting for the Eurozone as a whole, aiming at financial market 'credibility', provides the ECB with a powerful bargaining tool vis-à-vis member states and social groups over fiscal policy, wage, labour-market, and social policy. Initiatives in these spheres that contravene the ECB's conception of price stability are construed as bearing higher inflation risks, motivating higher interest rates. This is further underlined by the one area where monetary policy intergovernmentalism remains: national central banks, not the ECB, issue public bonds. There is no risk pooling of national public debts, and each member state is responsible for its 'credibility' in financial markets. Contrary to the Werner Plan, there is no meaningful federal transfer-payment system. EU fiscal arrangements are instead about setting constitution-like rules for national conduct. The 1996 SGP extended the fiscal aspects of the convergence criteria to the post-stage III era, hence replacing disciplinary functions served by interest-rate differentials in the EMS.

Developing alongside the EMU, liberalization of financial services was central to the SEM. Cockfield's White Paper estimated that financial service liberalization would generate 1/3 of SEM economies. The 1989 Second Banking Directive instituted a 'Single European Passport' for banks, consistent with mutual recognition and systems-competition between regulatory systems. It stipulated that any financial service provider licensed to operate in one member state could establish branches or provide cross-border financial services in any other member state subject only to the controls of the licensing state (home country control). A directive in 1988 banned two-tier systems of preferential shares, common in Rhineland capitalism. Three directives in 1989 (including the Second Banking Directive) established a minimum solvency ratio of 8 per cent, but with clear intent to facilitate securitization, it was even more permissive than the US in the range of business that it allowed Europe's universal banks to conduct (Tsoukalis, 1997: p. 98). While the 'Single European Passport' had been extended to non-bank financial services already with the 1993 Investment Services Directive, further and systematic liberalization in non-bank financial services was the primary objective of the 42 measures of the 1999 Financial Services Action Plan (FSAP) and then especially the 2004 Markets in Financial Instruments Directive (MiFID). While already called for at the Cardiff Summit of 1998, the FSAP became a central plank of the 2000 Lisbon

Agenda intended to make Europe not only 'the most competitive and dynamic knowledge-based economy of the world' (European Commission, 2000) but also 'the cheapest and easiest place to do business' (European Commission, 2001). The FSAP went beyond the competitive pressure exerted by mutual recognition by prohibiting 'gold plating' (regulatory standards above the minimum required by the single market that member states themselves voluntarily adopt). It also dovetailed with the broad orientation of Basel II and its emphasis on self-regulation in the financial sector (Bieling & Jäger, 2009).

Seemingly vindicating the EMU, there was no major turbulence during its first decade. The EMU outperformed the EMS on price stability, though unemployment rates remained high and growth rates anaemic (European Commission, 2015a). However, as the financial and Eurozone crisis revealed, developments were uneven and financial movements were highly distortive. The elimination of exchange-rate risks encouraged the investment of massive pools of accumulated capital in globalized financial markets (the 'banking glut') in assets with high rates of return in Europe's southern and eastern peripheries. Despite Article 104[1], private investors operated on the assumption that the Eurozone was irrevocable and that investments would have to be bailed out in the event of a financial crisis (Bordo & James, 2013: p. 232). The Basle II regulatory framework reinforced this assumption by permitting banks to hold government bonds with zero capital, encouraging 'carry trade' where cheap loans from the central bank could be invested in high yielding bonds in Europe's periphery (Acharya & Steffen, 2013). These problems were masked when the asset bubble developed on both sides of the Atlantic, increasing the nominal value of assets and compelling individuals holding these increasingly valuable assets to boost demand through additional spending (what is called an 'income effect'). High growth rates in peripheral states seen as largely compliant with the Lisbon Agenda and SGP were hailed as the 'Spanish Miracle', 'Celtic Tiger' (Ireland), and 'a giant in the making' (Greece) (Bordo & James, 2013: pp. 21–2). But problems revealed themselves with full force when the asset bubble burst, first in US subprime derivatives and then in European markets after the contagion effects from the collapse of major financial intermediary Lehman Brothers (Ioannou, Leblond, & Niemann, 2015). The subsequent repricing of risk and revisions of balance sheets revealed the high exposure of European banks to toxic assets in bad private debt in Eastern and Southern Europe. Over-exuberance during the boom turned into panic, the withdrawal of liquidity, the drying up of credit sources, and a sharp economic downturn.

As insolvency and default risk on a systemic scale became overbearing, threatening to reprise the Global Depression of the 1930s, states aggressively pursued countercyclical policies, extended guarantees, and nationalized or recapitalized major, 'too big to fail' banks through unconventional monetary policies ('quantitative easing'). The EU could achieve this only by unceremoniously breaching competition rules (on state aids) and the SGP. Nevertheless, keen to return its rules and norms, an 'exit strategy' was already being followed in the course of 2009. Though the ECB was injecting liquidity into the banking system, it did not yet conduct 'quantitative easing' and, given the Maastricht non-lending clause, had no convincing 'lender of last resort' function' – the crucial central bank role of lending to the banking system when it encounters potential insolvency. Bailout burdens fell instead on member states. Highly uneven capacities to carry these transformed the financial crisis into a sovereign debt crisis. Indeed, recently bailed-out financial actors soon turned on the weakest member states, speculating on their bonds' values (Weeks, 2014). The asymmetric shock resulted in rapidly increasing bond-yield spreads, bringing the EMU to the brink of collapse as what by then were disparagingly called the PIIGS faced insolvency or default.

Describing the progression of Council crisis summits – rapidly overtaken by events – would require its own chapter. Nevertheless, by 2013 EMU modifications were in place, stabilizing the common currency. Resulting from ECB President Mario Draghi's promise to do 'whatever it takes' to save the euro, the ECB's Outright Monetary Transactions (OMTs) Programme narrowed bond-yield spreads, signalling the ECB's resolve to stave off speculative attacks. Entailing ECB purchasing member-state bonds on secondary markets, OMTs balance finely and controversially what Article 104[1] permits. But the ECJ has confirmed OMTs' treaty compatibility, because of its conditionalities. These include fiscal conditionalities (see below) as well as demonstrable and full member state access to private lending markets. Furthermore, 'full sterilization' prevents quantitative easing. Money pumped into the system is reabsorbed through ECB deposit auctions. OMTs thus require neither state bailouts nor money supply increases, but they do require 'safeguarding an appropriate monetary transmission and the singleness of monetary policy' (ECB, 2012). Subtle legal debates aside, it is doubtful that the EMU would remain viable without OMTs. OMTs followed so-called Long Term Refinancing Operations (LTROs), announced in December 2011, providing massive liquidity injections into Europe's banking system. Offering 36-month loans, a 'liquidity cushion' should prevent interbank lending from seizing up. OMTs and LTROs that followed the creation of the European Stability Mechanism (ESM) proved insufficient – a €700 billion 'firewall', providing loans to Eurozone member states shut out of capital markets. Finally, and departing from mutual recognition in financial regulation, the Single Supervisory Mechanism (SSM) put the ECB in charge of a single resolution mechanism for banks and micro-prudential regulation in order to break the 'doom loop', where sovereign debt problems and bank vulnerability feed each other in a vicious cycle. At the time of writing, the fragility of Europe's securities markets continues, and it is unclear whether the envisaged Capital Market Union contains the instruments to address this (Grahl & Lysandrou, 2015). Facing deflation, diminished macroeconomic effects of LTROs as northern banks repaid their loans, and with the ECJ positive ruling on OMTs, the ECB finally commenced quantitative easing in 2015.

These monetary policy changes do not depart from neoliberalism, because conditionalities in fiscal and structural policy come under the umbrella heading of New Economic Governance. This consists of ESM Memorandums of Understanding, the 'Two Pack', 'Six Pack', and Fiscal Compact, which together facilitate neoliberal deepening. The Fiscal Compact tightens demands on budget balances: structural deficits must not be above 0.5 per cent of GDP. With the Six Pack, the EDP is now activated with reference to not only deficits but also debt. With what is called the 'reverse qualified majority voting principle', the Commission's executive power is significantly enhanced as decisions to activate EDPs automatically apply unless the Council votes against them by QMV. Finally, the legally binding Economic Partnership Programmes (EPPs) that states undertake when in EDP now include structural as well as macroeconomic policy, which significantly increases EU authority to impose privatization and flexibility reforms.

Liberal theories in trouble: the 'economics' of the EMU and financial liberalization

Traditional accounts of the EMU and financial integration in Europe failed to identify, let alone predict them, the factors that generated the Eurozone crisis. In the Introduction, we asserted that this had to do with blind spots resulting from the assumption that integration was a priori inherently rational. We elaborated on this point in Chapters 1 and 2, where we contrasted teleological understandings of integration in traditional theory with critical perspectives that assert that the EU, including the EMU and financial integration as central aspects, formed part of a dynamic and contradictory capitalist process. In this section, we will expand on this argument with a more specific review of mainstream analyses of the EMU and financial integration.

Seen primarily as belonging to the domain of economics, analysis of the Eurozone has been grounded in deracinated versions of Ricardian trade theory. This is not least the case in High Level Export Reports from Cecchini to Sapir. Money and finance are here treated as commodities like any other. Following the theory of sound money and the efficient market hypothesis, 'Anglo-Saxon' disintermediated financial markets are held to generate self-equilibrating and dynamic economies, reducing transaction costs and generating investments into new technology production (Sapir et al., 2003: pp. 34, 123, and 130, cited in Grahl, 2009: pp. 115–17). Most works in economics on the Eurozone are specialized refinements, sharing the assumptions made and agenda set by these reports. This does not mean that all economic analyses were mere mouthpieces of official reports and policies. Critiques were made early on about the macroeconomic crudeness and deflationary nature of the EMU's fiscal policy targets (e.g. Buiter, Corsetti, & Roubini, 1993). But these critiques did not question the self-stabilizing rationality of financial and socioeconomic structures enabled by financial market liberalization and the EMU.

According to this perspective, the economies promised by the SEM – optimal allocation of factors of production, economies of scale, technological development, competition, and learning – would be facilitated by the sturdy macroeconomic framework provided by the EMU. Here, 'advantage' was seen in governments 'tying their hands', hence preventing themselves from acting on the temptation to counter market forces (Giavazzi & Pagano, 1988). The common currency would reduce exchange-rate uncertainties and transaction costs. The independent ECB and the SGP would increase credibility in free and therefore efficient financial markets. Such markets would minimize costs of capital and allocate resources for investments according to their optimal utilization, especially clearing up lock-in effects in existing industries and providing resources for high-tech investments (Gianetti et al., 2002; London Economics, 2002). Lower rates of interest and transaction costs in a context of competition would produce higher rates of welfare-generating investments and innovation. These would be further induced by the liberalization of labour markets, welfare systems, and taxation regimes that in part would be the result of the discipline exerted by the EMU's strict macroeconomic regime and in part induced by Lisbon Process Best Practice diffused through the open method of coordination (see Chapter 5). The outcome would be a more flexible and mobile labour force, which could be better deployed with new investments. The overall result would be faster growth, better profitability, more employment, and in time, higher wages (Sapir et al., 2003; Sapir, 2007).

This perspective prizes the 'depth' of financial markets in terms of the volume traded and their 'mobility', and the more flexible the prices in these markets are, the better. True, these markets (like most) deviate from the perfect market model because of inherent information asymmetries, which in turn means that there are significant economies of scale, including 'network externalities' (like telephone systems, their merit resides in multiple users). Nevertheless, according to the neoclassical model, the solutions to these tendencies towards 'market failure' are found in the market itself or in regulation that makes actors behave according to market logic. It certainly merits integration into a single market at the European level. Information asymmetries inhere in the financial relationship because the debtor is in a better position to know their risk of defaulting on a loan than the creditor is. The creditor can respond to this by trying to accumulate as much information about the debtor as possible, and as we saw in Chapter 2, in the 'Rhineland Model', bankers become strategic owners in industry. But the efficient market hypothesis maintains that there is a superior market alternative to such quasi-planning by oligopolistic groupings, namely risk diversification. It is rational for creditors to divide up their assets and lend to a range of debtors with different profiles (portfolio spread), which means that lenders need contacts with a range of potential borrowers. A division of labour can also be refined between actors with different expertise and dispositions to take risks. Bond, equity, and securities markets serve the function of putting these agents in contact with one another, and according to neoclassical theory, this contact maximizes returns while minimizing lending costs because risk is optimally managed. Such diversification works better as more people are involved, which is an argument for making these markets as large as possible.

In this account, securitization that arose in American financial markets and was coveted by EU policymakers behind the SEMFC and the FSAP, represents the highest stage of development in the financial relationship between lenders, borrowers, possessors of knowledge about financial risk, the risk averse, and those with risk preference. Working according to the principle of hedging, financial institutions would lend to different lenders, seeking a higher return if the lender was a higher risk. However, these institutions, such as banks, would not necessarily take the default risk themselves but rather sell on the risk on a 'futures market' where specialized actors ready to take the risk would buy the loan at a certain price, hence allowing the bank to cash in at the expense of a lower rate of return (but lower risk). This process of 'securitization' and 'off balance sheet activities' was rendered highly complex as loans with different risks were divided up and packaged together in different 'exotic' financial products. The merit of such a system was supposed to be that it extended credit at the lowest possible cost for the highest possible return and with maximum mobility.

Hence, in the days when scholars and policymakers were celebrating Celtic tigers, Spanish miracles, and Greek giants in the making, it was therefore not extraordinary to raise the questions, as Blanchard and Giavazzi (2002) did, of whether the Eurozone signalled the end of the Feldstein-Horioka Puzzle. This puzzle refers to the well-established empirical observation that capital does not tend to move to poorer and less-developed regions, though according to liberal economic theory, it ought to because the rates of return are higher. Blanchard and Giavazzi pointed to evidence in the build-up of the asset-price bubble that capital flows now behaved according to theory. Hence, growing current account deficits should not be a concern but were instead a logical consequence of the rational properties of market-creation induced by the EMU's norms and macroeconomic prudence. The presumption is that inflows on the capital account will be efficiently allocated to business investments that, in time, will provide the foundations for repayment and balancing of accounts. However, the problem with this hubristic interpretation was that it failed to account for monumental misallocations of finance into speculative ventures, especially real estate, that would trigger a massive destruction of values in the crash.

The logical and empirical problems associated with the efficient-market hypothesis ought to lend credence to those pointing to profound problems in disintermediated financial markets. This way of managing risk leads to very short time horizons in financial decision making and tends to become highly speculative, and the movements intended to hedge and manage risk generate themselves price signals that are perverse for long-term investment and development. This argument was made with great eloquence more than 30 years ago by Susan Strange (1986) with reference to the euro–dollar foreign exchange market. The massive misallocation of resources, eventual default and contagion of the 2008 financial market can be seen as a vindication of that argument at a more general level.

Yet, the efficient-market hypothesis apparently contains formidable built-in resistance to any such criticism as it continues to inform Eurozone crisis management and New Economic Governance. In this account, the crisis resulted from a lack of economic discipline and reform in the PIIGS. The problem was not the policies pursued but that they were not pursued far enough. This is a move made by neoclassical theorists and neoliberal policymakers time and again (e.g. Grahl & Teague, 1989). Policy recommendations are generated from the standpoint of abstractly postulated, perfectly competitive free markets that do not exist and never have existed. When reforms fail to deliver, it is never the fault of the reform but some aspect that has not been fully reformed in accordance with the abstract model. Somewhat ironically, we confront a tautological form of theory-driven reasoning that never opens itself up to the possibility of being contradicted by evidence – a tendency that liberal philosopher of science Karl Popper associated with totalitarian reasoning.

The efficient-market hypothesis depends in this context on support from a version of the theory of sound money that is derived from a version of neoclassical Keynesianism (or neo-Keynesianism) used by senior analysts at the ECB. As noted in Chapter 1 (see p. 11), the assumption of spontaneous compulsion of the market towards balance and equilibrium is relaxed here because of 'sticky' prices in rigid oligopolistic markets and imperfect information in the short run. It focuses on the influx of monetary and financial resources that followed when the monetary union eliminated exchange rate risks, especially into member states in the European periphery, where stability culture was less entrenched than it was in the Eurozone core and, most notably, Germany. The attendant reduction of domestic savings, widening of indebtedness, and current account deficits should have been, according to this school of thought, countered with even more stringent and precautionary fiscal policy than was pursued to conform to SGP, and possibly ECB monetary policy. These proved insufficient in 'tying the hands' of member states and inducing macroeconomic prudence (cf. Giavazzi & Padano, 1988). Prominent advocates of this view include former ECB Chief Economist Otmar Issing and former ECB Research Director Vitor Gaspar. This is an important intellectual context that makes current crisis management intelligible – that is, the content of the ESM Memorandums of Understanding, the Two Pack, the Six Pack and the Fiscal Compact (Fagan & Gaspar, 2008).

These arguments are unconvincing. First, they do not account for the marginal status of these elements in the overall analysis. As late as 2008, the Pareto-optimal macroeconomic effects of the EMU are stressed. Second, indebtedness and current account deficits are seen exclusively as short-term adjustment problems caused by the regime shift to monetary union. Third, the fact that the financial resources are going to consumption rather than high-tech investments in supposedly more efficient financial services markets is noted, but no attempt is made to explain it. The two latter points do not address the fact that the financial crisis started as a massive misallocation of investments in the highly developed monetary and financial market systems of the United States, which, qua the Sapir Report, was the role model to be emulated in the Lisbon Agenda. Of course, it could be argued that the root of the problem resided in overly expansionary macroeconomic policies in the US, as well as in the PIIGS. But then one must entertain the possibility that it was this much more expansionary policy that explains the output and productivity gap between the US and the EU in the first place, and not the supply-side institutional differences of labour and capital markets that provided the impetus for the Lisbon Agenda and that the Sapir Report sought to eliminate. Finally, Eurozone economic growth would have been even more anaemic without US expansionary policies – Obama's significant albeit modest stimulus – and with a tighter fiscal policy stance in the PIIGS prior to the financial crisis. In other words, this perspective does not entertain the possibility that debt expansion is not an abnormality but instead an integral and necessary part of the sort of capitalism that the single market has promoted in Europe. But perhaps the case against this explanation is the most devastating when put in the simplest terms: It 'ignores that the EMU ... delivered exactly what the proponents of this ... framework wanted it to deliver, namely price and exchange rate stability in the context of moderate growth' (Schelkle, 2013: p. 42).

The 'politics' of the EMU and financial liberalization

As might be expected, there is a large body of work in the fields of political science and sociology on the causes and consequences of monetary union and (to a lesser extent) on financial liberalization across the 'optimism'/'pessimism' spectrum as reviewed in Chapters 1 and 3. Neo-functionalist and neo-Keynesian accounts have been fused to assert the necessity of monetary union to reduce trade-offs among currency stability, capital mobility, and macroeconomic policy space (Padoa-Schioppa, 1994). Querying the necessity of fixed exchange rates in the single market (consider the UK), supranationalists have pointed to cultivated spillover engendered by the Commission linking the EMU to capital liberalization (Jabko, 1999). Intergovernmentalists have seen the specific outcome resulting from lowest-common-denominator bargaining reflecting the balance of power among member states (Moravcsik, 1998: pp. 238–313). Multilevel analyses focusing on interest-group coalitions and leading financial as well as export-oriented sectors that are structuring compromises based in issue linkages between money, finance, and trade claim to explain why liberalization and stability culture could be generalized throughout the Eurozone (Frieden, 1991; Eichengreen & Frieden, 2001). Building on their analyses of the SEA as discussed in the previous chapter, constructivists have pointed to the *engrenage*-effects of ideas as a necessary condition (McNamara, 1998, 2006) or the centripetal symbolic effects of the EMU on national identity (Risse, 1999).

The relevance and centrality of the factors invoked are unquestionable. But in a disciplinary division of labour, analysts defer to the economists on how to understand the emergent properties and drivers of economic growth and stability. At most, analysts subscribe to a very thin 'states and markets' approach to political economy. Rather than seeking an integral analysis of production and power, the disciplinary split and a priori equilibrium biases are retained as economics and politics are treated as externally interactive realms. Above all, capital market mobility is treated as a non-political exogenously given 'condition' and not part of 'structural economic interests' (e.g. Moravcsik, 1998: p. 381). Neo-Keynesian economics is usually the starting point of this approach, which seeks to derive political implications from wedges created by sticky oligopolistic prices and imperfect short-run information. These create spaces in which interest-maximizing political actors, such as states and interest groups, can act on and affect outcomes.

Although analyses emerged soon after the fact to make sense of crisis management (e.g. Ioannou & Niemann, 2015; Schimmelfenning, 2015; Verdun, 2015), there was remarkably little interest in addressing questions that pertained to the build-up, breakout, and development of the Eurozone crisis itself. Moravcsik (2006) argued that the credible commitments in the Maastricht agreements had made the EU 'institutionally stable'. Falling in line with the ECB's analysis, McNamara (2006) went no further than to warn against corrosion of ideational consensus on fiscal policy.

The work of Benjamin Cohen is a notable exception. Together with Randall Henning, he saw the EMU as a mechanism to adjust to the vagaries of US policy priorities and to mitigate European sensitivity and vulnerability (Cohen, 2003; see also Henning, 1998, 2006). Cohen's argument rested on an analytical framework derived from the aforementioned wedges identified by neo-Keynesian economics and argues that states are endowed with differential power resources to delay and deflect balance of payment adjustments (Cohen, 2006). He argued – somewhat heretically at the time – that the EMU made the EU as a whole less vulnerable to the effects of changes in US policies. However, in the absence of a fully integrated bond market, the lack of anything equivalent to the US Treasury Bill, political fragmentation in the fiscal policy field, and an 'anti-growth bias' in its institutional setup, the euro was no serious contender against US hegemony in the monetary and financial field (Cohen, 2007, 2009).

The question is, though, whether the euro offers enough of an alternative vehicle for investment to deprive the US of power to delay and deflect. Invoking hegemonic stability theory with its root in the work of Kindleberger, Cohen suggests that this could be a profound source of instability in the world economy. This is a potentially appropriate context in which to consider the weak regime of international financial and monetary management, characterized by US passivity and unilateralism, in which the financial crisis emerged. It is also a potentially appropriate context in which to consider the inability of the US to avoid the contagion of the financial crisis and the difficulties of managing it, especially considering that the surplus pools now reside in potential geopolitical rivals to the US, such as China (Cohen, 2009; see also Helleiner, 2008; Kirshner, 2008; Otero-Iglesias, 2012). On the other hand, Cohen's analysis ultimately rests on a neoclassical economic conception. Consequently, he is sanguine about the merits and stability of the international monetary regime (Cohen, 2008). He has very little to say about the generative mechanisms and destabilizing dynamics behind the crisis, including those within Europe itself.

Post-Keynesian and regulation theoretical alternatives

The Eurozone clearly vindicates post-Keynesian and regulation theoretical analyses. As demonstrated in Chapter 2, these approaches assign central importance to effective demand as a cause for growth. The superior output and productivity growth performance of the US over the EU in the 1990s and 2000s was not a result of a better allocation in financial and labour markets, as argued by the Sapir Report. Rather, it resulted from debt-financed expansion of effective demand, albeit of a particular sort. Colin Crouch (2009) has called this 'privatized Keynesianism', to refer to macroeconomic expansion operating through the extension, not primarily through government expenditure, of private and public debt managed through securitization as discussed above. At the same time, the collapse of this system is also a vindication of Keynesianism in that it underlines Keynes' warnings about deregulated or lightly regulated financial markets.

In contrast to the neoclassical theory, which is the intellectual point of reference of the Single Market in financial services and the FSAP, Keynes argued that, left to their own devices, financial markets were inherently unstable and would not allocate investments efficiently. Hyman Minsky has elaborated on this argument in his Financial Instability Hypothesis (e.g. 1986; Kindleberger, 1978). Not unlike Marxist conceptions, this theory stresses the importance of capital development in an economy where the central motive is to invest money to make more money. This makes expectations of future profits essential to motivations. The stress on expectation makes it possible to account for the instability in financial markets with short time horizons, as well as their tendencies to generate manias and panics at the extreme ends of economic cycles. Manias follow lengthy periods of economic upturns, when credit is extended to ventures based on the expectation of rising (asset) prices. When substantial financial commitments have been made based on such assumptions and the rate of price increases slows down, lenders increasingly become 'ponzi-units', which are no longer able to pay off the interest, let alone principal, of their loans. The net worth of such ponzi-units decreases, and some of them may well default on their debts. This changes asset-price expectations rapidly and negatively. It prompts the selling of assets that adds momentum to the downward spiral of prices, which threatens to become a self-fulfilling prophecy and an all-out panic. The withdrawal of credit and liquidity affects investment and consumption rates adversely and threatens to draw the economy down into a deflationary spiral, which leads to further defaults and so on. This is consistent with developments in the 2000s that led up to the crisis, which may well be interpreted as a 'Minsky-moment'.

If one is to identify someone who offered a coherent and robust statement that the EZ crisis was in the making, one could do worse than consult the work of Engelbert Stockhammer (2008), working on the basis of formal macroeconomic modelling derived from what is called the Social Structure of Accumulation variant of regulation theory (Bowles & Boyer, 1995; Bhaduri & Marglin, 1990). The financial crisis should be understood as the crisis of such an accumulation regime, generated by financial markets driven into ever riskier segments of the market in the pursuit of profitable deployment of an ever expanding mass of accumulated capital (Aglietta & Breton, 2001; Altvater, 2012; Boyer, 2012. American capital accumulation was at the centre of this system, enabled by dollar seigniorage, the dominance of the US financial industry in financial intermediation, and institutional complementarity between global financial markets, American corporate governance, a residual welfare state (see Chapter 5), and the role of private loans and savings in everyday political economy (especially in housing and pensions) (Seabrooke, 2001; Schwartz, 2009; Konings, 2011). European capital accumulation was subordinated to American capital accumulation in two ways. The first was through export-led manufacturing in the competitive corporatist north, with wage increases set below productivity growth, which depended on the locomotive effect of the American economy (Bellofiore, Garibaldo, & Halevi, 2011; Lapavitsas et al., 2012; Onaran & Galanis, 2013). A leaner form of corporatism was promoted by financial liberalization, which included institutional investors among the stakeholders (Vitols, 2004). A second form of subordinated articulation was through so-called peripheral financialization whereby debt based consumption and growth were sustained for some time despite the absence of the relational density of the nodes of financial networks and the intermediary capacity found in financial centres such as New York and London (Konings, 2008: pp. 256, 262, 265, 270). As further elaborated in Chapter 6, surplus capital, from the US but above all from North-Western Europe, was invested in undervalued assets in Southern and Eastern Europe, not in productive enterprise, but above all in housing and mortgages in search of leverage opportunities (Becker et al., 2010; Becker & Jäger, 2012; Charnock et al., 2014; Raviv, 2008). Temporarily, access to cheap loans substituted as a lever of expanding demand also in Southern Europe, despite lower wage-shares (Milios & Sotiropoulos, 2010: p. 236). Financial market liberalization and the elimination of exchange rate risks by the EMU facilitated this development. This highlights that, in the absence of high productivity growth, finance-led accumulation has a decidedly extensive quality and has drawn on the opening of new frontiers of commodification in space but also in the increased scope of socioeconomic life, driven by commodification and privatization of previously public or common assets (Harvey, 2006: pp. 41–50, 52–3). It is important to stress the role of the US in this process as the consumer and clearer of balances in the last resort of the European economy (Bellofiore, Garibaldo, & Halevi, 2011).

Drawing on data from the Commission's own database, Stockhammer argued that the EMU and the single market in financial services were central to a mode of regulation that helped constitute a finance-led European accumulation regime that, like the American one, was fragile but that, unlike the American one, also suffered from mediocre growth performance. As expected in an economy where securitization makes loans readily accessible, just as in the US, household savings rates decreased. But in contrast to the US, the European consumption propensity did not increase (except in Greece). Stockhammer attributes this to two counteracting tendencies, namely rapidly falling wage-to-profit shares and retrenchment in pay-as-you-go state pension provisions.

Stockhammer and collaborators provided systematic evidence that wage moderation in fact leads to a contraction of output and does not stimulate employment. This is because growth in the Eurozone as a whole is wage-led (see also Onaran & Galanis, 2013). They also demonstrated, however, that the EMU compels member states to contain growth to protect the balance of payments, resulting in a collective-action problem which contains the expansion of aggregate demand (Stockhammer, Onaran, & Ederer, 2009: pp. 15–56). Just as in the US, investment rates did not increase despite increased profitability, which is quite consistent with the argument that increased mobility of financial capital puts premium on 'shareholder value'. This leads to demands for higher returns on investments in the form of higher asset-yield ratios in the here and now, prompting a change of management strategy from 'retain and reinvest' to 'downsize and redistribute' (Grahl, 2001). Europe's aggregate current account of international payments with the rest of the world was broadly in balance and did not effect much growth either way. But Stockhammer et al. were pioneering in pointing out the dangers of uneven development and the serious internal imbalances between export-oriented member states and those undergoing peripheral financialization. After a decade of the EMU, this problem was compounded by massively diverging relative unit labour costs caused by a 20 per cent internal devaluation by Germany after Agenda 2010 and the 'employers' offensive' of the early 2000s. Since German core inflation is close to zero, the only route of adjustment on the current account that was available to these countries (save a productivity growth miracle) would be highly destabilizing deflationary policies. Internal payments balances have therefore been dependent on highly volatile flows on the capital account. While the common currency kept the sort of turbulence associated with the ERM crisis at bay in the first decade of the EMU, Stockhammer presciently warned about the dangers entailed in the diverging unit labour costs and current account balances. Contrary to the US situation, and in accordance with Boyer's (1990) aforementioned warnings a decade and a half prior (as discussed in Chapter 3), the intended expansionary impulses did not materialize and did not generate a dynamic accumulation regime based on virtuous relations between productivity growth and aggregate demand. Indeed, estimates of so-called Verdoorn elasticities suggest that foregone attempts to boost growth by a percentage point in Europe equals just under 0.5 per cent of foregone productivity growth

(Storm & Naastepad, 2014: pp. 104–8). But the imbrication of global finance into Europe's socioeconomic relationships nevertheless meant that Europe shared the vulnerabilities of finance-led growth with the US. Stockhammer's only puzzle was that this configuration had not displayed the instabilities that one would have expected (Stockhammer, 2008: pp. 197–8). For him, there were two possible explanations: either (and according to Mabbett & Schelkle's (2007) research, implausibly) residual automatic stabilizers were still at work in Europe, or there was a major crisis around the corner. Indeed, the lead-time between his writing those lines and the actual publication debate would 'resolve' his problem since it coincided with the outbreak of the financial crisis.

These formal models of social structures of accumulation have now been extended to assess Eurozone crisis management and have painted rather catastrophic scenarios. Warnings are issued about a strategy based on trying to transpose the export-oriented models of Northern Europe to the rest of the Eurozone. These can be summarized by two key questions: (1) What will generate final effective aggregate demand? (2) And how are the polarization tendencies in the Eurozone to be mediated? The fallacy of composition is stressed: It is simply not possible for all Eurozone member states to run surpluses, unless there is a massive increase in the balance of payments to the rest of the world. John Grahl's estimate of the first fiscal semester has been that in the unlikely event that all national plans were successful, it would generate a Eurozone balance of payment surplus of 6 per cent of GDP (at the time of writing, roughly in balance) (2012). That is double the surplus that China is running for an economy half the size of the Eurozone. It is inconceivable that the rest of the world could or would absorb such surplus production, and the task is not rendered easier by austerity in the US, the export orientation of the BRICS, and growing signs of currency wars amid declining growth rates. Furthermore, with regard to internal Eurozone dynamics, a one-sided adjustment of relative unit labour costs of the periphery of 20 per cent to Germany, which runs an inflation rate of 1 per cent, as a strategy to consolidate financial balances through export orientation is inherently deflationary and self-defeating. According to Stockhammer's and Sotiropoulos' estimations (2014), this would require a contraction equal to two 1930-style depressions.

The (non-)optimal currency area problem

When the neoclassical assumption about the allocative efficiency of financial markets is abandoned, mainstream economics offers one important contribution to understanding the crisis – that is, the (non-) optimal currency area (OCA) problem. Monetary unions have the undoubted benefit of reducing uncertainty and transaction costs. But they are vulnerable to asymmetric shocks if they are not optimal currency areas: economic events and developments affect countries and regions differently. The most straightforward example of such shocks would be changes in the demand of key commodities, which might affect countries differently. Other factors that may generate asymmetric shocks include different growth rates (including a lack of synchronicity of business cycles), the workings of labour market institutions, and tax systems. Asymmetric shocks result in changes in the balance of trade, affecting economic output and the price level required to maintain a balance of payments. Only if the economy balances (or 'clears') 'spontaneously' do we have an OCA, which is supposedly ensured through fully integrated labour markets where wage levels and a free flow of labour supply adjust to the new situation.

OCAs are not as common as one might think. Indeed, the pioneer of OCA theory, Robert Mundell (1961), found that the United States was not an OCA. For that reason, monetary unions usually have mechanisms for transferring resources in response to asymmetric shocks. Fiscal transfer payments over the national budget constitute a standard mechanism in nation states, explaining perhaps why currencies tend to be nationally based. This mechanism is notable by its absence in the Maastricht setup of the EMU, which instead assumed that reforms would make labour markets sufficiently flexible and mobile so as to eliminate the problem. The sanguine response to the problem is also intelligible with reference to claims that the positive trade effects of the single currency were making the euro-area more like an OCA (e.g. Artis & Zhang, 1997; Rose & van Wincoop, 2001), with the implication that the problem would resolve itself. Other studies suggested that fully integrated financial markets would manage asymmetric shocks by spreading the effects more evenly over the entire euro-area because the spread of investors would be over the entire region and capital could flow to the best possible economic opportunities in the area as a whole (e.g. Arnold & de Vries, 1999; Angeloni & Ehrmann, 2003).

However, if the neoclassical arguments about markets as efficient allocators of capital do not hold, then the problem of asymmetric shocks is serious and indeed potentially dangerous if it is not backed up with fiscal federalism. Those who have maintained that that is the case (Bayoumi & Eichengreen, 1992; Krugman, 1993; de Grauwe, 2006, 2013) can reasonably see the effects of the financial crisis in the euro-area as a vindication of their position. Indeed, it may even be that financial movements have counteracted the tendencies towards an OCA generated by trade. As *The Economist* (2011a) acknowledged, speculative financial flows in search of higher returns in comparatively rapid growing Southern European economies, underpinned by a real estate bubble and the zero exchange rate risks that the EMU offered, exacerbated current account asymmetries, eventually bringing these into play in the mania–panic dynamic of the financial crisis. It is no wonder, then, that Southern European and Irish overheating, followed by the current debt-induced deflation in the PIIGS, is a central manifestation of the financial crisis in Europe. This is compounded by the fact that 'internal devaluation', marked above all by labour market flexibility, remains the only mechanism available to absorb asymmetrical shocks on the balance of payments. Yet, austerity is counterproductive since it holds back the expansion of internal demand and growth, which is the only path out of the debt crisis (Stockhammer, Onaran, & Ederer, 2009: p. 156).

Whither Rhineland capitalism?

Given the importance of the particular sort of relation between banks as direct lenders and strategic owners of corporations in Rhineland capitalism, questions arise with regard to the viability of this European variety of capitalism in the wake of monetary union and financial market liberalization. The intent of Frits Bolkestein, the commissioner of the Internal Market and Taxation under whose watch the FSAP was being implemented, is certainly clear in his famous remark that the EU 'must leave the comfortable surroundings of the Rhineland and move closer to the tougher conditions and colder climate of the Anglo-Saxon capitalism, where the rewards are greater but the risks also' (2001). But it is far from certain that this intention actually represents real developments. Arguing against the so-called strong globalization thesis that was fashionable at the time, some research on varieties of capitalism invoked the neo-institutionalist concept of path-dependence to suggest that Europe would continue to find its distinct method of asserting competitive advantage in the global economy (e.g. Rhodes & van Apeldoorn, 1998; Dore, 2000). And indeed, the idea that the European economy would simply become a carbon-copy of the American one does not hold up against empirical scrutiny. For instance, the use of corporatist social pacts to keep wage levels below productivity growth and social insurance concessions, when high unemployment puts centralized trade unions in a position of weakness, was a common tool in the 1990s (Fajertag & Pochet, 2000; Rhodes, 2001; Bieling & Schulten, 2003).

At the same time, although the neo-institutionalist concept of path dependence is helpful in striking a note of caution about hyperbolic claims about change, its primary weakness resides in its inability to deal with any change at all. Capital mobility has qualitatively changed the relationship between banks and non-financial corporations in Europe. Direct long-term lending to corporations and strategic ownership has decreased radically in importance to European banks and other financial institutions. Similarly, European so-called non-financial corporations are turning increasingly to self-finance and securities markets to meet their investment needs (Grahl, 2009; Raviv, 2011: chapter 4). Indeed, a larger portion of their own profits are coming from financial operations (Dumenil & Levy, 2004: pp. 110–18). But this has not resulted in an increased propensity to invest, since it correlates with the buying back of shares. Paradoxically, just as shareholder value as an ideology is becoming more pronounced, the importance of public shares as a source of finance is diminishing (Thompson, 2012: chapter 1). In the UK and the US, this has compelled corporations to turn to shadow banking or debt-financing in more 'exotic' forms, such as collateralized debt obligations and other 'off-balance sheet items'. It is less certain if this is the case with continental European corporations, which may just have resorted to more self-financing. In any case, the general tendency towards financialization has increased the demand for higher profit rates for any given investment and changed dramatically the terms under which capital is willing to negotiate with labour and the state in the corporatist process (Grahl, 2001).

There are, to be sure, different perspectives on this development. One evolutionary perspective suggests that Rhineland financing is an expression of a not fully developed economy, and it is only natural that when European economies have caught up fully with the American one that they will emulate it in terms of 'fully developed' capital markets (Raviv, 2011). Another interpretation follows the neo-institutionalist line of argument and eschews teleological explanations. The glass is still 'half full' for the Rhineland model, and it can productively accommodate itself to these new financial relationships (Vitols, 2004). Indeed, it is differential institutional comparative advantages between northern and southern member states that lies at the root of the crisis (Hall, 2014; Johnston, Hancké, & Pant, 2013). This assumption appears to be contradicted by arguments that turn the neo-institutionalist factor the other way and posit that financialization is itself a particular construct that emerged out of the American experience and is thus embedded in this particular social formation. For that reason, European companies struggle to compete in those markets which systematically favour the US (Konings, 2008; also Watson, 2001). One further variant of the argument accepts that Europe is disadvantaged in this context, but the structural power of these markets is overbearing, leaving Europe with little choice other than to adapt. Securitization is a structural necessity built into the post-Fordist regime of accumulation, because of the breakdown of information bottlenecks, making it possible to develop immense economies of scale in these markets. This is not possible in the nationally specific European models (Grahl, 2001). A final variant suggests that the turn away from the Rhineland model is simply an ideologically driven mistake (Hay, 2004). This brings us to the question of the political determinants of money and finance in Europe. And indeed, even those who insist on structures and institutions as determinants do not deny the role of politics in the process.

Social forces in the making of European money and finance

The potentially catastrophic macroeconomic implications of crisis management, as analysed by post-Keynesians and regulation theorists, raise questions about why the bumble-bee is still flying. A critical-theoretical explanation starts from their formal analysis of capital accumulation. By placing power and interests at the centre of analysis, it queries the chief objective of crisis management. It is unlikely to be primarily about eliminating payment imbalances, but more about mobilizing EU authority to deepen market reform. Crisis management serves the interests of the financial industry and is premised on a continuation of finance-led accumulation (Radice, 2014). The stalling of the agenda of financial regulation (Bieling, 2014) and Commission President Barroso's pronouncement of a market-oriented 'silent revolution' give credence to such an analysis (Haar, 2011). Ordoliberal crisis management is hence a manifestation of the shock doctrine (Klein 2009). The crisis serves as an occasion to move forward the boundaries of the possible. Privatization and making previously public assets available for financial leveraging, further enabled by legal authority through the structural provisions of the Fiscal Compact, is thus the chief policy priority. While such a policy orientation is likely to remain tension ridden and susceptible to another bubble-crisis dynamic eventually, its prospects should not be underestimated. It may prove viable for some time. The OECD world still has $2 trillion worth of state-owned enterprises that could be privatized (Christiansen, 2011). According to IMF estimates, public non-financialized assets in real estate and land, including subsoil resources, have a value equalling three quarters of the GDP of developed economies. Greek state-owned residential properties are currently estimated at €3.3 billion but could reach €20 billion in ten years. Creditor member states and consultants to the ESM are considering mechanisms through which such public assets could be brought to market from reluctant debtor states whose institutions sometimes cannot even account for them. Proposals include holding companies located in other member states and pledges of future cash flows from state assets (for instance, rents or ticket sales) as security against new bonds (*Economist*, 2014: p. 18).

The 'silent revolution' resonates with the perspective of the Amsterdam School on how transnational class agency exercises leadership in the transition from one accumulation regime to another. As outlined in Chapters 2 and 3, it emphasizes how 'private planning bodies' resolve differences and conflicts between different 'fractions' of capital and exert strategic leadership over the direction of single market reform. Interpreting rationales such as Giavazzi and Pagano's benefits of tying one's hands (see p. 85) as expressions of a dominant ideological rationality, or for that matter statements by senior ECB officials themselves (e.g. Issing, 2002: pp. 345–46), Stephen Gill (1992, 1998) has argued that the constitution-like rules of the EMS as well as the EMU have worked all along as a disciplinary device progressively to deepen market-conforming behaviour and identities on European societies. This is seen as reflecting an increasingly transnational power bloc of financial and export-oriented capital that also integrates skilled workers in high-value-added industries. Similar forces can be seen to be at play at present (van Apeldoorn, 2014), and with decreased judicial and Parliamentary checks and balances on transnational executive authority in the New Economic Governance, it is taking on an increasingly authoritarian form (Oberndorfer, 2015).

The Amsterdam School answers questions begged by those who, drawing on classical Marxist theories of imperialism, reduce the Eurozone crisis management to German dominance (e.g. Lapavitsas et. al., 2012). Although German origins of ordoliberalism are undeniable, the exclusive emphasis on Germany understates active elite internalization, consent, and the coordination of crisis management in other member states. It neglects the extent to which crisis management is the 'outcome of struggles between transnational social forces and shaped by the agency of a transnational capitalist class' (van Apeldoorn, 2014: p. 197). Bearing in mind that classical theories of imperialism anticipated sharpened inter-imperialist rivalry that only socialist transformation would resolve, the fundamental question to the German neo-mercantilist thesis is, how was European integration possible at all? As discussed in Chapter 2, the most significant contribution of the Amsterdam School is a theoretical breakthrough by van der Pijl (1998: pp. 9–24) that makes it possible to answer that question, which offers nothing less than a critical-theoretical counterpoint to Haas. Following the cue of a seminal piece by Poulantzas (1974), van der Pijl argues that while capitalist classes and societies, emerging out of late-feudal absolute states, originally see one another as part of external nature forming potential threats and objects of conquest, the molecular nature of capitalism creates strong tendencies towards 'interiorization'. Progressively, capitalist societies begin to interiorize each other's social relations, and international relations are transformed to become part of the management of internal nature. As Marxists, the Amsterdam scholars regard this development as uneven, imbricated by power relations, and sees 'network experts' as representing big capital who enjoy structurally privileged positions and exercise leadership over this process. Their perspective explains why inter-imperialist anarchy can be overcome in capitalism, and why transnational capitalist coordination was taken to a higher level after World War II under American leadership and the diffusion of Fordism. After the 1970s, the social content of transnational capitalist relations has become increasingly neoliberal (see also Overbeek, 1993).

The Amsterdam School is at its most convincing when it analyses the transnational, capitalist sources of international organization that shape interstate relations akin to Bull's (1977) 'international society'. However, it tends to 'bend the stick' too far and understate the importance of the state and interstate relations, which become understood as passive receivers of transnational ruling-class hegemony. This is empirically problematic. National fault lines remain relevant, even in as 'transnational' a policy area as European financial services (Macartney, 2011). Furthermore, Drainville's critique still stands: the Amsterdam School neglects that neoliberalism is not only a 'broad strategy of restructuring' but also 'a succession of negotiated settlements of concessions to the rigidities and dynamics of structures as well as the political possibilities of the moment' (Drainville, 1994). Drainville's critique has been borne out by research on the variegated nature of neoliberalism in different countries and sites (Birch & Mykhnenko, 2009). The critique is illustrated by simple examples such as Italy becoming more determined to join the EMU after the ERM crisis, while the UK decided to opt out (Talani, 2003). The theoretical implication is that states and interstate relations remain crucial to capitalism because of their roles as the ultimate sites of collectively binding decisions in a given territory, managing uneven development and reproduction, and maintaining social legitimacy by mediating the potentially antagonistic relations among classes and social groups. Hence, when focus changes from accumulation strategies to mass legitimacy through hegemonic projects, states and interstate relations remain essential.

It is in that context that the role of Germany, or rather Germany in relation to America, in ordoliberal Eurozone crisis management should be understood. Such understanding begins by posing the issue with reference to Poulantzas' interiorization thesis as outlined in Chapter 2. Recent research verifies that liberalized and global financial markets cultivated by US hegemony (Panitch & Gindin, 2012) are specifically organic to American corporate governance and liberal welfare residualism and enable the finance-led, consumption-based economic growth dynamic in the US (see also Seabrooke, 2001; Schwartz, 2009).

When posed in these terms, much insight can be gained from the most insightful neo-Keynesian inspired 'states and markets' approach to political economy of Henning and Cohen. The US capacity to shape global capitalism is underpinned by dollar seigniorage, which has given the US unique capacities in the post-Bretton Woods world to 'delay and deflect' adjustment costs (Cohen, 2006) for pursuing deficit-financed expansionary policies, especially low tax rates and military expenditure, to other parts of the world. In the absence of any challenge to this financial system, anything equivalent to the US Federal Treasury Bill and its 'anti-growth bias', the EMU simply does not pose a significant challenge to post-Bretton Woods US hegemony.

The pivotal role of German ordoliberalism in this method of adjustment can hence be specified, as can the reasons why, despite pernicious effects, ordoliberalism is so hard to escape. European monetary integration, culminating in monetary union, developed as a response to no less than six major adjustments to such US-induced externalities (Henning, 1998). For all intents and purposes, German foreign exchange reserves, the consequence of cumulative surpluses, offered buffers whereby a degree of protection from the externalities of US deflection could be secured (Jones, 2003). While benefits are of course rather more equivocal today than during the first decade of the euro, the threat of turbulence and lack of pooled protection against the vagaries of a US dollar that dominated global finance seems sufficient to keep Eurozone member states in line.

This method of adjustment originated with the Franco-German EMS. Turbulence on global money markets compelled West Germany to treat European monetary cooperation as a lever rather than a result of economic convergence. With the EMS, West Germany found a way to shield itself from dollar inflation and to revalue on acceptable terms. Given its composition, revaluation strengthened the German export sector as price increases had less of an impact on sales than reduced costs on imports, provided that European competitors could be locked into fixed exchange rate arrangements (Lankowski, 1982; Parboni, 1982). This is a formula that still applies and if anything to a more pronounced extent (Bellofiore, Garibaldo, & Halevi, 2011: p. 141). The general need to shield against dollar-induced turbulence, not least illustrated during the first years of Mitterrand's presidency in France, offered the inducement required for others to agree to an EMS on German terms. The continued relevance of this shield was in no little measure demonstrated when Syriza, despite the crippling effects of austerity and the ringing anti-austerity message of the 2015 Greek referendum, submitted to the Memorandum of Understanding.

Conclusion

This chapter has drawn on the theories introduced in previous chapters to review the literature on the causes and consequences of Europe's single market in financial services and monetary union in the context of the 2008 financial crisis and its aftermath. It has suggested that these developments have delivered a significant blow to the credibility of the efficient market hypothesis upon which the rationale of these initiatives was based. Instead, post-Keynesian and regulation theoretical accounts have been validated in their warnings about the fragile nature of finance-led growth in Europe. These conclusions, and the endurance of neoliberalism and finance-led growth in New Economic Governance, raise questions of power and interest. The chapter has argued that the arrangements were particularly conducive to the interests of financial and export-oriented transnational class interests, German capital groupings, and a post-Bretton Woods interstate hegemonic structure shaped by the relationship between Germany and the US. The EMU and the SEMFS, while designed by the Europeans themselves, continue to reflect subordination to American power and hegemony, with serious implications for societal legitimacy and uneven development – problems that will be addressed in the next chapter.

Chapter 5

The Welfare State: Whither the 'Social Dimension'?

This book started by invoking Jacques Delors' famous 1988 speech to the British Trades Union Congress (TUC). Delors argued forcefully that the single-market project should not only be about deregulation and dismantling welfare state arrangements that had formed an integral part of Europe's social market economies. Market-making must also have a 'social dimension' and be re-embedded in social policies and standards at the European level. It is clear from solemn incantations in major EU documents about 'social cohesion' and 'the social model' that there is a keen awareness of the importance of welfare state arrangements for legitimacy in European polities.

This concern with the 'social dimension' is warranted. The welfare state – a shorthand for public services, social-insurance schemes, protective legislation, industrial relations regimes, and employment promotion policies that are provided, guaranteed, or framed by the state as citizenship rights – is not merely some 'generosity', an optional extra charity or indulgence. Almost all social scientific research into the nature of advanced capitalism underlines that the welfare state is one of its essential components. This affirms the relevance of Lowi's discourse on modified liberalism (Chapter 1), Poulantzas' recasting theory of the state as a mediator of social and class conflict, Milward's research on the relationship between European integration and the 'rescue' of the (welfare) state, and the research programme on Rhineland capitalism that followed in the wake of Servan-Shreiber's *American Challenge* (all in Chapter 2).

The correlation between increased GDP per capita and public social expenditure as a proportion of GDP does not reflect merely the capacity to spend. More significantly, it reflects the *need* of advanced capitalist societies to spend to maintain social order (Wilensky, 1974). When societies industrialize, as was the case in Europe in the mid to late 19th century, the communal support structures and extended family networks characteristic of traditional agrarian society progressively eroded. As industrial capitalist market relations asserted themselves, these networks were not spontaneously replaced by other institutions. One might say that a deficit of care and reproduction emerged in societies where there was an increasing lack of synchronicity between the material needs as dictated by the human lifecycle and the capacity to engage in productive work through the labour market. Children could not earn an independent living, for instance, and the capacity of their parents to combine childrearing with work was decidedly compromised after extended family networks were attenuated. Hence, the need arose for state education and support for nuclear families through childcare benefits. At the other end of the lifecycle, the need arose for pensions and elderly care. Furthermore, novel problems emerged in industrial capitalism, such as the risk of industrial accidents, urban sanitary problems, and indeed unemployment. Illness is not a new risk in industrial society, but it took on new forms when it required the infirm to withdraw from waged work. The need to respond to these risks required the development of healthcare systems and forms of insurance against injuries, illness, and unemployment. The welfare state thus became a pivotal social stabilizer because it provided the means for satisfying the needs arising from the nature of capitalist industrialization. Given the further attenuation of family networks; the increase of single-parent households; the secular trend of increased aspirations of women to take full part in civil, societal, and working life; and the policy aspiration of boosting employment rates, these needs have increased rather than diminished over the last 150 years. Finding new ways of reconciling childcare provision with waged work was a primary concern of the Lisbon Agenda (Lewis & Giullari, 2005: pp. 79–83; Guerrina, 2015).

Of course, the degree to which these needs are met and on what terms is an open question. As a result of Eurozone crisis management and the politics of austerity, especially in Southern Europe, the retrenchment of public provision has been so severe that it may impose burdens on the nuclear family, and especially women, beyond what can be carried, thereby generating a crisis of reproduction (Salida, Carabana, & Torrejon, 2012; Guerrina, 2015). Moreover, while the focus in the Lisbon Agenda on 'activation' and supporting men as well as women in entering the labour market seems compatible with the feminist goal of financial independence, the reality is more equivocal. Unsurprisingly, the Lisbon Agenda is primarily concerned with commodification and enhancing supply on the labour market within tight budget constraints which seriously constrain genuine choice on the terms under which especially women enter the labour market and manage paid work with unpaid care work (Young, 2003; Lewis & Giullari, 2005; Wöhl, 2011). Research into 'welfare state regimes' as described in the next section confirms the general argument of this book that the terms under which welfare states perform reproductive functions are dependent on the balance of power among different social forces and classes. However, not providing for these reproductive needs at all is not an option in advanced capitalist societies if they are to maintain a modicum of stability.

Apart from satisfying such reproductive needs, the welfare state has also been essential for sociopolitical legitimacy in Europe. In Rhineland capitalist societies, it is no exaggeration to portray the welfare state as the 'consensus structure' par excellence (e.g. Schmid, 1998). The welfare state played a central role in reconciling capitalist markets with political democracy in the second half of the 20th century (Flora & Alber, 1981). To understand the significance of the welfare state for legitimacy, it is essential to appreciate the centrality of social citizenship and attendant rights, as well as their relationship to civic and political citizenship and rights. According to T.H. Marshall's seminal argument (1950), the great mass of the population that is materially dependent on waged work can effectively exercise civic and political rights only through social rights. In other words, it is only when the welfare state has either eliminated or substantially mitigated the risks of destitution associated with industrial capitalism that the broad mass of the population can fully obtain the status required to effectively exercise civic and political citizenship as envisaged in liberal democracy. This underpins with variations the societal accords across class, confessional, regional, linguistic, and gender cleavages in European states and societies (e.g. Esping-Andersen, 1990, 1999; Sainsbury, 1996; Arts & Gelissen, 2002).

It is possible, then, to specify the fear that arose with the SEM that Delors articulated and that European politicians and policymakers – at least nominally – continue to address. Negative integration based on mutual recognition results in 'social dumping', whereby cost competition compels the reduction in standards in social legislation and a shrinkage of the tax base, which in turn leads to reductions in social services and insurance provision (Scharpf, 2002). This fear is compounded by a monetary and financial regime that prioritizes high asset-yield ratios and price stability over high social wage rates, growth, and employment and that serves as a serious constraint on the fiscal capacities of member states to pursue redistributive policies (Grahl, 2001, 2009). The fear is intensified in periods of acute crisis, such as the Eurozone experienced starting in 2009. If welfare state research is correct, then the stakes are high since this goes to the very heart of societal reproduction and legitimacy.

Is there evidence of positive integration in the EU towards supranational harmonization of standards and tax bases, or perhaps the creation of European budgetary policies, that can counteract these dangers? Alternatively, might the fear be exaggerated? Can the welfare state compete, and is the question more about streamlining it, rendering it more rational and sustainable than it hitherto has been? This chapter will address these questions. It begins with an account of European welfare capitalist development in the first three decades that followed immediately after World War II, which sometimes are described as *les trentes glorieuses*, or 'the thirty glorious (years)'. It will then outline the key developments in social policy in the EU. These two sections set the scene for the crux of the matter, which is addressed in the final part of the chapter. This part reviews the academic debate in contemporary EU social policy between pessimists and optimists concerning the prospects of Europe's social dimension.

European welfare capitalism

European welfare state arrangements are most decidedly *national* phenomena. They are highly dependent on large public budgets that only nation states provide through the means of taxation. The total value of the EU budget is scarcely more than 1 per cent of EU GDP, as opposed to the 40–50 per cent public expenditure to GDP in most advanced capitalist nation states. In budgetary terms, the CAP, which serves welfare functions for farmers and regional supports to underdeveloped regions or regions with economic hardships, are the only exceptions to the EU's lack of relevance in the area of welfare expenditure. Apart from CAP, the Treaty of Rome was very modest in its ambitions in the social policy field. True, the European Social Fund (ESF) provided some modest retraining and resettlement allowances for workers who lost their jobs as a result of increased competition in the common market. But these were in effect used to augment national programmes. Since the EC had no meaningful resources of its own at the time, the extent to which this can be seen as a distinct EC-level policy is questionable. Apart from CAP and the ESF, the Treaty of Rome restricted itself to abstract formulations of principles in the social field, such as the objectives of 'social progress and a high level of employment'. Social policy decisions unequivocally required unanimity in the Council of Ministers. The fact that the Treaty of Rome required equal pay for men and women, free movement of workers with attendant rights to residence, social security, and non-discrimination in employment is sometimes seen as evidence of common EC social policy (e.g. Hix, 2005: p. 255). The importance of these requirements is not in question. However, they concern civic rights of equal treatment within a common market with free labour mobility rather than social rights per se.

A central reason why the welfare state is such an important factor for legitimacy in continental European societies, and why it has taken a national form, is to be found in the particular historical legacy of capitalist development and modernization in continental Europe that underpins the Rhineland variety of capitalism and its particular institutional logic. In contrast to Britain, industrialization in continental Europe did not occur until the latter part of the 19th century, at a time when the dominant production technologies and sectors most decidedly were based on economies of scale and the increased application of formal science in mechanical and chemical engineering. As discussed in Chapters 1 and 2, late industrialization led to collective action and state intervention in neo-mercantilist catchup strategies. Hence, when the reproductive deficit arose in the transition from agrarian society to industrial capitalism, manifesting itself in what is called the 'social question' in the late 19th century, even capitalist and state elites favoured the social integration of workers through national social programmes and state intervention. Consensus formation inspired by the preindustrial corporative tradition became particularly important, as did Christian norms of charity and a concern with the less fortunate, as well as geopolitical incentives to enhance mass mobilization capacity (e.g. Briggs, 1961). When the question of the origins of the welfare state is asked, analysts generally point to the Bismarck reforms in Germany in the 1880s, which were followed by similar reforms in other European nation states. Conversely, while proletarian revolutionary agitation was real enough, the nature of capitalist development in continental Europe generated reformist and corporatist dispositions in the labour movements. This provided the basis for the Rhineland model of interclass cooperation and quid pro quo, where social protection was provided in exchange for consent towards technological change and restructuring that facilitates productivity growth. This model continues to provide a normative orientation in European civil societies to this day. In the words of Hemerijck (2002: p. 39), 'At the cognitive level, the European social model is based on the recognition that social justice can contribute to economic efficiency and progress'.

National variations in the balance of social forces have also generated important variations of the terms under which welfare states perform their reproductive and legitimation functions. Gøsta Esping-Andersen (1990) identified three ideal types of social accords in Western Europe after World War II. Arguably, there is also a fourth type of more recent origin in Southern Europe, which experienced democratic transition as late as the 1970s (Ferrera, 1996; Arts & Gelissen, 2002). Furthermore, the even more recent capitalist and democratic transitions in Central and Eastern Europe have generated their own social policy and industrial relation patterns (Bohle & Greskovits, 2007; Bohle, 2009).

The liberal welfare state reflects sociopolitical accords where the bourgeoisie remains dominant not only in economic life but also in political life, where wage earners' demands are integrated as concessions and where as much as possible workers are socialized as mass investment subjects. This captures the essentials of welfare in the United Kingdom, Ireland, and the United States. Some universalist social programmes were developed (such as the National Health Service), but these provided services only at 'minimum standards', considering budget constraints and limited prospects of tax increases. Means tested benefits play a central 'residual' role in this type of system, but the default position is that those who are able should be encouraged to seek better private alternatives. Economic measures intended to combat unemployment are pursued, but with due regard for the policy conflict between this objective and that of price stability (as expressed by the Phillips Curve). The collective bargaining regime typically remains centred on the company level and is poorly integrated with other aspects of the welfare state. This is a 'residual' welfare state, where the principle of commodification remains dominant even in the provision of welfare. The welfare state is construed as a 'safety net' for those who are unable to fend for themselves adequately in the 'marketplace' (Titmuss, 1974). For those that can, private provision is often supported through tax breaks and state lender of last resort functions. In the era of finance-led capitalism, welfare state liberalization has been accentuated through the promotion of private pension savings and, with respect to private housing, through higher levels of mortgage debt (Langley, 2008; Seabrooke & Schwartz, 2008), even into the stratum of the poor and here via increasingly disciplinary means (Soederberg, 2014). Hence, 'asset-based welfare' has played an important role in promoting the accumulation regime based on extending debt via the increase of asset values and on securing labour supply in flexible markets, as also discussed in chapters (Crouch, 2009; Sturn & van Treeck, 2014: pp. 129–34).

By contrast, the social democratic welfare state is based on an unconditional commitment to full employment and universalist social policy provision at 'normal standards' that are intended to appeal to the entire population. The high cost of such provision is funded by high taxes. Highly organized, centralized, and strong trade unions provide leadership in the formulation of economic policy, managing to articulate it together with a coherent 'solidaristic wage policy'. In contrast to the other regimes, this welfare regime typically leads to the development of a high share of total employment in the state service sector. This reflects the post-war social accords in Scandinavian countries. These were the only countries in Europe where the 2nd international social democracy of the early 20th century became hegemonic in the political sphere, and the welfare state reflects the corresponding commitment to the de-commodification of labour through universal social rights. Economic power nevertheless remained with a highly centralized capitalist class and the political economy continued to be regulated through accommodation and negotiation between two power centres. It should be noted that while important social democratic path dependencies remain in the Scandinavian countries (for instance, in high levels of social service expenditure and social benefits), there have been important departures from the social democratic ideal type. Reforms in financial markets have introduced significant asset-based welfare components in pensions and housing (e.g. Schwartz & Seabrooke, 2008; Belfrage & Ryner, 2009; Belfrage, 2015). The emergence of high unemployment levels, coinciding with EU membership, has transformed industrial relations in a direction towards the Christian democratic regimes as described below (Pontusson, 1997; Ryner & Schulten, 2003; Ryner, 2013; Bengtsson & Ryner, 2016).

From the point of view of the Eurozone and the inner core of the EU in the western part of the continent, the Christian democratic welfare state is by far the most prominent one. It is in many respects 'functionally equivalent' to the social democratic one in terms of social expenditure and the generous replacement rates that it offers in social-insurance schemes (van Kersbergen, 1995). It also comes close to the social democratic regimes in terms of the status accorded to trade unions in wage determination and as a 'social partner' in corporatist deliberation on economic policy. Typically, collective agreements cover the entire labour market, and labour law grants 'co-determination' rights in the workplace. In other words, the degree of social protection from the vagaries of the market is substantial. But the qualitative nature of social programmes differs quite substantially from the social democratic variant. Rather than providing universalism and redistribution, the Christian democratic welfare state is geared towards income replacement and maintenance of *existing* social status groups, who pay into, and accrue benefits from, group specific funds. This type of welfare state not only lacks a universalist framework but also traditionally does not share the social democratic commitments to develop state services in welfare. This reticence reflects a commitment towards the reproduction of traditional civil societal institutions and the 'traditional' family with a housewife and a male breadwinner. Full employment is not an unconditional goal in this type of welfare state. Just as in the liberal type, price stability has been seen as an at least equally – indeed more – important economic policy goal, and this has been central as a social foundation of German leadership in central bank conservatism as institutionalized in the EMS and the EMU (Streeck, 1994; Crouch, 2000, 2002; Iversen & Soskice, 2012). This is a welfare state regime where 'de-commodification' is combined with a fundamental commitment to private property. In contrast to the social democratic conditional acceptance of private property, which reserves the option of challenging private property if social goals are not met, the Christian democratic welfare state *redeems* capitalism by furnishing it with social responsibility and reflexivity (van Kersbergen, 1995). This welfare state type expresses an accord where the sociopolitical power of both organized business and labour is substantial, but where neither is sufficient to achieve political hegemony. Christian democracy has, instead, become hegemonic here because of its exceptional capacity to assume the role of *mediator*. Interestingly, the development of asset-based welfare has been more limited and uneven in Christian democratic welfare states.

The effect of parametric retrenchment of social-insurance benefits to combat unemployment and monetary integration has instead been the further weakening of propensities for generating demand in the economy, resulting in a competitive corporatism based on extreme export orientation (Hall & Franzese, 1998; Soskice, 2006; Sturn & van Treeck, 2014: pp. 139–45; Lehndorff, 2015).

Christian democracy and social capitalism have thus demonstrated a remarkable capacity to mediate between these interests as well as those of confessional and/or linguistic groups. Indeed, Christian democracy can be defined quintessentially through this 'politics of mediation' as 'a religiously inspired, ideologically condensed and politically practiced conviction that conflicts of interests can and must be reconciled politically in order to restore the natural and organic harmony of society' (van Kersbergen, 1995: p. 2). This particular framework for managing cleavages has enabled Christian democracy to accumulate resources of political power and to inhibit the hegemonic capacities of liberalism and socialism. Christian democracy enjoyed remarkable success in the post-war period. This includes the reconciliation of class conflict in Germany (and Austria) within a liberal democratic framework – a conflict that had destroyed the Weimar Republic and paved the way for the Nazi regime. While 'social consensus' was less explicit and more ambivalent in Italy and France, the Italian Christian Democrats and the French Gaullists nevertheless achieved a remarkable degree of social integration and modernization within societies where fundamental social conflict between right-wing and left-wing extremes had previously been combined with economic stagnation. The Dutch and Belgian post-war experience built on the social compromises that had originated in the interwar period, which mediated not only between the left and right but also among Catholics, Protestants, and atheists, and between Dutch and French speakers. The welfare state was the central institutional expression and mechanism of this social peace formula (van Kersbergen, 1995).

The welfare states in the Mediterranean periphery of the Eurozone (Spain, Portugal, and Greece) resemble the Christian democratic ideal type insofar as social-insurance schemes are fragmented rather than universal and insofar as familialism and religion define their underlying norms. However, these welfare states do not have the same 'minimum standards' as their northern Christian democratic neighbours and the social expenditure per GDP is much lower. In addition, these states tend to have universal rather than status-based programmes for healthcare. There was no general retrenchment in these welfare states during the first two decades after Maastricht. But policies sought to 'iron out' benefit formulae, reducing benefits for insider groups while upgrading minimum benefits and – consistent with reproductive challenges – investing in family benefits and services (Rhodes, 2002: pp. 319–20). During the build-up of the asset bubble, these welfare state developments were made easier by peripheral financialization (Chapters 2, 4 and 6), whereby insider labour groups whose entitlements were reduced instead had access to cheap credit (Milios & Sotiropoulos, 2010: p. 236). This has dramatically changed in the course of the Eurozone crisis, wherein radical general retrenchment in welfare programmes (the reduction of unemployment and child benefits), employment security (the reform of legislation on dismissal, collective bargaining opt-outs, and the reduction of overtime-pay), pensions (indexing benefits to life expectancy, increased retirement age and contribution periods, and reduced replacement rates), and privatization have been undertaken in response to the conditionalities imposed for loans by the Troika (e.g. OECD, 2012: pp. 27–9).

Given the strict fiscal terms under which the transition from state socialism to capitalism took place in Central and Eastern Europe, and given the initial euphoric embrace of markets as a reaction to the collapse of central planning, it is not surprising that the welfare state is the least extensive in these parts of the EU. Indeed, social expenditure as a percentage of GDP is a mere 13 per cent in the Baltic States, and the trade union movement plays a very insignificant role. There is, however, considerable social policy variation in Central and Eastern Europe. With its gradualist transition to capitalism based on consensus, but within a strict macroeconomic regime, Slovenia's arrangements resemble in some respects the Christian democratic corporatist model. Social policy in the Visegrad Four (Poland, Hungary, the Czech Republic, and Slovakia) occupies an intermediary position between Slovenia and the Baltic States. Their market-friendly approach has been conditioned by the overall objective of attracting FDI, but has also at times called for selective protection. Social wages have also increased in some sectors, although these are highly dependent on the performance of the particular enterprise, and tripartite arrangements are at best embryonic. Social expenditure per capita is higher than in the Baltic, but the Visegrad states have experienced high levels of unemployment in a context of a meagre safety net (Bohle & Greskovits, 2007; Bohle, 2009: pp. 171–6). As discussed in the next chapter, peripheral financialization was central to developments in Central and Eastern Europe, which meant that the financial crisis had severe and dramatic effects here as well. At the outset of the crisis, the major responses were wage cuts and a reduction of public expenditure (Drahokoupil & Myant, 2010). As Chapter 6 will show, more recently, right-wing populist governments in Poland and Hungary have begun to mount significant attacks on neoliberalism through policies designed to enlarge welfare benefits, reverse privatizations, and re-regulate financial markets.

EU social policy

European welfare states are vulnerable in periods of economic instability and slow growth. Whereas the economic crises of the interwar
period generated repressive and authoritarian solutions, the establishment of a stable world economy after World War II provided the context
under which Rhineland capitalism could be made compatible with liberal democracy within a welfare capitalist framework (Milward, 1984,
1992). In a context of a Keynesian world of limited capital mobility,
the lack of a common social policy at the European Community level
was not a problem for the expansion of the welfare state, which indeed
underwent a historic expansion nationally, facilitated by high rates of
economic growth and full employment in the common market and in
the transatlantic economic area. However, when the decision was made
to form the single market on the basis of both negative integration and
mutual recognition, increased capital mobility, and a monetary order
that put a premium on price stability over employment, the prospects
for national welfare states became more questionable. Hence, the question arose whether a more ambitious EU-level social dimension would
be constructed, à la the vision of Jacques Delors.

The elimination of the national veto on welfare state issues would
potentially have had tremendous significance. But the SEA was clear
that qualified majority voting should be restricted to what was required
to complete the single market. On one count only, namely the one
stressed by Delors in Bournemouth, QMV was extended. Article 118A
of the SEA allowed for QMV in the Council only on issues pertaining
to health and safety at work as well as working conditions. While QMV
(and EP co-decision) now also applies in the area of workers' rights
to *information and consultation* about company decision making, this
still falls well short of the corporatist thresholds of co-*determination*
legislation in the national legislation of most member states in continental Western Europe and Scandinavia. Indeed co-determination itself,
social security legislation, protection of workers upon redundancy, and
conditions of employment for third-country nationals require unanimity, as do policies on tax harmonization. Reflecting the 'Rhineland
capitalist' corporatist arrangements of many member states, the Social
Protocol agreed in 1991 in Maastricht to provide a 'social dialogue'
on EU policy with the European peak-level employers' organization
(Union of Industrial and Employers Organizations in Europe [UNICE],
and trade unions such as the European Trade Union Confederation
(ETUC)). At the 1999 Summit in Cologne, it was augmented by a 'macroeconomic dialogue'. The social dialogue requires the European Commission to consult these 'social partners' on any legislative initiatives
in the social policy field. The Social Protocol also provided an enabling
framework for 'Euro-agreements' between employers and employees on

social policy. That is, it gave the social partners the legislative capacity to negotiate their own settlements should they choose to do so. These could then, depending on the particular social policy traditions in each country and welfare policy regime, be implemented by nation states or the social partners themselves, or become the basis of a common European legislative proposal by the Commission to be tabled by the Council. It should be said, however, that it takes two to dance this tango, and the employer side has been very reticent in taking up this possibility. In addition, the complex relationships between EU-level organizations and national affiliates on the employers as well as the trade union side make it very difficult to find common ground for social dialogue (Leonard et al., 2007). Consequently, with very few exceptions, the social dialogue generated joint opinions and declarations rather than collective agreements (Welz, 2008). Similarly, ECB, the Economic and Financial Affairs Council (ECOFIN), and the Euro-Group have paid scant regard to the macroeconomic dialogue (Janssen, 2005: pp. 230–3).

Turning from legislative rules and procedures to actual policy outcomes and decisions, even those who stress significant developments on the former concede that substantive pieces of EU social legislation have been 'few and far between' (Hix, 2005: p. 256). Directives have established a framework for general health and safety at work. In the area of working conditions, a directive in 1992 stipulated the rather modest threshold that there should be proof of an employment contract. There have also been directives on the protection of pregnant women, working time, parental leave, and equal rights for temporary and fixed contract workers. Again, it should be stressed that these tend to fall below the threshold of most national legislation. The most substantial EU welfare measures are, despite the minuscule relative size of the EU budget, the regional supports – which we will discuss in further detail in the next chapter. These are the supports given by the ESF to so-called objective 1 regions – that is, regions that only have a GDP per capita of less than 75 per cent of the EU average, and objective 3 regions to modernize 'human resource' infrastructure in the field of education and training. It should be stressed, however, that regional support has been spread considerably thinner since eastern enlargement, which increased claims with a total budgetary envelope that remained more or less the same.

The most significant developments in EU social policy arose out of the 1999 Lisbon Agenda and more recently from the fiscal provisions on Eurozone crisis management. The former have at best had an equivocal effect on welfare state developments, and the latter have unequivocally promoted retrenchment. As noted in the previous chapter, the Lisbon Agenda linked social policy closely to financial liberalization in a bid to revitalize the European economy on the American model. In form and technique, the Lisbon Agenda was based on the application of non-binding 'soft regulation', known as the Open Method of Coordination (OMC). Rather than relying on formal sanction, the OMC is based on defined codes of conduct, benchmarking, and policy coordination in a process of policy learning intended to disseminate best practice (e.g. Wincott, 2003). Based on the principle of 'invited dutifulness', it is premised on a measure of policy consensus of what could be construed as the 'best' policy, and the purpose is to generate the rational conditions that make it possible to implement it and regulate such implementation. And, that consensus is very much based on the 'third way' reform in social democracy that also had an impact on Christian democracy that sought to make welfare policy more market conforming and compatible, stressing the idea of no social rights without responsibility (Büchs, 2007). In substantive terms, the emphasis is on promoting an asset-based welfare system in response to fiscal, reproductive, and demographic problems that slow growth rates generated for pension systems and supply-side policies of 'activation' and 'employability' to reduce unemployment through increased market flexibility. In other words, welfare provision is not conceived in opposition to capitalist commodification but as being provided through the constitution of markets through a set of discursive and disciplinary practices promoted through policy networks operating on a European scale (Walters & Haahr, 2005: pp. 114–36; Wöhl, 2011).

The 'Jobs Summit' in Luxembourg in November 1997 was a significant precursor to the Lisbon Agenda (Tidow, 2003). It was called in response to the newly elected Socialist Jospin government in France, committed to signing the Amsterdam Treaty only if more was done to address the problem of unemployment. Notably, the Jobs Summit eschewed any review of the Maastricht agreement on monetary union and its macroeconomic framework. The European Employment Strategy (EES) launched at the jobs summit did not identify or address systemic issues that might restrict employment opportunities. Treating such opportunities as exogenously given, the EES instead assumed that the unemployment problem had to do with deficiencies of individuals, such as their skill sets and motivation to work, and focused exclusively on activation and employability (Hager, 2009: p. 116). Eschewing 'hard' and 'binding' common policies, the EES sought instead to render member state policies transparent to one another and subject them to peer review and mutual learning. Hence, the EES engaged member states in ongoing reflection on their policies. Fixed guidelines and timetables, country-specific recommendations, 'National Action Plans', and periodic monitoring are devised for that purpose. Hence, the blanket term Open Method of Coordination was conceived, and the Lisbon Agenda formalized these practices while also extending their scope beyond the area of employment policy to social policy more generally. Crucially, social policy in general was to be closely related to conditionalities and exigencies of activation and employability in the labour market (Wincott, 2003: esp. pp. 535–6, 542). On that basis, reforms were proposed in areas such as family policy, unemployment insurance, and pensions (Sapir, 2006). Crucially, the Lisbon process links social policy to a central theme of the previous chapter, namely Europe's strategy to create a 'new economy' on the basis of finance-led growth. The transformation of the pension systems from defined benefit to market-based actuarial schemes to market-based actuarial schemes, à la the Anglo-Saxon liberal model, was a crucial aspect of reform (e.g. Clark, 2002: pp. 78–84; Ebbinghaus, 2011).

Clearly, the Lisbon Agenda is something altogether different from the protective social provisions that Delors seemed to conceive in his Bournemouth speech. In fact, just as in the case of the monetary union, it can be seen as a complement to negative integration. But even in these terms, its success is questionable. The convening of the Sapir High Level Expert Group, and others such as the Wim Kok Committee, reflected a sense of impatience and lack of progress. From that point of view, New Economic Governance, arising out of the post-Eurozone crisis – which we discussed in the previous chapter, with reverse majority voting and remits to pursue 'structural policy' – can be seen as a return to executive authority, hard law, and regulation to achieve the substantive goals of Lisbon in an overt process of welfare state retrenchment (Oberndorfer, 2015).

Debates over the social dimension: the pessimists versus the optimists

The pessimistic case

The relative lack of 'hard' protective supranational regulation and collectively binding social policy, industrial relations, and fiscal federalism gives credence to those who are pessimistic about the prospects for a meaningful social dimension to the EU. As discussed in chapter 3, Fritz Scharpf's rational choice institutionalism outlines incisively the essence of the case in the most parsimonious of terms (2002). He argues that in the very institutional design of the treaty structure, there is an asymmetry between market efficiency and competition policies enabled by negative integration and welfare policies that would require positive integration to be effective. Cost competition exerts pressures on social standards, wages, and levels of taxation on national welfare states. At the same time, the diversity of European welfare states, which differ not only in terms of levels of development (that is continental Western Europe as compared to Southern Europe and even more so Eastern Europe) but more importantly in their institutional design (the different welfare policy regimes), results in a 'joint decision-making trap':

While most member states agree that the pressures exerted by the single market on their welfare policies are a problem, they cannot agree on an effective regulation or directive. What is more, member states will not agree on more supranational procedures because they fear that they will be constrained by European rules devised from templates and perspectives that reflect welfare policy regimes that are different from their own. The pressure exerted by market competition means that the expansion of the welfare state programme cannot rely on tax increases but only on more rapid economic growth (George, 1998). Hence, the anti-growth bias of the EMU compounds the problem.

For Scharpf, the joint decision-making trap can be explained with reference to institutional path dependence, caused by European welfare capitalism being organized on a national basis prior to the single-market programme. Already, the 1957 Messina IGC, which produced the Treaty of Rome, was a crucial watershed when French Socialist Prime Minister Guy Mollet's position was rejected. Mollet had argued that any integration of industrial markets would need to be accompanied by the harmonization of social regulations and tax burdens (Scharpf, 2002: pp. 645–6). In explaining why Mollet's position was not adopted, it is possible to take the argument about path dependence one step further and suggest that although European welfare states would not expand in quantitative terms until the 1950s and especially the 1960s and 1970s, the qualitative diversity of welfare institutions had arguably been crystallized already prior to World War II. For instance, the resilience of the Bismarckian social-insurance model has proven to be a remarkable constant in Germany's turbulent 20th-century history, surviving the transition from Empire to the Weimar Republic, to the Nazi state, allied occupation, and the formation of the Federal Republic.

Accounting for Eurozone crisis management, Scharpf's assessment has become even more pessimistic. The receivership nature of the Memorandums of Understanding hits at the very heart of political citizenship (overruling representative politics) as well as social citizenship (welfare retrenchment), posing profound problems for maintaining legitimacy (Scharpf, 2011: p. 31). Scharpf's assessment has been accepted by most critical political economists (e.g. Grahl & Teague, 1997; Holman, 2004). However, as discussed in chapter 3, while these scholars acknowledge the impact of path dependence, they also stress the central role played by dominant classes and elites in the context of capitalist structures that determine the 'limits of the possible'. While he would not be counted among them, Wolfgang Steeck has most felicitously captured the contention by critical political economists that the asymmetrical institutional arrangement in question reflects a pre-constitutional 'double compromise', excluding labour, between European business and national governments (1995: p. 390).

Thus, in critical political economy terms, this pre-constitutional settlement and resultant asymmetrical regulation express the dominant hegemonic strategy of Europe's transnational fractions of capital, articulated most clearly by the ERT (van Apeldoorn, 2002; Holman, 2004; Hager, 2009; van Apeldoorn & Hager, 2010). Far from being merely the product of a random formative institutional moment, asymmetrical regulation was a deliberate attempt to change the terms of Europe's welfare settlements so as to assert a higher degree of market discipline and commodification at a juncture in European history when the power of organized labour had been weakened. This also entailed recasting citizenship bargains and community in a manner that increasingly discounts Marshallian social citizenship and that emphasizes individual rights and responsibilities to perform in the market. Apart from market pressures on social standards, the increased instrumentalization of welfare in the Lisbon Agenda as a public good for market performance (whether in the form of increasingly using corporatism exclusively as a mechanism to coordinate wage restraint or seeing retraining as an exclusively positive externality on the labour market) is symptomatic of this (Hager, 2009; van Apeldoorn & Hager, 2010; Bieling, 2003).

On the basis of this core argument, critical political economy research on EU social policy has concerned itself with three main areas. First, it has concerned itself with how social policy initiatives at the EU level, such as the Social Protocol, the social dialogue, and the Open Method of Coordination have served symbolic and ideological functions to ensure a modicum of appeal to trade unions and other partners in social consensus mechanisms, who from a position of weakness are 'locked into' this route as the only available alternative. Hence, the 'yes, but' position of the unions help in forging mass consent to the EU project (e.g. Schulten & Ryner, 2003; Bieling & Schulten, 2003). Second, with particular reference to the FSAP and the Lisbon Agenda, critical political economy has highlighted attempts to reform welfare programmes, most notably pensions, so as to make them serve direct accumulation functions for finance-led growth (Bieling, 2003; Beckmann, 2007), a tendency intensified by Eurozone crisis management (Busch et al., 2013; Ryner, 2015: pp. 283–4). A final area of research has highlighted the diminished capacities of these initiatives to recast the terms of legitimacy in European societies and highlighted an emergent crisis of social mediation that is reducing the appeal of mass parties in favour of right-wing populism and thereby facilitating increasingly authoritarian forms of governance (e.g. Cafruny & Ryner, 2007; van Apeldoorn, 2009; Holman, 2004; Bruff, 2014).

More supranational social policy than supposed?

These pessimistic assessments are contested in the literature by two versions of relative optimism, both of which assert that the pessimists underestimate the complexity of the institutional logic of EU social policy. The first of these is more optimistic about what actually has been achieved at the EU level. Writing from a neo-functionalist perspective, Carsten Strøby-Jensen argues that the Social Protocol of the Maastricht Treaty has encouraged significant spillover in the social policy and labour market fields, in the sense that member states have begun to do together what they previously did individually (Strøby-Jensen, 2000: p. 77). In particular, he refers to the inclusion of the right to information and consultation and to the integration of persons who have been excluded from the labour market, among the areas subject to QMV. He also considers areas that require anonymity but that are nevertheless included in the Social Protocol as indicative of spillover, since many of these were not within the remit of EU policy at all prior to the Protocol. Moreover, whatever the social dialogue may or may not have achieved, its existence is itself indicative of spillover (Strøby-Jensen, 2000: pp. 82–3). Focusing on jurisprudence in the ECJ, Caporaso and Tarrow (2009) have found evidence of significant supranational market correction as rulings have interpreted labour mobility provisions so as to extend universal social citizenship rights to non-national residents (see also Armstrong, 2010; Hay & Wincott, 2012: pp. 162–3).

Similar arguments have been made by historical institutionalists, although here, as one may recall from Chapter 3, it is not the rationality of decision making, but rather its limitations, that are held to explain the outcome. In other words, the Commission has been able to extend its competence because of the short-termism of member state governments in the Council and a lack of command of the implications of the agreements that they sign, including the legal implications as interpreted by the ECJ (e.g. Pierson & Leibfried, 1995). For instance, the Commission, the ETUC, and the European Parliament have at times been able to assert an expansive reading of what falls under the distortion of competition regulation and health and safety, as was the case in the passage of the 1992 Maternity Directive (Leibfried & Pierson, 1995: p. 48; Rhodes, 1995). Furthermore, as noted above, civic rights of equal treatment under labour mobility in the single market do have social policy implications, for instance on the transnationalization of income transfers and more generally social citizenship rights (Leibfried & Pierson, 1995: pp. 53–65). It is not impossible that problems associated with this, such as the disarticulation of a clear relation between taxation and benefits, will ultimately require solutions at the EU level. Daniel Wincott (2003) has proposed a more careful variant of the historical institutional argument. Although he does reject a pessimistic reading of the balance sheet, he nevertheless suggests that even the soft regulation associated with the OMC in the Lisbon Agenda marks a departure from the strict separation of economic efficiency regulation from social regulation and that a blurring of the open method and the community (or Monnet) method – that is, cultivated spillover – cannot be ruled out as a possibility. Furthermore, the meaning of terms such as 'activation' and 'employability' vary with the institutional context of the particular welfare regime. This is the case for instance in Scandinavian versions of 'flexicurity', and one should not underestimate their resilience vis-à-vis neoliberal intentions (e.g. Andersen et al., 2002; Andersen, 2007).

It should also be noted that there is an optimistic critical political economy variant, which stresses sectoral variation and the dialectical quality of historical development. Most notably, these emphasize the impetus that the single market has given organized labour in different sectors to organize transnationally, not primarily within but also outside formal Euro-corporatist structures such as the social dialogue (Bieler, 2006). While acknowledging that this is not the predominant trend, Roland Erne (2008) points to the real impact of informal wage coordination in the construction and metalworking sector in the Eurozone and of intra-union mobilization on job security issues in mergers and acquisitions. These are instances where unions have been able to politicize the decisions of supranational corporations or executives. While being careful not to infer any significant general effects on current neoliberal austerity policies, Bieler and Erne (2015) do point to relative instances of success in forging transnational solidarity campaigns by service sector unions.

These literatures primarily focus on decision making and the spatial scale on which agents organize rather than focus on welfare state performance. Regarding the latter, questions can be raised about the treatment of standards of measurement in these literatures, and as such, they do not really seriously challenge the assessment of the pessimists. They address neither the retrenchment that actually has taken place in European welfare states nor the fact that common EU social policies are generally set at levels that fall short of national legislation. Above all, they do not face up to the standard of welfare state performance that would need to be reached if effective entitlements are to be maintained. Furthermore, as Leibfried and Pierson themselves point out (1995: pp. 70–4), some unintended consequences, such as the disarticulation between taxation and transfer payments to residents in other jurisdictions that are the results of equal treatment, may actually increase the pressure on welfare states. The latter point is revisited and expanded on in Höpner and Schäfer's (2010) critique of Caporaso and Tarrow's interpretation of ECJ rulings, which as stated above are restricted to extending rights according civic citizenship non-discrimination criteria rather than maintaining the extent and quality of social citizenship rights per se. With regard to effective transnational working-class agency, even those who point to it concede that at best these are embryonic developments and that little evidence is provided that there are mechanisms in place that will cumulatively upscale them. In the end, the fragmentation of trade union action during the crisis bears all the marks of the joint decision-making trap (Dribbusch, Lehndorff, & Schulten, 2016). This is indeed the conclusion of Erne himself (2015).

A social model fit to compete?

Another response to the pessimists comes from those who make no major claims about significant developments towards 'hard' common EU social policy but who instead suggest that the dangers of the single market and the EMU to national welfare state are exaggerated. The single market and EMU have generated complex and surprising outcomes. More often than not they have addressed welfare state problems that have needed to be resolved anyway, thereby placing the welfare state on a more rational and sustainable footing (Ferrera, Hemerijck, & Rhodes, 2000). Indeed, rather than posing a threat, the SEM and the EMU have facilitated reform and 'self-adjustment' in the welfare state and are, if anything, contributors to stability.

This literature makes two basic points. The first is an empirical one. It emphasizes the 'remarkable continuity' of social expenditure after the inception of the SEM and the EMU in relation to previous decades, made possible by reduced interest payments, expansion of the tax base, and revenues generated from privatization (Rhodes, 2002: pp. 311–12, 317–18). Furthermore, it contends that there is scant evidence of 'social dumping' and a 'race to the bottom' where economic competition from less developed welfare states in Southern and Eastern Europe would compel the Northern European welfare states to 'retrench'. In fact, developments in Southern Europe in the 1990s and early 2000s even pointed to a 'race to the top' insofar as the southern welfare state – notably Portugal – extended coverage to groups which previously were not protected by a safety net (Rhodes, 2002: pp. 319–20).

One important subset of this empirical argument has been that, rather than marking the decline of collective bargaining and industrial relations, the EMU increased the *need* and the *scope* for strengthening corporatist collective bargaining. The *need* increased because coordinated wage policy was one of the few areas where nation states could recover economic policy autonomy and macroeconomic steering capacity. The *scope* for agreements has also simultaneously increased since the reduction of policy tools under the formal discretion of the state decreased the agenda of distributive conflict between the social partners. In short, competitive advantage within the Eurozone became contingent on strong collective bargaining regimes (Hancké, 2013; Hall, 2014). The conclusion and readjustment of 'social pacts' also mushroomed after the 1990s throughout the EU, after a decade of corporatist decline in the 1980s (Fajertag & Pochet, 2000; Rhodes, 2001; Bieling & Schulten, 2003; Enderlein, 2006).

To be sure, the relationship between the SEM, the EMU, and welfare state retrenchment is complex. As we noted at the outset of this chapter, the welfare state is an institution that is constitutive of the essence of the modern European social order. Hyperbolic claims that the SEM and the EMU would result in an outright 'end' of the welfare state are off the mark, and if nothing else the empirics that these contributions invoke usefully remind us of this. Indeed, under conditions of uneven development in some locales, at some junctures welfare state efforts could be maintained at existing levels or perhaps even expanded within the single market.

However, leaving aside the rather obvious rejoinder that this upbeat assessment of Southern European welfare states had to be reassessed after the Eurozone crisis, the implications for welfare regimes, the terms under which reproductive and legitimation functions operate– in short for *social citizenship*– conveyed by the empirical evidence provided by this literature is highly misleading. As Esping-Andersen put it in a memorable turn of phrase, it is hard to find any instance where social forces have struggled for spending as such. 'Expenditure is epiphenomenal to the substance of the welfare state' (Esping-Andersen, 1990: p. 19). What matters are rather *effective entitlements*, and the extent to which they correspond to the norms of distributive justice and legitimacy that are contained in the social citizenship accords.

When considered from this point of view, the stability of social expenditure levels may actually be an indicator of significant welfare state retrenchment. This is because from the point of view of prevailing norms of *unchanged* social citizenship, there are good grounds to suppose that there should be an *increase* of claims. First and foremost, the European population is ageing, and there has been a marked increase in pensioners ready to make claims on programmes that they see themselves as having contributed towards in their working lives. The level of claims has been raised by previous rationalization strategies in Christian democratic welfare states, based on early retirement. Second, as noted in the introduction to this chapter, reproductive needs have grown. Divorce rates have soared, leading to an increase in single-parent households (mostly 'headed' by single mothers). These factors, along with the efforts to increase employment rates and the aspiration of women to become full economic citizens, have increased the demand for family services. It is no wonder, then, that Rhodes' more disaggregated figures point to a marked shift of resources towards areas such as these (Rhodes, 2002: pp. 312–13). Similar reforms were pursued in Christian democratic regimes, but the record of extending or maintaining social citizenship rights is highly equivocal (Lewis & Giullari, 2005; Lewis et al., 2008; Wöhl, 2011).

From the point of view of social citizenship norms, then, it makes more sense to focus on the interrelationship of welfare state programmes and what they provide in terms of entitlement. Given the increased demand for, and claims on, these programmes despite fixed resources, we can expect that there has been significant retrenchment. Even before the Eurozone crisis, there was a marked reduction of the net replacement rates for benefits received during sickness, work accidents, and unemployment in Europe (Korpi & Palme, 2003; Korpi, 2003: p. 597). But above all, as Korpi rightly points out, it is the end of the full employment commitment, progressively consolidated by the EMS and the EMU, and the understanding of employment in terms of 'a right to work' at a certain standard, that *in and of itself* is a decisive factor in welfare state retrenchment.

> [U]nemployment ... [is] ... a central variable [of the welfare state] ... because for categories of citizens with labour power as their main basic power resource, the efficacy of this resource in distributive conflict and bargaining is to a major extent determined by the demand for labour and by the level of unemployment. ... [T]he maintenance of low levels of unemployment empowers citizens and is an essential preventative part of the welfare state. ... In Western Europe, the emergence of full employment as well as the expansion of social transfers and social services ... emerged approximately at the same time. ... [C]ontemporaries saw this triplet as constituting a unity, the full employment welfare state, where expanding social insurance and services were combined with unemployment rates below the 3 percent maximum level set by the British social reformer William Beveridge .... It was a manifestation of what can be called an implicit social contract between the main interest groups in these countries .... The return of mass unemployment must be seen as ... the eradication of one of the corner stones of the Western European welfare states. (Korpi, 2003: pp. 592–4, 596)

In light of this, it is not surprising that inequality among individuals and between capital and labour has increased, nor is it surprising that the Fordist formula of almost perfect proportionality of social wage increases with economic growth has been broken, indicating that the wage relation is increasingly defined as a 'market variable' as opposed to a means to disseminate the 'fruits of progress' and to ensure the 'virtuous' Fordist relationship between mass production, productivity growth, and mass consumption, inter alia, as described in Chapter 4 of this book. When considered against the backdrop of the latter point, the corporatist bargains of the 1990s hardly represent continuity or even 'self-transformation'. In contrast to previous periods, when the raison d'être of corporatist bargains was to contain price increases at full employment, they are now used in order to secure wage settlements below rates of productivity growth at levels of high unemployment.

Unions have signed up to these bargains from a position of exceptional weakness in order to increase the probability – but not guarantee – that this will boost employment. This puts serious strain on the 'moral economy' that makes workers join unions in the first place, because unions are perceived to contain rather that increase wages and because concessions attenuate internal representative structures within unions at the expense of peak-level concertation. All of these problems are exacerbated when the bargains *fail* to significantly boost employment and increase involuntary participation in non-standard employment (Heyes & Lewis, 2014), since they contribute to the dynamic of competitive austerity, as analysed in the previous chapter.

When matters are considered at this more disaggregated level of entitlement, this version of the optimistic argument also concedes that there has been significant retrenchment. There has been 'some' increase of inequality, mainly due to increased incidence of ageing, single parenthood, and unemployment. It is conceded that in France, Germany, Belgium, and Austria, there have been important changes in entitlements that are more or less directly linked to the Maastricht convergence criteria. In Finland, the Netherlands, and Ireland, such changes preceded Maastricht (Rhodes, 2002: pp. 318–22). It is also conceded that there have been adverse deflationary effects on employment rates (ibid.: p. 305). But this is where this literature makes its second major move: it views retrenchment as necessary. The single market, the EMU, and the Open Method of Coordination (and perhaps the Troika Memorandums of Understanding?) have served as a catalyst for this necessary retrenchment in order to put European welfare states on a more secure footing (Ferrera, Hemerijck, & Rhodes, 2000; Esping-Andersen, 2002).

The question is whether this is a purely normative judgement in favour of a neoliberal adjustment of European welfare capitalism as advanced by the policymakers in the EU or whether it is as claimed an objective assessment made with reference to necessity. After all, the authors concerned have played a central role in the policy process as advisers (for an overview, see Jenson & Saint-Martin, 2005).

There are two possible lines of argument with regard to objective necessity. Wisely, the usual suspect, 'globalization', is not pursued because it would be circular. After all, as this book shows, globalization is a structural necessity forged in no little respect by social forces themselves. Moreover, it is Europeanization (policies promoted by authors such as these) rather than globalization that has had such a discernible impact on European welfare states (Hay & Wincott, 2012). The preferred argument is instead that 'post-industrialism' imposes a logic of 'no alternative' to welfare retrenchment and that the SEM, the EMU, and Lisbon were beneficial for the welfare state because they compelled social groups to come to their senses and participate in the policy process of adjustment. Although this is a stronger argument, it is an overly deterministic one.

The argument is derived from a simple two-sector model developed in the 1960s by the economist William Baumol (1967): As industrialization progresses, the 'manufacturing sector' becomes increasingly capital intensive and sheds labour. This labour surplus can be absorbed only by an emerging 'service sector'. However, it is held that services, by their very nature, are not amenable to the same kind of continuous productivity growth as in manufacturing. This means that wage and benefit rates in the service sector cannot match those of the manufacturing sector, at least at 'normal' rates of profit. This has sharpened policy trade-offs, and a thorny 'trilemma' has emerged where it is becoming impossible to obtain simultaneously low unemployment, income equality, and fiscal balance (Iversen & Wren, 1998). Analysts agree that the Christian democratic and Mediterranean welfare state characteristics of the Eurozone are facing particularly severe crisis tendencies in this context. These 'social-insurance states' with high wage and non-wage labour costs, the latter of which are exacerbated as unemployment (and claims on social insurance) increases, are simply pricing the production factor labour out of the market, which then fiscally destabilizes the entire welfare system. In this environment, it is impossible to develop a sizeable service economy, because high wage costs serve as a severe barrier to entry. In contrast to the residual liberal state type, there is insufficient flexibility in terms of allowing wage dispersion and hence sufficiently cheap labour for a market-based service economy. In contrast to the social democratic welfare state, there are not sufficient tax-financed investments in social services and in active labour market policies to expand public-sector service employment (Esping-Andersen, 1990: pp. 191–220; Esping-Andersen, 1996, 1999: pp. 99–142; Hemerijck, 2002). However, the experience with the competitive corporatism of the 1990s has demonstrated that reform is nevertheless possible. Such reforms require containing wage costs *as well as* accepting wage segmentation in order to achieve a measure of 'liberal' wage flexibility combined with Scandinavian-inspired emphasis on active labour market policy (under the heading 'reactivation'), as opposed to 'passive' unemployment benefits. It is in this context, then, that the discipline imposed by the SEM, the EMU, and Lisbon served as a catalyst (ibid.: p. 9; Rhodes, 2002: p. 311).

But this somewhat Malthusian view is flawed. First, on an empirical level, it is rendered problematic by significant instances of productivity growth in economies with significant service sectors, including not only the US but also Scandinavia. This suggests that there is also a problem of a more conceptual nature. First and foremost, the blanket term 'services' cannot capture such diverse activities as investment banking, legal advice, marketing, haircutting, computer maintenance, healthcare, and childcare. Quite a few of these activities actually contribute to productivity growth indirectly or find mechanisms through which to charge the manufacturing sector clients for these services (whether in the form of fees or taxation) (Ryner, 2009). Finally, services can provide demand that triggers further productivity in manufacturing in complex 'systems of innovation' (Mahon, 1987, 2006). Viewed from this perspective, there is no reason to suppose that a new, post-Fordist phase of capitalist growth in output and productivity, based on communications and computer technology, is not possible, provided that an adequate and coherent institutional framework – or mode of regulation – is instituted. This conclusion reinforces the central argument of the previous chapters: the EMU as presently constituted is part of the problem rather than the solution.

There is, in other words, no reason to assume the existence of an objective, hyper-structural, 'post-industrial' constraint beyond social relations that makes it impossible to expand social consumption and general taxation in order to boost public-service sector employment and provide childcare, healthcare, and service provision for the elderly and single-parent households. These are measures that would increase tax receipts, reduce claims on social insurance, and most likely also contribute to productivity growth through what in the previous chapter was termed 'Kaldor-Verdoorn' dynamics. If nothing else, niche strategies in Scandinavia provide prima facie evidence for the presence of these dynamics. Rhodes (2002) is aware that these strategies are an option but argues that there was 'little scope' for such expansion, due to 'fiscal overload'. But inadvertently, this makes our point. The reduction of scope is institutional and caused by structural social power relations as institutionally expressed through the design of the SEM and the EMU.

A broader problem with the idea of a successful 'self-adjustment' of the European welfare state facilitated by the EMU is the definition of 'self'. At what moment does retrenchment challenge the very quality and identity of the social citizenship accord? This is not a question that can be answered in the abstract, and most certainly not simply with reference to social expenditure levels and budgetary balances. Rather, it depends on the extent to which reforms can also be rendered compatible with the terms of legitimacy in broader civil society. Here, the problem is that an essentially neoliberal project has been presented in mass political discourse as compatible with social citizenship and the European social model. The preliminary answer, however, is that EMU-induced retrenchment does not accord with the political logic of the Christian democratic welfare state (van Kersbergen, 1995: pp. 235–46): As European societies became secularized, Christian democracy became increasingly reliant on reproducing the power resources that are connected to the institution that it has assumed leadership in creating, namely the welfare state. In such a situation, economic stagnation and austerity are particularly damaging to a social order defined by

Christian democratic norms, as the welfare institutions that are threatened by such stagnation and austerity are intimately connected to the very stability of the social and political order itself.

Conclusion

After having outlined the essential nature of European welfare capitalism and its regimes, as well as developments in EU social policy, this chapter has reviewed the scholarly debate between those who are optimistic and those who are pessimistic about the social dimension of the EU. While the optimists in the historical institutionalist tradition make a number of valid points that should make us wary about simplistic predictions that the EU implies an end of the welfare state, the chapter ultimately sides with the pessimists. In particular, the chapter stresses the reduction of effective entitlements resulting from anaemic growth and distributive implications of finance-led growth in the face of increased reproductive needs driven by demographics and changing gender relations. These have taken an acute form in the wake of the politics of austerity and the Eurozone crisis. Given the central importance of social citizenship for mass legitimacy, this is a profound source of instability for European democracy.

Chapter 6

Core and Periphery in an Enlarged European Union

The European Community was founded by six states that, with the exception of southern Italy, are situated within the relatively confined and homogenous socioeconomic space in north-western Europe. Since 1973 the EU has expanded dramatically to encompass a vastly larger population and geographical area. Following the enlargements of 2004, 2007, and 2013, the number of member states increased from 15 to 28 and included a much wider range of socioeconomic structures and political cultures than 'the original six'. Whatever the current and fraught accession negotiations may bring, the prospective memberships of Turkey and Serbia will not diminish this reality. More generally, the striking growth of nationalism and Euroscepticism throughout the EU, generated by the Eurozone and migration crises, pose major obstacles to further enlargements. As the British referendum on 'Brexit' indicates, it is possible that one or more member states might withdraw from the EU, a process that was given a legal mechanism in the Lisbon Treaty.

The successive enlargements have dramatically transformed the EU. The entry of the UK along with Ireland and Denmark in 1973 simultaneously raised the EU's global profile while exposing it to greater American influence. The accession of Greece in 1981 followed by Portugal and Spain in 1986 helped to consolidate democratic transitions, but increased socioeconomic heterogeneity. The process of enlargement and expansion into Central and Eastern Europe that started in the 1990s with the collapse of the Soviet Union, and that continues today in the form of European Partnerships, also greatly enhanced the EU's global weight even as it further entrenched American power across the continent. The fault lines of the eastern enlargements alongside the southern enlargements of the 1980s cast a long shadow over the Eurozone crisis. This chapter offers a critical political economy analysis of these developments.

The EU's ambitious enlargement over the three decades from the 1980s and the 2000s coincided with the implementation of the SEA and the EMU. Thus, it was accomplished within the context of the neoliberal project and played a very important role in its consolidation. Enlargement was accompanied by extremely modest compensatory measures in the form of regional policy, the absence of a deliberate industrial development policy, and above all the absence of fiscal federalism in the form of sizeable transfers between regions. The 1977 MacDougall Report had concluded that monetary union would require the EC budget to increase significantly to 7.5–10 per cent of GDP to ensure cohesion in a much less diverse and more closely integrated economic space (European Commission, 1977: p. 14), while currently the EU budget remains no more than 1 per cent of EU GDP. Moreover, it is the 'old' member states, many of which were hit hardest by the Eurozone crisis and the lack of adjustment mechanisms provided by monetary sovereignty, that have been and will remain the major recipients of the relatively modest cohesion funds (Lepesant, 2014).

The chapter begins with a description of the most important policy instruments that were mobilized to integrate new member states. It then reviews the experience of what we call the Southern European semi-periphery. Although Southern and Eastern European member states have followed very different economic and political trajectories, important commonalities in the experience of both regions illustrate the profound limitations of liberal theory as a guide to enlargement policy. Liberal approaches to enlargement are described and then challenged from a critical political economy perspective that draws on key concepts that have a long lineage in the historical materialist (and Keynesian) traditions, namely uneven development and core-periphery relations. We argue that the absence of fiscal federalism has reinforced the control of the core, itself overwhelmingly dominated by German capital, over the southern semi-periphery as it seeks to enlarge the domain of finance-led accumulation. However, finance-led accumulation is inherently polarizing and, hence, *disintegrative*. Part III applies these perspectives to the 'real existing' developmental trajectory of the Central and Eastern European (CEE) member states. Here similar mechanisms have served to reinforce core-periphery relations. The chapter then addresses the EU's evolving strategy towards the former republics of the Soviet Union through the European Neighbourhood Policy (ENP) and Eastern Partnerships. We focus here on the EU's evolving economic relationship with Ukraine, which is experiencing what we have called the first shock therapeutic stage of semi-peripheral development. Finally, we introduce a critical political economy perspective to address two profoundly important yet neglected questions with respect to the eastern enlargement: was there a viable alternative to liberal development? If so, why was such a project not pursued? In the sixth and final section of the chapter, we link our findings to that of neo-institutionalist scholar Martin Heidenreich and his concept 'enlargement trilemma', which enables a parsimonious formulation of the structural limitations of neoliberal enlargement.

Key policy instruments and enlargement

In considering the enlargement process, it is useful to distinguish between the rules, process, and policy substance that the EU applies before new members are admitted and those that are applied to manage affairs once an enlargement has taken place. With regard to the former, it is important to note that the admission of new member states is essentially treated as treaty amendment (Preston, 1997: pp. 8–22). Hence, the process of enlargement occupies the extreme intergovernmental end of the spectrum, with formal authority residing with the European Council and the member states. Each member state needs to ratify the admission of any new member and hence enjoys the power of veto. Because applications for membership are addressed to the Council, the policy initiative lies with it and not the Commission. Furthermore, it is the Council that decides on the EU's common position on the basis of the principle of unanimity (though the Commission and Parliament must be consulted). The Maastricht Treaty mitigated somewhat the Council and member state focus by mandating that the admission of new member states also requires assent by the European Parliament. With so many potential veto points, it could be considered remarkable that enlargement takes place at all. It is an outcome that needs to be explained with reference to the interrelationship between neoliberal transformation and geopolitics.

It is especially telling that the current member states of Central and Eastern Europe – and in the case of the Baltic States, former Soviet republics – became EU members only a decade and a half after the collapse of Soviet communism and the dissolution of the Soviet-sponsored Council for Mutual Economic Assistance (COMECON). Prior to the 1988 Trade and Cooperation Agreement between the EC and COMECON, these states did not even diplomatically recognize the EC. Indeed, even after the revolutions of 1989, it seemed inconceivable that the former communist states would become EC members anytime soon. To be sure, with the formation of the European Bank of Restructuring and Development (EBRD) and the Poland and Hungary: Assistance for Restructuring the Economies (PHARE) programme, the EC contributed significantly to the loan and aid programme that Western powers committed to 1989–90 in support of the reform process. Furthermore, the Europe Agreements reduced tariffs and barriers to capital and labour mobility and institutionalized political dialogue. But these were bilateral, hub-and-spoke relationships that excluded 'sensitive industries' (e.g. Mayhew, 1998) and were designed 'to restrict access to key Western markets rather than to integrate them' (Bidelux & Jeffries, 2007: p. 582). When the EU then responded to the incoming applications for membership with the Copenhagen Criteria in 1993, there were good reasons to believe that eastern enlargement was off the immediate agenda. This is because the path that was staked out followed closely the 'classical method' of enlargement whereby accession involves joining a club with definite rules to be followed rather than a pact between two parties, where these rules are up for negotiation (Preston, 1997: p. 9). In other words, the eastern enlargements have assumed that the applicant states adjust to the EU. Since the SEA and the Maastricht Treaties were already mandating stringent market discipline, it was hard to see how states that were transforming themselves from an entirely different mode of production might be able to satisfy these rules in the foreseeable future. The Copenhagen Criteria stipulated not only that the Central and Eastern European applicants would need to accept the full *acquis communitaire* in a general sense but also that they must be able to take on the obligations of membership of political, economic, and monetary union (Mayhew, 1998: p. 162). While most CEE members have not joined the third stage of the EMU and adopted the single currency, it is a testament to the power of the interests favouring enlargement and neoliberal shock therapy and to the strength of belief in the integrative power of markets that prevailed at the time (e.g. Schimmelfennig, 2001) that full EU membership was nevertheless achieved by these applicants only a decade later.

Regarding the post-enlargement phase, regional policy stands out as the instrument that the EU has developed to deal with a larger and more heterogeneous body of members. Indeed, together with the CAP and claiming about one-third of the overall EU budget, it is the only area where EU budgetary policy plays a significant role. Regional policy underwent major reform and became a significant factor in 1988, after southern enlargement had been achieved with the accession of Greece (1981), Spain (1986), and Portugal (1986) just as the EU was completing the single market. Regional policy was a compensatory measure that recognized that at least initially the adjustment costs would outweigh the benefits of the single market in many parts of Southern Europe as well as in Europe's western Atlantic rim. The 1988 reforms doubled the size of the regional policy budget within an unchanged budgetary envelope that depended on reduced spending on the CAP.

The 1988 reforms also established the three principles that should inform what now became known as 'cohesion policy' (e.g. Hix, 1999: pp. 256–60). First, according to the principle of additionality, Community funds were not to replace but rather to augment those of national regional policy, and they were to be paid directly to the regions. Second, according to the principle of partnership, the programmes generated by the policy were to be administered jointly by the Commission, the member states, and the regions. Hence, in marked contrast to highly intergovernmental pre-accession politics, regional policy is often celebrated as the quintessential example of post-Westphalian multilevel governance (e.g. Hooghe, 1996). A direct link is established between the supranational level and regional level, and not all policy deliberation goes through the central national state. Third, according to the principle of concentration, regional policy is to focus on 'priority objectives'. Initially, there were six such objectives. Objective 1 was to support structural adjustment in 'laggard' regions with an average GDP/capita less than 75 per cent of the EU average. Objective 2 was to support regions in industrial decline (drawing on the European Regional Development Fund – ERDF). Overlapping with social policy, Objectives 3 and 4 were to draw on the ESF to combat long-term unemployment and discrimination against women (Ob. 3) and adapt workers to industrial change (Ob. 4). Overlapping with the CAP, and drawing on the European Agriculture Guarantee Fund (EAGF), Objectives 5 and 6 were to promote rural development and to assist regions with low population density.

Regional policy is programme specific and consists of targeted measures, with budgets that are not of sufficient size to have any significant macroeconomic effects. As such, it should not be confused with macroeconomic management in fiscal federalism. The claims for a putative 'multi-levelled governance' need to be assessed in this context. In contrast to 1 per cent of EU GDP of the EU budget, modern European states have a budget equivalent to one-third to half of total GDP. Between 2004 and 2006 the average net transfer from the EU to the CEE countries was about 1 per cent of GDP, with the available funds rising to 3 per cent (Rae, 2011: p. 256). Although these funds are not insignificant, they are not 'automatic stabilizers' of fiscal and welfare transfers that facilitate cohesion within nation states (MacKay, 1995). The European Investment Bank (EIB) notwithstanding, there is no significant EU-level industrial policy. As discussed in Chapter 3, the single market was based on the assumption that spontaneous market forces would have a stabilizing effect. This is reinforced by the constraints on national fiscal transfers imposed by the Stability and Growth Pact and now the Fiscal Compact, both of which water down the 'additionality' principle (e.g. Barnett & Borooah, 1995).

These assumptions were relied upon even more after EU eastern enlargement, since the overall envelope of regional policy – in line with the so-called Agenda 2000 – was not increased, compared to the 1988 settlement. The obviously increased demand for regional policy funds, when such a large group of much poorer economies joined, was managed by a reduction of policy objectives from six to three. Objective 1 was retained, but with a lowering average GDP, many Southern European areas became ineligible for Ob. 1 funding. Objectives 2 and 4 were merged to form a new Objective 2 devoted to 'areas experiencing structural difficulties'. In line with the employability principle of the supply-side economics of the Lisbon Agenda, the new Objective 3 was devoted to the modernization of education, training, and employment policies in regions not eligible under Objective 1 (Hix, 2005: p. 290).

Diffusion and polarization in the single market: uneven development and Europe's north–south dynamics

Thus the transformational EU developments over the two decades from 1985 to 2005 – the EMU and enlargement – took place without the expansion of the EU budget that had been considered essential by the MacDougall Report. The rationale behind the integration strategy that facilitated this development was based on a neoliberal synthesis of Balassian trade theory (see Chapters 1 and 3), the efficient market hypothesis, and endogenous optimal currency area theory (see Chapter 4). As discussed in Chapter 4 (see pp. 84–89), from such a perspective liberalized and therefore efficient financial markets would solve the problem through optimal capital allocation. For that reason, current account deficits within a common currency area are not a problem. Inflows on the capital account would finance investment in the businesses that would provide the basis for financing and amortizing the accumulated debts in the future (Blanchard & Giavazzi, 2003). While reservations were issued, not least by analysts associated with the ECB to the effect that fiscal policy should do more to generate precautionary savings in upturns, the essential thrust of this analysis was widely shared (e.g. Fagan & Gaspar, 2008).

This analysis essentially reduced the determination of the economic geography of Europe to one of transaction and communication costs. With liberalized and integrated product and factor markets, reduced uncertainty through institutional integration (competition policy, the single market, and the EMU would be the key cases in point), and the cost-advantages of less developed economies in Southern and Eastern Europe, there would be a considerable diffusion of investments to these regions (e.g. Dluhosch, 2000; Kaminski, 2001). Barbara Dluhosch offered a particularly explicit statement of this rationale. 'Getting the institutions right', by which she meant ensuring the economies of competition, and reduced costs of communication that allow corporations to coordinate economic activities in distant places, would ensure that economies of scale can be diffused in the single market. Dluhosch directed her argument against the new trade theory of Paul Krugman, who had otherwise suggested that economies of scale tend to work against competition and comparative advantage and also polarize free trade areas by clustering investments in already developed areas (e.g. Krugman & Venables, 1990).

Dluhosch used the rhetoric of 'in practice', 'experience', and 'evidence' to make her point. However, the practice, experience, and evidence of the Eurozone crisis have shown the exact opposite. The capital flows that were the cause for Blanchard's and Giavazzi's sanguine conclusions were not expressions of such a fortuitous positive feedback loop between economies of competition, scale, and comparative advantage. In this respect, the impact of financial flows to Europe's southern periphery observed by Blanchard and Giavazzi had a similar perverse effect. Far from providing the business-fixed investments that would provide the foundations for financing the flows, it is now clear that these flows were highly speculative, akin to the Minskyan 'mania' phase described in Chapter 4, mainly in real estate. With reference to Barcelona, for example, Charnock, Purcell, and Ribera-Fumaz (2013) offer an especially vivid account of how these financial market dynamics fail to foster industrial development. In the mania phase of the bubble, the access to cheap loans compensates for welfare state retrenchment and wage moderation, helping to maintain consumption-based demand growth (Milios & Sotiropoulos, 2010). When the bubble burst and became transmitted into a fiscal and payments crisis via bailouts of banks in the context of austerity, the result was, as explored in Chapter 4, an acute crisis.

Europe's industrial structure has not been diffused but has in fact been increasingly polarized and concentrated in the north-western core and with the Southern European states progressively deindustrializing through a 'quiescence trap' (Simonazzi, 2016). This gives credence to those who argue that post-Fordist economies of elimination of communication bottlenecks and flexible specialization (see Chapter 2) generate significant counter-tendencies that concentrate high value-added production and relative surplus-value augmentation in certain districts and regions, especially in urban metropoles. These 'agglomeration economies' include the imperative of customer networking for product development and 'just-in-time' delivery, labour-pooling, proximity to research and development centres generating 'knowledge spillovers', intermediary goods and service provision, and the clustering of administrative functions. These can make economies of scale work against diffusion generated by lower factor costs in the periphery (Dunford & Perrons, 1994: esp. pp. 165–68, 172–73; Agnew, 2001: pp. 34–35; Dunford, 2005: p. 160).

The single market as structured by the broader macroeconomic austerity framework of the monetary union has generated a dynamic of competitive austerity. This policy mix has above all fostered mergers and acquisitions motivated by increasing the global competitiveness of capital-intensive European multinational corporations. At the same time, this restructuring has resulted in massive labour shedding (Ramsay, 1995). Regions are compelled to cut costs, but by doing so they mutually undercut aggregate demand. This often has perverse effects, including the inability to establish economies of scale and resultant higher than anticipated production costs, and higher budget deficits because of reduced tax revenues. In turn, these factors compel further austerity. But in line with the dynamics of agglomeration economics, regions have different capabilities in engaging in such competition, which has enforced a core-periphery structure (Dunford, 1995: p. 141). The politics of austerity following in the wake of the Eurozone crisis is, then, merely the most recent and dramatic expression of a more long-standing tendency.

The high value-added activities of these multinationals, as well as some small to medium size niche producers, are located in Europe's core, where there are positive feedback loops between competition, specialization, and economies of scale that are facilitated by the afore-mentioned agglomeration economies and where high value-added pro-duction for European and world markets (in Marxist parlance, relative surplus-value augmentation) facilitate high wages, comparatively high levels of employment, and high levels of service provision. Crucially in these districts, demand pull from the world market and supply-side policies of training, education, and industrial policy facilitated by infor-mal networks may generate sustained and high rates of local economic growth. Notably, these regions only rarely correspond with nation states anymore, and if they do, only to small states. Hence, even large states such as Germany, France, and the UK contain significant core-periphery divides – for instance, between regions or metropoles such as Baden-Würtemberg versus former East Germany; Rhône-Alpes versus deindustrialized northern France; metropolitan London versus north-east England. The key core region of Europe overlaps these national borders and runs from Piemonte in the Italian north-west along the Rhine basin up into south-eastern England (e.g. Dunford & Perrons, 1994). Birch and Mykhnenko (2009: pp. 10–15) expand on this picture by suggesting that regions that have combined the retention of high value-added manufacturing with high value-added services provision have enjoyed higher growth rates than those depending exclusively on high value-added manufacturing, because this has improved demand-side effects (see also Baccaro & Pontusson, 2015). It is in this core where one finds the sociopolitical alliances and power blocs that support aus-terity politics and export-oriented development strategies.

'Really existing' transitions in Central and Eastern Europe

Socioeconomic trajectories: semi-periphery and periphery

The developmental trajectory of the Central and Eastern European countries since the accession agreements also serves to illustrate the profound disconnect between the expectations of liberal development theory and their actual experience (Bohle, 2016). To be sure, generali-zations about the transition to capitalism throughout the former Soviet bloc must be made with caution. The outcomes of transition have in important respects been country specific and dependent on the prior position within COMECON, as well as historical and cultural factors and the political means by which transition was carried out. Moreover, an important aspect of dependent incorporation has been the afore-mentioned tendency towards uneven development operating *within* the post-communist region. Thus, some CEE countries and regions have managed to achieve significant growth rates through trade, FDI, and capital flows. The restructured post-communist industrial regions that are connected to the core through subcontracting chains and which offer relatively low wage and highly skilled labour forces may be said to form part of Europe's semi-periphery. This includes most notably the border regions of the Czech Republic, Slovakia, and Slovenia, as well as second-tier business and financial-services centres formed in capital and other major metropolitan regions, especially in the Visegrad states (the Czech Republic, Poland, Slovakia, and Hungary) (Birch & Mykhnenko, 2009: pp. 19–20).

However, much of the CEE is experiencing peripheralization, dein-dustrialization, and underdevelopment, and there is little evidence of diffusion. The Baltic new member states have been cited as a success story for 'internal devaluation' and shock therapy as a path to devel-opment (Åslund & Dombrovskis, 2011). However, between 2004 and 2013 Latvia experienced a loss of 200,000 migrant workers, or 9.5 per cent of its population, despite experiencing an unemployment rate of 20 per cent in 2013 (International Organisation for Migration, 2014; see also Lepesant, 2014: esp. pp. 4–5). Estonia and Lithuania have experienced similar patterns. The demographic crisis arising from shock therapy will have lasting effects into the mid to late 21st cen-tury. Finally, the outer rim of the periphery encompasses backward agricultural regions, especially in the Balkans and areas of the former Soviet Union, characterized by clientelism. As the Ukrainian case nota-bly illustrates, these latter states and regions are also gradually being incorporated into an EU-organized division of labour through what is called 'primitive accumulation', whereby extra economic means, ranging from state coercion to organized criminal activity, are used to strip common and public property and to privatize and commodify it (Agnew, 2001; Yurchenko, 2012). Such 'accumulation by dispossession' forms an integral part of finance-led accumulation as an extensive accumulation regime (Harvey, 2003).

Germany has played a central role in CEE enlargement. In the post-Fordist era, and especially since reunification was accomplished, Ger-man capital has pursued a strategy of relentless cost cutting and austerity in support of export mercantilism (Kinderman, 2005). A crucial ele-ment of this strategy has been extensive foreign direct investment in the CEE countries. Although Western European capital as a whole has pursued this strategy, German firms are by far the most successful and dominant, taking advantage of unit labour costs between one-quarter and one-half of those in Germany and, as a result of 'vertical disintegration', facilitating the reorganization of German labour relations on the basis of significant concessions (Krzywdzinski, 2014: pp. 12, 13). Key stages of German manufacturing and commodity supply chains have been relocated throughout Central and Eastern Europe in what the IMF has called the 'German–Central Europe Supply Chain' (IMF, 2013; Gross, 2013). This involves 'just-in-time' production in multiple countries and in which only final assembly may take place in Germany. As Rainer Hundsdoerfer, CEO of the German engineering firm EBM-Papst, has noted, 'Nothing in German industry, regardless of whether its automotives or appliances or ventilators, could exist without the extended workbenches in Eastern Europe' (Follain, Look, & Campbell, 2016). The successive enlargements have provided a more secure institutional and legal basis for this enlarged manufacturing base. Thus, Germany's modest political-military profile as a *geo-economic* power (Kundnani, 2011; Luttwak, 1990; Cafruny, 2015) belies its economic hegemony throughout Central and Eastern Europe, as we will explore in Chapter 7. Yet, as we will show in Chapter 8, the collapse of Schengen under the pressure of large-scale migration constitutes a serious threat to this enlarged manufacturing base and the underlying export-oriented strategy.

Enabling capitalist transition: three phases of transnational neoliberalization

Although the experience of transition has by no means been uniform, it is nevertheless possible to identify common features in a process that has passed through three distinct phases. With the exception of Hungary, at the behest initially of the United States and the IMF, all of the CEE countries passed through an initial phase of shock therapy involving price and trade liberalization, currency devaluation, austerity through restrictive monetary and fiscal policies as well as welfare state retrenchment, and the breaking of COMECON - links. Shock therapy paved the way for the entry of foreign capital into the region by greatly diminishing state capacity and, hence, national projects. By plunging formerly state-owned enterprises into bankruptcy and causing a precipitous drop in domestic demand and supply, it facilitated a rapid privatization of assets at 'fire sale' prices to foreign capital and domestic 'insiders' drawn variously from the formerly communist elites or *nomenklatura* (as in Bulgaria and Romania), oppositional groups (as in the Czech Republic and Poland), or individuals from both groups. This phase initially propelled the entire region 'into the greatest depression known anywhere in peacetime since the Great Depression' (Gowan, 1999: p. 227). In Poland, for example, the freeing of imports and prices in January 1990 precipitated hyperinflation. In one month, wages fell to 57 per cent and consumption to 58 per cent of the previous month's levels. Industrial output shrank by 68.5 per cent. Throughout 1990 real wages declined by 75 per cent, and consumption fell to 82 per cent of the 1989 level. The Czech Republic, Hungary, and Slovakia followed roughly similar patterns. The initial phase of shock therapy set the stage for a second phase of FDI-based development as the transition economies signed the Europe Agreements and faced EU conditionality.

At the outset of this phase, the initial volume of FDI in the region was meagre as a result of the devastating blow to former state institutions and consequent high risk, and the initial defensive posture towards FDI as states sought to develop national economic projects. However, by the second half of the 1990s under the pressure of severe stagnation, national development strategies were abandoned in favour of FDI, which came to be seen as the only available recourse to spur growth. The result was ruthless competition to attract FDI in the form of generous incentive schemes in the hope that embedding FDI might increase the market power of the state, positioning it closer to the core while pushing its competitors towards peripheral status. Moreover, if FDI inflows were initially modest, they nevertheless purchased massive assets in the context of devaluation. During this period multinational corporations followed a strategy of *market seeking* rather than *production seeking*. MNCs made investments contingent on protection from competitors. A study by the EBRD found a strong correlation between high levels of FDI and those sectors which received high import protection (Bohle, 2009: p. 175).

Over time, however, the vast pools of cheap labour served as a potent incentive for Western multinationals to restructure and outsource in search of higher profit rates. Hence a growing volume of FDI became increasingly linked to the cost-cutting strategies of German firms especially, first in light industries but later in automobile, electronics, machinery, and pharmaceutical industries (Bohle & Greskovits, 2007: p. 11). The FDI-led growth strategy would ultimately propel the Visegrad countries (Hungary, the Czech Republic, Slovakia, and Poland) into semi-peripheral status. Yet, although these countries export higher value-added products to other peripheral countries, they remain dependent on more sophisticated imports from the core for both their consumer and input markets. Chronic current account deficits and the need for importing capital goods suggest that backward linkages between FDI and domestic suppliers have been precarious, significantly undermining the potential for technological spillover effects from FDI. To be sure, FDI has contributed to the upgrading and expansion of their industrial bases. However, their economic structures are still subordinate to the global strategies of MNCs, setting barriers to autonomous growth, as became clear at the onset of the global financial crisis.

A third phase, that of finance-led accumulation, began to develop in the late 1990s with the invasion of Western European banks. The incorporation of Central and Eastern Europe has provided nothing short of a bonanza for Western financial capital. Approximately 80 per cent of bank assets in the CEE are foreign owned (Rae, 2011: p. 252). In 2011 of the total banking assets in the following nations, foreign banks owned 96 per cent in the Czech Republic, 95 per cent in Hungary, 70 per cent in Poland, and 84 per cent in Bulgaria (IMF, 2012). The driving force has been high levels of return on assets but foreign control of their banking has created numerous problems for the CEE economies (Becker et al., 2010). First, foreign banks have been reluctant to lend to the domestic corporate sectors, which they deem to be high credit–risk. In Poland, for example, the ratio of private-sector credit to GDP stabilized at 27 per cent from 2000 to 2006. The average for Poland, Hungary, and the Czech Republic was 40 per cent, or the same as 1993 (Raviv, 2008). Meanwhile, household credit as a share of total domestic lending expanded dramatically. It has taken the form of unsecured consumer credit and mortgage lending, predominantly in euros, which has imposed currency and interest rate risks onto households. In this respect, the financial flows to CEE had similar perverse effects as those to Southern Europe.

If the Visegrad countries have achieved a precarious status as Europe's semi-periphery, the record for many others, including the Baltic States, Romania, and Bulgaria, has been even more dismal. Notwithstanding advances in the first years of the 21st century, these countries have in no sense escaped their peripheral status. Bulgaria, for example, was never able fully to take advantage of the limited opportunities afforded by FDI-led accumulation. Tightly incorporated within COMECON, it had specialized in high-tech industries such as computers, electronics, transport, and nuclear energy, achieving growth rates of 6 per cent in the late 1970s and 1980s. Termination of COMECON linkages delivered a massive shock that could not be compensated by increased exports to the EU. By 1996 Bulgaria was unable to service its foreign debt, and 'The IMF refused to provide assistance until the government had agreed both to selling assets to foreign investors and to closing down non-profitable enterprises' (Gowan, 1999: p. 291). The government monetized the debt, and hyperinflation peaked at 241 per cent in 1997 (Ivanova, 2007: p. 160). At the IMF's insistence, the government established a currency board, which paved the way to foreign-led capital accumulation. Public debt increased by 345 per cent from 2003 to 2008, and debt service peaked in 2005 at 46 per cent of export revenue. Indebtedness and foreign ownership of the banking sector have become the key features of Bulgaria's transition (Ivanova, 2009: p. 160). By 2008 the market share of foreign banks was 84 per cent; the five largest banks were entirely foreign owned.

These foreign subsidiaries spurred a property and consumption bubble through expansive credit supply. The ratio of private-sector credit to GDP reached 74.5 per cent in 2008 with the lion's share going to households for mortgage loans denominated in euros.

Unable to compete with other CEE countries in attracting FDI, Bulgarian production has been pushed down the value-added production chain, specializing in labour intensive low-tech sectors. The overvalued currency has contributed to extensive deindustrialization. Massive capital outflows have resulted from the Eurozone crisis and its effects on Greek banks, which own 30 per cent of banks' total assets, 20 per cent of bank loans, and one-third of all deposits in Bulgaria (Novinite, 2011). Faced with chronic high unemployment, Bulgaria has experienced a 'demographic shock'. Between 1989 and 2011, 5.1 per cent of Bulgarians emigrated and Bulgaria experienced an overall population decline of 13.7 per cent (Usheva, 2011). Romania similarly experienced rapid growth in the years immediately preceding the global financial crisis, in part as a result of FDI in areas such as IT and automobiles but also capital inflows to finance the consumption and property boom, resulting in an exploding current account deficit. The crisis exposed the depth of financial instability. In 2009 the bottom fell out of the Romanian economy. An IMF loan was conditioned on deep austerity, resulting in mass unemployment and increasing levels of emigration (Mihut, 2012: pp. 117–19).

Indeed, just as the global financial crisis exposed the internal contradictions and limitations of the EMU, so also it might be said to have delivered a verdict on the liberal transition model. Prior to the crisis, proponents of the liberal development model pointed to the strong growth rates experienced by new member states that coincided with their accession. The CEE countries as a whole registered 6.7 per cent growth between 2004 and 2007 as against the EU-15 average of 2.7 per cent (from a much higher base). Countries such as Latvia and Estonia, whose growth rates peaked at 12.2 per cent and 10 per cent respectively in 2006, were celebrated as neoliberal avatars. Overall GDP per capita in the CEE countries increased from 56 per cent to 61 per cent of the EU average, and unemployment declined from 10.8 per cent to 6.8 per cent (Rae, 2011: p. 255).

Yet, these advances were brought to a halt in 2009. All of the CEE countries experienced comparatively more severe downturns than the rest of the EU countries, as per capita income gains were reversed and unemployment soared. The previous growth rates had disguised current account deficits and acute dependency on foreign borrowing to support consumption. The bursting of the finance-generated bubble proved especially devastating to the neoliberal avatars: GDP fell by 13 per cent in Estonia and 18 per cent in Latvia, plunging these countries into a depression and precipitating the aforementioned extraordinarily high levels of emigration. Capital outflows led to large currency depreciations in countries that had consumer and household loans in foreign currencies. All of this resulted in decreases in FDI and contraction of credit to households and consumers. Thus in many CEE countries, levels of GDP have not advanced significantly beyond those of 1989. Although the Visegrad countries have experienced partial recoveries, they retain 'a high level of dependence on developments in more wealthy economies' (Drahokoupil & Myant, 2011: p. 331). Given their previous experience and their proximity to Germany, this was to be expected. Yet, even here, much of the catchup was in the hitherto badly neglected service sector, while industry performed relatively worse compared to the EU as a whole. The resultant heightened political tensions and authoritarian tendencies have reflected the underlying growth of inequality and mass unemployment that have resulted since the onset of the global financial crisis.

Summarizing the results of the two-decade-long transition for the CEE countries, Drahokoupil & Myant (2011: pp. 331–2) conclude that 'the transition economies missed a chance, or at best, only some of them took advantage of the possibilities that the world offered at the time. There is plenty of evidence ... of where alternatives existed but were not chosen. ... Taking account of contrasts between transition economies and of developments elsewhere in the world, the key mistake would appear to have been excessive faith in, and reliance on, free markets'. Where state intervention and civil society were strongest, as in Poland, higher growth rates and more equal income distribution have been achieved. By contrast, with respect to both the peripheral and semi-peripheral Visegrad countries,

> Where private enterprise was given the freest hand, controlled the least by a state, a legal framework, or an active civil society, the outcome was enrichment for some individuals, without much accompanying economic development .... Opportunities were missed by the reluctance to accept the benefits of an active state in helping to create better environments for business, helping to improve the physical infrastructure, and helping to maintain and develop a research base. These are normal state roles in mature market economies and in rapidly developing economies. They were either avoided or undertaken only on a small scale, as governments complied with fashionable theories on the dangers of state involvement. This did not prevent rapid growth, especially in the last years up to 2008, but the result was a dependent status as outposts for foreign MNCs. (Drahokoupil & Myant 2011: p. 332)

With banking is in foreign hands, weak states are unable to intervene to prevent capital outflows. The explosion of government deficits has precluded anti-cyclical fiscal policies and subsidies to sustain consumption. IMF support has been predicated on further deficit reduction and other steep austerity measures, further reinforced by the relentless discipline of the bond markets.

Capitalism and democracy

The impact of EU accession on democracy – a key goal of the Copenhagen Criteria – has been, at best, mixed. At the outset, EU membership arguably served to promote democratic consolidation in the new member states, just as it did in the Iberian Peninsula in the 1980s. Yet, developments in Hungary and Poland challenge the assumption that the democratic credentials of member states can be taken for granted and indicate the wide gap between the rhetoric of democracy and the realities of neoliberalism in Europe's eastern semi-periphery and periphery. In 1989 Hungary was widely considered to be the most advanced candidate for market-liberal principles and, hence, membership in the EU. Since 1989 Hungary has experienced wholesale privatization, the reorganization of the Hungarian economy under Western European and German MNCs, and a massive increase in the growth of foreign trade, centred on the EU. While Hungary has registered significant gains in absolute GDP, it has shown no sign of 'catching up' with Western Europe: From 1989 to 1992 Hungary's per capita GDP declined from 135 per cent to 107 per cent of the world average. By the advent of the government of Viktor Orban in 2010, Hungary had still not recovered to its 1989 level (Borocz, 2012; see also Pogatsa, 2016). Orban, who was elected to a second four-year term in 2014 and who enjoys a two-thirds majority in Parliament, has silenced the Constitutional Court and passed a series of laws restricting freedom of the press, purging public servants connected to opposition parties and curbing the activities of NGOs.

Similar developments are occurring in Poland. The shock therapeutic first stage of transition saw the collapse of two-thirds of the country's medium and large industrial enterprises, resulting in the loss of two million jobs. Although 45 per cent of the country's workers remain inactive, more than two million have emigrated since 2004 (Rae, 2016). In December 2015 the newly elected Law and Justice Party effectively eliminated the Constitutional Court and imposed restrictions on media, widely believed to infringe on basic freedoms of the press. These growing challenges to EU norms and principles as enshrined in the Charter of Fundamental Rights illustrate the 'Copenhagen Dilemma': EU candidates for membership are vetted by the European Commission on the basis of the Copenhagen Criteria on the rule of law, human rights, and minority protection. Once they are members, however, the Union has difficulty enforcing these policies. Article 7 of the Treaty on European

Union spells out penalties for a 'serious and persistent breach' of common values, most notably the suspension of voting rights in the Council, but enforcement is left to the Council (Myers-Resende, 2013), which has been unwilling to take action. In the case of Poland, for example, Hungarian Prime Minister Orban has threatened to veto proposed sanctions against Poland. It should be noted that these challenges to liberal democratic norms in the form of increasingly popular xenophobic and nationalist parties, although most advanced within the eastern enlargement sphere, preceded the migration crisis of 2015, and are occurring throughout the Union.

To be sure, in many member states, liberal democratic norms have proven more resilient, and the new member states were not simply passive objects of neoliberal structural adjustment. In the post-socialist conjuncture, it was conducted in highly propitious conditions characterized by active consent by elites and the public, at least initially. But also, this process is varied. Following Bohle and Greskovitz (2007), the different outcomes can be understood in terms of a complex interaction of commodification and socialization conducted through the agency of transnational and domestic social forces.

Transnational neoliberalism has been implemented in its most radical and least mediated form in the Baltic States. Identity politics focusing on independence from Russia has been the main principle of social mobilization and has not been oriented towards mitigating market pressure. Hence, there is a high social tolerance towards levels of inequality and openness to transnational and social costs induced by macroeconomic stability policy. Slovenia, by contrast, represents the polar opposite, and if one is to identify a corporatist social-market type of post-socialist state, this is the case in point. Here, the legacy of Yugoslavian market socialism and workers' self-management was resilient. National companies that survived the transition process enabled the Slovenian state to partially shield itself from the excesses of transnational and European neoliberalism. This is confirmed by comparison with union density, industrial relations, and welfare legislation in the Visegrad states, which is not significantly different from that in the Baltics.

Nevertheless, despite a high level of dependence on transnational investments, the Visegrad states are themselves not entirely devoid of the use of protective measures such as the use of investment agencies, investment support funds, tax exemption regimes and public development banks or indeed a measure of tariff and non-tariff barriers. One of Viktor Orban's most popular policies was the forcible conversion of housing loans made by Swiss banks from the Swiss franc to the forint. In January 2016 the Law and Justice Party fulfilled its campaign pledge to impose a bank tax to fund child benefits, provoking resistance from the ECB. The persistence of policies that provided a measure of social protection even within the context of highly constraining transnational pressures was a result of the gradual process of transformation to markets that had commenced even before the collapse of communism, the rise of social protest, and the emergence of electoral politics (Bohle & Greskovits, 2007).

Further to the east: European partnerships

As noted at the beginning of this chapter, the momentum towards further EU enlargement appears to have come to a halt under the impact of prolonged economic stagnation, migration, and resultant increasing xenophobia and nationalism. Yet, the general logic of 'widening' has persisted in the form of less comprehensive but still significant institutional projects. Recognizing that successive enlargements were greatly expanding the territory of the EU and establishing new boundaries, in 2004 the EU introduced the ENP. The ENP established close bilateral relations, supplemented with more specific agreements in specific sectors with the EU's 'closest neighbours' in Eastern Europe and the Middle East. Within the framework of the ENP in 2009 at Prague the EU launched the Eastern Partnerships and in 2008 in Paris the Euro-Mediterranean Partnership (EuroMed). Although both of these programmes were introduced under the umbrella of the ENP, they are very different. The Eastern Partnerships, in the main, apply to former Soviet republics that have achieved a relatively high level of industrial development. Moreover, the Eastern Partnership countries are in principle considered potential EU members as well as candidates for NATO, which has historically served as the EU's antechamber. By contrast, the EuroMed applies to a much poorer subset of peripheral countries in North Africa and the eastern Mediterranean. The EU's relations with this group will be explored in Chapter 8 on North–South Relations.

While the Eastern Partnerships do not provide a path to EU membership, they nevertheless establish an institutional and, in some respects, normative basis for the further extension of transatlantic and EU economic power. At the same time, insofar as the NATO Lisbon Summit of 2010 institutionalized links between NATO and the EU by declaring the latter a 'strategic partner', inclusion in the Eastern Partnerships has not only economic but also geopolitical implications, a topic that we will explore more comprehensively in Chapter 7.

The Russo-Georgian war of 2008 marked a defeat for the strongest advocates of Georgian and Ukrainian entry into NATO and the EU, most notably Poland, the Baltic States, and Sweden. Largely at the behest of these states, the Eastern Partnership programme in 2009 was initially designed to associate Ukraine and five other former Soviet countries (Armenia, Georgia, Moldova, Belarus, and Azerbaijan) more closely with the EU. However, whereas the EU envisaged a 'ring of friends', the Russian Federation perceived these partnerships as threatening economic and political incursions into its sphere of influence.

In August 2013, then-President Viktor Yanukovych of Ukraine declared his intention to sign the EU–Ukraine Association Agreement, a key aspect of which is the 'Deep and Comprehensive Free Trade Area' (DCFTA). However, unable to secure sufficient financial support from Brussels to compensate for the resultant substantial costs to Ukrainian industry, in November 2013 Yanukovych abruptly changed course, accepting a $3 billion loan under extremely favourable terms and declaring his intention to join the Russian-led Eurasian Economic Union instead. This decision sparked protests in Kiev among masses of ordinary people for whom closer association with the EU was viewed as a way out of poverty, corruption, and oligarchic rule. When these protests were joined by more radical nationalist forces, they became violent and took on an anti-Russian tone, ultimately leading to a forcible seizure of power from the government of Victor Yanukovych in February 2014 and the establishment of a new government in Kiev led by Western-leaning oligarchs that appeared threatening to Ukraine's Russian-speaking regions. Russia responded by annexing Crimea and providing military and humanitarian support for a separatist rebellion among ethnic Russians in the Donbass region of Eastern Ukraine. Following his election on 27 June 2014, Ukrainian President Petro Poroshenko signed the partnership agreement with the EU. The European Commission asserts that the DCFTA will increase Ukraine's national income, while adopting EU rules on government contracts and completion will reduce corruption and make the economy more investor-friendly. Although the DCFTA went into effect provisionally on 1 January 2016, a subsequent 'advisory' referendum in April held as a result of a petition organized by populist forces saw the Dutch vote to block it, leaving formal ratification uncertain.

Notwithstanding optimistic predictions, together with IMF and EU aid packages, the DCFTA represents an extreme version of the aforementioned first phase of the neo-liberal transition model of shock therapy. Prime Minister Arseny Yatsenyuk proclaimed that 'everything that was not done in the past 23 years needs to be done in 23 months' while acknowledging that his government represented 'political suicide'. The DCFTA states that the key purpose of the agreement is the removal of all barriers to EU trade and capital, including the privatization of oil and gas pipelines and their sale to foreign investors:

> The DCFTA, linked to the broader process of legislative approximation will contribute to further economic integration with the EU's internal market. This includes the elimination of almost all tariffs and barriers in the area of trade in goods, the provision of services, and the flow of investments (especially in the energy sector). Once

Ukraine has taken over the relevant EU acquis, the EU will grant market access for example in areas such as public procurement or industrial goods. (EEAS, 2016: p. 3)

The EU Commission asserted that the DCFTA would allow firms in both the Ukraine and the EU to realize significant cost savings by eliminating tariffs and other barriers. Yet, as Josef Borocz notes (2013), given the massive large disparities between Ukraine and even the CEE enlargement countries, virtually all of the savings will accrue to EU operators. The liberalization of investment will have a much greater impact. Here the implications of adopting the *acquis communautaire* are massive: it would pave the way for the penetration of transnational capital into Ukraine, including in the strategically important energy sector. Indeed, one of the first laws passed by the new government was to allow 49 per cent of Ukraine's gas and oil pipelines to be privatized and sold to foreign investors. Ukraine's vast agricultural sector will also be opened up to foreign investment and ownership. Ukraine is the largest entirely European country by area and the sixth most populous. Not only does it possess a highly educated workforce and sophisticated technological base, but it also contains one-third of Europe's arable land and one-quarter of the world's black earth land. Although Ukraine has imposed a moratorium on land purchases, the law has been subverted through widespread leasing arrangements that have allowed Western (and Chinese) agribusiness to enter full force into the sector. For example, Clause 404 of the Association Agreement permitted 'the use of biotechnologies in agriculture' and states that Ukraine must 'facilitate conditions of investment' and open Ukraine's agriculture to a 'framework of international organizations' (Oakland Institute, 2014). In 2016 the US agricultural conglomerate Cargill signed an agreement with Kiev to build a $100 million grain export terminal on the Black Sea near Odessa as part of a long-term strategy to turn the country into an agricultural 'superpower' (Cargill, 2016), even as the World Food Programme estimates that 1.5 million people are hungry and 300,000 food insecure as a result of two years of civil war.

The main reason that President Yanukovych rejected the Association Agreement and turned towards Russia was the failure of the EU to provide significant financial aid to compensate for the loss of trade and financial linkages to Russia as well as the costs of structural adjustment to EU standards and markets. Following the removal of Yanukovych, Western institutions and the EU recognized that such aid would be required. According to the IMF Standby Agreement with Ukraine (IMF, 2014), the IMF was to provide $14–18 billion in financial support, with an additional $9 billion coming from other countries, $2 billion of which was to be provided by the EBRD and $1–2 billion by the US. Given the projected $17 billion trade deficit estimated for 2014, the IMF proposed that Ukraine's currency should 'float more freely', thereby leading to a sharp rise in the cost of imports and inflationary tendencies that were to be combated through a reduction of the money supply. As natural gas prices increased, subsidies to households – currently amounting to 7.5 per cent of GDP – were to be phased out over two years. The IMF agreement also stipulated that Kiev should 'implement deeper fiscal adjustment', in the form of tax cuts and government spending cuts, including pensions. A further $6.5 billion of the IMF aid was to cover payments to Western banks in debt servicing payments. Continuing IMF support for the Kiev government was jeopardized by Ukraine's default on the $3 billion loan to Russia. However, in December 2015 at Washington's behest, the IMF revised its rules that had prohibited lending to countries that are in arrears to other governments.

It is also important to note what is lacking in the DCFTA for Ukraine. Whereas actual EU membership provides significant compensatory policies in the form of free movement, references to such movement in the case of Ukraine are extremely vague: 'The importance of the introduction of a visa free travel regime for the citizens of Ukraine in due course, provided that the conditions for well-managed and secure mobility are in place is recognized in the Agreement' (pp. 1, 2). The agreement stipulates merely that the EU and Ukraine 'commit through the Association Agreement to increase their dialogue and cooperation on migration, asylum and border management'. Finally, the document in 1500 pages never mentions the possibility of EU membership. In conclusion, the DCFTA represents not a means of closer integration but instead extreme dependent status. The Ukrainian economy will be exposed to the full force of Western European capital and trade.

Consent and coercion in EU enlargement: beyond the integration telos?

The previous sections of this chapter have described processes of uneven development and deepening stratification between the core and periphery. Although they are of course most visible in the context of the Eurozone crisis in Southern Europe and the eastern enlargement and partnerships extending into the former Soviet empire, they are occurring throughout the EU. Enlargement and, more generally, the process of widening have developed on the basis of market-based, negative integration, reflecting erroneous and dogmatic assumptions about economic diffusion and the self-regulating nature of markets. The absence of fiscal federalism and industrial policy, virtually nullifying the possibility of a cohesion policy (Dunford & Smith, 2000), have generated this highly uneven, unequal, and crisis-prone constellation whose institutional viability is very much in question. How are we to understand the reasons why the EU's regional relations took such a form? What social forces were the drivers behind this development? The eastern enlargements of 2004 and 2007 represented a significant new development for the EU. They dramatically increased the disparity levels of economic development across the Union. At the same time, they have created a larger European economic space for finance-led accumulation while also reinforcing Europe's geopolitical dependence on the United States.

Not surprisingly, mainstream debates about enlargement remain confined within parameters confined by the integration telos. The transition and modernization literatures in the sub-discipline of comparative politics have concerned themselves with the speed and extent to which new member states after enlargement are likely to converge towards a liberal democratic pluralist template. They assume the more or less inevitable march towards pluralism as a universal ideal (e.g. Lijphart et al., 1988; Fischer & Gelb, 1991; for a critique with reference to Southern Europe, see Holman, 1993: pp. 22–3; for a critique with reference to Eastern Europe, see Shields, 2014: pp. 132–33).

The European integration literature represents the other side of the same coin, asking whether optimism about the formation of a solidarist community of pluralist states within the framework of the EU is warranted. Not surprisingly, liberal intergovernmentalists remain at the pessimistic end of the register, explaining enlargement in terms of national interests, the relative power of existing member states and candidate countries, and domestic and sectoral interests (Moravscik & Vachudova, 2003; Copsey & Haughton, 2009). The relative weakness of the candidate countries accounts for their acquiescence to substantial economic and social costs imposed by draconian terms of accession, but even so, it is assumed that over the long term, the benefits will outweigh the costs (e.g. Mandelbaum, 1993). As Jan Komarek has written,

> The 'There is No Alternative' to the liberal democracy and market economy narrative presented the people in post-communist Europe with something that was disturbingly familiar to them. When they lived in 'really existing socialism' they were left with no choice but to submit to the laws of historical necessity steering them to a better (socialist) future. Throughout the 1990s they were again simple 'marionettes' in a historical process that takes place independently of their will and drags them with it to a better future – this time liberal democracy and market economy, which awaited them at the end of history (2014: p. 195).

Constructivist theory has been mobilized to make the strongest possible case for 'optimism'. This literature asked why the member states of the EU would themselves agree to sustain significant costs to enable eastern enlargement. Given the asymmetries in bargaining position, and the availability of alternative arrangements short of full membership, they argue that the agreement to enlarge cannot be explained exclusively through material factors or rational interests (Schimmelfennig, 2001; Diez, 2001; Fierke & Wiener, 1999). Some scholars working within this school of thought point to the causal significance of European identity: only a community such as the EU, based on norms of inclusion and solidarity, would be willing to make the sacrifices necessary for enlargement. In addition, the logic of following rules – itself a function of discourse and the 'social construction of interests' – establishes strong imperatives for establishing compliance criteria on the part of both accession states and existing members (Schimmelfennig & Sedelmeier, 2002). The latter argument invokes the sociological-institutionalist concept of 'logic of appropriateness' to bring home the point of the resilience of EU institutions. However, neo-institutionalism is also invoked to stress the endurance of national specificities (Bryant & Mokrzycki, 1994). Hence, consistent with developments in EU scholarship in general, neo-institutionalism is increasingly the theoretical site on which debates take place.

From a critical political economy perspective, these approaches are not entirely without merit. Both constructivists and intergovernmentalists provide important insights concerning the willingness of CEE countries to bear the significant costs of enlargement. Clearly, the underlying assumptions of liberal developmentalism – and neoliberalism more generally – found its strongest proponents throughout formerly socialist countries and seemed even more convincing in light of the experience of the recent southern enlargement. Given the strong presumption that there was 'no alternative', it was reasonable to hope that the costs could be – and to some extent have been – mitigated by access to regional and agricultural funds, the free movement of labour, and the possibility that membership in the EU might buttress democratic institutions and reduce corruption. To be sure, costs were indeed borne by Western Europeans. Enlargement has served to reinforce market discipline throughout the Union – either through migration, outsourcing, or competitive taxation policies, all of which have reduced the power of labour (Blanchflower, 2009 & Shadforth, 2009; Krzywdzinski, 2014). As Daimler Chrysler CEO Jürgen Schrempp noted in collective bargaining with IG Metall, the German metal works union, 'We were very clear in the talks: We said, "We have Poland. We have Hungary. We have the Czech Republic"' (cited in Boudette, 2004: p. 1).

At the same time, constructivism and intergovernmentalism do not adequately capture the substantive socioeconomic power relations that inhere in the enlargement process itself (see especially Agnew, 2001; Bieler, 2002; Bohle, 2016; Dale, 2011). Assessments on whether or not new member states will close the development gap are based exclusively on highly problematic comparative advantage and diffusion conceptions. Such conceptions also colour assessments of costs and benefits that different social groups and states may have with regard to successful enlargement: some are seen as agents for progressive change and others as obstacles in the defence of their particular interests. Enlargement has been shaped not only by states but also by actors with their own special interests, notably different fractions of transnational capital. The necessity of a 'return to Europe' has justified the market-building project in the east just as it has austerity in the name of the euro in the west and south.

Intergovernmentalist and constructivist approaches have thus tended to focus on the development of institutions, *forms*, and rhetorical bases of interactions but have overlooked the structural power of capital and underlying social purposes of arrangements. The emphasis on solidarity does not adequately explain the power relations between member and candidate states and societies. Moreover, enlargement has resulted in nominal equality among all member states, but it has also served to reproduce the power of transnational European capital over the new member states and, more generally, over European society as a whole. Full Union membership and (potentially) the Association Agreements play an important role in facilitating market discipline and the penetration of Western capital on a scale that might otherwise not have been possible. Nominal equality also had an important compensatory function for populations whose standard of living declined precipitously due to enlargement. Emerging from more than four decades of Soviet domination, the widespread disenchantment with the 'Washington consensus' that swept over much of Latin America and Asia in the last 25 years found, at least until recently, little echo among Eastern European elites or populations. The community norm of solidarity undoubtedly played an important role in mobilizing public opinion behind the decision to admit the Eastern European states to full membership. Yet, 'the impact of solidarity on the EU's enlargement policy is weaker at the level of substantive policy-making than at the start of the enlargement process' (Jileva, 2004: pp. 18–19). As a result, conflicts that are suppressed through appeals to 'Europe' and 'necessity' metamorphose into the politics of identity and the nation.

For critical political economy, then, the transition and integration processes of enlargement are not an expression of *objective reason* as such. A prima facie case for this can be made with reference to Western strategic planning documents themselves, such as a Pentagon *Defence Planning Guidance* document made public in 1992, stating that it is necessary to

> show the leadership necessary to establish and protect a new order that holds the promise of convincing potential competitors that they

need not aspire to a greater role or pursue a more aggressive posture to protect their legitimate interests .... We must account sufficiently for the interest of the advanced industrial nations to discourage them from challenging our leadership or seeking to overturn the established political and economic order. (cited in van der Pijl, 1997: p. 195)

The key term here is 'leadership'. It refers to the management and structuring of relations between associations between powerful business interests and states in the post-Cold War era. In Europe, the European Round Table of Industrialists (ERT) would play a pivotal role in influencing the Commission and the Council in that regard (Bohle, 2006: p. 71) but only, as we will show in the following chapter, when potential opposition to neoliberal Atlanticism had been neutralized in a process that included both coercion and consent, involving narrow economic issues but also geopolitical ones.

Was there an alternative?

Could eastern enlargement have taken a different path? During the turbulence of 1989–91, this possibility presented itself. Mikhail Gorbachev's concept of a 'common European home' was predicated on a vision of social democracy along Scandinavian lines and a recognition that the 'German miracle' had not been simply a result of 'free markets' but rather a social-market economy. Many dissidents in the CEE countries supported this vision. Even within the citadels of power there were doubts about neoliberalism, especially within Germany itself. An indication of developments more in line with Rhineland capitalism and negotiated involvement forms of post-Fordism that might have been is contained in the programme of Deutsche Bank Chief Alfred Herrhausen, who also was a close confidant and adviser to Helmut Kohl. Herrhausen's vision was one of a more gradual transition and an extension of the infrastructure investment programme advocated by the ERT at a time when Rhineland fractions had the upper hand on the east (see Chapter 2, pp. 49, 55–57 and Chapter 3, pp. 78–79). A showcase component of this would be an extension of the high-speed rail-line between Paris and Berlin to Moscow. Notably, Herrhausen opposed the establishment of a European Bank for Reconstruction and Development (EBRD) along Washington Consensus/World Bank lines. Instead, he proposed a model based on the Marshall Plan, geared towards the cancellation of existing Eastern European debt and the channelling of Western loans through public credit institutes designed to provide dedicated long-term capital. The model he had in mind in that regard was the West German Kreditanstalt für Wiederaufbau, which has the mandate to provide long-term dedicated loans in the 'public interest', which is possible because its loans are underwritten by the Federal Government. In time, Herrhausen envisaged that the ownership of these institutes would be transferred to the individual Eastern European states themselves (Herrhausen, 1989).

Given his leading position in the German house bank with the most independent structure vis-à-vis Anglo-American capital, and its strategic ownership in leading German industries, Herrhausen was a powerful actor within the German elite. He was powerful especially because of his close association with Helmut Kohl (Dyson & Featherstone, 1999). His vision was not unlike that of leading politicians at the time in both German political parties – especially Oskar Lafontaine in the Social Democratic Party (SPD) and Lothar Späth in the Christian Democratic Union (CDU) – nor for that matter that of Jacques Attali (van der Pijl, 2001) at a time when there was growing concern about the impact of shock therapy in the former Soviet bloc. As first president of the EBRD, Jacques Attali opposed neoliberalism and sought to orient the bank towards public finance, but he was removed in 1993 in favour of the former Managing Director of the IMF Jacques de Larosiere (van der Pijl, 2006: p. 268) when the United States threatened to suspend its contributions to the fund.

Yet, these voices were very much 'off message'. They played into tropes about a 'fourth German Reich' in a 'fortress Europe', especially in Anglo-Saxon neoliberal circles. Given investments of the Deutsche Bank into strategic industries and inroads into Gorbachev's Soviet Union, there was – and perhaps remains – a definite material dimension to these conflicts. Nevertheless, in the end this alternative concept was overwhelmed by the forces of Atlanticism. Herrhausen himself was assassinated a few days before his speech was to be delivered in New York, reportedly at the hands of Red Army Faction terrorists. As we will show in Chapter 7, the conflict in Yugoslavia and the US decision to expand NATO underscored and deepened the EU's Atlanticist dependency. To be sure, the heirs of Herrhausen continued to exert influence, not least through the residual 'special relationship' between Berlin and Moscow cultivated by German export interests and cooperation in the energy sphere, symbolized by the presence of Gerhard Schröeder on the board of Gazprom. The presence of *Russlandverstherer* in the debate over Ukraine and sanctions continues to exist, albeit in the shadow of American hegemony (Steingart, 2014; Taggesspiegel, 2014a).

Underpinning the political economy of enlargement and corresponding NATO expansion, then, was the structural configuration and power of US-dominated transnational capital. Although the Commission took the lead in the negotiation with candidate countries and the implementation of the enlargements, the ERT played a 'pivotal' role, just as it had with the EMU: 'Of the crucial issues that have dominated the ERT's agenda since its formation in 1983, eastward enlargement is on a par with the creation of the single market in the 1980s and of the single currency in the 1990s' (Bohle, 2006: p. 71). In this context, it is important to emphasize the striking contrast between the policies of the international financial institutions and the EU towards the reconstruction of Central and Eastern Europe with those of the United States towards the reconstruction of Europe after World War II. As Maria Ivanova has written,

> Financial assistance to Eastern Europe has largely been of a symbolic nature and was never meant to play a significant economic role. It is quite obvious that massive amounts of foreign aid coupled with debt relief would have been inconsistent with the strategy of maximizing profit opportunities for foreign investors and Western credit agencies. Moreover, the meager aid that was made available was disbursed in a way which secured that the bulk of it went into the pockets of Western firms and consultants for capitalism, with the whole enterprise amounting to a symbolic 'Marshall Plan of advise'. (Ivanova, 2007: p. 363)

Indeed, the market itself, in the form of FDI, became reconstruction policy. As the US Ambassador to Hungary explained,

> I have often been asked why there isn't a new Marshall Plan to help Central and Eastern Europe. Well, there is – it is here – and it is called private foreign investment. FDI creates jobs, enhances productivity, generates economic growth and raises the standard of living. It brings new technology, new management techniques, new markets, new products and a better way of doing business. (quoted in Ivanova, 2007: p. 361)

The enlargement trilemma

Neoliberal Europe's crisis thus has a regional dimension. It challenges not only the deepening narrative but also the widening narrative: the process of uneven development is generating conflicts that are becoming more acute, and not less. Indeed, the EU stands as much a chance of shrinking – or seeing its centralizing powers and distinctive characteristics radically diminished – as it does of achieving further enlargement. The final section of this chapter follows Heidenreich (2003) and sets out in schematic form what might be called an *enlargement trilemma*. That is, it is possible to have only two of the following three: enlargement, deeper political cooperation, and budget neutrality. Budgetary neutrality (that is the absence of federal fiscal transfers) was compatible with deeper political cooperation in the small, relatively cohesive EC that existed before enlargement. However, enlargement has created a more diverse and stratified political-economic structure. This structure can only be maintained through deeper cooperation in the form of either fiscal federalism or budget neutrality that accepts deep cleavages between regions and that creates joint decision-making traps and therefore produces conflicts among and within member states.

There can be no doubt that developments since the 1990s have prioritized enlargement and budget neutrality. Once the Rhineland option was abandoned in the early 1990s, the ambition of deeper political cooperation was very much discounted. The problem that the EU faces, however, is that the one area of strong political cooperation that came in this package – the EMU – was based on the premise that financial markets were self-equilibrating and were in effect making the Eurozone an optimal currency area. When that is not the case, deeper political cooperation is necessary and budget neutrality needs to be sacrificed if the euro is to survive. The problem is, however, that the conditions for such a transition are absent. In fact, one can argue that the developments of the past decades have rendered their recovery that much more difficult.

It is axiomatic that the social cohesion required for fiscal federalism presupposes that social cleavages are no longer primarily geographical but rather functional. That is, the terms of negotiation and compromise are no longer between regions but rather among distributive groups and classes that feel solidarity with one another across space. It is becoming emphatically clear that that is not the case in the Eurozone today. For Heidenreich, there are two possible ways out of the dilemma. One way out would be a 'trickle down' development that evens out disparities over time, eliminating the need for fiscal transfer mechanisms. Proponents of financial integration expected this result; this is what Blanchard and Giavazzi thought that they were seeing. Perhaps the sort of managed financial intermediation and industrial policy structure – in short a European Marshall Plan – that Herrhausen envisaged could have generated such an outcome, but we cannot undo the developments of the last 30 years.

The other way out that Heidenreich envisaged was one of uneven development but one where core regions in the new member states (the core of the periphery and semi-periphery) would reach sufficient degrees of prosperity and development. This is probably the most accurate description of what seemed to be happening in the first decade of the euro. The urban regions of Southern and Eastern Europe experienced comparably rapid growth, together with certain industrial districts such as those in the Eastern European border regions tied through subcontracting arrangements to Western industrial structures. This would make it possible for these states to create *internal* regional transfer payment systems. For example, Spanish core regions would be able to support Spanish periphery regions within an integrated Europe without a federal budget. This configuration, perhaps above all else, has been damaged by the Eurozone crisis, and the politics of austerity as the financial bubble has generated a collapse in urban centres such as Madrid, Barcelona, Lisbon, Rome, Athens, and Budapest. Notably, this is corrosive for transregional solidarity not only between member states but also within member states, making functional cleavages increasingly regional. Here one can observe the rise of regional movements in Spain and then not only in Catalunya and the Basque country but also Italy, for instance.

In other words, from a geographical perspective, neoliberal, finance-led accumulation has brought the EU to a situation where the commitment to the EMU has put the EU in a position where more political cooperation is required. However, at the same time, the imperative of budget neutrality is stronger than ever not only because of the ideology of austerity but also because the prevalence of regional over functional cleavages, certainly between states but also increasingly within states, renders the situation very inopportune for such cooperation. It is hard to find a better case of a crisis-generating contradiction without a mechanism for internal solution: the very mirror image of spillover.

Conclusion

As this chapter has shown, the strategy of enlargement based on negative integration has precluded fiscal federalism and industrial policy, two essential characteristics of a stable economic and political union. As a result, the EU is dividing politically between North and South, and East and West. With respect to the southern enlargement countries, the seeds of the Eurozone crisis were planted long before the bursting of the finance-generated bubble of the 2008 global financial crisis and the subsequent debt crisis. The similarities between the experiences of the Southern European countries and those of the CEE countries, where semi-peripheral development has taken place outside the Eurozone, confirm that while exit from the Eurozone may be a necessary means of escaping semi-peripheral status, it is by no means sufficient.

Thus, the enlargement process has not expressed an objective or universal rationality. Nor, given its structural constraints, could it have realized fully the expectations that were set out in the conclusions of the 1993 European Council when the goal of eastern enlargement was established. Rather, transnational neoliberalism, Atlanticism, and finance-led accumulation, representing the dominant social forces, have constructed a project that has conformed to their particular interests. The project represented the defeat of a distinctive European alternative based on Rhineland principles that were articulated in the early days of post-socialist transition in favour of a project premised on the self-regulating powers of financial markets.

If the 2008 financial crisis dramatically exposed the economic limitations of this project, the Brexit vote exposed its ominous political implications. The Leave campaign persuaded a majority of British voters to associate the effects of austerity with substantial migratory flows from Central and Eastern Europe that followed the 2004 and 2007 enlargements. Although it is highly unlikely that immigration has impacted negatively on the British economy as a whole, it has undoubtedly served to tighten local labour markets and strain local public services in the context of the full spectrum of neoliberal austerity policies pursued by successive British governments since 2010, including steep cutbacks in healthcare, education, and welfare. Neither this surge of (mostly) young workers nor the nationalist backlash was a 'natural' or inevitable result of integration per se. Rather, it was a consequence of the particular form that it took: neoliberal development policy absent a social dimension.

The *imperial* metaphor has been a persistent theme in scholarship on the EU ever since the initial enlargement of 1973 (Galtung, 1973; Waever, 1997; Zielonka, 2006; Anderson, 2007), and it accords with the argument of this chapter. Unlike the essentially descriptive widening narrative, the concept of empire suggests the salience of socio-economic power relations that have shaped enlargement. But, what kind of empire? In 2007 then-EU Commission President Jose Manuel Barroso candidly acknowledged that 'We have the dimensions of empire' while asserting that 'Empires were usually made with force, with a center imposing a *diktat*, a will on others. Now what we have is the first non-imperial empire' (BBC, 2009). Our assessment of EU enlargement indicates the fallacy of Barroso's interpretation. The southern and eastern enlargements have indeed established an EU diktat, providing an institutional basis for an expanding semi-periphery reorganized after the fall of fascism in the south and the Soviet Union in the east, designed to conform to the requirements of core Western banks and multinational corporations: in short, a Europe of capital. Barroso is of course correct that this diktat has been implemented through geo-economic means, and not through the direct use of military power, which is unavailable to the EU. Indeed, given the formal equality of member states, the imperial diktat is most often exercised structurally rather than instrumentally. However, it became utterly transparent during the negotiations between the Troika and Southern European heads of state in the context of the Eurozone crisis.

At the same time, however, the eastward movement has also been profoundly geopolitical: it has crucially depended on the coercive powers of the American superpower in the form of the corresponding expansion of NATO, and it has propelled the EU into a progressively more confrontational posture towards Russia. Thus even as enlargement has extended the EU's imperial diktat, it has done so by lengthening the shadow of the American superpower over the European continent. We will explore more fully the origins and dynamics of Europe's continuing transatlantic subordination in the next chapter.

Chapter 7

The American Challenge Revisited: The Lengthening Shadow of US Hegemony

The significance of the transatlantic relationship for the origins and development of the EU is a central theme of this book. In Chapter 2 we saw that the transition to Fordism in Europe was carried out through American hegemony after World War II. Traditional theories designed to make sense of EU integration originated during this period within a distinctively American intellectual milieu. The unravelling of Bretton Woods in the 1960s gave rise to debates about the nature and extent of US power, such as those animated by the publication of Servan-Shreiber's *The American Challenge*. These still resonate, albeit within a very different historical conjuncture. Mandel concluded that the EU was developing greater autonomy and power in relation to the United States. Poulantzas, by contrast, contended that the penetration of US money capital in conjunction with a host of corporate practices involving deepening commodification was not leading to the establishment of an autonomous European pole of capitalism but rather to the formation of an 'interior bourgeoisie' still subordinated to the United States. Our analyses of the single market and the EMU in Chapters 3 and 4 confirm the enduring relevance of Poulantzas' analysis. To the extent that Europe's neoliberal relaunch expressed to an internal dynamic, this was ultimately subordinated to finance-led growth.

At the present time, the transatlantic relationship is experiencing great turbulence as a result of not only the global financial crisis but also two related developments that are simultaneously geopolitical and economic in nature. The first is the apparent decline of US power in relation to China, which we will explore further in Chapter 8. This was expressed vividly in March 2015 by the failure of the United States to prevent its closest European allies from joining the Chinese-led Asian Infrastructure Investment Bank. For former US Treasury Secretary Lawrence Summers, this 'may be remembered as the moment when the United States lost is role as the underwriter of the global economic system' (Summers, 2015: p. 1). The second development is the 'return of geopolitics' to Europe through the return of the 'German question' and the escalating conflict between Russia and the West.

167

Charles de Gaulle is famously reported to have told Konrad Adenauer that 'Europe is France and Germany, the rest are just trimmings.' France's economic problems have escalated under conditions of German-led competitive austerity. Consequently, France is now only nominally an equal in decision making on key issues, which are in fact made in Berlin. At the same time, the special relationship that Germany formed with the USSR and then Russia, starting with Ostpolitik, has also withered even as German capital has pushed eastward and Europe remains heavily dependent on Russian gas and oil exports. Germany finds itself once again on the frontline of geopolitical confrontation.

This chapter starts by contrasting liberal and realist perspectives on the transatlantic relationship with that of critical political economy, the latter of which we argue provides a deeper and more comprehensive analysis. The chapter is then organized historically, starting by reviewing the arc of European imperial decline following World War I and culminating in the Suez Crisis, the significance of which was noted already in Chapter 2 and that will be revisited in Chapter 8. The second part addresses the geopolitical underpinnings of Europe's post-war institutions. The Luxembourg Compromise called a halt to supranational integration while paradoxically providing the basis for the high point of post-war European assertiveness and autonomy in world affairs during the 1960s and 1970s, which is the topic of the third part. The fourth part considers the mirror image of this paradox, expressed by the geopolitics of the extended neoliberal relaunch. Far from empowering the EU, the end of the Cold War ultimately gave rise to NATO expansion and the further consolidation of US power and neoliberalism across the European continent. The fifth part documents the EU's inability to devise a common foreign and security policy. The chapter concludes by assessing the nature and scope of German power. In the absence of a political-military counterpart to its geo-economic sphere of influence in Central and Eastern Europe, Germany – and hence the EU as a whole – remains tethered to Atlanticism and the American superpower.

Imperialism: Europe and the US

Academic scholarship on transatlantic relations has been, just as on the EU, conducted within the traditional perspectives of liberalism and realism. Indeed, the assumptions made by traditional theories about European integration – mutual gains and the density of social relations, on the one hand, and the primacy of 'security', on the other – find their parallel in studies of the origins and development of Atlanticism. Since the 1950s liberals have emphasized the significance of an increasingly dense, quasi-functionalist of web of communication and 'interconnectedness' as the basis for an Atlantic 'security community' (e.g. Deutsch et al., 1957). While acknowledging the centrality of US hegemony in constructing liberal international institutions, they argue that these institutions can endure even as the hegemonic power of their progenitor gradually erodes (Keohane, 1984; Ikenberry, 2001). Realists, by contrast, have rejected the assumption that deepening global economic interdependence implies greater cooperation at either the global or European level. Whereas for liberals the unification of markets underpins the transatlantic security order (Rosecrance, 2013), realists understand it as reflecting a Cold War (Gilpin, 1987) or 'new cold war' (Levy, 2015) balance of power and the persistent of conflict between the United States and its two strongest competitors, China and Russia (Frölich, 2012). The liberal and realist perspectives are synthesized in their understanding of the Transatlantic Trade and Partnership Agreement (TTIP), conceived as an 'economic NATO', a topic that we will address specifically in Chapter 8.

A critical IPE approach to the transatlantic relationship, by contrast, departs from the Marxist concept of imperialism, thereby rejecting the assumption of a harmony of capitalist interests or the primacy of 'power politics' narrowly conceived. While acknowledging the relative autonomy of geopolitical competition arising from the struggle for power, transatlantic relations are understood in terms of the logic of capital accumulation and the functions that the capitalist state acquires as capital pushes beyond the national boundaries. The concept of hegemony refers to the systemic supervisory function that leading states have performed during certain historical periods. Because interstate relations have historically co-constituted the capitalist world economy, and there is no 'higher authority', rivalry has been a permanent feature of the world capitalist system (Wood, 2002). Hence, 'there is, necessarily, a realist moment in any Marxist analysis of international relations and conjunctures: in other words, any such analysis must take into account the strategies, calculations and interactions of rival political elites in the state system' (Callinicos, 2007: p. 542).

The fact of rivalry requires a non-reductionist approach that incorporates both geopolitical and economic competition into the analysis of the imperatives of capital accumulation. Rivalry can be moderated either through the actions of a hegemonic power willing and able to maintain global order (Block, 1977; Varoufakis, 2011) or through the emergence of a 'transnational capitalist class' that reduces the coercive aspects of intraregional and perhaps even international conflict. Bieler and Morton (2015: p. 105), for example, contend that 'one has witnessed the emergence of a transnational capitalist class (TCC) meaning that it is no longer possible to simply speak in terms of a rivalry between "German" capital, "French" capital, or "American" capital, etc.' (see also, inter alia, van der Pijl, 1984; Gill, 1990; van Apeldoorn, 2003; Robinson, 2004; Hardt & Negri, 2000). However, if different capitalist groupings in the transatlantic sphere now view each other, as van der Pijl would have it (see Chapter 2), as part of 'internal nature', hegemony has nevertheless been exercised through various regulatory projects that arise at the national level and are then reproduced within subordinate states. This also involves political-military supervision. Hence, 'internationalization of policy regimes' (Jessop, 1994) has not generated supranational state forms that eliminate geopolitical rivalry. Poulantzas sums up the complex interplay of unity and rivalry in the following terms:

> The current internationalization of capital neither suppresses nor by-passes the nation states, either in the direction of a peaceful integration of capitals 'above' the state level (since every process of internationalization is effected under the dominance of the capital of a definite country), or in the direction of their extinction by the American super-state, as if American capital purely and simply directed the other imperialist bourgeoisies. This internationalization, on the other hand, deeply affects the politics and institutional forms of these states by including them in a system of interconnections which is in no way confined to the play of external and mutual pressures between juxtaposed states and capitals (1973: p. 167).

The end of the European era and the rise of the American imperium

On the eve of World War I, the four greatest European powers – Britain, France, Germany, and Russia – possessed half the earth's surface and ruled more than 80 per cent of the world's population. Great Britain's vast domain included India, large areas of the Middle East, China, Africa, and the English-speaking dominions. France controlled most of Indo-China and the North African littoral, as well as large parts of sub-Saharan Africa. Russia's colonial empire extended throughout much of Eastern Europe, the Caucasus, and Central Asia. Chancellor Otto von Bismarck began seizing in the 1870s large areas of East and West Africa for the new German Empire. Still, Germany lagged behind in the struggle for colonies as a result of its late political integration and industrialization. By the beginning of the 20th century, the contrast between Germany's relatively modest share of colonies and markets and its burgeoning economic and military power was fuelling Anglo-German rivalry.

Notwithstanding the variety of inventive doctrines to justify their conquests, including humanitarianism, Christianity, and nationalism, as argued in Chapter 2, the drive towards empire in the late 19th century was ineluctably connected to the logic of capital accumulation that generated growing competition among national capitalist classes for markets, cheap labour, and raw materials. This logic applied not only to the colonies, where the great powers carried out openly extractive and predatory economic policies alongside systematic campaigns of what would today be called genocide, but also to Europe itself, where the brief moment of 19th-century free trade – roughly 1850–1880 – had been eclipsed by a wave of protectionism. As classical Marxist theorists of imperialism argued, the inexorable tendency towards concentration of ownership and the corresponding steady growth in the size of firms closely tied to states meant that economic competition would no longer be pursued exclusively or even primarily through commercial means or within the national economy. Rather, it would be pursued globally through the use of state power and thus become inextricably bound up with foreign policy.

Anglo-German rivalry gave rise to an increasingly tight alliance system. Germany aligned with the decaying Austro-Hungarian 'Dual Monarchy', itself struggling to retain its empire in South-eastern Europe, in a 'Triple Alliance' of 'Central Powers' against the 'Triple Entente' comprising Great Britain, France, and Russia. In the end, the 'struggle for mastery in Europe' (Taylor, 1980) compelled virtually all the nations of the world to choose sides (Stevenson, 2011) in a global war that brought about the 'end of the European era' (Gilbert, 2008). The terrible carnage in turn inspired the dream of a United States of Europe, which gained many adherents during the 1920s and of course would flourish after the even greater catastrophe of World War II.

After three years of bloody stalemate in World War I, two seminal events occurred in 1917 that would define European politics for the remainder of the 20th century. First, the advance guard of a two-million-soldier American Expeditionary Force (AEF) arrived in France. The AEF would turn the tide in favour of the Entente and establish the United States as the ultimate arbiter of European affairs, a role it has yet to relinquish. Second, the devastation of war greatly intensified class conflict throughout Europe, provoking the October Revolution in Russia and popular uprisings in most of the defeated Central Powers.

The arrival of the AEF signified the end of Europe's domination of world politics but did not result in an immediate or straightforward 'hegemonic transition' to American leadership. The League of Nations was enshrined in the Versailles Treaty at the behest of US President Woodrow Wilson amid torrents of idealist rhetoric, but the US Senate blocked American ratification and the League ultimately had little practical effect on international affairs. Rather, the victors quickly carved up the 'spoils of war', such as through the secret clauses of the 1916 Sykes-Picot agreement of 1916 that divided the collapsing Ottoman Empire among France, Britain, and Russia, allocating the richest oil deposits to Britain. Britain and France reneged on promises to give Italy territories in Istria and Africa, fanning the flames of Italian nationalism and ultimately fascism. Article 22 of the Versailles Treaty divided Germany's overseas empire among Britain, France, Belgium, and Japan. France recovered Alsace-Lorraine and occupied the industrially strategic Ruhr valley while imposing crippling reparations. As John Maynard Keynes predicted in 1919, the Carthaginian peace of Versailles led ineluctably to inflation and mass unemployment. Humiliated by the war guilt clauses of Versailles, and crippled by reparations, Germany forged close political-military and economic ties with the Soviet Union at Rapallo in 1922.

If the 'isolationism' of US interwar foreign policy is arguably more myth than reality (Panitch & Gindin, 2012), it is nevertheless the case that once the revolutionary tide in Europe subsided, the United States abandoned comprehensive plans for post-war stabilization. The United States did sponsor two initiatives that, in some respects, prefigured the Marshall Plan. The Dawes (1924) and the Young (1927) plans facilitated loan repayments and thereby sought to promote political stability in Weimar Germany, always viewed as the first line of defence (and potentially offence) against the Soviet Union. Yet, the complex transatlantic financial circuitry was broken by the wave of speculation in the United States in the latter half of the 1920s. US loans to Germany and Austria were recycled into reparations to Britain and France. These payments in turn enabled Britain and France to service their war debts to the United States. The speculative boom in the United States meant that external lending ceased and capital flooded into the United States (Kindleberger, 1973). The bubble burst in 1929 and Austria's Kreditanstalt Bank crashed two years later, triggering a wave of bank defaults across the European continent.

Absent decisive US leadership, the Great Depression ultimately provoked a return to protectionism in the United States, sparked by the Smoot–Hawley tariff of 1930. Franklin Roosevelt's New Deal was predicated on the withdrawal from the gold standard and the construction of a nascent Fordist system and welfare state shielded by protectionist trade policies. Not until the short-lived Tripartite Monetary Agreement of 1936 did the United States attempt to reconstruct a global monetary system. Falling back on their empires and traditional spheres of interest, the European powers countered with their own 'beggar thy neighbour' trade policies and imperial currency blocs: At the Ottawa Conference of 1932, Britain erected an imperial tariff. France established a Francophone zone in Africa. Germany sought to carve out its own regional bloc, first through trade and monetary arrangements, and then with panzers and stukas. The United States imposed crippling sanctions on Japan for its invasion of China in 1932, reinforcing Japan's expansionary tendencies in Asia.

The failure of the US Senate to ratify the League of Nations treaty was not simply a reflection of traditional 'nativism' or 'exceptionalist' expressions of American identity, however important these sentiments were and, to some extent, remain. It also arose out of the tensions and contradictions that were arising from capitalist transition. The development of Fordism was not fully consummated at either the corporate or the political level until World War II. Absent a comprehensive global settlement along the lines of the post-World War II Bretton Woods system, protectionism served to underpin American capitalism during the presidency of Franklin Roosevelt. The resultant regulatory order described in Chapter 2 would not cross the Atlantic until after World War II through the Marshall Plan, US military occupation, and the embryonic institutions of the European Union. At that time US planners, haunted by the 'nightmare of depression' (Williams, 1972), would adopt a more comprehensive and liberal approach to the problem of international order, resurrecting the concept of the 'open door' that originated in the 1890s and that remains the central tenet of US foreign policy.

From the ECSC to the Treaty of Rome

At one level the ECSC represented a set of highly technical economic arrangements and institutions. Yet, the significance of these arrangements was by no means technical, and the term 'low politics' that is sometimes applied to these arrangements can be misleading. From the point of view of France, the ECSC provided a more durable means of containing Germany than traditional power politics, which would have meant essentially reprising the disastrous Versailles arrangements.

Integrating the coal and steel industries across Western Europe's borders was not something new as it had previously been accomplished through German conquest. As German forces advanced to the Marne, the 1914 September Program of War Aims read as follows:

> Russia must be thrust back as far as possible from the German eastern frontier. France must be so weakened as to make her revival as a great power impossible for all time ... economically dependent on Germany. A central European customs association (including France) would stabilize Germany's economic dominance. Belgium would become a 'vassal state', and economically a 'German province'. (Fischer, 1967: pp. 103–4)

During both world wars, the coal and steel resources of West Germany, France, and Belgium had been integrated and administered by Germany, with participation from French industrialists. France had thus participated in a highly subordinate way in a German-led 'common market'. Despite substantial cooperation among French and German industrialists, however, these previous common markets had proved highly damaging to French interests because of punitive 'occupation costs' imposed on France (Gillingham, 1991: esp. pp. 65–86; Hirschfeld, 1989). Indeed, in 1945 'The Franco-German imbalance of economic power was even greater than before' (Gillingham, 1991: p. 95). Thus, after World War II, France once again confronted the spectre of a potentially stronger Germany. If the institutional development of the EU has in important respects always corresponded to the logic of Franco-German leadership (Krotz & Schild, 2012), it has also served as a means of containing German power.

Containment was a central aim of French policy. Because disarmament alone could not accomplish this aim, France sought to restrict Germany's economic development. Initially, this was accomplished by delaying recovery and sabotaging the work of the Allied Control Commission. France also sought to drive a stake into the heart of the German economy by seizing the Rhineland, annexing the coal-rich Saar region, and internationalizing the Ruhr valley. Still, a durable policy of containment required deeper institutional measures. As principal adviser to Robert Schuman and director of planning, Jean Monnet sought to avoid what would have been essentially a replay of Clemenceau's punitive and ultimately self-defeating post-World War I strategy.

At the London Conference on Germany in 1948, France agreed to permit Germany to form a provisional government, and muted its demands to internationalize the Rhineland (Gillingham, 1991: p. 159). The United States and Britain agreed to establish an International Authority for the Ruhr (IAR) that would monitor German production of coal and steel. Nevertheless, it was increasingly apparent to France that the United States and Britain wanted a prosperous Germany to become the centrepiece of post-war European reconstruction and the advance guard against the Soviet Union. Monnet convinced Schuman that a more conciliatory policy was necessary to maintain US support and defuse growing German nationalism. Just a few months after agreeing to the establishment of the IAR, the United States and Britain announced, without notifying France in advance, that German industrial restrictions would be relaxed and that a future German government would determine the ownership structure of the Ruhr coal mines. Schuman feared that the United States would privilege German recovery at the expense of France and Western Europe as a whole (Gillingham, 1991: pp. 159–161). The ECSC thus forestalled an American-German axis that might impede French industrial modernization. While restrictions on German production would be lifted, at the same time all six countries would negotiate price and investment levels. Hence the ECSC was, as with all subsequent EU developments, an expression of Franco-German relations in the context of triangular diplomacy between Bonn/Berlin, Washington, and Paris. As Schuman wrote in his proposal for an ECSC (the Schuman Declaration) on 9 May 1950, 'The solidarity in production thus established will make it plain that any war between France and Germany becomes not merely unthinkable, but materially impossible.' The purpose of the proposal was 'eminently political', as Konrad Adenauer noted in his memoirs (Adenauer, 1983: p. 45). The ECSC was made in Paris, but it was a key element of American grand strategy.

Supranational cooperation in the political-military sphere represented a parallel French attempt to Europeanize and thereby reduce German power, but this strategy was less successful, and it ultimately – and perhaps inevitably – would serve to reinforce US authority in Europe. France and Britain had signed the Treaty of Dunkirk in 1947; the Brussels Treaty of 1948 added the Benelux countries. As early as 1948, the United States had been pushing for the formation of a unified Western European defence structure. In 1949, NATO was formed, and one year later the United States proposed bringing the Federal Republic into the alliance. When the Korean War broke out in June 1950, pressure intensified. The Pleven Plan for a European Defence Community (EDC), supported by the United States, envisaged a multinational European army. Although a treaty was signed among the six in 1952, it could not be ratified in the National Assembly and gave way to a far less ambitious Western European Union (WEU). However, the WEU, essentially an extension of the Brussels Treaty, allowed France to influence German rearmament and thereby join NATO in 1955. As with all of its successors, including the Fouchet Plan, EPC, and the CFSP, European political and military cooperation was essentially subordinated to NATO and nominal.

Although formally a Benelux initiative, the Treaty of Rome also served the French containment strategy, and was ultimately a result of complex negotiations between Mollet and Adenauer. An even more comprehensive common market could be seen as the logical development of the ECSC. With the signing of the Treaty of Rome, Germany gained access to French markets while undertaking to support French agriculture and increase its food imports from France. French acquiescence to an open market was encouraged by the prospect of a free trade area that was being offered by London to Bonn – a prospect that threatened France's strategic imperative of close commercial ties between France and Germany. At the same time, Germany gained support for eventual reunification. But it was not economic considerations alone that convinced Mollet to proceed to ratification in the National Assembly.

In October 1956 Egyptian President Nasser nationalized the Suez Canal, owned jointly by France and Britain since 1886. In response, France, Britain, and Israel conspired to destroy the Egyptian air force, carried out large-scale terror bombings on civilians in Cairo and Port Said (Varble, 2003: p. 89), invaded the Canal Zone, and sought to remove Egyptian President Gamel Abdel Nasser from power. However, less dependent on the canal for oil supplies and fearful of growing Soviet influence and backlash from the Arab world, the United States opposed the invasion. In the midst of the tripartite negotiations, Eisenhower compelled Mollet and a tearful Anthony Eden to call off the invasion by supporting an Arab-led oil embargo against both countries and threatening to precipitate a Sterling crisis (Love, 1969). Britain and France drew opposite lessons from this American military and financial coercion that would set the tone for the next 50 years. Britain, which had close financial and commercial ties to the United States – not least in global petroleum markets – resolved to pursue the 'special relationship' at all costs. Recognizing that France could no longer depend on US support for its empire, as it had in Indo-China, Mollet drew a different conclusion: greater European unity coupled with an independent French nuclear deterrent – the *force de frappe* – was essential to French imperial goals.

But the Treaty of Rome and, more generally, the process of European integration was nevertheless decisively conditioned by American initiative. It expressed American interests and was inconceivable without US support. As noted in Chapter 1, American political scientists supplied much of the rationale for the fledgling EEC. Archival evidence confirms the conclusion of scholars such as Alan Milward (1984) and John Gillingham (1991): the US State Department, CIA and its precursors, and transatlantic elite organizations and informal networks based in the United States provided crucial financial support, much of it covert, for the architects of European unity (Aldrich, 1997). The most important European organization in this respect was the European Movement, an umbrella organization which focused on the Council of Europe and which included as its 'presidents of honour' Winston Churchill, Paul-Henry Spaak, Konrad Adenauer, Leon Blum, and Alcide de Gasperi. Financial support was provided by the American Committee on United Europe (ACUE), established in 1948 and Washington's key instrument of influence under the leadership of Allen W Dulles, future CIA Director, and William J. Donovan, former head of the Office of Strategic Services, precursor to the CIA. Jean Monnet is remembered as a European visionary but he was – along with his assistant Robert Marjolin, Vice President of the European Commission – simultaneously a French nationalist and a transmission belt from Wall Street to Brussels. Churchill, who served as the 'vital link between the ACUE and the European Movement', believed that European unity was the 'unofficial counterpart to the Marshall Plan' (Aldrich, 1997: p. 195; see also Anderson, 2009: pp. 1–9). As Eisenhower proclaimed, the Treaty of Rome would be 'one of the finest days in the history of the free world, perhaps even more so than winning the war' (quoted in Milward, 1984: p. 375). For Monnet, on the other hand, US patronage was essential in realizing his goals for modernization and Atlantic partnership.

The high point of Europe

The Treaty of Rome consecrated the American vision of a US-led Atlantic economic area that complements the NATO geopolitical one. Yet, ironically, even as it determined the content of Europe's first project of integration, it also set the stage for the phase of greatest European autonomy and influence in the post-World War II period. Having overcome the domestic struggles over Algeria, and with the key Franco-German question resolved, de Gaulle soon moved to contain the power of European institutions, as he did with the empty chair crisis and subsequent Luxembourg Compromise as described in Chapter 1. The Elysee Treaty inaugurated a subsequent decade of European prosperity and relative power. Indeed, during this period 'Europe' would exert its most sustained global influence, long before the EU's 'relaunching' which, as we showed in Chapter 3, would ultimately tether Europe more closely to Wall Street and Washington.

This was the high point of European assertiveness, but it was in no sense either supranational or, as recognized by Poulantzas, based on a putative European capitalist class. Rather, it was entirely 'intergovernmental' and outside the purview of the Commission. Indeed, in the case of France especially it was based on a strong state, hostility to the Commission and lingering suspicions of West Germany, as affirmed by de Gaulle in the empty chair crisis. Nor did it necessarily imply a unity of purpose or coordination between France and Germany: indeed, if the Elysee Treaty provided a basis for greater freedom of action, such actions were seldom concerted and often produced frictions. It was these limitations that motivated the likes of Servan-Shreiber, as discussed in Chapter 2, to seek a concerted European response to the 'American challenge', but which never materialized.

European assertiveness during this period was evident not only in 'high' political diplomacy but also in relations with the Global South and, of course, its consolidation of distinctive Rhineland and associated varieties of capitalism. Charles de Gaulle's call in 1962 for a 'Europe from the Atlantic to the Urals' promoted a vision of autonomy from the American superpower. In 1964, France recognized the People's Republic of China; in 1966 de Gaulle expelled US forces from French territory and withdrew from the military command structure of NATO. Strongly opposed to the US war in Vietnam and deeply resentful of the 'exorbitant privilege' the dollar-gold standard conferred on the US economy, French Finance Minister Jacques Rueff embarked on a campaign of speculation against the dollar. In August 1971 French President Pompidou dispatched a French destroyer to Fort Lee in New Jersey to redeem gold for dollars and transport it from Fort Dix in New Jersey back to France (Varoufakis, Halevi, & Theorcarakis, 2011: p. 320). Even as France challenged the superpower 'condominium', it also attempted to assert French power in the international oil regime.

Throughout the 1960s Iraq had engaged in a long-running effort to break the power of the international oil companies over its economy. When these companies reduced Iraqi oil output, a showdown ensued in which the Iraqi state nationalized the Western-dominated Iraq Petroleum Company, supported by French undertakings to purchase Iraqi oil and not participate in any blockade such as Iran had faced in the 1960s (Hellema, 2004). Placed on the defensive as a result of the Vietnam War, the United States acquiesced to Iraqi nationalization, helping to convince the Saudi-led members of OPEC to launch their long-dormant 'oil weapon' with the October 1973 oil embargo against the United States, the UK, the Netherlands, and the IOCs. President Pompidou prodded other European countries to join an EC–Arab direct dialogue with the express intent of creating a more independent European role in world affairs. Ultimately, however, this effort was unsuccessful. With Dutch and British support, the United States established the Paris-based International Energy Agency (IEA) in 1974 and vigorously supported bilateral deals that enabled it to recapture petrodollars with sales of ordinary goods, weapons, and large-scale infrastructural and engineering services.

This period also witnessed the growing assertiveness of West Germany, albeit in more muted form. In the general context of Ostpolitik, itself a precursor of the broader US–Soviet détente, German Chancellor Willy Brandt and his foreign minister, Egon Bahr, pursued a 'negotiating offensive' towards Moscow designed to open up markets in the Soviet bloc and establish closer relations with the German Democratic Republic (GDR). This combined commercial and political project initially caused serious frictions in US–West German relations, provoking schemes in the Nixon White House to destabilize the Brandt government, although ultimately Nixon and Kissinger supported Ostpolitik in the interests of détente (*Zeitonline*, 2012). By contrast, West Germany's reaction to US-dollar hegemony was far less strident, a result not only of the weaker position of Germany vis-à-vis the United States but also the unwillingness to accept French monetary leadership in Europe. Even as France speculated against the dollar with seeming impunity Nixon and Kissinger threatened West Germany with NATO troop reductions if it dared to follow suit. Nevertheless, by refusing to prop up the dollar by devaluing the DM, in May 1971 West Germany was the first European country formally to exit the Bretton Woods system (Calleo, 1982; Parboni, 1982).

The significance of these European initiatives should not, of course, be overstated. France never renounced its political membership in NATO and de facto dependence on American military support. The collapse of the Bretton Woods system deepened chronic monetary divisions among the Western European states. European exports continued to depend on the open US market; the US growth locomotive survived the demise of Bretton Woods. More generally, the overall lack of European power and coherence – reinforced by perennial British and Dutch adherence to Atlanticism – continued to frustrate attempts to develop a 'European' foreign policy (van der Pijl, 1984, 2006). Nevertheless, Europe's relative assertiveness during the 1960s and 1970s, notwithstanding institutional 'sclerosis', contrasts strikingly with the deepening subordination to the American superpower that would occur in the context of the 'relaunching'. This perspective illustrates the limitations of teleological approaches to European integration that assume a steady, one-dimensional march towards an 'ever closer union' and the widespread tendency in EU studies to draw conclusions on the basis of formal institutions and rhetoric rather than on substantive socioeconomic, and political relationships.

After the Cold War: neoliberalism and NATO expansion

Chapters 3 and 4 situated Europe's neoliberal relaunching in the form of the single market and the EMU within the broader structural changes in European and global capitalism. The Maastricht Treaty in particular also had important geopolitical causes and effects. EMU inevitably became closely linked to a global process of post-Cold War restructuring. Moreover, negotiations over the Maastricht Treaty in 1990 and 1991 ran concurrently with the 'two plus four' talks in which the occupying powers – France, Britain, the United States, and the Soviet Union – negotiated the terms of German reunification with the Federal Republic of Germany (FRG) and the GDR.

In 1952 Lord Ismay, NATO's first secretary general, had famously declared that NATO was created to 'keep the Americans in, the Russians out, and the Germans down'. Yet, after 1991 the spectre of communism no longer haunted European ruling classes, and Germany's resurgence could conceivably be contained within the institutions of the EU. It seemed possible that the United States might substantially reduce its role in Europe. Indeed, during the first Bush administration (1989–1993) and the first year of the Clinton administration, some leading policymakers in the United States contemplated the downsizing or even elimination of NATO in favour of European security cooperation amid high hopes for CFSP, perhaps realizing the original intent of the EDC: large-scale withdrawal of US forces to realize a 'peace dividend', and a policy of accommodation with a compliant Russia. This policy accorded with the Clinton administration's core project of financial liberalization, free trade agreements, and domestic fiscal retrenchment. The first Gulf War (1991), endorsed in the UN Security Council by Russia, and the subsequent UN-supervised post-war settlement, appeared to reaffirm this stance, which did not, however, last long.

There is a great deal of controversy surrounding commitments that may have been given by the United States to Mikhail Gorbachev during the 'two plus four' talks concerning NATO expansion (Sarotte, 2014; Shifronson, 2014). Some scholars have claimed that Secretary of State James Baker declared unambiguously that NATO would not extend 'one inch to the east' (Zelikow & Rice, 1995: p. 183), but no such declaration was put in writing. Moreover, although the Soviet delegation ultimately preferred a 'common European home', as a practical matter, it saw the advantages of a reunified Germany fully within the embrace of NATO (Sarotte, 2014: p. 2).

The brief 'interregnum' of the first years of the Clinton Administration saw a vigorous debate in Washington over the abolition of NATO. But by 1994 the advocates of abolition were clearly marginalized. The Clinton administration settled on a forward strategy designed to expand American power across the European continent, including first the establishment of Partnership for Peace Programs followed by the expansion of NATO into Eastern Europe and then into former republics of the USSR (Latvia, Lithuania, Estonia). The sources of this transition were multiple and complex, including fragmentation among the EU powers; war and instability in South-eastern Europe; American domestic politics; and the tremendous lobbying power of the US military-industrial complex. Underlying these objectives, moreover, was the crucial interdependence of Atlanticism and neoliberalism.

The wars in former Yugoslavia (1992–5; 1999) played a central role in the expansion of NATO and its transformation from a regional defence organization to global arm of US policy. Initially designed as a test-case of a common EU foreign policy, the policy towards Yugoslavia and its successor states clearly showed the limitations and illusions of an independent European security order. When Serb units of the Yugoslav National Army mobilized in Croatia and Slovenia, the prime minister of Luxembourg (that then held the rotating Presidency of the Council), Jacques Poos, rashly proclaimed that 'This is the hour of Europe, not of the US', outlining a policy stance and transatlantic division of labour that accorded with the American position at that time: that the USSR should remain intact and that NATO should not be enlarged.

In fact, the EU was paralysed: Germany's decision to recognize Croatian and Slovenian sovereignty in the context of debates over reunification provoked serious conflicts with Britain and France, who together feared a 'German offensive' in South-eastern Europe (Cafruny, 2003). However, German diplomatic and legal declarations were not accompanied by broader initiatives, and certainly not a political-military project for regional stability. Prodded by the United States, Bosnia proclaimed its own independence in the context of Serb uprisings and a campaign of ethnic cleansing and genocide supported by Belgrade. France and

Britain offered plans for the de facto partition of Bosnia that provoked further ethnic cleansing by Serb and Croat forces. Massive human rights violations, the failure of EU and UN forces to protect 'safe havens' and refugee flows to Western Europe generated pressures for a settlement, eventually provoking US military intervention within the framework of NATO, including air assaults on Bosnian Serb forces and assistance to Bosnian Muslim and Croat forces. In November 1995 a peace treaty was signed in Dayton, Ohio, establishing a nominally independent Bosnia that comprised semi-autonomous Croat, Bosnian Muslim, and Serb cantons. The treaty was initially enforced with large numbers of NATO troops. However, since 2003 Bosnia has effectively been a NATO protectorate under EU administration.

The US intervention in Bosnia catalysed the transition to a more expansionist strategy for NATO. It indicated that, notwithstanding EU aspirations in the area of military cooperation, the United States was not willing to accept NATO retrenchment, to cede European security to the EU, or to recognize a Russian 'sphere of influence' in Eastern Europe or, for that matter, anywhere outside the boundaries of Russia itself. This policy would be clearly implemented in the subsequent US-led NATO war against Serbia in 1999, and it remains in place at present. NATO's 50th anniversary celebrations at the 1999 Washington Summit inaugurated Poland, Hungary and the Czech Republic as members amid bombings in Serbia in which thousands of civilians were killed or maimed. Since then, the Baltic States (Estonia, Latvia, Lithuania), Slovenia, Croatia, Montenegro, Romania, and Bulgaria have joined NATO.

As a result of the wars against Serbia, South-eastern Europe has gradually been integrated into Atlantic structures. In 2004, Slovenia joined NATO and the EU. Croatia joined NATO in 2009 and the EU in 2013, while Montenegro joined NATO in 2015. Kosovo and Bosnia remain effectively protectorates of NATO and the EU, with the former patrolled by 5,565 NATO troops and the latter governed under the terms of a Stabilisation and Association Agreement and the prospect of EU membership in the distant future. In April 2013 the EU brokered a 'normalization' agreement between Kosovo and Serbia that would allow Serbia to begin negotiations on EU membership. However, it is no exaggeration to consider Kosovo a 'failed state'. Even as its leaders are under investigation for war crimes, Kosovo is the largest per capita contributor of forces to rebel groups in Syria (Economist, 2015).

While the Washington Summit of 1999 established a rationale for NATO operations in South-eastern Europe, the Prague Summit of 2002 – taking place in the context of the unfolding 'global war against terror' – promulgated an even more ambitious doctrinal basis for NATO's transformation, pushing NATO beyond its Atlantic origins into Eurasia, Central Asia, the Middle East, and Africa. In August

2003 NATO took control of the International Security Assistance Force (ISAF) in Afghanistan, which included significant French and German participation.

The United States began moving forces into Eastern Europe, establishing bases in Romania and Bulgaria to serve as potential 'lily pads' on the Black Sea for potential operations in the Caucasus, Central and South Asia, and the Persian Gulf. The accession of Eastern European countries was preceded by extensive US weapons exports and long-range procurement and training packages, especially with Poland and the Czech Republic. These weapons sales were complemented by the unilateral American renunciation of the ABM (Anti-Ballistic Missile) Treaty under President George W. Bush and the placing of interceptor missiles in Poland and a radar base in the Czech Republic, ostensibly to defend against Iranian nuclear missiles, a policy that produced significant tensions with Moscow. By 2006 Ivo Daalder, former US ambassador to NATO, was calling for the establishment of a 'global NATO' (Daalder & Goldgeier, 2006). At present 21 of 28 EU member states are also members of NATO, with the five Nordic countries intensifying cooperation with NATO. NATO is gradually being integrated into a more diffuse but global network of multilateral and bilateral pacts, centred in Washington. In Zbigniew Brzezinski's words, 'The essential point regarding NATO expansion is that it is a process integrally connected with Europe's own expansion' (1997: pp. 79–80).

A central feature of the United States' forward movement was the plan to integrate Georgia and Ukraine in NATO and the EU. Former US Deputy Assistant Secretary of State for Europe Ronald Asmus set out the strategic vision with great candour and clarity: Anchoring Ukraine to the West would facilitate NATO's 'strategic shift away from defending the old European heartland' and create 'a new platform better positioning the US and Europe to tackle ... the major challenge of the 21st century – dealing with the instability and threats emanating from the Greater Middle East.' It would give the West 'an enhanced capacity from which to radiate its political influence and stability into the Caucasus and Central Asia and further into the Middle East' (2004: p. 2).

The US-sponsored 'Orange Revolution' of 2004, propelling the pro-Western Viktor Yuschenko to power, was viewed as a serious challenge by Russia. The industrial belts and agricultural systems of Russia and Ukraine are integrated. Russia's Black Sea fleet is based in Sevastopol in the Crimean peninsula that had been administratively reallocated to Ukraine by Nikita Khruschev in 1954 but annexed by Russia in 2014 in the context of the Ukrainian civil war. Ukraine remains a major conduit for natural gas exports to much of Europe. For its part Georgia is the key strategic link in the British Petroleum-dominated Baku–Tbilisi–Ceyhan (BTC) gas pipeline running from the Caspian Sea to the Mediterranean, the Baku–Tbilisi–Erzurum (BTE) gas pipeline; and the Kars–Tbilisi–Baku (China to London) railway. The US-sponsored 'Rose Revolution' of 2003 paved the way for extensive military and economic ties between Georgia and the United States.

Whereas President Boris Yeltsin (1991–2000) pursued an accommodating stance towards the West, especially in the energy sector, under President Vladimir Putin (2000–2008; 2012–) and President Dmitry Medvedev (2008–12), Russia became more assertive with respect to its patrimonial interest in energy resources and transit within Russia and its 'near abroad'. In 2008, responding forcefully to the incursion of Georgian military units into south Ossetia in the aftermath of extensive Georgian-US military exercises, Russia sent forces deep into Georgia, traversing the BTC pipeline, recognizing Abkhazian and south Ossetian sovereignty and constructing a naval base in Abkhazia. The United States sought to grant Georgia (and Ukraine) an 'action plan' for NATO membership, but France and Germany refused to endorse it. Nevertheless, the Lisbon Summit of 2010 explicitly confirmed the centrality of NATO to the EU, including the establishment of a pan-European ABM system, the expansion of NATO to embrace 'a wide network of partner relationships with countries and organizations around the globe' (NATO, 2010) and the call by Herman Van Rompuy to 'break down the remaining walls' between NATO and the EU (European Council, 2010).

Towards a common European foreign policy?

Ever since the founding of the ECSC, there has been a desire to match the supranational dimension of economic policy with parallel coordination in foreign policy. Under the terms of the 'pillar structure' of the Maastricht Treaty CFSP remained essentially intergovernmental but codified ambitious plans for a common foreign and security policy alongside the EMU. As a European constitutional process began to unfold, many observers discerned the outlines of an embryonic 'polity' that was a precondition of genuine regional self-determination and autonomy: appointment of a high representative for CFSP and External Action Service; consensus on a set of international humanitarian tasks; formation of European military units ('common defence'); and the regional integration of European defence industries through the European Defence Agency (EDA). Under the terms of the treaty, 'joint actions' and 'common positions' – resulting from consensus – were supposed to be legally binding on the member states. Moreover, the treaty called for the 'eventual framing of a common defense policy, which might in time lead to a common defense' (Treaty on European Union). However, notably, Britain insisted that CFSP must be designed to strengthen the

European pillar of NATO and, most tellingly, that the treaty must allow for member-state veto power.

The Amsterdam Treaty (1997) rechristened the CFSP as the European Security and Defense Policy (ESDP) and resulted in a further modest strengthening of the supranational dimension. It provided for EU participation in the Petersburg Tasks, essentially humanitarian and peacebuilding measures that would be implemented by the WEU and also established the position of high representative. In 1998 a joint Franco-British St Malo initiative allowed the ESDP to undertake autonomous missions in areas where the United States was not involved. At the Helsinki Summit (1999) the member states established a Rapid Reaction Force of 60,000 peacekeeping troops along with a non-military response capacity of 5000 police officers. The Lisbon Treaty (2009) terminated the WEU in favour of a new formal mechanism, the Common Security and Defence Policy (CSDP), with the establishment of the European External Action Service (EEAS, the diplomatic arm of the CSDP), and the appointment of a high representative of the Union for Foreign Affairs and Security Policy (McCormick & Olsen, 2014: esp. pp. 296–305). As with all previous institutional developments in the area of foreign policy, the CSDP enshrines the principle of unanimity in the Council and remains entirely with the framework of Atlanticism:

> The CSDP shall include the progressive framing of a common Union defence policy. This will lead to a common defence when the European Council, acting unanimously, so decides …. The policy of the Union with respect to this article shall not prejudice the specific character of the security and defense policy of certain member states which see their common defense realized in the NATO, under the North Atlantic Treaty, and be compatible with the security and defense policy established within that framework (TEU, Article 17, 1997).

There is no shortage of academic scholarship that links a putative European global political identity to the integration telos. (e.g. Ginsberg, 2001; 2010) Scholars commonly argue that despite occasional setbacks, the EU is gradually on course to expand its military capability and global influence. On paper, the EU has the second largest military force in the world. By 2011 the EU was conducting no less than 16 separate operations in Africa, Iraq, the Caucasus, Afghanistan, and South-eastern Europe (McCormick & Olsen, 2014: pp. 296–305). These interventions are in addition to NATO operations 'out of area' in Afghanistan and Libya (see below) in which the EU played a significant role. Substantial foreign aid programmes endow the EU with significant influence, most notably with respect to the Palestinian Authority. In 2004 the EDA was established as part of the CSDP to strengthen European military-industrial cooperation. By 2006 four European firms – BAE systems, the European Aeronautical and Defense Systems (EADS), Thales, and Finnmeccanica – were among the top ten global armaments firms.

Franco-German cooperation – and hence the dream of an independent foreign policy – reached its apex in response to the US invasion of Iraq at the Summit of Four in April 2003, when President Jacques Chirac and Chancellor Schröder followed up their declaration of January 2003 (calling for joint decision making) with an appeal – with Luxembourg and Belgium – for an EU autonomous military planning headquarters. A single headquarters system would have replaced current arrangements whereby EU military missions are run out of national centres in the UK, Germany, Greece, and Italy. Although pushed by the 'Weimar countries' (Poland, France, and Germany) a single military headquarters was vetoed by Britain. Franco-German initiatives during the Iraq War were predicated in part on the desire for closer military collaboration but also on the creation of Franco-German 'national industrial champions'. However, as the aforementioned section indicated, neither in the realm of military affairs nor industry has there been significant collaboration.

Although Germany, France, and the UK are respectively the world's third, fourth, and fifth largest armaments exporters, a significant European military capability is not emerging, and indeed, Europe is becoming increasingly subordinated to US/NATO structures, as confirmed by the Lisbon Treaty. The 'Rapid Reaction Force' was quietly abandoned. The proposed deployment of the 5000-person Franco-German brigade to Mali in 2012 was blocked by Germany. While Russia and China have embarked on significant rearmament programmes, EU defence spending declined by 10 per cent between 2006 and 2016, falling below 2 per cent of GDP. The United States spends seven times more on research and development than all of the 28 member states collectively and accounts for 75 per cent of NATO military spending (EDA, 2015). The United States maintains 180 tactical B-61 nuclear gravity bombs in Germany, Belgium, Netherlands, Italy, and Turkey. NATO defence doctrine declares that 'Nuclear weapons are a core component of NATO's overall capabilities for deterrence and defence alongside conventional and missile defense' (NATO, 2012). Moreover, as will come as no surprise given the assessment on Servan-Shreiber's vision of a joint industrial policy in Chapter 3, the European military-industrial complex remains fragmented. European firms have become more heavily dependent on the highly restricted US market. BAE systems, Britain's largest defence contractor, is the seventh largest American armaments manufacturer and recently had considered becoming a US firm (Cafruny, 2009). Surveying this landscape, Commission President Jean Claude Juncker confessed that 'A bunch of chickens looks like a combat formation compared to the foreign and security policy of the EU' (*DefenseNews*, 2015: p. 1).

The NATO-led 'Operation Unified Protector' assault on Libya in 2011 vividly illustrates the dynamics of the US-European political-military relationship. President Sarkozy proclaimed that 'Europeans have shown for the first time that they are capable of intervention in a decisive way, with their allies, in an open conflict on their doorstop' (quoted in Rettman, 2011). The war did signify a new activism for French, British, and (to some extent) Italian policy in the Middle East and North Africa (MENA) regions. However, this activism was and remains clearly situated within the framework of NATO. At the outset, France and Britain sought to enlist US support for intervention in the form of UN Resolution 1973, designed only to establish a 'no-fly zone'. However, along with Russia, China, Brazil, and India, Germany opposed intervention and abstained in the UN Security Council. France and Britain then sought to undertake a joint action. EUFOR Libya (European Union Military Operation in Libya) was proposed instead as an EU military humanitarian mission, but it was never launched, because it depended on a request from the UN that was never received. Only after an intensive diplomatic confrontation did France ultimately agree to 'Operation Unified Protector' with NATO's full control and command of forces. In the end, the United States played a critical role in all phases of the operation, providing three-quarters of the tanker aircraft, reconnaissance planes, ammunition, intelligence, and drone aircraft. US fighter planes played a pivotal role by destroying Libyan air defence systems. The operation ultimately facilitated Gadhafi's overthrow and execution, clearly violating the terms of Resolution 1973, which had limited the intervention to humanitarian aims and the enforcement of a 'no-fly zone'. In 2013 the EU launched a border control mission for Libya (EUBAM), but in 2014 it was compelled by the civil war in Libya to retreat to Tunisia and then suspended in January 2015 as the country fell into anarchy.

While acknowledging the limits of the EU as a military power, many scholars assert that the significance of the Union's foreign policy derives not from traditional conceptions of military security or 'hard power' but rather 'soft power' (Nye, 2003; Reid, 2004; Leonard, 2005) or 'human security' in which Europe is a 'normative power' that leads by 'attraction' and example (e.g. Laidi, 2008; Manners, 2002, 2008; Forsberg, 2011). These conceptions of the EU as a novel entity received official recognition as a central objective of the 2008 Report by the European Council on the European Security Strategy (ESS) (Martin & Kaldor, 2012). The 2003 ESS and the 2012 Agenda for Change – the EU's security and development 'bibles' – call for greater linkages between development cooperation, humanitarian aid, and CSDP. To be sure, this type of influence has sometimes been brought to bear, especially in the EU's periphery through the European Neighbourhood Policy. As noted in Chapter 6, the goal of accession has in the past undoubtedly served to reinforce democratizing tendencies and reduced levels of corruption in Central and Eastern Europe (Vachudova, 2009).

However, as Chapter 6 also showed, the EU's eastern enlargements and ENPs in Eastern Europe and the Mediterranean reinforce existing core-periphery relations. Chapter 8 will show that the EU's relations with the Global South remain essentially post-colonial. More generally, the limitations of 'soft power' are widely recognized, not least within the European military establishment. As former NATO Secretary General Anders Fogh Rasmussen noted, 'soft power is really no power at all. Without hard capabilities to back up its diplomacy, Europe will lack credibility and influence …. [T]hen all talk about a strengthened European defense and security policy will just be hot air' (quoted in Rettman, 2013). Two decades ago, American policymakers commonly expressed concerns over the potential development of European defence capabilities, which they feared might serve as a counterweight to Washington. Their concern today is very different: Their calls for European military spending increases reflect their view that EU military capabilities have diminished to the extent that NATO's mission is becoming imperilled.

The German question redux

The Ukraine crisis opened up a new chapter in relations between Russia and the West. Notwithstanding the strong pro-Russian sentiments of Crimea's residents, Russia's actions in Crimea represented the first time since World War II that a territory was clearly and unambiguously seized and annexed as a result of force. Harsh US and EU sanctions and Russian support for the ethnic Russian rebellion in Eastern Ukraine have greatly damaged not only the Russian economy but also that of many member states of the EU. Chancellor Angela Merkel's support for sanctions over the objections of German (and other EU) export interests and the debate between Atlanticist and enduring pro-Russian forces within the German elite (Tagesspiegel, 2014a, 2014b) suggest that the war in Ukraine has shattered the longstanding consensus on the need for collaborative relations with Russia and the need for attempts to moderate the US's more confrontational policies, as occurred, for example, during the Russo-Georgian war of 2008.

During 2015 a series of negotiations in Belarus involving France, Germany, Russia, and Ukraine (Minsk I and II) led to ceasefire in Ukraine. Although the violence diminished as positions were frozen, the EU appeared condemned to confront three interlocking crises for years to come: not only that of the monetary union but also the return of great power rivalry in Europe and migration crisis that we will explore in Chapter 8. The three crises have distinctive origins and logics, but a common denominator is growing German primacy in the EU. They raise fundamental questions about basic European and Euro-Atlantic political-military structures. How will they be answered, and what are the implications for the EU and the transatlantic relationship?

The problems for Western Europe represented by growing conflict with Russia are magnified by energy dependence. The EU currently imports approximately 50 per cent of its oil and gas from Russia. For CEE countries, however, dependence on Russian gas is almost total. Contrary to the ambitions of EURATOM, the Treaty Establishing an Atomic Energy Community signed alongside the EEC treaty, or Servan-Shreiber's vision, there is no single market for energy; European energy policy represents "commercial great-power politics" (Abdelal, 2010: p. 31). Although the European Commission has for many years sought to promote energy liberalization, EU energy policy remains at an embryonic stage. It is essentially organized along national lines and infused with intra-member-state rivalry in which the centrality of the German state and the power of German energy firms are increasing. During the Cold War, Soviet exports to the CEE and Western Europe flowed through Ukraine, but political instability and civil war have rendered this highly unstable and unacceptable to both Russia and Germany.

Completed in 2011, the Nord Stream gas pipeline is a joint venture in which Russia's Gazprom holds 51 per cent of the shares, with the remainder held by the Dutch Gasunie and the German company Wintershall, the energy division of the German chemicals group BASF, and E.ON Energie, chaired by former Chancellor Gerhard Schröder. It extends from Ukhta, 350 kilometres from the Arctic Circle, through the Baltic Sea to Greifswald, Germany and then across the German–Czech border and eventually back to a border delivery station in Walhaus, Germany. Poland, the Baltic States, and the Czech Republic bitterly opposed the pipeline on the grounds that it would deepen European dependency on Russian gas and 'disintermediate' their countries from primary pipelines linking Russian to Western Europe. In 2009 Polish Foreign Minister Radek Sikorski compared Nord Stream to the Nazi-Soviet Pact of 1939.

A second proposed gas pipeline project, South Stream, represented a joint Gazprom–Italian ENI venture that would have run from the Black Sea through Bulgaria to Southern Europe. South Stream was also opposed by Brussels and Washington, which had unsuccessfully lobbied for the construction of the gas pipeline Nabucco, which would have brought natural gas to Europe from central Asia and reduced dependence on Russia but was ultimately commercially unviable. Absent a sufficiently powerful state lobbyist in the EU, South Stream was eventually torpedoed in the context of the Ukraine crisis. In the summer of 2014 the European Commission and the United States, with strong German support, pressured Bulgaria to break its contracts with Gazprom. The

EU Commission invoked the Third Energy Package, a set of competition rules prohibiting suppliers of gas from owning the pipelines that deliver it, according to which South Stream was incompatible. An alternative Turkish Stream Project became a casualty of tensions over the civil war in Syria but could be revived in the context of a Russo-Turkish rapprochement.

In 2015 an agreement was made between Gazprom Russia and a consortium of German (BASF and E.ON), French (ENGIE), Anglo-Dutch (Royal Dutch Shell), and Austrian (ÖMV) companies on the construction of 'Nord Stream II', traversing the same route as the original Nord Stream pipeline. Scheduled for completion in 2019, the project would further reduce Ukraine's role as a transit corridor and deprive it of 3 billion euros in annual transit fees, concentrating two-thirds of Russian gas exports to Western Europe in one route. It would further consolidate German primacy in a hub-and-spoke system of Russian gas exports throughout Europe.

Like its predecessor, Nord Stream II has elicited widespread hostility from the strongly pro-Ukranian European Commission as well as from Poland, the Baltic States, and Slovakia, who are demanding more 'solidarity' from Germany. Because the pipeline runs along the same route as the original Nord Stream, the project does not apparently contravene the anti-monopoly restrictions of the Third Energy Package (O'Donnell, 2015). The project also apparently enjoys the full support of the German state. During his meeting with President Vladimir Putin on 28 October 2015, German Vice-Chancellor Sigmar Gabriel expressed the German position with extraordinary candour:

> What's most important as far as legal issues are concerned is that we strive to ensure that all this remains under the competence of the German authorities, if possible. So if we can do this, then opportunities for external meddling will be limited. And we are in a good negotiating position on this matter. (President of Russia, 2015)

However, in response to the decision of Polish authorities in August 2016 to apply competition regulations to the proposed pipeline, Gazprom's European partners have pulled out of the project, raising questions concerning Gazprom's ability to finance the project on its own and enhancing the significance of an alternative Turkish Stream project.

In conjunction with the centrality of German capital in CEE production chains (see Chapter 6) and its leadership role in the EMU, these energy projects have profound geopolitical implications. Reflecting on the changing European balance of power as well as cultural shifts in

Germany, Hans Kundnani (2015a) imagines a 'post-Western German foreign policy' that implies a tectonic shift in global power relations:

> Post-Western Germany could take much of the rest of Europe with it, particularly those central and eastern European countries with economies that are deeply intertwined with Germany's. If the United Kingdom leaves the EU, as it is now debating, the union will be even more likely to follow German preferences, especially as they pertain to Russia and China. In that event, Europe could find itself at odds with the United States – and the West could suffer a schism from which it might never recover. (Kundnani (2015a), p. 116)

The causes of such a shift for Kundnani and others (inter alia, Wallerstein, 2014) are both economic and cultural. According to these scholars, Germany has become increasingly dependent on emerging country markets, especially China, whose weight in Germany's export and investment portfolio vastly exceeds that of Russia. At the same time, anti-American sentiments within European and German society have deepened, in part as a result of revelations of the activities of US intelligence services in Germany. The civil war has damaged Germany's 'special relationship' with Russia, but it has also strengthened underlying Russophile strains in German society. However, if these trends suggest limits to Germany's pro-American policy (see also, Schlapentokh, 2014), the evidence from the Ukraine crisis suggests that they have probably been overstated, not least by Russia. As Russian Foreign Minister Lavrov acknowledged with reference to German support for sanctions, 'Frankly, we have overestimated the independence of the EU from the United States' (TASS, 2014).

To be sure, German foreign trade patterns are gradually shifting. German exports remain concentrated on the EU. However, the Eurozone share of German exports has gradually declined while Asia's share increased. The TTIP is projected to accelerate this trend. In 2015 the United States replaced France as the principal trading partner to Germany. China now receives more German FDI than France and appears poised to overtake France as Germany's second largest trade partner. It is the largest market for Germany's machine-tool industry; almost one-half of China's exports go to Germany. These data not only illustrate the centrality of the United States for the German economy, but also the development of a 'special relationship' between China and Germany outside of EU structures (Kundnani & Parello-Plesner, 2013).

There is clearly a linkage between Germany's global economic interests and power and the emergent strategy of 'selective multilateralism' in which Germany no longer marches in lockstep with the United States. In 2003 Germany voted in the UN Security Council against

US military intervention in Iraq. Germany (along with France) refused to grant Georgia an action plan for NATO membership following the Russo-Georgian war of 2008. In March 2011 Germany abstained in the UN Security Council – effectively siding with China and Russia – over the Anglo-French-US proposal (Resolution 1973) to establish a 'no-fly zone' in Libya. With the exception of Serbia (1999) and Afghanistan (2001–14), Germany has refused involvement in all actual or proposed NATO military interventions. However, the significance of these abstentions should not be overstated. While Germany pulled its four warships in the Mediterranean out of NATO patrols in response to the 2011 attack on Libya, it cooperated with France and the United States in significant ways. Foreign Minister Guido Westerwelle did not interfere with North Atlantic Council meetings. The Luftwaffe sent 300 military personnel to Afghanistan, thereby relieving pressure on NATO. Three hundred German soldiers participated in the assault, mainly identifying bombing targets in Libya. Chancellor Merkel asserted that Germany's position should 'not be confused with neutrality' (IPS, 2011).

As noted in Chapter 6, during the last two decades, German banks and corporations expanded into Central, Eastern, and South-eastern Europe, where they obtained privileged status within strategic financial and industrial structures that were denationalized and privatized as a result of shock therapy and, later, the terms of the *acquis communautaire* with the EU. German-Russian relations in particular also began to assume a quasi-colonial division of labour with the partial conversion of Russia into a market for industrial exports and source of raw materials imports resulting from Russia's own denationalization and deindustrialization during the 1990s.

In the context of German economic primacy in Europe, there is a rhetorical consensus within foreign policy circles that 'Germany will have to take the lead more decisively and more often' (SWP-GMF, 2014) and abandon the 'culture of restraint' that has defined its international outlook since 1945 (Sonne, 2014). However, and unsurprisingly within the EMU macroeconomic regime, this has found only modest expression in the German defence budget, which notwithstanding increases announced in the German Defence White Paper of July 2016 appears likely to remain under the NATO norm of 2 per cent for years to come. At the same time, notwithstanding rhetorical appeals to Franco-German military unification in the wake of the Brexit vote, EU defence policy appears destined for further marginalization. German security concerns extend well beyond Ukraine. As a 'geo-economic' power, Germany cannot independently pursue a forward strategy in a sphere that is contested by Russia. In this respect, it is notable that, having surrendered its economic leadership role in the EU to Germany, France has strengthened the Atlantic vector of its policy, abandoning its Gaullist stance, reintegrating with NATO's military structures in

2009, signing a defence cooperation treaty with the UK in 2010, and, as Chapter 8 will show, concentrating its ambitions on North Africa and the Middle East in close cooperation with the United States.

Conclusion

This chapter has traced the evolution of transatlantic relations from World War I to the present. Rejecting economism, it demonstrates the significance of the political – or in Callinicos' words, the 'realist moment' – as a determining factor in the evolution of the capitalist world system and the EU. A critical political economy perspective must account for the mutual constitution of elite rivalry and power politics, on the one hand, and the interests of capitalist classes and phases of capitalist accumulation, on the other hand. This co-constitution can be seen most vividly in the role played by NATO's wars and expansion and the consolidation of neoliberalism.

This perspective makes it possible to conceptualize both necessity and contingency in history. Fordism as a mode of regulation and social set-tlement represented a 'solution' to capitalism's internal contradictions within a particular historical conjuncture. It was therefore 'functional' but at the same time quintessentially geopolitical, contingent, and by no means inevitable. During the 1930s and 1940s, the American state consolidated the Fordist settlement in the United States (and Western Europe) in the interests of capital in general but against the will of recalcitrant and strongly organized capitalists. A similar if more muted process took place in Western Europe after 1945. Thus, Fordism was implemented within a geopolitical context of superpower rivalry and ideological challenge to Western capitalism posed by communism and socialism. Indeed, in the United States, anti-communism was mobilized and arguably 'oversold' as a means of legitimizing the post-war settle-ment in the face of obstructionist and isolationist US Congress (Lowi, 1967). Similarly, the neoliberal 'resolution' of the Fordist crisis starting in the 1980s was by no means inevitable or a given in the functional sense. It was ushered in on the strength of capital's grand offensive starting in the late 1970s, further emboldened by the collapse of the USSR and crisis of social democracy and fully confident that there could be 'no alternative'. The absence of a systematic challenge to capitalist power looms increasingly large as the crisis of neoliberalism deepens. It certainly contributes to an explanation for the extraordinary intel-lectual complacency in academia and EU institutions concerning the establishment of the EMU and the unwillingness on both sides of the Atlantic – but especially in Europe – to consider even modest Keynesian initiatives in the context of stagnation and mass unemployment.

The centrality of American power in the transatlantic relationship, spanning two very different regulatory modes, is a striking element of continuity. A second element of continuity is uneven development throughout the EU and Euro-Atlantic space, exacerbated and not reduced as a result of the neoliberal transformation. Germany's regional ascendance, reflecting the tremendous and distinctive productivity of German capitalism throughout its history, is a more cyclical development. Since the collapse of the Bretton Woods system, all European monetary orders, including the EMU, have sought unsuccessfully to contain German power. Yet, because Germany is powerful but not hegemonic in the Gramscian sense – an argument we advance in the concluding chapter – it is playing a destabilizing role in Europe and the EU. Finally, even if the sun is slowly setting on the American imperium, a thesis we will explore critically in the next chapter, it continues to cast a lengthening shadow across the whole European continent. c

Chapter 8

The European Union, the Global South, and the Emerging Powers

The previous chapter underlined the geopolitical significance of the Suez Crisis for the European powers and for the creation of the EC. Suez confirmed that France and Great Britain had been reduced to subordinate status within a bipolar world and that the United States would not necessarily support their efforts to retain their colonies or help them to exercise primacy over them after formal independence was achieved. The shock of Suez strengthened France's determination to move forward with the EC as a countervailing power to the United States, and therefore to reach a positive agreement at the Messina IGC. Although Britain sheltered under the umbrella of the 'special relationship' even Harold Macmillan, who replaced the chagrined Anthony Eden as Prime Minister, would soon apply for EC membership, setting in motion a long and stormy courtship that would culminate in Britain's entry in 1973.

That the Suez Crisis also served as a catalyst for the Treaty of Rome indicates that Europe's postcolonial condition was an important factor in European integration. Not only did the EC provide a new institutional framework through which to manage advanced capitalist social relations that, by their nature, could not be confined within nation states of the moderate European size; it also furnished a new means of collectively managing relations with the capitalist periphery of the former colonies.

This chapter continues to focus on Europe's external relations, a focus that began in the previous two chapters on enlargement and transatlantic relations. It shows that a narrative of transformation from Fordism to finance-led accumulation and neoliberalism makes sense of developments in the EU's relationship to the Global South and emerging markets, just as it did with respect to the EU's eastern enlargement and transatlantic relations. In the first section, we will review the general history of the relationship between the EU and the Global South, starting with the Treaty of Rome. The second section will explore the EU's multilateral relations, first with formerly French colonies through the Yaoundé Agreement of 1963 and followed by two agreements that the EU negotiated with the so-called African, Caribbean, and Pacific (ACP) states: a series of Lomé Conventions beginning in 1975; the more recent Cotonou Agreement of

2000; and finally the Euro-Mediterranean Partnership as the southern tier of the European Neighbourhood Policy. The chapter will then turn to the crisis of migration that erupted in 2015 in the context of the EU's relationship with the Middle East and Maghreb and assesses its implications for free movement throughout the EU, an important component of European neoliberalism. We will then address the impact of the BRICS (Brazil, Russia, India, China, and South Africa) on the EU, followed by a more detailed exploration of the significance of China's dramatic rise for the EU and the transatlantic condition of global hegemony. Finally, we analyse three strategic trade negotiations: the aforementioned TTIP alongside the Trans-Pacific Partnership (TPP) and the Trade in Services Agreement (TISA). These projected agreements have major significance for the transatlantic relationship and also for the EU's relations with emerging markets and China. They do not, however, provide a means of overcoming growing instability in the European or world economy. The conclusion synthesizes the findings in these sections and returns to the question of Europe as a 'normative power'. It confirms what was argued also in Chapter 7, namely that the dream of a European external policy that is post-imperial remains elusive.

The EU and the Global South

The EU's relations with the Global South have been managed primarily through the core international economic institutions that were established under American leadership: the GATT, the WTO, the World Bank, and the IMF. However, since the Treaty of Rome, the EU and member states have also sought to develop their own arrangements with the Global South through multilateral agreements and foreign aid. The postcolonial developmental strategies pursued by the Global South can be understood schematically in terms of a broad transition from nationalization and import substitution inaugurated in the 1950s and symbolized by Nasser's nationalization of the Suez Canal, to globalization and neoliberal policies that are commonly referred to as the 'Washington consensus', which started in the late 1970s and were consolidated as a result of the massive debt crisis of the early 1980s. This transition corresponded to the movement in advanced capitalist countries from Fordism to finance-led accumulation.

Raúl Prebisch, the chief economist of the UN Economic Commission for Latin America (ECLA), perceptively discerned the implications of Fordism for the capitalist periphery. His sobering conclusions contrasted with early-days optimism about economic development – that is, that such development could be achieved through participation in the world market on the basis of comparative advantage. Although Prebisch did not use the term Fordism, he nevertheless recognized the significance of the growing integration of mass production and mass consumption of consumer durables that was taking place after World War II within the advanced capitalist countries. He concluded that this development would cause stagnation in the periphery because it would result in deteriorating terms of trade. Increased income-levels among the mass of consumers in the core, characterized by rising productivity and strong labour movements, would lead to a relative decline of income spent on food and the other primary commodities that were the backbone of peripheral economies. In the peripheral countries with undiversified economies dependent on the export of raw materials, producers would respond to declining prices by increasing their output, thus driving down prices even further and leading to a further deterioration in the terms of trade. Moreover, capital investments in the periphery would lag because the integration of production and consumption – which in regulation-theoretical parlance is called 'intensive accumulation' (see Chapter 2) – reduced the compulsion of territorial expansion of core capital accumulation (Prebisch, 1950).

Thus, in important respects, formal independence in itself would not overcome colonial or 'neo-colonial' economic dependency. However, Nasser's nationalization programme and the resultant Suez Crisis showed that postcolonial regimes were developing counterbalancing strategies, in no small measure as a result of the influence of analyses such as that of Prebisch. Confronted by deteriorating terms of trade, they pursued to varying degrees interventionist models of development, of which Nasser's nationalization programme was a case in point. These models would range from 'modified liberal' versions of industrialization through import substitution to revolutionary socialism inspired by the Soviet Union and China. In the context of the Cold War, moreover, they received some support for these strategies from the United States, as in the Suez Crisis, and also the Alliance for Progress in Latin America. Hence, the EC's relationship to the Global South was shaped not only by such interventionist developmental strategies but also by geopolitical systems competition between the capitalist and socialist superpowers. As a result of the Russian and Chinese revolutions, the capitalist world had shrunk considerably. The Cuban revolution in 1959, the wars in Indo-China, and proxy wars throughout the world cast some doubt on the future of capitalism. These concerns provided the context for novel European and Western efforts to secure their economic and political interests in the Global South.

To be sure, the military option was by no means off the table, as exemplified by the bloody wars in Korea and Vietnam. Individually and collectively, the United States and the most powerful Western European states carried out numerous overt and covert interventions. In 1953 the United States (with the UK as a junior partner) orchestrated a coup against Mohammed Mussadeq's regime in Iran and would continue to sponsor or provide support for coups, especially in Latin America, for decades to come. Relying on massive American financial support, France fought for years against the Viet Minh in Vietnam before suffering a humiliating defeat at Dien Bien Phu in 1954. France's seven-year-war against Algerian independence, waged with indiscriminate violence and terror, led to the death of 350,000 Algerians and 25,000 French soldiers, including hundreds of Algerians slain by the French National Police in the 'Paris Massacre' of 17 October 1961. An abortive coup d'état in France resulted in the establishment of the Fifth Republic, under Charles de Gaulle, who presided over France's withdrawal from Algeria in 1961. France continues to deploy military forces in Africa and the Middle East, including most recently in Libya, Mali, and Syria. In 2007, France established a naval base on the Straits of Hormuz in Port Zayed, Abu Dhabi.

However, military methods were not exclusive or even primary in exerting control. As an institutional expression of capitalist interiorization (see Chapter 2), national development agencies, and international institutions, not least in the UN system, were designed to facilitate economic relations of consent between the capitalist core and periphery. Essentially, these institutions served to secure market access on Western terms, especially in primary commodities. They also served as forums to negotiate terms through which policy space and even Western support for national development could be secured in the periphery, provided that they were compatible with Western objectives and interests. Together, these methods served to shore up supportive local elites (Magdoff, 2003). Here, it is important to note that these novel methods corresponded to the mixed-market norms of Fordism that were being consolidated throughout Western Europe. While the Western European states conducted a great deal of development policy through bilateral relations outside the remit of EC institutions, the agreements forged in Yaoundé, Lomé, and Cotonou played an important role. Rather than being based on formal colonial authority, they offered an institutional relationship of 'discrete entente' where the postcolonial relation could be reproduced through more subtle means (Lister, 1988: p. 189, cited in Hurt, 2003: p. 162).

Yaoundé, Lomé, and Cotonou

Formal development cooperation between the EC and the ACP group of states began with the Treaty of Rome itself, which granted associate status to 31 countries and colonies and established a European Development Fund (EDF). With the first cycle of the EDF coming to an end and many colonies becoming independent states, the Yaoundé (Cameroon) Agreement was signed in 1963 between the EC and 17 African states. Yaoundé granted preferential treatment to signatories in the form of technical assistance and preferential access to the European market alongside increased EDF and European Investment Bank (EIB) assistance. The agreement essentially corresponded to the neo-colonial settlement outlined above.

The Lomé (Togo) Convention of 1975 represented a far more ambitious development. It coincided with what Chapter 7 labelled as the high point of European assertiveness in the transatlantic relationship. The terms of the convention reflected a new conjuncture in which peripheral and postcolonial states had become more assertive in the context of demands for the New International Economic Order (NIEO) made by the 'Group of 77' developing countries (Hurt, 2003: pp. 161–2) and the OPEC oil cartel. The NIEO was based on the principle of mutual responsibility for economic and social development. It envisioned the radical reform of the Bretton Woods international organizations such as GATT, the World Bank, and the IMF. In the context of a still-unresolved Fordist crisis, state capitalist, social, and left-Christian democratic parties in Europe supported the NIEO. The Lomé Convention was a compromise that sought to address some of the concerns of the NIEO movement. It contained a price-stabilization system intended to guarantee a certain level of export earnings for raw-material producing states (STABEX – Stabilization of Export Earnings) funded by the EDF, and it provided preferential access to the common market. The countries covered by the Convention increased to include former colonies throughout Africa, the Caribbean, and the Pacific (ACP states) including former British colonies because the UK had become an EC member in 1973.

As the NIEO movement collapsed in the context of the Third World debt crisis starting in the early 1980s, successive rounds of the Lomé Convention (from Lomé II to Lomé IV) saw these reforms gradually weakened (Brown, 2000). Ultimately, Lomé was replaced by the Cotonou (Benin) Agreement in 2000. Cotonou represented a marked change in the relationship between the EU and the former European colonies (Flint, 2008, 2009; Stevens, 2006). In institutional terms, it was shaped by the conclusion of the Uruguay Round of GATT in 1995 and the creation of the WTO. In principle, the WTO opposes trade preferences, and hence the main agenda of the Cotonou negotiations concerned the terms of their repeal. Furthermore, EU aid was made conditional on 'good governance' (Hout, 2010). Thus EU policy towards the ACPs followed the so-called Washington Consensus Structural Adjustment Programmes (SAPs). Developed by the IMF and the World Bank after the so-called Baker and Brady Plans in the mid 1980s (Gill & Law, 1988: pp. 184–5, 298–9), SAP became the template for opening markets, the privatization of public assets, and macroeconomic prudence in Third World countries in payment difficulties (Brown, 2000). As Chapter 6 showed, the neoliberal Washington Consensus has also been the leading norm in the policies that the EU has applied to its immediate external border areas in Europe under the terms of the ENP and Eastern Partnerships. As we will show below, a similar dynamic can be observed with respect to the EuroMed dimension of the ENP (Kniou, 2013).

From the standpoint of orthodox scholarship, the Washington Consensus reforms were assumed to represent a movement away from 'politics' and towards rational adjustment to market-deepening trends. The question then became one of consent: were the states of the Global South sufficiently committed and resilient to withstand political challenges arising from the assumed short-term dislocations resulting from these reforms (e.g. Forwood, 2001)? However, as the process of transition from Fordism to finance-led accumulation in the transatlantic sphere indicates, the reforms themselves were profoundly political. The NIEO coalition had to be politically defeated, and this included potential allies within the EC itself that continued to hold social democratic or mercantilist views. Thus, the imposition of Washington Consensus reforms in the Global South represented the external face of the neoliberal finance-led developments undertaken through the single-market project itself (Hurt, 2003; Bretherton & Vogler, 1999: p. 7).

The SAPs imposed tremendously harsh terms of adjustment, especially in Africa (e.g. Davis, 2006). As the 1997 Libreville Declaration indicates, even the most market-friendly elites of these countries were concerned about transition costs (Hurt, 2003: pp. 169–70). Hence, ACP enthusiasm for Cotonou has been very limited. The agreement struggled to obtain a requisite hegemonic aura of consent, rendering it a more purely coercive construct at a time after the Cold War when the EU and the West were the 'only game in town' as an economic partner. At the same time, Washington Consensus policies greatly reduced the infrastructural and hegemonic capacities of these already weak states (Graf, 1995: pp. 151–2). This indicates that core capitalist powers increasingly put premium on imperatives of capital accumulation, especially access to resources that could be turned into assets, and increasingly discounted the postcolonial imperative to support the legitimacy claims of allied domestic elites. In the most acute cases in Africa, this has resulted in state collapse and protracted civil conflict associated with immeasurable human suffering and countless human deaths. Consequently, the EU has found it difficult to secure Economic Partnership Agreements (EPAs) to eliminate the remaining preferential access waivers from WTO rules (Hurt, 2012). This is in part because of the weakness of the ACP states themselves, which has created spaces for civil-society organizations to embed themselves in the negotiation process, helping to block agreements (Trommer, 2013). This outcome needs to be seen in a broader geopolitical context, where especially China has become a major player in Africa and has offered itself as an alternative partner to that of the EU (Hurt, 2012: p. 500).

EuroMed: the southern tier of the European Neighbourhood Policy

Chapter 6 introduced the European Neighbourhood Policy (ENP), which was launched in 2004 to enhance the political and economic reach of the EU within states of the former Soviet Union that were not considered candidates for EU membership. Within Europe, the ENP gave rise to the Eastern Partnerships. The ENP also incorporated the countries of North Africa and the Eastern Mediterranean in the Euro-Mediterranean or 'EuroMed' Partnership or 'Barcelona Process'. The Barcelona Process had been launched in 1995 to provide a comprehensive European policy towards the region. The Partnership expanded to include the 28 members of the EU alongside Algeria, Egypt, Israel, Jordan, Lebanon, Libya, Morocco, Palestine, Syria, and Tunisia. The main aspects are political and security dialogue, economic, financial, social, and cultural partnership.

In the wake of developments after the 'Arab Spring' uprisings in 2011, the results of the Barcelona Process must be deemed a failure. With spikes in food prices generated by financial speculation in grain markets (Baines, 2014) as a key immediate cause, the Arab Spring brought about the collapse of the 'halfway house' neoliberal 'passive revolutions' that the EU had promoted in the region (e.g. Roccu, 2013). It is particularly telling that the Arab Spring started in the relative 'success case' of Tunisia. At the political level, the composition of member states – including Israel and Palestine – indicates the difficulty of developing common or cooperative policies, especially in an arena ultimately dominated by the United States.

The inability to devise a unified policy beyond a lowest common denominator Washington Consensus is even more tragically apparent with respect to the 2011 intervention in Libya spearheaded by France and Britain. As Chapter 7 noted, the mission, which extended well beyond UN Resolution 1973 calling for the enforcement of a 'no-fly zone', was opposed by Germany. While the French and British (and American) justification was framed in terms of humanitarian concerns and the 'Responsibility to Protect' (R2P), these objectives were never seriously pursued while geopolitics and oil loomed large. Colonel Ghaddafi had placed numerous restrictions on international oil companies and also represented an obstacle to the exploitation of oil in the Chad Basin, surrounded by Chad, Cameroon, and Niger, all of which are former French colonies.

In response to the Arab Spring, the European Commission and the European External Action Service (EEAS) updated the ENP to establish the '3M' programme, which included opening markets in areas where the MENA countries enjoyed a comparative advantage, politically targeted foreign aid, and investment. However, a projected free trade area was put on hold. Foreign direct investment has been very low, and the EU continues to maintain high tariff barriers on a range of agricultural commodities. In fact, the MENA region moved backwards over the past decades: experiencing not even dependent incorporation but rather marginalization that has ultimately deepened poverty and inequality while simultaneously reducing state capacity (Talani, 2014). The massive growth of urban slums, caused by the push factor of rural enclosures and a dearth of formal employment opportunities, has created rich breeding grounds for organized crime as well as millenarian movements (Davis, 2006; Hurt, Knio, & Ryner, 2009). Long before the crisis of 2015, the region's economic stagnation was causing large migratory outflows and associated brain drain. The EU has contributed substantial development aid to the MENA region and beyond. However, as with the limited scope of action and resources of the EIB and structural funds as cited in Chapter 6, the compensatory impact of aid within a broader framework of neoliberalism has been very weak.

In 2014 the EU and its member states were collectively the world's largest aid donor, providing more than one-half of the total official development assistance. The total sum of 58.2 billion euros represented 0.42 of the EU's gross national income (GNI), although aid to the poorest countries continued to decline, and the EU continued to lag well behind its stated goal of 0.7 per cent (OECD, 2015a). Although EU development policy – and the status as largest global donor – includes both member state and EU funds, the former account for more than 75 per cent of aid. Although the European Commission is charged with the overall coordination of aid, it is simply one actor among many, and member state funds are disbursed according to national economic and political interests.

Approximately 25 per cent of this combined national and EU aid was granted to the Western Balkans and European Neighbourhood. With respect to the latter, Germany and the CEE countries have sought to prioritize the six eastern countries while the Mediterranean countries have sought to increase funds to the states of the Maghreb. Just as in the case of limited industrial policy, these relatively modest funds do not offset the broader framework of dependent development and, in the case of much of the MENA countries, marginalization as noted above.

There is a contradiction between the stated goals of development aid and overall trade policies: subsidized agricultural exports that flood southern markets, exposing local farmers to impoverishment and greater dependence on humanitarian aid; policies designed to foster large-scale agribusiness and foreign investment in raw materials thus displacing small farmers; and selective tariffs on the Global South designed to encourage exports of primary commodities (European Parliament, 2010). The EU's Court of Auditors, furthermore, has issued a series of reports detailing massive corruption and inefficiency in EU aid programmes (European Union Court of Auditors, 2013), especially with respect to the MENA region and, in particular, Egypt and the Palestinian Authority. In sum, the member states of the EU have been unable individually or collectively to abandon postcolonial attitudes and strategies towards the Global South, much less to devise a coherent strategy for the MENA region, leaving them vulnerable to the charge that the EU has 'lost its southern neighbourhood' (Techau, 2014), an observation fully borne out by the migration crisis of 2015.

Migration

During the post-World War II boom, Northern European countries experienced acute labour shortages, leading governments to sponsor large-scale immigration programmes. In the case of Britain and France, these programmes were organized in the context of relationships with former colonies, whose citizens enjoyed privileged access to labour contracts offered in the country of origin (McMahon, 2015). West Germany established a 'guestworker' programme for Turkish workers, assumed initially to be temporary, and it also received substantial immigration from Yugoslavia. At present five million French citizens are Muslims, mainly from North Africa. There are three million people in Germany with at least one parent of Turkish descent, approximately one-half are German citizens. Northern European countries also hosted large numbers of immigrants from Spain, Portugal, Greece, and Italy and, more recently, from Central and Eastern Europe.

Even under conditions of full employment, there was widespread and sometimes violent opposition to immigration. However, as resistance intensified in the context of recession and growing unemployment, the EU and member states gradually began to restrict illegal immigration. Although the Schengen Agreement of 1985 abolished internal border controls among participating member states, it also sought to harmonize controls over the community's external borders. In 1997 Schengen was incorporated into the Maastricht Treaty, thereby establishing as an *acquis* the principle of free movement for EU citizens as well as third parties with valid visas. The Maastricht Treaty established guidelines for asylum, borders, and immigrant entry under the Justice and Home Affairs pillar, thus defining asylum and migration as security issues (McMahon, 2015: pp. 292–5). The Dublin Convention, also incorporated into the Maastricht Treaty, decreed that asylum seekers could apply to only one member state and that the terms and conditions of asylum would remain the prerogative of the state. The Dublin II Regulation of 2003 mandated that an asylum application must be made in the first country in which a refugee arrives. The EU also applied transitional measures that temporarily restricted the rights of Bulgarians and Romanians to work following the 2007 accession. Finally, in 2004 the European Council established Frontex to conduct surveillance and coordinate national and EU policies towards the EU's 14,000 km border, deploying helicopters, naval vessels, and drones to combat smugglers, leading to a gradual process of militarization of the borders.

While these measures did little to prevent illegal immigration, they gave rise to the establishment of lucrative and dangerous trafficking operations which, since 2002, have been estimated to generate 16 billion euros (Migrants Files, 2015). The EU has prioritized sealing its borders – in part by paying neighbouring countries such as Turkey, Morocco, and Libya (before 2011) – to establish buffer zones. These zones, however, do not guarantee the rights of refugees, and they serve to erode refugee status. Most European states have not respected even minimum standards of asylum as codified in the Geneva Convention and the 1951 Refugee Convention. The EU has also made it virtually impossible for refugees to arrive legally at its borders; the Dublin system applies only when a refugee has reached a border. The absence of a coherent EU policy towards migrant rescue operations has placed the responsibility on those member states that are experiencing the rise of mass anti-immigration movements and anti-immigration parties and, in particular, on front line states in the Mediterranean that are experiencing austerity. These states have been demonstrably unable or unwilling to devote the resources to provide for safe passage across the Mediterranean and Aegean seas.

During the early 2000s, migration flows centred on Spain, as people from the Maghreb and from sub-Saharan Africa made the dangerous voyage across the Strait of Gibraltar; as Frontex operations increased in this area the geographical focus of would-be immigrants shifted to Italy, Malta, and Greece. The Arab Spring uprisings and subsequent interventions and civil wars sparked a significant increase in migration from the Middle East, southern Mediterranean, and sub-Saharan Africa. In 2015, however, in large part as a result of the intensification of the chaos and civil wars in Syria, Iraq, Afghanistan, Eritrea, and Libya, 1.3 million refugees entered the EU through six countries (Greece, Bulgaria, Italy, Spain, Malta, and Cyprus), the vast majority by sea, largely transited by smugglers. The flow of refugees was greatly encouraged by German Chancellor Angela Merkel's declaration in August 2015 to provide refuge to all Syrians as well as others fleeing from persecution and war. During 2015 more than 3700 people drowned in the Mediterranean Sea and a further 700 in the Aegean while 3200 perished in these seas during the first eight months of 2016. This human tragedy was dramatized by the body of a three-year-old Syrian boy found washed up on a Turkish beach and 71 dead bodies in a lorry in Austria. The largest numbers arrived from Syria, followed by Afghanistan and Iraq. However, the great majority of displaced people either remained within their own countries or within the region. Lebanon, Turkey, and Jordan have received almost four million Syrians. During 2015 Germany took in more than one million migrants, many coming from Balkan countries not counted in the sea of arrivals, and registered more than 316,000 asylum claims. However, Sweden registered by far the highest number of claims per capita, followed by Hungary and Austria (European Commission, 2015b). These numbers provoked a moral panic in Europe that threatens the basic principle of free movement and has greatly accelerated the rise of right-wing populism throughout the EU. CEE countries challenged Schengen rules. Poland and Hungary declared that Muslim asylum seekers would be rejected. In the summer of 2015, invoking emergency clauses in Schengen that allow for border closure 'in case of serious threat to public order or internal security', Hungary sealed off its border with Macedonia, followed by similar measures in Slovenia, Croatia, France, Germany, Austria, Sweden, and Denmark.

More generally, the political backlash against migration, reinforced in 2015 and 2016 by attacks in Brussels, Paris, and Nice and by widespread criminal and sexual assaults in Cologne, called into question the fundamental principle of free movement as enshrined in Schengen. The crisis illustrated clearly that within the present political environment, Schengen could survive only if the EU exerted centralized effective control over its border and the number of migrants was closely monitored and regulated. EU leaders and Chancellor Merkel warned that the EMU and Schengen are indivisible (*Financial Times*, 2016). The European Commission proposed amendments to the Dublin II Regulation, whereby the existing de facto abrogation of Schengen would be accepted in law: the first country that a refugee enters would no longer bear responsibility for shelter, and those granted asylum could be distributed throughout the member states. Frontex was replaced by a European Border and Coast Guard with vastly greater resources and centralized authority, including the right to apply intervention forces within member states. While these measures were intended to relieve frontline states and, in principle, provide a basis for the survival of Schengen, they were resisted by many member states. As noted in the introduction to this volume, in March 2016 the EU and Turkey agreed on a plan to reduce the flow of migrants from the MENA region to Europe. Migrants arriving illegally in Greece would be sent back to Turkey. For every such returned migrant, the EU agreed to grant one migrant in Turkey asylum in the EU. Notwithstanding the plan's many problematic ethical aspects and the willingness of Turkey to continue to abide by it, it is not clear that it will lead to a significant decline in migrants entering Europe. The plan capped the number of Syrians who can be sent to the EU at 72,000. The chief architect, Angela Merkel, has been notably unsuccessful in establishing quotas for each member state. Moreover, even if the plan can be enforced, there are many alternate routes to the EU, including

Albania, Bulgaria, the central Mediterranean route connecting North Africa and Italy, and the Caucasus. Indeed, by mid April of 2016 there was evidence of increasing migrant flows to Italy.

A de facto or de jure repeal of Schengen not only raises significant symbolic issues concerning European unity but would also have important consequences for the European economy. Enshrined in the Treaty of Paris in 1951 and then in the Treaty of Rome in 1958, the right to free movement has been considered the foundation of European identity and 'ever closer union'. However, its practical realization in the Schengen Agreement of 1985 was in important respects a reflection the transition of European capitalism to the post-Fordist era. There is in fact a significant degree of spillover from the single market and the monetary union to the free movement of labour and goods. Schengen was signed by France, Germany, and the Benelux states in 1985 to resolve the crisis caused by French and Italian customs workers who had deployed 'work to rule', thereby effectively restricting trade and labour mobility. Schengen thus also was a response in the functionalist sense to the growth of intra-Europe trade alongside labour mobility and, perhaps even more importantly, the development of German-dominated regional production chains. Reinstating internal border controls would impose massive costs on the European economy (France Strategie, 2016). These costs are especially relevant to German industry (Euractiv, 2016; European Parliament, 2016).

Yet, if reinstating border controls is a precondition of preserving Schengen, then at the same time, such a policy poses what is arguably an even more serious danger to Europe's long-range economic prospects and the fiscal viability of welfare states, and not least to Germany. Since the 1970s, Europe's demographic transition has resulted in an ageing population and low birth rates. By 2030 one in four Europeans will be 65 or older; in 2014 European women gave birth to an average of 1.6 children, well below the replacement rate of 2.1. Among the largest EU countries, the demographic crisis has hit Germany the hardest (IMF, 2016: pp. 30, 31). In 2010 EU Commissioners Cecilia Malmström and Laszlo Andor concluded that 'Europe will not survive without immigration', noting that Europe's working-age population was expected to shrink by 50 million by 2015 (European Voice, 2011). The demographic problem is most acute in areas such as Saxony, where anti-immigrant sentiments have discouraged investment (Handelsblatt, 2016). Chancellor Merkel's fateful invitation in August 2015 to Syrian refugees to come to Germany must be understood in this context. The potential contribution of Syrian refugees, whose educational levels may not be dissimilar to those of Germany (IMF, 2016: p. 17; Eakin, 2015; OECD, 2015b: p. 8) is clearly understood by German big business and think tanks as well as the IMF (IMF, 2016; IFO, 2015, 2016; Frantzscher, 2014, 2015; Connolly, 2015). Recognizing that the refugee flows provide an opportunity to increase labour market flexibility, the IMF and German business associations have called for the abolition of the minimum wage for refugees, effectively giving wage subsidies to companies (IMF, 2016: pp. 17–19).

In principle, refugee flows could be absorbed within an EU of 508 million people; the one million arrivals in 2015 represented less than 0.2 per cent of the EU population. Although the present situation is unprecedented in numbers, similar surges of immigration occurred after the fall of the Berlin Wall in 1989 and the wars of former Yugoslavia (OECD, 2015b). The problem is ultimately not numbers but rather capacity and political will. The present political climate characterized by deepening nationalism – clearly not anticipated by Chancellor Merkel in the summer of 2015 – thus makes it highly unlikely that migration can resolve Europe's demographic problems.

Emerging markets and emerging (?) powers

The role played by Chinese investments and presence in Africa on the EU's attempt to forge EPAs raises the broader question of the impact of emerging markets and emerging powers on the EU. The 'emerging market' concept arose as a result of the successful industrial development of the 'Asian Tigers' in the 1980s and the 1990s through a combination of export orientation and mercantilist industrial policy (Deyo, 1986). Similar developments in very large states in the 2000s suggested the possibility of emerging powers challenging the transatlantic terms of global hegemony.

The emerging global powers are usually referred to as the BRICS (Brazil, Russia, India, China, and South Africa), the acronym coined by Goldman Sachs economist Jim O'Neill in 2001 to generate investor interest in these countries. The term has gained a great deal of purchase because it represents what now is a self-conscious formal international political grouping. The members of the BRICS Forum have tried to articulate a distinct position based on the assumption that they are the avatars of a nascent global multi-polarity (Desai, 2015). In 2015, for example, the BRICS under Russia's presidency established a goal of achieving a fully-fledged mechanism of cooperation in the key issues of global economy and politics, including the New Development Bank and a foreign currency pool. Furthermore, some analysts suggest that these large states have some common institutional characteristics that allow us to talk about a distinct ideal type, namely a 'state-permeated market economy', based on foreign direct investments tempered by 'dense relationships between public authorities and major domestic enterprises' dominated by national capitalists and 'clan-based' coordination (Nölke, 2010: p. 3). Notwithstanding these considerations, the concept of BRICS is problematic because it deceptively attributes uniformity to radically different development trajectories and different state forms. It also overlooks significant underlying conflicts of interests among the BRICS. Furthermore, accounting for roughly two-thirds of the total 15 per cent BRICS contribution to global trade and now representing by some measures the largest economy in the world, China is clearly the towering giant among the BRICS.

To be sure, China and Russia have shown signs of greater cooperation. Russia is the leading exporter of sophisticated weapons and military technology to China. The two countries cooperate on some aspects of foreign policy, including voting in the UN Security Council where they generally defend state sovereignty principles and non-intervention. They participate in joint military manoeuvres through the Shanghai Cooperation Organization (SCO). In 2014, Russia and China concluded a $400 billion long-term contract for the delivery of natural gas to China, to be paid for in renminbi, although many questions remain concerning the terms of the contract and financing. Facing growing conflict with the EU and NATO, Russia has adopted a Eurasian strategy, seeking to reorient its economy and society towards Asia and the Pacific. Notwithstanding these instances of cooperation, it is not clear that China and Russia have much in common apart from being post-communist states with a fractious relationship with the West. As noted in Chapter 7, Russia will remain heavily dependent on oil and gas exports to Europe for years to come, as indicated by the proposed construction of Nord Stream II. This indicates a more general point that Russia and China are articulated in very different ways into the global capitalist order. China's extraordinarily rapid industrialization and dependence on the US market contrasts with Russia's partial deindustrialization following the collapse of the USSR. Russia is in economic terms arguably a declining power increasingly dependent on energy exports that appear to be in long-term decline.

Having moved closer to the United States in economic and strategic terms, and negotiating free trade arrangements with the EU on a strict mutual recognition basis (Khandekar, 2013), India has not sought to challenge the basic framework of transatlantic hegemony, although it has taken a strong stand against the United States and the EU in the WTO Doha negotiations. Having also challenged the EU and the US in the Doha Round, Brazil has been perhaps more assertive in seeking to develop closer regional ties. As is the case with respect to many ACP states as discussed above, EU initiatives to secure deeper trade-links with Brazil and the Latin Comun Mercado del Sur (MERCOSUR) failed in 2004 and 2011, and the 2007 Strategic Partnership agreement agreed between Brazil and the EU has not delivered much (Gratius, 2012). However, Brazil's assertiveness has been closely linked to developments in Asia and then especially the growth of the Chinese economy.

This is not only because Brazil is asserting itself through the BRICS Forum (Keukeleire et al., 2011). It is also because its model of development is increasingly dependent on exports of primary commodities and processed raw materials (such as cellulose, paper, cement, iron, and steel) to the Chinese economy (Gratius, 2012: p. 10; Nölke, 2010: p. 7). Indeed, with the partial exception of China, the impressive growth rate of the BRICS has been correlated to the rising price of commodities and may itself be a symptom of, rather than a challenge to, the US and the finance-led world economy. Since 2012, growth has slowed dramatically in all of the BRICS, tempting one analyst to suggest that, except for China, the appropriate phrase is 'forever emerging' (Sharma, 2012: p. 2).

The question of China

The challenge to the US-led transatlantic global hegemony is thus really about China. The late Giovanni Arrighi (2005a, 2005b), a critical political economist synthesizing more classical variants of Marxism with so-called world systems and neo-Gramscian theory, contended that China does in fact represent a significant challenge to what he called an 'unravelling' or 'terminal' American hegemony. Basing his conclusions on the historical and comparative analysis of American, British, and Dutch hegemony, Arrighi focused on the dialectical developments resulting from finance-led accumulation. Each of these hegemonic phases ended with a financial era. Like an ageing red star before it collapses and becomes a black hole, the financial era is in many respects the most spectacular period in the hegemonic cycle. But it is also the beginning of the end because the hegemon lives on borrowed time on the basis of rents accrued from the previous phase of industrial supremacy. Arrighi concluded that American finance-led capitalism will share the fate of its Dutch and British historical antecedents. Just as Britain displaced the Netherlands in the 17th century and emerged as hegemonic in the 19th, so the American and German states emerged as contenders in the late 19th century, and China now challenges the United States.

Theoretically, Arrighi's dialectic is indebted to the work of David Harvey (2003), who contrasts the 'molecular' logic of capital accumulation with the territorial logic of states. Finance-led capitalism has compelled the US to draw on its favourable position in finance and exchange relations to expand its territorial sphere of influence. That was especially so as it allowed the production of manufactured goods to be increasingly subcontracted to East Asia and above all China. However, in the long term this has allowed China to develop a highly productive economy itself, upon which the US is dependent. Therefore, it might become more difficult for the US to service the cavernous current account deficit and, more generally, to manage the increasingly complex, intricate, and vulnerable territorial arrangements upon which it is based.

This analysis has much in common with neo-realist or 'basic force' models of power projection and hegemonic leadership (Friedberg, 2011). In 2013 President Xi Jinping asserted that China should be treated as an equal in a 'new kind of great power relationship', a statement widely interpreted as bringing an end to the phase of China's relative deference and representing a direct challenge to American hegemony in both economic and geopolitical terms. China has taken limited steps to diminish American naval primacy in the western Pacific by claiming sovereignty over islands constructed on coral reefs in the South China Sea and developing a 'blue water navy' that includes aircraft carriers. The government-sponsored 'Silk Road' or 'one belt one road' initiative seeks to create a comprehensive system of land and sea routes between Europe and Asia – including ports, pipelines, railways, and power stations. It has included multibillion-dollar loans to Kenya, Cambodia, Myanmar, Thailand, and Laos for infrastructure projects. In addition, China has provided $5.5 billion to the Ecuadoran government for infrastructure and $4.7 billion to Argentina for hydroelectric projects. China has also been very active in purchasing privatized Greek assets (Bermingham, 2015).

While state policy is decisively influenced by the interests of economically dominant groups, the state is nevertheless understood by realists as analytically distinct or external to the economy. One corollary of this assumed externality is that the national economy provides basic resources that the state converts to state power. Hence, realists point to China's status as the world's largest economy in terms of GDP at purchase power parity (PPP) as a key indicator of emergent Chinese pre-eminence. Caveats are issued with respect to contingencies of policymaking and to diminishing returns of China's export-oriented development model and attendant risks for social instability. However, provided that these challenges can be surmounted, China can convert economic capabilities into military capabilities should it perceive a US threat to contain its rise. Some predict that Chinese military expenditure could equal that of the US in 20 years (Casarini, 2012: pp. 4–5). In monetary affairs, China is challenging US capabilities by diversifying out of the dollar and into the euro and by promoting the international role of the renminbi in pursuit of a multipolar monetary order (Casarini, 2012: p. 9).

The rise of China has important implications for the EU and for the transatlantic relationship. These include the potential political effects of Chinese foreign direct investments in Europe, whereby China is assumed to increase its leverage in the EU (e.g. Brown, 2012). Chinese portfolio investments and diversification into the euro, on the other hand, might actually serve to increase the EU's power in world affairs insofar as it would make the euro a challenger to the top-currency status of the dollar (Eichengreen, 2011). While working in different directions with regard to the EU's autonomy and power, these

developments would be corrosive to the economic and political foundations of Atlanticism and by extension US hegemony. Notably, China has
also played a role in Eurozone crisis management through the acquisi-
tion of hard assets, especially as collateral for investment in Eurozone
bond markets (Steinbok, 2012). Finally, Beijing has preferred to negotiate with individual European states outside of EU structures. This has
been especially evident in China's 'special relationship' with Germany,
whose trade patterns are gradually shifting from Europe to Asia and
the growing Chinese market for capital goods (Kundnani & Parello-
Plesner, 2012). For these reasons, EU states failed to heed American
objections and subscribed to the Chinese-sponsored Asian Industrial
Development Bank (AIIB). The EU is strongly considering granting
China 'market economy' status, again over Washington's objections. In
December 2015 the United States agreed to include the renminbi in the
IMF's special drawing rights, a clear demonstration of China's growing economic power. At the same time, European companies are much
less integrated with China than are US companies. The former have
not taken advantage of the potentials that the Chinese market offers in
terms of production capacity to the same extent as American or Asian
firms. European companies have used China mainly as a marketplace
for final sale, rather than as a site for 'processing-trade' and value-added
augmentation through commodity chains (Coriat, 2009: p. 228).

Thus, although predictions of the EU's own superpower status that
arose in the context of the EMU have not been borne out, as a result
of the rise of China and other BRICS, it has become an article of faith
that global economic power is shifting from the Atlantic area to the
East and the South, or to 'a world without the West' (Barma, Ratner,
& Weber, 2007). The thesis of American hegemonic decline has been
a mainstay of Western scholarship in the field of international political
economy for more than 40 years (e.g. Gilpin, 1987; Keohane, 1984;
Kennedy, 1988). However, the thesis is not consistent with a large body
of empirical evidence based on more conceptually sophisticated assumptions concerning global power in the contemporary era of globalization.
As noted above, the empirical evidence for China's hegemonic ascent
relies primarily on inferences drawn from long-range trends in GDP
and exports. However, although the assumption that national power
can be inferred from national accounts made sense in previous historical periods, it may be highly misleading in a world characterized by the
globalization of not only financial but also productive capital (Starrs,
2013, 2014) and in which the strategies of the leading powers, not least
the hegemonic power, are based on the establishment of multinational
production chains enabling them to outsource labour while maintaining ultimate control over the production process.

Sean Starrs has illustrated the limitations of the realist 'basic force'
model by comparing China's ascent with that of Japan. During the

1960s and 1970s, Japan's massive exports of automobiles and electronics to the West resulted not only in a rising trade surplus and growing GDP but also the strengthening of Japan's corporations on a global scale. The situation for China is very different. In 2010 three-quarters of China's top 200 exporting companies were foreign owned, and 90 per cent of China's high-technology exports are produced by foreign-owned corporations (Starrs, 2014: pp. 88–90; Coriat, 2009: pp. 224–6). In the crucial electronics sector, for example, China's profit share is 3 per cent compared to 25 per cent for Taiwanese companies and 33 per cent for US companies (Starrs, 2014: p. 91). American firms continue to hold a commanding position over global supply chains and the highest value aspects of production. Apple's iPad is perhaps emblematic in this regard: Entirely designed and owned by Apple, a US corporation, iPads are assembled in China by Foxconn, a Taiwanese firm. The total production cost of the iPad adds $275 to the American trade deficit with China, but the cost to Foxconn of the value added in China is only $10. In 2011 iPads added $4 billion to the US trade deficit with China, but only $150 million if measured on a value-added basis. Regarding profits, Apple receives 30 per cent of the sales price and other US firms another 20 per cent. The South Korean firms Samsung and LG receive another 7 per cent. The financial benefit to China is largely the wages paid to Chinese workers representing 2 per cent of the sales price (*Economist*, 2011b).

To be sure, these data must be treated cautiously. China's developmental trajectory cannot be described within the terms of dependency theory, and its ruling elite is by no means a 'comprador class'. Nevertheless, China's staggering rate of growth has been based in no small part on subordination to global production chains. US (and European and Japanese) firms have outsourced production – and environmental degradation – to China, even as they retain control over technology and the labour process. A significant Chinese challenge to US hegemony would require it to develop world-class corporations. A precondition of this turn would be a massive leap in indigenous innovation for which there is very little evidence (e.g. Starrs, 2014: pp. 92–5).

These significant weaknesses are in some respects linked to underlying structural problems in the Chinese economy that may also prove to be a limiting factor in China's rise (Norloff, 2014; Overbeek, 2016). China's extraordinary ascent has been fuelled by massive public investment flowing from state banks and unregulated 'shadow banks' into construction, heavy industry, and infrastructure. This investment boom has generated massive overcapacity, unsustainable debt levels, and a series of speculative bubbles: first in infrastructure, real estate, and property, and then in the stock market. This process bears certain comparisons to Japan's experience during the 1980s and 1990s (Murphy, 2014). The shift to a more consumption-based economy is not, however, a technical matter but would require sharp political attacks on strongly entrenched elites in the export sector based in the Ministry of Finance and local party and state organizations in the coastal provinces (Hung Ho Fung, 2009, 2013). It would also drive corporations to countries offering even cheaper labour, a process that is already taking place. China's extraordinary stimulus of 2008 was supposed to spearhead this transition, but the vast majority of the stimulus flowed into infrastructure instead. The massive 'one belt one road' projects arguably represent an extension and consolidation of Chinese status quo rather than transition.

There has been a great deal of speculation concerning the possibility of the Chinese challenging the dollar as the international reserve currency. However, in this respect Chinese policymakers have been very cautious, setting very modest aims with regard to the international role of the renminbi and in terms of influencing the development of global financial markets (Bao, 2013). It is true that China is keen to diversify the portfolio of its reserves from the dollar into the euro, in order to escape the 'Dollar Trap'. However, in the absence of Eurobonds and a liquid integrated Eurobond market, this becomes a self-defeating strategy, and hence the limited global ambitions of the EMU constrains the extent to which China can obtain leverage vis-à-vis the US or indirectly propel the EU into contender status. The dollar derives its reserve currency status not primarily because of its role in international trade but rather as a result of the size and depth of US financial markets. At the most, the euro demonstrates that a transnational currency can be forged, which may in the long run motivate Chinese designs for an Asian monetary union and a global system based on special drawing rights (Otero-Iglesias, 2014). However, in the foreseeable future, one is above all struck by the limits of the Chinese challenge to dollar hegemony (Norloff, 2014: esp. chapter 5; Schwartz, 2016). Notwithstanding the renminbi's inclusion in the IMF's special drawing rights, China's financial and bond markets are underdeveloped and highly unstable. China's ascent is unmistakable but unpredictable. The United States' ambitious trade initiatives represent an attempt to contain it and channel it within the US hegemonic orbit.

TTIP: consolidation of the Atlanticist bloc?

The more assertive role played by emerging economies in international trade negotiations has been symbolized by the eclipse of the G7/8 by the G20, a much larger and more representative group of countries, and the modest rebalancing of voting rights in the IMF. However, the Doha Round of WTO negotiations, initiated in the aftermath of 9/11, has stalled amid US and EU reluctance to abandon agricultural protectionism and resistance on the part of the Global South to the liberalization of services. After some hesitation, both the United States and the EU Commission have fully embraced and, indeed, spearheaded the trend towards 'megaregional' trade agreements (Siles-Brugge, 2014).

At the Nairobi WTO meeting in 2015, the United States officially called for the Doha Round to be terminated. The new regime envisioned by Washington is based on three prospective trade agreements. In addition to the TTIP, the TISA is arguably the largest component of Atlanticist neoliberal strategy, embracing 51 countries and all of the advanced capitalist economies. Services account for 80 per cent of the US economy and 75 per cent of the EU economy. The TISA represents an extension of the WTO's General Agreement on Trade in Services, including further liberalization of financial services, healthcare, education, engineering, and telecommunications. The Trans-Pacific Partnership, embracing 11 Pacific countries – including the United States, Japan, and South Korea – and 40 per cent of global GDP, resembles the TTIP in its deregulatory effects but would also serve to divert trade and investment towards a US bloc in South East Asia.

In its 2006 communication entitled 'Global Europe: Competing in the World', the EU Commission directorate-general for trade asserted that while multilateral trade liberalization remained the EU's main objective, bilateral agreements should also be sought. This strategy, the precursor in many respects to the TTIP, is notable also for introducing the competitiveness discourse directly into EU trade policy. The communication 'explicitly linked Europe's economic well-being to its ability to *compete* in the global economy. In doing so, policymakers were invoking the ideas embodied by the Lisbon Agenda of competitiveness' (Siles-Brugge, 2014: p. 3). Thus since the advent of the Doha Round, the EU has signed bilateral agreements with a host of countries, including Mexico, South Korea, and Chile. The Canada–EU Comprehensive Economic and Trade Agreement (CETA) that was agreed on in February 2016 and is expected to come into effect in 2017 serves as a template for the TTIP.

Although the TTIP has provoked massive opposition, especially in Europe, the support given to it by the EU Commission, member state governments led by Germany, and transnational capital on both sides of the Atlantic indicates that there is a great deal of momentum towards a further 'deep and comprehensive' integration of the transatlantic economy in some institutional form. Since the mid 1990s, big business on both sides of the Atlantic has called for closer economic integration. The Transatlantic Business Dialogue composed of chief executives of major US and European corporations was created in 1995 to advocate the removal of remaining trade barriers and the harmonization of regulations, and in 2007 it called for the establishment of a Euro-Atlantic free trade area. The TTIP constitutes a joint US-European economic strategy to further liberalize labour and product markets, both domestically and throughout the world with all the trappings of new constitutionalism locking in state commitments and sealing the agreements from democratic deliberation (de Ville & Siles-Brugge, 2015). TTIP also has important geopolitical implications insofar as closer transatlantic cooperation is viewed as a means of confronting the growing challenges from the BRICS, especially China (Rosecrance, 2013; Kundnani, 2015b; Telis, 2014), envisioned by then-Secretary of State Hillary Clinton as an 'economic NATO' (Ignatius, 2012).

The transatlantic space represents by far the most important 'region' in the global economy. In 2015 the United States and EU accounted for 35 per cent of global GDP, 25 per cent of global exports, and 30 per cent of global imports. US–EU merchandise trade was $600 billion in 2014, twice the level of 2000. However, a focus on trade greatly understates the nature and scope of transatlantic integration. In 2014 FDI flows across the Atlantic outpaced those to China by a factor of 10. The sales of US-owned foreign affiliates in Europe were greater than US exports to the world, and 60 per cent of US imports consisted of intra-firm trade, compared to 30 per cent of US exports to Europe. The United States runs a substantial trade deficit with the EU, offset by a surplus in services (Hamilton & Quinlan, 2014, 2016). The TPP accounts for a further 30 per cent of global GDP. Together, these two US-centred pacts would account for 65 per cent of global GDP and exports, 80 per cent of weapons-related spending, and 90 per cent of weapons-related research and development (Hamilton & Quinlan, 2014).

From the point of view of American corporations, liberalization provides opportunities for further penetration into the European market, especially in politically sensitive sectors such as agriculture, services, and public procurement. It would further consolidate transatlantic ties in the military-industrial sector. A similar logic applies to the large European banks and corporations, whose long-range growth strategies remain focused on the American marketplace. The EU Commission also seeks to protect its own more liberalized banking regulations, thus allowing European banks to operate in the United States according to national and EU rules. The EU has now begun to import liquid natural gas from the United States; the US Congress recently repealed legislation restricting oil exports, a key objective of the EU.

Thus, the TTIP also serves as a joint US-European neoliberal strategy, ultimately designed to deregulate labour and product markets not only in the transatlantic space but throughout the rest of the world (de Ville & Siles-Brugge, 2015). It would have significant implications for the survival of the WTO and, more generally, the principle of a multilateral trading order. Standing at the centre of two exclusive rings, the United States (with Europe in tow) could set standards for world trade to which BRICS and the rest of the world would be compelled to adjust not unlike the Cobden–Chevalier Treaty in the 19th century under British hegemony. The intent of these pacts is not to *exclude* the rest of the world but rather to incorporate them into the global division of labour on Western terms. As President Obama said of the TPP, 'When more than 95 per cent of our potential customers live outside our borders, we can't let countries like China write the rules of the global economy. We should write those rules' (*Financial Times*, 2015).

The methodological approach of mainstream studies of the impact of TTIP bear an uncanny resemblance to previous studies of the SEM and the EMU, all of which greatly exaggerated the benefits for employment and growth (see Chapters 1, 3, and 4; Scott, 2003; Boltho & Eichengreen, 2008; de Ville & Siles-Brugge, 2015). The two most prominent studies of the TTIP conducted by the Centre for European Policy Research (2013) and the Bertelsmann Foundation (2013) estimate respectively that a 'deep liberalization' scenario of TTIP would lead to 0.5 per cent (CEPR) or 5.7 per cent (Bertelsmann) additional growth by 2027 along with very modest increases in employment. Bertelsmann predicts a 'strong increase in trade flows between Germany and the USA' (pp. 13, 14; Table 1) and also that Germany's trade with many other countries and regions would decline significantly. This is because trade among EU members is barrier-free while US–EU trade is subject to both trade and non-trade barriers. Increased transatlantic integration would significantly raise German exports to Japan and the BRICS because the availability of cheaper intermediate products from the USA would increase the competitiveness of German firms. At the same time, German trade with China would decline by 13 per cent and its imports from the other BRICS would also decline significantly. Finally, trade between the member countries of the southern Eurozone and Germany would decrease substantially, accelerating a process that was set in motion by the crisis; in 2012 Greece ranked 44th among German trading partners, just behind Vietnam. In sum, the TTIP might increase Germany's (and the EU's) dependence on the transatlantic economy while actually having a disintegrative effect on the EU.

Both of these studies employed a general equilibrium model that assumed that a new macroeconomic equilibrium would automatically be reached after trade had been liberalized and that more competitive sectors of the economy would absorb all of the resources – including labour – released by the shrinking sectors. Conclusions based on these assumptions need to be treated with great caution. More recently, Jeronim Capaldo (2014) obtained very different results by assuming that employment and growth are driven through demand rather than based on productive efficiency and by factoring in assumptions about the path of the real economy in different regions: for example, fiscal austerity. He concluded that the impact of TTIP on Europe would be very negative, including significant reductions in employment, net losses in GDP, loss of labour income, a reduction in the labour share of GDP, a reduction of government revenue, and greater financial instability:

> With export revenues, wage shares, and government revenues decreasing, demand would have to be sustained by profits and investment. But with flagging consumption growth, profits cannot be expected to come from growing sales. A more realistic assumption is that profits and investment (mostly in financial assets) will be sustained by growing asset prices. The potential for macroeconomic stability of this growth strategy is well known after the recent financial crisis. (Capaldo, 2014: p. 3)

The negotiations over the TTIP have been protracted and contentious (Siles-Brugge, 2014), and the outcome is very unclear. Conducted under a shroud of secrecy that has served only to deepen suspicions, they have provoked intense domestic opposition among NGOs, trade unions, environmental groups, and other civil-society groups on both sides of the Atlantic, but especially in Europe. The key issues of concern include the further liberalization of agriculture, especially with respect to genetically modified organisms; the liberalization of public procurement as a means of privatizing key sectors of the welfare state, including social services, healthcare, and education; 'investor-state dispute settlement' (ISDS) clauses (suspended in January 2015) that would limit the scope of national laws and courts and would thereby greatly enhance corporate power; the deregulation of banking, including trading in derivatives; and also the fallout from revelations concerning US surveillance, especially in Germany. Although the TTIP (and CETA) is commonly referred to as a *trade* pact, the overall impact on trade through the removal or reduction of regulatory and other nontariff barriers is likely to be relatively modest (although important for given sectors). The average US tariff is 3.5 per cent and the average EU tariff is 5.2 per cent. Unlike traditional trade pacts such as those concluded under GATT and NAFTA, the TTIP derives its significance from 'behind the border' policies: the removal or reduction of regulatory and other nontariff barriers, where the effect on economy and society is potentially far-reaching and radical.

It is notable that, compared to previous liberalization projects, such as the SEM and the EMU, the TTIP has elicited much greater opposition and mobilization in civil society, especially among trade unions, NGOs, and environmental groups, not least in Germany. NGOs and trade unions have challenged key assumptions of corporate- and Commission-sponsored studies on the impact of the TTIP. Hundreds of thousands have marched and demonstrated against the agreement and millions have signed petitions against the TTIP directed to the European Commission.

Indeed, anti-TTIP fervour contrasts significantly with the rather more muted support of civil-society groups over the EU's austerity policies with respect to the Mediterranean member states, as exemplified by Syriza's lonely struggles against the Troika. One explanation for this is that opposition in the EU to previous neoliberal initiatives – such as the single market, various fiscal pacts, and competitiveness agenda – and austerity programmes has been discouraged though appeals to 'Europeanization' reinforced by anti-Americanism. The TTIP, by contrast, can hardly be marketed as a 'European' project.

Deeper transatlantic integration, whether in the shape of a TTIP or more modest institutional forms, would thus appear to represent for the EU the next logical step in a process of neoliberal consolidation that started with the SEM and the EMU. It represents a strategy designed to resolve the problems of stagnation through competitiveness patterned on the model of German export mercantilism and, more generally, further accumulation via dispossession, as we will argue in the conclusion. However, not only does the strategy have to reckon with the rising tide of nationalism in Europe, but it also depends on exports into a world market that is full of uncertainties and tending towards slower growth and competitive devaluations.

Conclusion

Liberalism and realism struggle theoretically to make sense of the overall trend in the EU's relations with the Global South since decolonization, and especially the transition in development strategy that took place in the 1980s. Liberalism finds it hard to understand on its own terms the economic nationalism and protectionism of the 1950s and 1960s, and realism has difficulty coming to terms with the neoliberal direction of policies since the 1980s. By contrast, this chapter has shown that critical political economy can elucidate how the dynamics of Fordism established a structure of dependency that the newly independent states – and their allies within the social and Christian-left – sought to counter, albeit with limited success. The era of finance-led accumulation made it imperative for core states to open up markets in the periphery, and liberalization and SAPs were fit for purpose. EU-level arrangements and policies were not the primary ones in this context, but Lomé, Cotonou, EuroMed, and bilateral free trade agreements all played a significant role in this context. In a post-WTO world, the joint EU–US project of the TTIP alongside the TPP and TISA would serve to consolidate all of these relationships.

The rise of the BRICS, and China in particular, clearly constitutes a challenge to US-led transatlantic hegemony of which the EU of course forms a part. However, we ultimately took a sceptical view of the 'basic-resource' model that has been advanced primarily by realists but also some critical political economists who are sanguine about the rise of China and the fall of the United States. A more consistently structural reading of the relationship between capital, the state, and power suggests a more cautious assessment, a topic to which we will return in the conclusion.

It seems appropriate against this backdrop to end with a few words about what our assessment says about the EU as a 'normative power' – a concept that has been advanced by constructivist scholars in security studies and which also has been embraced in official EU self-description. Proponents of this concept advance an argument that is not unlike Barroso's aforementioned notion of the EU's benign imperium: although the EU lacks significant military capabilities, it exerts influence through norm diffusion and decouples actions and policies from narrow material interests (Manners, 2002, 2008). Perhaps the clearest statement in support of Europe as a normative superpower is that by Andrew Moravscik (2002: p. 12):

> Europeans already wield effective power over peace and war as great as that of the United States, but they do so quietly through 'civilian power' [which] does not lie in the development of battalions or bombs, but rather in the quiet promotion of democracy and development through trade, foreign aid and peace-making.

To be sure, the leading proponents of the normative power concept might reject a sharp dichotomy between norms and interests and are quite amenable to the proposition that normative power operates in a way akin to the Gramscian notion of hegemony (Manners, 2010). Even so, our analysis in this chapter, as well that of Chapter 6, on the EU's relations with its eastern and southern flanks throws a very harsh spotlight on the concept of 'normative power Europe'. When the concept of normative power is deployed ideologically and is seen as being in opposition to material self-interest – the idea of the EU as an altruistic force for good – then it is deeply problematic (see also de Zutter, 2010). When structural adjustment policies from the Washington Consensus are added to a list that includes trade and aid policies, migration, and European military interventions in the Middle East and Maghreb, it is evident that where significant amounts of blood and treasure are at stake, the universalist, altruistic, and emancipatory potentials of EU norm diffusion are sacrificed on the altar of capitalism and geopolitics.

Conclusion: The Ordoliberal Iron Cage

On the eve of the global financial crisis, most observers considered Europe's prospects for closer economic and political integration to be virtually limitless. The reality that the single market had failed to deliver on economic growth (see Chapter 3), reservations about structural and institutional flaws in the EMU design (see Chapter 4), and the EU's growing economic and political subordination to the American superpower (see especially Chapter 7) received very little attention from official European or establishment economists and political scientists. Indeed, as late as 2009 – one year into the global financial crisis – a study sponsored by the European Commission epitomized the stunning hubris and intellectual complacency within the academic world of EU studies.

> This unparalleled experiment in monetary unification is a milestone in the European integration process. By now, the euro has emerged as a major currency, even challenging the U.S. dollar as the global reserve currency. In a very short period of time, it has transformed the European economic and political landscape. Never before have sovereign nation states surrendered their national currencies to a common central bank, abstaining from monetary sovereignty. In short, the euro is one of the most exciting experiments in monetary history. (Jonung & Drea, 2009: p. 1)

Similarly, the directors of the prestigious Peterson and Bruegel Institutes proclaimed at a high profile event organized to mark the first decade of the euro that

> In the midst of the greatest financial crisis of the last 70 years, the world's only transnational major currency has delivered price stability to the people of the euro-area, retained its value in international markets, and proven capable of weathering the storm – which at present came from internal as well as external asset price bursts and imbalances. While a few increasingly shrill and lonely naysayers remain, the euro has amply demonstrated its sustainability. (Pisani-Ferri & Posen, 2009: p. v)

These glowing assessments – steeped in the teleological thinking accounted for in Chapter 1 – of the future prospects of Europe's monetary union were accompanied by corresponding confidence in Europe's growing geopolitical profile. The enlargements of 2004 and 2007 alongside European Partnership programmes propelled the EU across the entire European continent and into territories of the former Soviet Union (see Chapter 6). Ambitious new programmes were also being developed for Maghreb and the Middle East (see Chapter 8). If the EU was not a traditional superpower or a traditional empire, it might be considered, in Barroso's words, a normative one.

From this we can infer two emphatically positive answers to the questions that we posed in the Introduction to this book. Servan-Shreiber and Willy Brandt may well have been dead and buried for a long time and Jacques Delors' vision of welfare supranationalism was passé and ultimately misguided. Furthermore, there were problems of implementation of activation-inducing policies in individual member states. Nevertheless, the single market, the monetary union, and the Lisbon Agenda were facilitating a rational 'self-transformation' of national European welfare states, making them more fit for the terms of global competitiveness (Hemerijck, 2002). Taking Robert Kagan's (2003) insult as a compliment, if the US was from Mars, then Europe was now from Venus and normative-power Europe could indeed be seen as *post*-imperialist.

But developments have cruelly exposed these Panglossian assessments. They register Europe's own instances of massive and tragic blow-back (Johnson, 2001) – the Eurozone crisis, the migration crisis, and the geopolitical conflagration of the civil war in Ukraine – shedding a less flattering light on Europe's second, neoliberal project of integration. This book has made the case for considering the EU from the perspective of critical theory. Such a perspective, we believe, offers a deeper and more comprehensive understanding of the forces that have brought the EU to the situation it finds itself today, and one which provides an entirely different answer to the questions posed.

On the question of whether the EU is part of the solution to the challenges posed by globalization so as to protect and extend the achievements of the social-market economy, the answer is not only negative. Whatever benefits 'another Europe' could contribute on that score (see below); it is becoming increasingly clear that the 'real existing Europe' is part of the problem. The compensatory welfare mechanisms that the EU offers are not only inadequate in relation to the challenge that globalisation poses for social citizenship in Europe, as Chapters 5 and 6 showed. Attempting to manage the Eurozone crisis within the parameters of the finance-led capitalism that caused it, the New Economic Governance accounted for in Chapter 4 is subjecting European societies to further bouts of privatization and commodification. What is more, this is done through increasingly authoritarian means. Draconian austerity programmes aggravate simmering conflicts between east and west and north and south as the Brussels–Berlin axis replaces the velvet glove of the 'open method of coordination' with an iron fist. It is in this context that one should pose the problem of the increasingly fraught equation of capitalism and democracy in Europe today. Authoritarian tendencies in Europe, such as the rise of the far right, may not be reducible to this, but nor can these tendencies be seen, as the integration telos would, as something external to 'integration'.

We have demonstrated in this book that this mode of crisis management reflects German priorities as conditioned by an enduring European subordination to American leadership. Indeed, the US Federal Reserve played a decisive role in avoiding Eurozone collapse. It is no small irony that the US Treasury and the IMF have sought unsuccessfully to soften the Troika's draconian austerity policies, and that the epicentre of global neoliberalism is now the Berlin–Brussels axis. The negative answer to the second question posed – Can Europe's 'soft power' be seen as a radical break with and transcendence of its imperial past? – follows as a corollary to this. As detailed in Chapters 6 through 8, at best the EU projects soft power is a complement to American hard power in a broader strategy of imperial control of the world economy. Again, though the outcome cannot be reduced to this, structural adjustment policies pursued in Partnership Programmes, Neighbourhood Programmes, and trade negotiations, have played central roles in generating the crises in Ukraine and the Middle East. The spike of food prices generated by financial speculation was a key proximate cause to the Arab Spring, which despite its initial promise, generated a tragic chain of events that – in conjunction with Western interventions – have brought about the migration crisis. The brutal conflicts between rival oligarchs in Ukraine are in the last instance a symptom of primitive accumulation, and hence not disconnected from the extensive nature of finance-led growth (Yurchenko, 2012).

Thus the dream of a superpower, postmodern or otherwise, has given way to a nightmare of disintegration and struggle for survival. From the perspectives of both widening and deepening, Europe is experiencing profound centrifugal tendencies. The US-led transatlantic order is experiencing challenges in the form of a rising China as well as its ability to restore global financial stability and growth. With respect to Europe, the post-Cold War system that saw NATO/EU expansion into the former sphere of an acquiescent Russia has ended. Tensions have arisen over Ukraine, a tremendously significant economic and geopolitical state, and sanctions have greatly damaged both the Russian and EU economies. The United States has expanded significantly its military presence in Central and Eastern Europe. The EU's energy strategy towards Russia has also greatly exacerbated conflicts between Germany and new member states. At the same time, as the previous chapter indicated, Chancellor Merkel's de facto suspension of the Dublin Accords and invitation to (mostly) Syrian refugees set off a firestorm of unintended consequences that will torment Europe for years to come. Each of these crises has a distinctive logic, but one common denominator is the collapse of Franco-German shared leadership and the central role played by German power.

If the integration telos has been extinguished, it is not yet clear whether these crises will result in an actual breakup of the Union. Leading EU politicians, from Merkel to Draghi to Juncker, have warned that each is existential for the EU and that the death of Schengen would destroy the monetary union. What is certain is that the EU will not last much longer in its present configuration. Various scenarios for exits and multi- and two-speed 'variable geometry' are discussed – and even endorsed by leading national politicians and EU officials – but each contains contradictions and dangers (Euractiv, 2015). The crises over Ukraine and migration are in principle susceptible to resolution. Our assessment of the Eurozone crisis – the epicentre of a deeper crisis of capitalist regulation – is more sombre. The analysis presented in Chapter 4 has shown, we believe, the superiority of critical political economy for understanding the origins and evolution of the crisis of the Eurozone. Therefore, it is appropriate to conclude this book by asking what this theoretical perspective has to say about resolving it.

Another Eurozone? Another Europe?

Current Eurozone crisis management and New Economic Governance are informed by ordoliberalism as a particular variant of neoliberalism. Ordoliberalism provides an ideological point of reference for moral and intellectual leadership (Gramsci, 1971: p. 181) that distances rule from the corporate-economic interests served by engendering an intersubjective framework for deliberation in the EU over the general economic good. The theory of ordoliberalism emerged out of the crisis of interwar Weimar Germany. It postulates that market society does not emerge spontaneously but that its autopoiesis must be politically framed by constitution-like rules. Hence, it is a theory of how market society can be depoliticized through politics and attendant entrepreneurial socialization through what it calls *Vitalpolitik* (Bonefeld, 2012b). While historical change in ordoliberalism can be debated, there are essential features that continue to give intellectual content to Eurozone crisis management. When translated into stylized tropes such as Merkel as the prudent 'Swabian housewife', it also elicits popular appeal in Northern European civil societies that have enjoyed export-oriented recoveries (Young, 2011). Such tropes played a crucial role in recasting the narrative of the financial crisis from one of dysfunctional financial markets to one of public finances and competitiveness (Heinrich & Kutter, 2014). Ordoliberalism has long informed EU governance, notably in competition and monetary policy (Gerber, 1998; Dyson & Featherstone, 1999). In current crisis management, it influences the disciplinary conditionalities as codified in New Economic Governance.

As Chapter 4 showed, heterodox economists working in the interfaces of the post-Keynesian and Marxist traditions deserve credit for having identified the emergent properties and mechanisms that generated the Eurozone crisis (see especially Stockhammer, 2008). They have also issued warnings against the ordoliberal Eurozone crisis management based on achieving export-led recoveries in the states in crisis – in other words, a one-sided adjustment of the deficit countries. Formal econometric projections that such adjustment would require the equivalent of two 1930s-style depressions can perhaps be debated. Depreciation of the euro and lower oil prices have no doubt mitigated the situation in recent years, although the former has served to export austerity. Nevertheless, they do point to a formidable impasse, and while the outright monetary transactions programme announced in 2012 and the belated ECB quantitative easing have seen off an imminent collapse, the banking system and economy cannot, eight years into the crisis, manage without life support.

In that context, critical political economists have offered widely discussed policy alternatives. For example, the Euromemorandum Group (e.g. 2014, 2015), calls for the mutualization of debt (Eurobonds), EU-wide industrial policy, fiscal transfer payments and a substantially larger EU budget, EU-wide capital controls, EU-wide wage coordination norms, a common expansionary fiscal policy, and external policies that require collective European agency such as new approaches to Association Agreements and the WTO, and a rejection of the TTIP, at least in its present form. Macroeconomic projections suggest that these policies would result in higher, more evenly, and environmentally more sustainable development (Eatwell, McKinley, & Petit, 2014).

However attractive these alternatives would be, notably connecting one way or another with the spirits of Servan-Shreiber and Brandt, there are two fundamental problems with proposals such as these. First, these highly federalist alternatives raise questions about the normative public order that could legitimate them. Second, conceiving existing crisis management simply in terms of 'policy mistakes' is problematic. A given policy might have more method to its madness. The rationality of a policy depends on the interests and objectives that it serves.

Regarding the first problem, the leading European critical theorist of our times, Jürgen Habermas, offers a compelling vision of 'constitutional patriotism' (1992, 2001). Whether one subscribes to prevailing crisis management or the heterodox alternative, he calls for federal legitimating institutions that can either overrule national systems of democratic representation in the name of economic discipline or that can legitimate economic federalism.

Habermas, in other words, proposes a European constitution that replaces current treaty structures. Such a constitution would have merits not only based on the letter of the law. More important, it would serve as a point of reference for a post-national public sphere, where 'conventional' norms and modes of attachment, most notably nationalism, would be replaced by post-conventional norms. Such norms challenge ('discursively thematize') not only nationalism but also traditional 'received wisdoms' about the social roles of men and women in gender relations and human domination over the environment. Populated by a broad range of civil society associations, such a post-conventional public sphere would furnish the euro-polity with enhanced reflexive capacities to meet challenges of social regulation.

However, with regard to the second question, Habermas has very little to offer. At an earlier stage of his career, Habermas drew on dramatic tragedy to define crisis as a turning point in a fateful process:

> Fate is fulfilled in the revelation of conflicting norms against which the identities of the participants shatter, unless they are able to summon up the strength to win back their freedom by shattering the mythical power of fate through the formation of new identities. (Habermas, 1975: p. 2)

A progressive European fiscal federalism such as that outlined by the Euromemorandum Group and embedded in a European constitutional patriotism (Habermas) or sovereign and democratic pan-European Parliament as called for by Yanis Varoufakis' Democracy in Europe Movement 2025 (DIEM25, 2016) would certainly represent a 'winning back of freedom' from the 'mythical power' of disciplinary neoliberalism, or ordoliberalism. But there is no compelling account of how the real balance of social forces has created the conditions for the agency required to 'summon' the requisite 'strength'. To be sure, there is enough critical sentiment in Habermas and Varoufakis to rage against the injustices of the financial crisis and the 'business as usual' of conventional party politics. However, this is overshadowed by the increasingly Kantian influence on both that leads to a reading of the drivers of European integration that is not unlike traditional political sociology accounted for in Chapter 1, and it produces a rather fanciful overestimation of the transnational capacities of power mobilization of post-conventional civil society organizations. One wonders whether the following passage was written by Habermas or Haas:

> Expanding and intensifying markets or communication networks ignite a modernisation dynamic of opening and closure. The proliferation of anonymous relations with 'others' and the dissonant experience with 'foreigners' have a subversive power. Growing pluralism

loosens ascriptive ties to family, locality, social background and tradition, and initiates a formal transformation of social integration. With each new impulse toward modernisation, intersubjectively shared lifeworlds open, so that they can reorganise and then close once more. (Habermas, 2001: pp. 82–3)

A second approach to the problem of collective order proceeds not from within the liberal or Kantian integration telos but rather within the assumptions of intergovernmentalism and the conversion of German geo-economic power into benevolent leadership. Can the structural interests of German capital accommodate the developmental needs of the Eurozone as a whole? Could Germany reprise in the Eurozone the hegemonic leadership role played by the United States in the Bretton Woods system? This more 'realistic' strategy has no shortage of champions from various points on the political spectrum (Soros, 2012; Varoufakis, 2013; Maier, 2012, Blyth & Matthijs, 2011; *Economist*, 2013; Wolf, 2014; Flassbeck & Lapavitsas, 2015). Indeed, this general strategy is advocated in some form almost everywhere but in Brussels and Germany itself, including the US Treasury (US Department of Treasury, 2013). Perhaps the strongest and most sustained presentation of this argument from the standpoint of critical political economy has been made by Heiner Flassbeck and Costas Lapavitsas (2015).

The essential macroeconomic building blocks of a left-Keynesian alternative would be constructed under German leadership as a matter of enlightened self-interest. Recognizing that 'the entirety of its economic policy is based on export surpluses', Germany would need to radically revise its model towards strengthening aggregate domestic demand and weakening foreign demand, restoring wage growth and increasing corporate tax rates and using the proceeds to invest in infrastructure (Flassbeck & Lapavitsas, 2015: p. 48). Such a turn would require 'an honest and serious discussion inside the country' (p. 36). Flassbeck and Lapavitsas are fully aware of the weakness of the European Left, which has been unable to put forward a coherent programme on either a national or a pan-European basis. They are also aware of the strength of German capital and the German state. Acknowledging that such changes would provoke massive resistance from Germany, Flassbeck and Lapavitsas propose two possible scenarios within the framework of a radically reformed EMU: First, 'combined political pressure by other European countries, including France' might be sufficient to compel Berlin to accept such a leadership role. Second, an EMU implosion in which one or more countries moved towards exit might generate 'a coalition of debtor countries led by France and threatening to bring the end of EMU' (p. 49). If this proved impossible, then the alternative must be exit, most likely in an atmosphere of extreme hostility.

There are, however, reasons to doubt that the German state has the capacity to carry out this type of policy. Germany's present incremental strategy of crisis management through bailouts and austerity has itself become increasingly costly. The Bundesbank remains liable for massive contributions to the Target2 credit system. The ECB has already bought large quantities of sovereign bonds and is now carrying out significant asset purchases through its quantitative easing. The mutualization of debt via the introduction of Eurobonds would represent a significant new liability. The establishment of a debt redemption fund – pooling debt over 60 per cent of GDP – would require massive new spending, which explains why Germany has categorically rejected joint liability in the form of a genuine banking union. Germany's financial liability would also have increased substantially if it had not rejected a European deposit-guarantee scheme in an act of "brutal power politics" (Spiegel, 2013). At the end of 2015, Germany's own public debt was 75 per cent of GDP. Reflation would increase budget deficits and debt, reducing the ability to recapitalize Germany's banks, many of which are in serious trouble. Higher wages would increase unit labour costs, thereby undermining international competitiveness. The moral hazard implicit in Eurobonds would be likely to expand significantly the cost of these programmes. The popularity of Eurosceptic and conservative nationalist parties and movements in Germany – soaring in the wake of the migration crisis – greatly strengthens resistance to a 'transfer union'. In addition, Germany faces a host of longer-term structural challenges, including extremely low growth rates far into the future, population decline, and the legacy of years of low public investment (Fratszcher, 2014). Annual costs of migration are projected to represent 2 per cent of the national budget in 2016 and 2017 (Cologne Institute for Economic Research, 2016), a figure that could increase substantially in the coming years.

The point here is not to rehearse ordoliberal arguments but to indicate that they have a real underpinning in the geopolitical realities that Germany confronts. This is another way of saying that, short of challenging the seigniorage status that is afforded the United States as a result of the dollar being the global reserve currency. Germany may have the power to subordinate other European states to the imperatives of its export-oriented, competitive austerity, but it does not have the power to act as a Keynesian leader. In other words, an intergovernmental Euro-Keynesianism cannot escape the limitations that put the question of monetary union on the agenda in the first place. The most salient factor in accounting for the persistence of Germany's support for austerity is neither the strength of the state as such, nor specifically German cultural norms, but rather long-term vulnerability. It is this vulnerability that makes it doubtful that the German state could summon sufficient resources to serve as a 'benevolent hegemon' even if it faced more formidable challenges than that of Syriza from within the Eurozone.

This leaves the option of an acrimonious exit from the Eurozone under conditions of finance-led US hegemony, a prospect that gains further credence in the context of the Brexit vote, itself a harbinger of the ominous rise of nationalism in Europe. One should recall that turbulence arising from post-Bretton Woods American strategy has been a key motivator for European monetary integration (Henning, 1998). For all intents and purposes, German foreign exchange reserves, the consequence of cumulative surpluses, offered buffers whereby a degree of protection from the externalities of US deflection could be secured, not least for states vulnerable on the capital account (Jones, 2003). While benefits are far more equivocal today than they were during the first decade of the euro, the threat of turbulence and lack of pooled protection against the vagaries of a dollar-denominated global finance seems sufficient to keep Eurozone member states in line, including that of Syriza's Greece. This method of adjustment originated with Franco-German agreement on the European Monetary System (EMS) in 1978. The general need to shield against dollar-driven turbulence, not least illustrated during the first years of Mitterrand's presidency in France, offered the inducement required for others to agree to an EMS, and later EMU, on German terms. There is little evidence that the logic of inducement has lessened since the 1980s.

If critical political economy aspires to unity in theory and practice, this raises some extremely thorny conundrums. In their analysis of the formidable normalizing capacities of capitalist society, the Frankfurt School that Horkheimer helped to form would appreciate these conundrums. Its members did not hesitate to be bearers of bad news. One does not have to agree with Adorno that escape can be found only in highly esoteric aesthetic experiences as induced by Schoenbergian tonal scales. Nevertheless, the implication of this analysis about how current forms of rule are *both* deeply imbricated in transnational capitalism *and* in the state system is sobering. It is not easy for any member state to exit a German-dominated regional system, because the costs of doing so are real and potentially more catastrophic than remaining within it. Nor is it simply a matter of finding an alter-transnational agency to counter a transnational ruling class. The various transnational protest groups that have developed worldwide and in Europe face formidable structural limitations (Scholl & Freyberg-Inan, 2013). Arguments that ignore these limitations seriously underestimate the degree to which the states and the state system still integrate, yet at the same time divide, mass society. Moreover, while marginalization certainly means that the integrative capacities have diminished, opposition movements that grow out of this situation often generate paradoxical results. And that is the point with iron cages. They are not easily escaped.

References

Abdelal, R. (2010) 'The Profits of Power: Commercial Realpolitik in Eurasia', *Harvard Business School Working Paper* (September).

Acharya, V. & S. Steffen (2013) 'The "Greatest" Carry Trade Ever? Understanding Eurozone Bank Risks', *NBER Working Paper* 19039.

Adenauer, K. (1983) *Memoirs 1945–53* (London: Regnery).

Adorno, T.W. & M. Horkheimer (1944 [2002]) *Dialectic of Enlightenment: Philosophical Fragments* (Stanford, CA: Stanford University Press).

Aglietta, M. (1979) *A Theory of Capitalist Regulation* (London: New Left Books).

Aglietta, M. (1982) 'World Capitalism in the Eighties', *New Left Review* 136 (old series), pp. 1–41.

Aglietta, M. (1998) 'Capitalism at the Turn of the Century: Regulation Theory and the Challenge of Social Change', *New Left Review* 232 (old series), pp. 41–90.

Aglietta, M. & R. Breton (2001) 'Financial Systems, Corporate Control and Capital Accumulation', *Economy and Society* 30 (4), pp. 433–66.

Agnew, J. (2001) 'How Many Europes? The European Union, Eastern Enlargement and Uneven Development', *European Urban and Regional Research* 8 (1), pp. 29–38.

Albert, M. (1993) *Capitalism Against Capitalism* (New York: Wiley).

Aldrich, R. (1997) 'OSS, CIA and European Unity: The American Committee on United Europe, 1948–1960', *Diplomacy and Statecraft* 8 (1) March, pp. 184–227.

Altvater, E. & B. Mahnkopf (2007) *Konkurrenz für das Emire: Die Zukunft der Europäischen Union in der globalisierten Welt* (Münster: Westfälisches Dampfboot).

Altvater, E. (2012) 'From Subprime Farce to Greek Tragedy: The Crisis Dynamics of Finance Driven Capitalism' in L. Panitch, G. Albo & V. Chibber (eds) *The Socialist Register 2012* (London: Merlin Press), pp. 271–87.

Andersen, J.G., J. Clasen, W. van Oorschot and K. Halvorsen (eds) (2002) *Europe's New State of Welfare: Unemployment, Employment Policies and Citizenship* (Bristol: Policy Press).

Anderson, J. (1997) 'Singular Europe: An Empire Again?' in W. Armstrong and J. Anderson (eds) *Geopolitics of EU Enlargement: the Frontier Empire* (New York: Routledge).

Anderson, P. (1964) 'Origins of the Present Crisis', *New Left Review* 23 (old series), pp. 26–53.

Anderson, P. (2002) 'Force and Consent', *New Left Review* 17 (new series), pp. 5–30.

Andersen, J.G. (2007) 'The Danish Welfare State as "Politics for Markets": Combining Equality and Competitiveness in a Global Economy', *New Political Economy* 12 (1), pp. 71–8.

Anderson, P. (2009) *The New Old World* (London: Verso).

228

Angeloni, I. & M. Ehrmann (2003) 'Monetary Policy Transmission in the Euro-Area: Any Changes after EMU?', *ECB Working Papers* 240.

Armstrong, K. (2010) *Governing Social Inclusion: Europeanization through Policy Coordination* (Oxford: Oxford University Press).

Armstrong, P., A. Glyn, and J. Harrison (1991) *Capitalism since 1945* (Oxford: Basil Blackwell).

Arnold, I. & C. De Vries (1999) 'Endogenous Financial Structure and the Transmission of ECB Policy', *Tinbergen Institute Discussion Papers* 99–021/2.

Arrighi, G. (2005a) 'Hegemony Unravelling I', *New Left Review* 32 (new series), pp. 23–80.

Arrighi, G. (2005b) 'Hegemony Unravelling II', *New Left Review* 33 (new series), pp. 83–116.

Artis, M. & W. Zhang (1997) 'International Business Cycles and the ERM: Is There A European Business Cycle?', *International Journal of Finance and Economics* 2 (1), pp. 1–16.

Arts, W. & J. Gelissen (2002) 'Three Worlds of Welfare Capitalism or More? A State-of-the-Art Report', *Journal of European Social Policy* 12 (2), pp. 137–68.

Åslund, A. & V. Dombrovskis (2011) *How Latvia Came Through the Financial Crisis Peterson Institute for International Economics* (Washington, DC).

BBC (2009) 'Lisbon Treaty: What They Said', accessed at http://news.bbc.co.uk/2/hi/europe/8282241.stm, accessed on 30.04.2016.

Baccaro, L & J. Pontusson (2016) 'Rethinking Comparative Political Economy: The Growth Model Perspective', *Politics & Society* 44 (2), pp. 175–207.

Baehr, P. (2001) 'The "Iron Cage" and the "Shell as Hard as Steel": Parsons, Weber and the *Staalhartes Gehäuse* Metaphor in *The Protestant Ethic and the Spirit of Capitalism*', *History and Theory* 40, pp. 153–69.

Bailey, D.J. (2006) 'Governance or the Crisis of Governmentality? Applying Critical State Theory at the European Level', *Journal of European Public Policy* 31 (1), pp. 16–33.

Baines, J. (2014) 'Food Price Inflation as Redistribution: Towards a New Analysis of Corporate Power in the World Food System', *New Political Economy* 19 (1), pp. 79–112.

Balassa, B. (1961 [2011]) *The Theory of Economic Integration* (London: Routledge).

Bao, M. (2013) 'The RMB Internationalisation and Sustained Growth in China', Lecture by the Deputy Governor General of the People's Bank of China, 'Towards a Sustainable Financial System', London School of Economics, March 21.

Barma, N., E. Ratner, & S. Weber (2007) 'A World Without the West', *The National Interest*, July/August.

Barnett, R.R. & V. Borooah (1995) 'The Additionality (or Otherwise) of European Community Structural Funds' in S. Hardy et al. (eds) *An Enlarged Europe* (London: Jessica Kingsley), pp. 38–46.

Baumol, W.J. (1967) 'Macroeconomics of Unbalanced Growth: The Anatomy of Urban Crisis', *The American Economic Review* 57 (3), pp. 415–26.

Bayoumi, T. & B. Eichengreen (1992) 'Shocking Aspects of European Monetary Unification', *NBER Working Paper,* 3949.

Becker, J., J. Jäger, B. Leubolt, & R. Weissenbacher (2010) 'Peripheral Financialisation and Vulnerability to Crisis: A Regulationist Perspective', *Competition and Change* 14 (3/4), pp. 225–47.

Beckmann, M. (2007) *Das Finanzkapital in der Transformation der Europäische Ökonomie* (Münster: Westfälisches Dampfboot).

Belfrage, C. (2015) 'The Unintended Consequences of Financialisation: Social Democracy Hamstrung? The Pensions Dilemma', *Economic and Industrial Democracy DOI: 10.1177/0143831X15586070.*

Belfrage, C. & M. Ryner (2009) 'Renegotiating the Swedish Social Democratic Settlement: From Pension Fund Socialism to Neoliberalization', *Politics & Society* 37 (2), pp. 257–87.

Bellofiore, R., F. Garibaldo, & J. Halevi (2011) 'The Global Crisis and the Crisis of European Mercantilism' in L. Panitch, G. Albo, and V. Chibber (eds) *The Socialist Register 2011: The Crisis this Time* (London: Merlin Press), pp. 121–46.

Bengtsson, E. & M. Ryner (2015) 'The (International) Political Economy of Falling Wage Shares: Situating Working Class Agency', *New Political Economy* 20 (3), pp. 406–30.

Bengtsson, E. & M. Ryner (2016, forthcoming) 'Why No Wage Solidarity *writ large*? Swedish Trade Unions under Conditions of European Crisis' in H. Dribbusch, S. Lehndorff, and T. Schulten (eds) *Trade Unions under the Conditions of the European Crisis* (Brussels: ETUI Press).

Berminghan, F. (2015) 'Will China Come to Greece's Rescue?' Global Trade Review 6 July, accessed at http://www.gtreview.com/news/asia/will-china-come-to-greeces-rescue/, accessed on 30.04.2016.

Bertelsmann Foundation (2013) 'Transatlantic Trade and Investment Partnership: Who Benefits from a Free Trade Deal?', *Global Economic Dynamics*, Berlin.

Bertrand, H. (2002) 'The Wage-Labour Nexus and the Employment System', in R. Boyer & Y. Saillard (eds) *Régulation Theory: The State of the Art* (London: Routledge), pp. 80-86

Bhaduri, A. & S. Marglin (1990) 'Unemployment and the Real Wage: The Economic Basis for Contesting Political Ideologies', *Cambridge Journal of Economics* 14, pp. 375–93.

Bhagwati, J. (2008) *Termites in the Trading System: How Preferential Agreements Undermine Free Trade* (New York: Oxford University Press).

Bidelux, R. & I. Jeffries (2007) *A History of Eastern Europe: Crisis and Change*, 2nd edition (London: Taylor and Francis).

Bieler, A. (2002) 'The Struggle over EU Enlargement: A Historical Materialist Analysis of European Integration', *Journal of European Public Policy* 9 (4), pp. 575–97.

Bieler, A. (2006) *The Struggle for a Social Europe: Trade Unions and EMU in Times of Global Restructuring* (Manchester: Manchester University Press).

Bieler, A. & R. Erne (2015) 'Transnational Solidarity: The European Working Class in the Eurozone Crisis' in G. Albo and L. Panitch (eds) *Transforming Classes: Socialist Register 2015* (London: Merlin Press), pp. 157–77.

Bieler, A. & A. D. Morton (2015) 'Axis of Evil or Access to Evil: Spaces of New Imperialism and the Iraq War', *Historical Materialism* 23 (2), pp. 94–130.

Bieling, H.-J. (2003) 'Social Forces in the Making of the New European Economy: The Case of Financial Market Integration', *New Political Economy* 8, pp. 203–24.

Bieling, H.-J. (2010) *Die Globalisierungs und Weltordnungspolitik der Europäischen Union* (Wiesbaden: VS Verlag).

Bieling, H.-J. (2014) 'Shattered Expectations: The Defeat of European Ambitions of Global Financial Reform', *Journal of European Public Policy* 21 (3), pp. 346–66.

Bieling, H.- J. & J. Jäger Jäger (2009) 'Global Finance and the European Economy: The Struggle over Banking Regulation' in B. van Apeldoorn, J. Drahokoupil, and L. Horn (eds) *Contradictions and Limits of Neoliberal European Governance: From Lisbon to Lisbon* (Basingstoke: Palgrave Macmillan), pp. 87–105.

Bieling, H.-J, J. Jäger & M. Ryner (2016) 'Regulation Theory and the Political Economy of the European Union', *Journal of Common Market Studies* 54 (1), pp. 53–69.

Bieling, H.-J. & T. Schulten (2003) '"Competitive Restructuring" and Industrial Relations within the European Union: Corporatist Involvement and Beyond' in A. Cafruny and M. Ryner (eds) *A Ruined Fortress? Neoliberal Hegemony and Transformation in Europe* (Lanham, MD: Rowman and Littlefield), pp. 231–60.

Bieling, H.-J. & J. Steinhilber (1999) *Die Konfiguration Europas Dimensionen Einer Kritischen Integratientherie* (Munster: Westfalisches Dampfboot).

Birch, K. & V. Mykhnenko (2009) 'Varieties of Neoliberalism? Restructuring in Large Industrially Dependent Regions across Western and Eastern Europe', *Journal of Economic Geography* 9 (3), pp. 355–80.

Blanchard, O. & F. Giavazzi (2002) 'Current Account Deficits in the Euro Area: The End of the Feldstein–Horioka Puzzle?', *Brookings Papers on Economic Activity* 2/2002.

Blanchflower, D. & C. Shadworth (2009) 'Fear, Unemployment, and Migration', *Economic Journal* 119 (535), pp. 136–182.

Block, F. (1977) *The Origins of International Economic Disorder* (Berkeley and Los Angeles, CA: University of California Press).

Blyth, M. & M. Matthijs (2011) 'Why Only Germany Can Fix the Euro: Reading Kindleberger in Berlin', *Foreign Affairs*, 17 November.

Bohle, D. (2006) 'Neoliberal Hegemony, Transnational Capital, and the Terms of the EU's Eastward Expansion', *Capital and Class* 30 (1), pp. 57–86.

Bohle, D. (2009) 'Race to the Bottom? Transnational Companies and Reinforced Competition in the Enlarged European Union' in B. van Apeldoorn, J. Drahokoupil, and L. Horn (eds) *Contradictions and Limits of Neoliberal European Governance: From Lisbon to Lisbon* (Basingstoke: Palgrave Macmillan) pp. 163–86.

Bohle, D. & B. Greskovits (2007) 'Neoliberalism, Embedded Neoliberalism and Neocorporatism: Towards Transnational Capitalism in Central-Eastern Europe', *West European Politics* 30 (3), pp. 443–66.

Bohle, D. & B. Greskovits (2009) 'Varieties of Capitalism and Capitalism, Tout Court', *European Journal of Sociology* 50 (3), pp. 355–86.

Bolkestein, F. (2001) 'European Competitiveness', *Speech to the Ambrosetti Annual Forum*, Cernobbio, September 8.

Boltho, A. & B. Eichengreen (2008) 'The Economic Impact of European Integration', *Discussion Paper* 6820, Centre for Economic Policy Research.

Bonder, M., B. Röttger, & G. Ziebura (1992) *Deutschland in einer neuen Weltära* (Opladen: Leske and Budrich).

Bonefeld, W. (2002) 'European Integration: The Market, the Political and Class', *Capital and Class* 26 (2) (Summer), pp. 117–42.

Bonefeld, W. (2012a) 'Neo-liberal Europe and the Transformation of Democracy: On the State of Money and Law' in P. Nousios, H. Overbeek, and A. Tsolakis (eds) *Globalisation and European Integration: Critical Approaches to Regional Order and International Relations* (London: Routledge), pp. 51–69.

Bonefeld (2012b) 'Freedom and the Strong State: On German Ordoliberalism', *New Political Economy* 17 (5), pp. 633–56.

Bordo, M.D. & H. James (2010) 'The European Crisis in the Context of the History of Previous Financial Crises', *NBER Working Paper*, 19112.

Borocz, J. (2012) 'Hungary in the EU: "Catching Up" Forever', *Economic and Political Weekly*, Mumbai, 15 (7), pp. 22–25.

Boudette, N. (2004) 'As Jobs Head to Eastern Europe Unions in West Start to Bend', *Wall Street Journal*, March 11.

Bowles, S., D. Gordon, & T. Weisskopf (1983) *Beyond the Waste Land: A Democratic Alternative to Economic Decline* (New York: Anchor Books).

Bowles, S. & R. Boyer (1995) 'Wages, Aggregate Demand, and Employment in an Open Economy: A Theoretical and Empirical Investigation' in G. Epstein & H. Gintis (eds) *Macroeconomic Policy after the Conservative Era: Research on Investment, Savings and Finance* (Cambridge: Cambridge University Press), pp. 143–71.

Boyer, R. (1990) 'The Impact of the Single Market on Labour and Employment: A Discussion of Macro-Economic Approaches in the Light of Research in Labour Economics', *Labour and Society* 15 (2), pp. 109–42.

Boyer, R. (2012) 'The Four Fallacies of Contemporary Austerity Policies: The Lost Keynesian Legacy,' *Cambridge Journal of Economics* 36 (1), pp. 283–312.

Boyer, R. (1991) 'The Eighties: The Search for Alternatives to Fordism' in B. Jessop, H. Kastendiek, K. Nielsen, and O.K. Pedersen (eds) *The Politics of Flexibility* (Aldershot: Gower), pp. 106–32.

Boyer, R. (2000) 'Is a Finance-led Growth Regime a Viable Alternative to Fordism? A Preliminary Analysis', *Economy and Society* 29 (1), pp. 111–45.

Boyer, R. and Y. Saillard (eds) (2002) *Régulation Theory. The State of the Art* (London: Routledge).

Braudel, F. (1958 [1980]) 'History and the Social Sciences: The *longue durée*', in *On History* (Chicago: University of Chicago Press), pp. 25–54.

Braverman, H. (1974) *Labour and Monoply Capital: The Degradation of Work in the Twentiety Century* (New York: Monthly Review Press).

Brenner, N., J. Peck, & N. Theodore (2010) 'Variegated Neoliberalization: Geographies, Modalities, Pathways', *Global Networks* 10 (2), pp. 182–222.

Brenner, R. (2006) *The Economics of Global Turbulence* (London: Verso).

Bretherton, C & J. Vogler (1999) *The European Union as a Global Actor* (London: Routledge).

Brewer, A. (1980) *Marxist Theories of Imperialism: A Critical Survey* (London: Routledge and Kegan Paul).

Briggs, A. (1961) 'The Welfare State in Historical Perspective', *European Journal of Sociology* 2 (2), pp. 221–58.

Brown, K. (2012) 'Chinese Overseas Investment in the European Union', *International Spectator* 47 (2), pp. 1–13.

Brown, W. (2000) 'Restructuring north-south relations: ACP-EU development co-operation in a liberal international order', *Review of African Political Economy* 85 (27), pp. 367–83.

Bruff, I. (2011) 'What About the Elephant in the Room? Varieties of Capitalism, Varieties in Capitalism', *New Political Economy* 16 (4), pp. 481–500.

Bruff, I. (2014) 'The Rise of Authoritarian Neoliberalism', *Rethinking Marxism* 26 (1), pp. 113–29.

Bryant, C. & E. Mokrzycki (1994) The New Great Transformation? *Change and Continuity in East-Central Europe* (London: Routledge).

Brzezinski, Z. (1997) *The Grand Chessboard: American Primacy and its Geostrategic Imperatives* (New York: Basic Books).

Buch-Hansen, H. & A. Wigger (2010a) 'Revisiting Fifty Years of Market Making: The Neoliberal Transformation of European Competition Policy', *Review of International Political Economy* 17 (1), pp. 20–44.

Buch-Hansen, H. & A. Wigger (2010b) *The Politics of European Competition Regulation* (London: Routledge).

Büchs, M. (2007) *New Governance in European Social Policy: The Open Method of Coordination* (Basingstoke: Palgrave Macmillan).

Buiter, W., G. Corsetti, and N. Roubini (1993) 'Excessive Deficits: Sense and Nonsense in the Treaty of Maastricht', *Economic Policy* 8 (16), pp. 57–100.

Bull, H. (1977) *The Anarchical Society* (Ithaca, NY: Columbia University Press).

Bulmer, S. (1993) 'The Governance of the European Union: A New Institutionalist Approach', *Journal of Public Policy* 13 (4), pp. 351–80.

Burley, A.-M. and W. Mattli (1993) 'Europe Before the Court: A Political Theory of Legal Integration', *International Organization* 47 (1), pp. 41–76.

Busch, K., C. Herrmann, K. Hinrichs, & T. Schulten (2013) 'Euro-Crisis, Austerity Policy and the European Social Model', *Friedrich Ebert Stiftung International Policy Analysis*.

Cafruny, A. (2003) 'Europe, the United States, and Neoliberal (Dis)Order: Is There a Coming Crisis of the Euro?' in A. Cafruny and M. Ryner (eds) *A Ruined Fortress: Neoliberal Hegemony and Transformation in Europe* (Boulder, CO: Rowman and Littlefield) pp. 285–306.

Cafruny, A. (2009) 'Geopolitics and Neoliberalism: U.S. Power and the Limits of European Autonomy' in B. van Apeldoorn, J. Drahokoupil, and L. Horn (eds) *Neoliberal European Governance and Beyond—The Contradictions and Limits of a Political Project* (London: Palgrave), pp. 63–83.

Cafruny, A. (2015) 'The European Crisis and the Rise of German Power' in J. Jäger and E. Springler (eds) *Assymetric Crisis in Europe and Possible Futures: Critical Political Economy and Post-Keynesian Perspectives* (London: Routledge), pp. 61–73.

Cafruny, A. & M. Ryner (eds) (2003) *A Ruined Fortress: Neoliberal Hegemony and Transformation in Europe* (Lanham, MD: Rowman and Littlefield).

Cafruny, A. & M. Ryner (2007) *Europe at Bay: In the Shadow of US Hegemony* (Boulder, CO: Lynne Rienner).

Calleo, D. (1982) *The Imperious Economy* (New York: Basic Books).

Calleo, D. (2001) *Rethinking Europe's Future* (Princeton, NJ: Princeton University Press).

Calleo, D. (2003) 'Balancing America: Europe's International Duties', *International Politics and Society* 1, pp. 1–18.

Callinicos, A. (2007) 'Does Capitalism Need the State System?', *Cambridge Review of International Affairs* 20 (4), pp. 533–49.

Cameron, D. (1997) 'Economic and Monetary Union: Underlying Imperatives and Third Stage Dilemmas', *Journal of European Public Policy* 4 (3), pp. 455–85.

Capaldo, J. (2014) 'Transatlantic Trade and Investment Partnership: European Disintegration, Unemployment, and Instability', Global Development and Environment Institute, *Working Paper* 14 (3), Tufts University, October.

Caporaso, J.A. & S. Tarrow (2009) 'Polanyi in Brussels: Supranational Institutions and the Transnational Embedding of Markets', *International Organization* 63 (4), pp. 593–620.

Cargill (2016) 'Cargill & MV Cargo take final steps to build port terminal in Yuzhni, Ukraine', 24 February, accessed at http://www.cargill.com/news/releases/2016/NA31931055.jsp, accessed on 03.11.2016.

Carr, E.H. (1961 [1990]) *What Is History?* (Harmondsworth: Penguin).

Casarini, N. (2012) 'Editorial Note: Special Issue on A Rising China and its Strategic Impact', *International Spectator* 47 (2), pp. 1–13.

Center for Economic Policy Research (2013) *Reducing Transatlantic Barriers to Trade and Investment* (London).

Charnock, G., T. Purcell, & R. Ribera-Fumaz (2014) *The Limits to Capital in Spain* (Basingstoke: Palgrave Macmillan).

Checkel, J.T. (2003) '"Going Native" in Europe? Theorizing Social Interaction in European Institutions', *Comparative Political Studies* 36 (1/2), pp. 209–31.

Christiansen, H. (2011) 'The Size and Composition of the SOE Sector in OECD Countries', *OECD Corporate Governance Working Papers* 5.

Churchill, W. (1946) 'The Tragedy of Europe', Speech to the Academic Youth, Zürich, September 19.

Cini, M. & L. McGowan (1998) *Competition Policy in the European Union* (Basingstoke: Palgrave Macmillan).

Clark, G.L. (2002) 'European Pensions and Global Finance: Continuity or Convergence?', *New Political Economy* 7 (1), pp. 67–91.

Clift, B. (2014) *Comparative Political Economy: States, Markets and Global Capitalism* (Basingstoke: Palgrave Macmillan).

Cocks, P. (1980) 'Towards a Marxist Theory of European Integration', *International Organization* 34 (1), pp. 1–40.

Cohen, B. (2003) 'Global Currency Rivalry: Can the Euro ever Challenge the Dollar?', *Journal of Common Market Studies* 41 (4), pp. 575–95.

Cohen, B. (2006) 'The Macrofoundations of Monetary Power' in D. Andrews (ed.) *International Monetary Power* (Ithaca, NY: Cornell University Press), pp. 31–50.

Cohen, B. (2007) 'Enlargement and the International Role of the Euro', *Review of International Political Economy* 14 (5), pp. 746–33.

Cohen, B. (2008) 'The International Monetary System: Diffusion and Ambiguity', *International Affairs* 84 (3), pp. 455–70.

Cohen, B. (2009) 'Dollar Dominance, Euro Aspirations: Recipe for Discord?', *Journal of Common Market Studies* 47 (4), pp. 741–66.

Cologne Institute for Economic Research (2016) 'The Influence of Demographic Developments in Germany', May, accessed at https://www.iwkoeln.de/en/topics/demografie/zuwanderung.

Connolly, K. (2015) 'Refugee Influx a Major Opportunity for Germany, Leading Economist Says' *The Guardian*, 5 November.

Copsey, N. & T. Haughton (2009) 'The Choices for Europe: National Preferences in New and Old Member States', *Journal of Common Market Studies* 47 (2), pp. 263–86.

Coriat, B. (2009) 'Between China and the USA: Which Future Strategies for EU-based Enterprises?' in M. J. Rodrigues (ed.) *Europe, Globalisation and the Lisbon Agenda* (Cheltenham: Edward Elgar), pp. 223–33.

Corrigan, P. & D. Sayer (1985) *The Great Arch: English State Formation as Cultural Revolution* (Oxford: Basil Blackwell).

Cox, R.W. (1976) 'On Thinking About Future World Order', *World Politics* 28 (2), pp. 175–96.

Crouch, C. (2000) 'National Wage Determination and European Monetary Union' in C. Crouch (ed.) *After the Euro: Shaping Institutions for Governance in the Wake of European Monetary Union* (Oxford: Oxford University Press), pp. 203–26.

Crouch, C. (2002) 'The Euro and Labour Market and Wage Policies', in K. Dyson (ed.) *European States and the Euro* (Oxford: Oxford University Press) pp. 278–304.

Crouch, C. (2009) 'Privatised Keynesianism: An Unacknowledged Policy Regime', *British Journal of Politics and International Relations* 11 (3), pp. 382–99.

Daalder, I. & J. Goldgeier (2006) 'Global NATO' *Foreign Affairs*. September–October.

Dale, G. (2011) *First the Transition, Then the Crash* (London: Pluto).

Davis, M. (2006) *Planet of Slums* (London: Verso).

DefenseNews (2015) 'Juncker: EU Military Forces? All Squawk and No Bite' 7 May, accessed at http://www.defensenews.com/story/defense/2015/05/07/juncker-eu-military-forces-all-squawk-no-bite/70951584/, accessed on 30.04.2016.

De Grauwe, P. (2006) 'What Have We Learnt about Monetary Integration since the Maastricht Treaty?', *Journal of Common Market Studies* 44 (4), pp. 711–30.

De Grauwe, P. (2013) 'Design Failures in the Eurozone: Can They Be Fixed?', *London School of Economics 'Europe in Question' Discussion Paper Series* 57/2013.

De Ville, F. & G. Siles-Brugge (2015) *TTIP: The Truth about the Transatlantic Trade and Investment Partnership* (Cambridge: Polity Press).

Delors, J. (1988) '1992: The Social Dimension', *Address to the Trades Union Congress (TUC)*, Bournemouth, 8 September.

Delors Report (Committee for the Study of Economic and Monetary Union) (1989) *Report on Economic and Monetary Union in Europe* (Luxembourg: Office for the Official Publications of the European Union).

Deppe, F. (ed.) (1975) *Arbeiterbewegung und westeuropäische Integration* (Cologne: Pahl-Rugenstein).

Desai, R. (2013) *Geopolitical Economy: After U.S. Hegemony, Globalization, and Empire* (London: Pluto).

Deudney, D. & G.J. Ikenberry (1999) 'The Nature and Sources of Liberal International Order', *Review of International Studies* 25 (2), pp. 179–96.

Deutsch, K., S. Burrell, R.A. Kann, M. Lee Jr., M. Lichterman, R.E. Lindgren, F.L. Loewenheim, & R.W. van Wagenen (1957) *Political Community in the North Atlantic Area* (Princeton NJ: Princeton University Press).

Deyo, F. (ed.) (1986) *The Political Economy of the New Asian Industrialism* (Ithaca, NY: Cornell University Press).

De Zutter, E. (2010) 'Normative Power Spotting: An Ontological and Methodological Appraisal', *Journal of European Public Policy* 17 (8), pp. 1106–27.

Dicken, P. (2010) *Global Shift: Mapping the Changing Contours of the World Economy,* 6th edition (London: The Guildford Press).

DIEM25 (2016) Democracy in Europe Movement, http://diem25.org/.

Diez, T. (2001) 'Europe as a Discursive Battleground: Discourse Analysis and European Integration Studies', *Cooperation and Conflict* 36 (1), pp. 5–38.

Dluhosch, B. (2000) *Industrial Location and European Integration* (Cheltenham: Edward Elgar).

Doré, R. (2000) 'Will Global Capitalism be Anglo-Saxon Capitalism?', *New Left Review* 6, pp. 101–19.

Drahokoupil, J. & M. Myant (2011) *Transition Economies: Political Economy in Russia, Eastern Europe, and Central Asia* (Hoboken, NJ: Wiley Blackwell).

Drainville, A. (1994) 'International Political Economy in the Age of Open Marxism', *Review of International Political Economy* 1 (1), pp. 105–32.

Dribbusch, H., S. Lehndorff, and T. Schulten (eds) (2016, forthcoming) *Trade Unions under the Conditions of European Crisis* (Brussels: ETUI Press).

Dumenil, G. & D. Levy (2004) *Capital Resurgent: Roots of the Neoliberal Revolution* (Cambridge MA: Harvard University Press).

Dunford, M. (1995) 'Cohesion, Growth and Inequality in the European Union', in A. Amin (ed.) *Behind the Myth of European Union: Prospects for Cohesion* (London: Routledge), pp. 125–46.

Dunford, M. (2005) 'Old Europe, New Europe and the USA: Comparative Economic Performance, Inequality, and Market-Led Models of Development', *European Urban and Regional Studies* 12 (2), pp. 149–76.

Dunford, M. & D. Perrons (1994) 'Regional Inequality, Regimes of Accumulation, and Economic Development in Contemporary Europe', *Transactions of the Institute of British Geographers* 19, pp. 163–82.

Dunford, M. & A. Smith (2000) 'Catching Up or Falling Behind? Economic Performance and the Trajectories of Economic Development in an Enlarged Europe', *Economic Geography* (April 2000), pp. 169–95.

Dunning, J.H. (1997a) 'The European Internal Market Programme and Inbound Foreign Direct Investment', *Journal of Common Market Studies* 35 (1), pp. 1–30.

Dunning, J.H. (1997b) 'The European Internal Market Programme and Inbound Foreign Direct Investment', *Journal of Common Market Studies* 35 (2), pp. 189–203.

Dyson, K. (2000) *The Politics of the Euro-zone: Stability or Breakdown* (Oxford: Oxford University Press).

Dyson, K. & K. Featherstone (1999) *The Road to Maastricht: Negotiating Economic and Monetary Union* (Oxford: Oxford University Press).

Eakin, H. (2015) 'The Terrible Flight from the Killing', New York Review of Books, October 2, accessed at http://www.nybooks.com/articles/ archives/2015/oct/22/terrible-flight-killing, accessed on 30.04.2016.

Easton, D. (1953) *The Political System: An Inquiry into the State of Political Science* (New York: Alfred A. Knopf).

Eatwell, J., T. McKinley & P. Petit (eds) (2014) *Challenges for Europe in the World, 2030* (London: Ashgate).

Ebbinghaus, B. (ed.) (2011) *Varieties of Pension Governance: Pension Privatization in Europe* (Oxford: Oxford University Press).

ECB (2012) 'Technical Features of Outright Monetary Transactions', Press Release, 6 September, accessed at http://www.ecb.europa.eu/press/pr/ date/2012/html/pr120906_1.en.html, accessed on 30.04.2016.

Economist (2011) 'Ipadded: The Trade Gap between America and China is Much Exaggerated', 21 January, accessed at http://www.economist.com/ node/21543174.

Economist (2011a) 'A very short history of the crisis', http://www.economist. com/node/21536871, accessed 15.10.2016

Economist (2013) 'Europe's Reluctant Hegemon' 15 June, accessed at http:// www.economist.com/news/special-report/21579140-germany, accessed on 30. 04, 2016.

Economist (2014) 'Setting out the Store: Briefing State Owned Assets', 11–17 January, pp. 17–20.

Economist (2015) 'Fight the Good Fight: With the Western Balkans at Peace, Some Go Abroad to Look for War', 18 April, accessed at http://www.econo-mist.com/news/europe/21648697-western-balkans-peace-some-go-abroad-look-war-fight-good-fight.

EDA (2013) *Defense Data 2012*, Brussels, accessed at http://www.eda.europa. eu/docs/default-source/eda-publications/defence-data-booklet-2012-web, accessed on 30.04.2016.

EDA (European Defence Agency) (2013) *National Defence Data* (Brussels), accessed at https://www.eda.europa.eu/docs/default-source/documents/ national-defence-data-2013---27-eda-ms_updated.pdf.

Eichengreen, B. (2007) *The European Economy since 1945* (Princeton: Princeton University Press).

Eichengreen, B. (2011) *Exorbitant Privilege: The Rise and Fall of the Dollar and the Future of the International Monetary System* (Oxford: Oxford University Press).

Eichengreen, B. & J. Frieden (2001) 'The Political Economy of European Monetary Unification: An Analytical Introduction' in B. Eichengreen and J. Frieden (eds) *The Political Economy of European Monetary Unification* (Boulder, CO: Westview Press), pp. 1–22.

Eichengreen, B. & P. Temin (2010) 'Fetters of Gold and Paper', *NBER Working Paper*, 16202.

Enderlein, H. (2006) 'Adjusting to EMU: The Impact of Supranational Monetary Policy on Domestic Fiscal and Wage Setting Institutions', *European Union Politics* 7 (1), pp. 113–40.

Engels, F. (1884 [1976]) 'The Origins of the Family, Private Property and the State' in K. Marx and F. Engels (eds) *Karl Marx and Frederick Engels: selected works in one volume* (New York: International Publishers).

Erne, R. (2008) *European Unions: Labor's Quest for a Transnational Democracy* (Ithaca, NY: Cornell University Press).

Erne, R. (2015) 'A Supranational Regime that Nationalizes Social Conflict: Explaining European Trade Unions' Difficulties in Politicizing European Economic Governance', *Labour History* 56 (3), pp. 345–68.

Esping-Andersen, G. (1990) *The Three Worlds of Welfare Capitalism* (Cambridge: Polity Press).

Esping-Andersen, G. (1999) *The Social Foundations of Post-Industrial Economies* (Oxford: Oxford University Press).

Esping-Andersen, G. (2002) *Why We Need a New Welfare State* (Oxford: Oxford University Press).

Esser, J., W. Fach, G. Junne, F. Schlupp, & G. Simonis (eds) (1979) 'Das "Modell Deutschland" und seine Konstruktionsswächen', *Levithan* 7 (1) (special issue).

Euractiv (2015) 'French, German Ministers Spell Out Plans for Two-Speed Europe', Brussels, 4 June, accessed at http://www.euractiv.com/sections/eu-priorities-2020/french-german-ministers-flesh-out-plans-two-speed-europe-315123, accessed on 30.04.2016.

Euromemorandum (2014) *The Deepening Divisions in Europe and the Need for a Radical Alternative to EU Policies*, Euromemo Group.

Euromemorandum (2015) *What future for the European Union - Stagnation and Polarisation or New Foundations?*, Euromemo Group.

European Commission (1977) *Report of the Study Group on Public Finances in the European Integration, Volume I* (Brussels: European Commission).

European Commission (1985) *Completing the Internal Market*, COM 85 (310).

European Commission (1988) *Europe 1992: The Overall Challenge* (Brussels: The Commission of the European Communities), SEC 88 (524) Final, 13 April.

European Commission (1990) 'One Market, One Money: An Evaluation of the Potential Benefits and Costs of Forming and Economic and Monetary Union', *European Economy* 44.

European Commission (2000) 'The Lisbon European Council – an Agenda of Economic and Social Renewal for Europe', *Contribution of the Commission to the special European Council in Lisbon*, 23–4 March. DOC/00/7

European Commission (2001) 'Realising the European Union's Potential: Consolidating and Extending the Lisbon Agenda', *Contribution of the Commission to the European Council*, Stockholm, 23–4 March.

European Commission (2014) *EU-Ukraine Deep and Comprehensive Free Trade Area*, Brussels, accessed at 27 June http://trade.ec.europa.eu/doclib/docs/2013/april/tradoc_150981.pdf, accessed on 30.04.2016.

European Commission (2015a) *Statistical Annex of the European Economy*, Autumn, Brussels: European Commission.

European Commission (2015b) *Asylum in the EU*, accessed at http://ec.europa.eu/dgs/home-affairs/e-library/docs/infographics/asylum/infographic_asylum_en.pdf, accessed on 30.04.2016.

European Council (2010) The President, *Remarks by Herman van Rompuy* (Brussels), accessed at http://www.consilium.europa.eu/uedocs/cms_data/docs/pressdata/en/ec/117890.pdf.

European External Action Service (EEAS), 2016   EU-Ukraine Association Agreement, "Quick Guide to the Association Agreement" (Brussels), accessed at https://eeas.europa.eu/.

European Parliament (2010) *Report on the EU Policy Coherence for Development and the 'Official Development Assistance Plus' Concept*, Session 2009–2014, Rapporteur Franziska Keller 5 May 2010, A7–0140/2010.

European Parliament (2016) 'The Economic Impact of Suspending Schengen', Research Service, April, accessed at http://www.europarl.europa.eu/Reg Data/etudes/ATAG/2016/579074/EPRS_ATA%282016%29579074_EN.pdf, accessed on 03.11.2016.

European Union Court of Auditors (2013) *EU Cooperation with Egypt in the field of Governance*, Brussels 18 June.

European Voice (2011) 'EU Must Remain Open to Immigration' 9 December.

Fagan, G. & V. Gaspar (2008) 'Macroeconomic Adjustment to Monetary Union', *ECB Working Paper* 946.

Fajertag, G. & P. Pochet (eds) (2000) *Social Pacts in Europe: New Dynamics* (Brussels: European Trade Unions Congress).

Ferrera, M. (1996) 'The 'Southern' Model of Welfare in Social Europe', *Journal of European Social Policy* 6 (1), pp. 17–37.

Ferrera, M., A. Hemerijck, & M. Rhodes (2000) 'Recasting European Welfare States for the 21st Century', *European Review* 8 (3), pp. 427–46.

Fierke, A. M. & Wiener, A. (1999) 'Constructing Institutional Interests: EU and NATO Enlargement', *Journal of European Public Policy* 5 (2), pp. 721–42.

Financial Times (2014) *Voting Will Not Change Europe's Real Power Balance,* 4 May.

Financial Times (2015) *U.S., Japan, and Ten Pacific Countries Strike Pacific Trade Deal,* 10 November.

Financial Times (2016) 20 March, http://www.ft.com/intl/cms/s/0/ff442fb6-ecfc-11e5-bb79-2303682345c8.html#axzz43XCKRZ5B

Fischer, F. (1967) *Germany's Aims in the First World War* (London: Chatto and Windus).

Fischer, S. & Gelb, S. (1991) 'The Process of Socialist Economic Transformation', Journal of Economic Perspectives 5 (4), pp. 91–105.

Flassbeck, H. & C. Lapavitsas (2015) *Against the Troika* (London: Verso).

Fligstein, N. (2009) *Euro-Clash: The EU, European Identity and the Future of Europe* (Oxford: Oxford University Press).

Fligstein, N. & A. Stone-Sweet (2002) 'Constructing Politics and Markets: An Institutional Account of European Integration', *American Journal of Sociology* 105 (5), pp. 1206–43.

Flint, A. (2008) 'Marrying Poverty Alleviation and Sustainable Development? An Analysis of the EU-ACP Cotonou Agreement', *Journal of International Relations and Development* 11 (1), pp. 55–74.

Flint, A. (2009) 'The end of a "special relationship"? The new EU-ACP economic partnership agreements', *Review of African Political Economy* 36 (119), pp. 79–92.

Flora, P. & J. Alber (1981) 'Modernization, Democratization and the Development of Welfare States in Western Europe' in Peter Flora and Arnold Heidenheimer (eds) *The Development of Welfare States in Europe and America* (New Brunswick, NJ: Transaction Publishers), pp. 37–80.

Follain, L., C. Look & M. Campbell (2016) 'The Trucker's Nightmare that Could Flatten Europe's Economy' Bloomberg, 17–04, accessed at http://www.bloomberg.com/news/articles/2016–04–17/the-trucker-s-nightmare-that-could-flatten-europe-s-economy

Forsberg, T. (2011) 'Normative Power Europe once again: a Conceptual Analysis of an Ideal Type', *Journal of Common Market Studies* 49 (6), pp. 1183–204.

Forwood, G. (2001) 'The Road to Cotonou: Negotiating a Successor to Lome', *Journal of Common Market Studies* 39 (3), pp 423–42.

France Strategie (2016) 'The Economic Cost of Rolling Back Schengen', Paris, 5 February, accessed at http://www.strategie.gouv.fr/sites/strategie.gouv.fr/files/atoms/files/the_economic_cost_of_rolling_back_schengen_0.pdf, accessed on 30.04.2016.

Fratzscher, M. (2014) *The Germany Illusion* Institute for Economic Research, Berlin.

Freyssenet, M. (1998) "Reflective Production': An Alternative to Mass Production and Lean Production?', *Economic and Industrial Democracy* 19, pp. 91–117.

Friedberg, A. (2011) *A Contest for Supremacy, China, America, and the Struggle for Mastery in Asia* (New York: W.W. Norton).

Frieden, J. (1991) 'Invested Interests: The Politics of National Economic Policies in a World or Global Finance', *International Organization* 45 (4), pp. 425–51.

Frölich, R. (2012) *The New Geopolitics of Transatlantic Relations: Coordinated Responses to Common Dangers* (Baltimore: Johns Hopkins University Press).

Fung, H. (2009) 'America's Head Servant: The PRC's Dilemma in the Global Crisis', *New Left Review* 60 (November–December), pp. 5–25.

Fung, H. (2013) 'China's Rise Stalled?', *New Left Review* 81 (May–June), pp. 154–60.

Galtung, J. (1973) *The European Community: A Superpower in the Making* (New York: Harper Collins).

Garrett, G. (1995) 'The Politics of Legal Integration in the European Union', *International Organization* 49 (1), pp. 171–81.

Garrett, G. & G. Tsebelis (1996) 'An Institutional Critique of Inter-governmentalism', *International Organization* 50 (2), pp. 269–99.

Garrett, G. & B. R. Weingast (1993) 'Ideas, Interests, and Institutions: Constructing the European Community's Internal Market', in J. Goldstein & R. O. Keohane (eds) *Ideas and Foreign Policy: Beliefs, Institutions, and Political Change* (Ithaca: Cornell University Press), pp. 173–206.

George, V. (1998) 'Political Ideology, Globalisation and Welfare Futures in Europe', *Journal of Social Policy* 27 (1), pp. 17–36.

Gerber, D. (1998) *Law and Competition in Twentieth Century Europe: Protecting Prometheus* (Oxford: Oxford University Press).

Gianetti, M. et al. (2002) 'Financial Integration, Corporate Financing and Economic Growth', Final Report by the Centre for European Policy Research to the European Commission, 22 November.

Giavazzi, F. & M. Pagano (1988) 'The Advantage of Tying One's Hands', *European Economic Review* 32, pp. 1055–82.

Gilbert, F. (2008) *The End of the European Era 1890 to the Present*, 6th edition (New York: W.W. Norton).

Gilens, M. & B. Page (2014) 'Testing Theories of American Politics: Elites, Interest Groups, and Average Citizens', *Perspectives on Politics* 12 (3), pp. 564–81.

Gill, S. (1990) *American Hegemony and the Trilateral Commission* (Cambridge: Cambridge University Press).

Gill, S. (1992) 'The Emerging World Order and European Change' in R. Miliband and L. Panitch (eds) *The Socialist Register 1992* (London: Merlin Press), pp. 157–96.

Gill, S. (1998) 'European Governance and New Constitutionalism: EMU and Alternatives to Disciplinary Neoliberalism in Europe', *New Political Economy* 3 (1), pp. 5–26.

Gill, S. (2003) 'A Neo-Gramscian Approach to European Integration' in A. Cafruny and M. Ryner (eds) *A Ruined Fortress? Neoliberal Hegemony and Transformation in Europe* (Lanham, MD: Rowman and Littlefield), pp. 47–70.

Gill, S. & D. Law (1988) *The Global Political Economy: Perspectives, Problems and Policies* (Baltimore, MD: Johns Hopkins University Press).

Gillingham, J. (1991) *Coal, Steel, and the Rebirth of Europe, 1945–1955: The Germans and French From Ruhr Conflict to Economic Community* (Cambridge: Cambridge University Press).

Ginsberg, R. (2001) *The European Union in International Politics: Baptism By Fire* (Lanham, MD: Rowman and Littlefield).

Gilpin, R. (1987) *The Political Economy of International Relations* (Princeton, NJ: Princeton University Press).

Ginsberg, R. (2010) *Demystifying the European Union: The Enduring Logic of Regional Integration*, 2nd edition (Lanham, MD: Rowman and Littlefield).

Gowan, P. (1999) *Global Gamble: Washington's Bid for Global Dominance* (London: Verso).

Graf, W. (ed.) (1992) *The Internationalization of the German Political Economy: Evolution of a Hegemonic Project* (New York: St. Martin's Press).

Graf, W. (1995) 'The State in the Third World', in L. Panitch (ed.) *The Socialist Register 1995: Why Not Capitalism* (London: Merlin Press), pp. 140–62.

Grahl, J. (2001) 'Globalized Finance: The Challenge to the Euro', *New Left Review* 8 (new series), pp. 23–47.

Grahl, J. (ed.) (2009) *Global Finance and Social Europe* (Cheltenham: Edward Elgar).

Grahl, J. (2011) 'The Subordination of European Finance', *Competition and Change* 15 (1), pp. 31–47.

Grahl, J. (2012) 'The First European Semester: An Incoherent Strategy', Paper Presented at the Political Economy Research Group Workshop 'Europe in Crisis', April, Department of Economics Kingston University, London.

Grahl, J. (2015) 'Social Europe and the Crisis of the European Union' in J. Jäger and E. Springler (eds) *Asymmetric Crisis in Europe and Possible Futures*, pp. 168–85.

Grahl, J. & P. Teague (1989) 'The Cost of Neoliberal Europe', *New Left Review* 174 (old series), pp. 33–50.

Grahl, J. & P. Teague 1990, *The Big Market: The Future of the European Community* (London: Lawrence and Wishart).

Grahl, J. & P. Lysandrou (2015) 'Financial Reforms in the EU: A Critical Appraisal', *Presentation at Workshop on 'Smart and Sustainable Growth'*, King's College London, 30 June/1 July.

Grahl, J. & P. Teague (1997) 'Is the European Social Model Fragmenting?', *New Political Economy* 2 (3), pp. 405–26.

Gramsci, A. (1971) *Selections from the Prison Notebooks* (New York: International Publishers).

Gratius, S (2012) 'Brazil and the European Union: Between Balancing and Bandwagoning', European Strategic Partnership Observatory *Working Paper* 2, July.

Gross, S. (2013) 'The German Economy Today: Exports, Foreign Investment, and East-Central Europe', *Center for European and Mediterranean Studies* (New York University).

Guerrina, R. (2015) 'Socio-Economic Challenges to Work-Life Balance at Times of Crisis', *Journal of Social Welfare and Family Law* 37 (3), pp. 368–77.

Haar, K. (2011) 'EU's Silent Revolution in Economic Governance Undermines Democratic Control', *Corporate Europe Observatory*, accessed at http://corporateeurope.org/pressreleases/2011/eus-silent-revolution-economic-governance-undermines-democratic-control, accessed on 30.04.2016.

Haas, E.B. (1964) *Beyond the Nation State: Functionalism and International Organization* (Stanford, CA: Stanford University Press).

Haas, E.B. (1968) *The Uniting of Europe: Political, Social and Economic Forces*, 2nd edition (Stanford, CA: Stanford University Press).

Haas, E.B. (2001) 'Does Constructivism Subsume Neo-functionalism?' in T. Christiansen, K.E. Jørgensen, and A. Wiener (eds) *The Social Construction of Europe* (London: SAGE), pp. 22–31.

Habermas, J. (1975) *Legitimation Crisis* (Boston, MA: Beacon Press).

Habermas, J. (1992) 'Citizenship and National Identity: Some Reflections on the Future of Europe', Praxis *Interternational* 12 (1), pp. 1–19

Habermas, J. (2001) *The Postnational Constellation* (Cambridge Mass.: The MIT Press).

Hager, S.B. (2009) "New Europeans' for the 'New European Economy': Citizenship and the Lisbon Agenda' in B. van Apeldoorn, J. Drahokoupil and L. Horn (eds) *Contradictions and Limits of Neoliberal European Governance: From Lisbon to Lisbon* (Basingstoke: Palgrave Macmillan), pp. 106–24.

Hall, P.A. (2014) 'Varieties of Capitalism and the Euro Crisis', *West European Politics* 37 (6), pp. 1223–43.

Hall, P.A. & R.J. Franzese, Jr (1998) 'Mixed Signals: Central Bank Independence, Coordinated Wage Bargaining and European Monetary Union', *International Organization* 52 (3), pp. 505–35.

Hall, P.A. & R.C.R. Taylor (1996) 'Political Science and the Three New Institutionalisms', *Political Studies* XLIV, pp. 936–57.

Hallstein, W. (1962) *United Europe* (Oxford: Oxford University Press).

Hamilton, D. & J. Quinlan (2014) *The Transatlantic Economy 2013: Annual Survey of Jobs, Trade, and Investment between the United States and Europe*, Center for Transatlantic Relations, Johns Hopkins University Paul Nitze School of Advanced International Studies.

Hamilton, D. & J. Quinlan (2016) *The Transatlantic Economy 2016: Annual Survey of Jobs, Trade, and Investment between the United States and Europe*. Washington, DC: Center for Transatlantic Relations.

Hansen, L. & M.C. Williams (1999) 'The Myths of Europe: Legitimacy, Community and the 'Crisis' of the EU', *Journal of Common Market Studies* 37 (2), pp. 233–49.

Hancké, B. (2013) 'The Missing Link: Labour Unions, Central Banks and Monetary Integration in Europe', *Transfer: European Review of Labour and Research* 19 (1), pp. 89–101.

Hardt, M. & A. Negri (2000) *Empire* (Cambridge, MA: Harvard University Press).

Harvey, D. (2003) *The New Imperialism* (Oxford: Oxford University Press).

Harvey, D. (2006) *Spaces of Global Capitalism: Towards a Theory of Uneven Geographical Development* (London: Verso).

Hay, C. (2000) 'Contemporary Capitalism, Globalization, Regionalization and the Persistence of National Variation', *Review of International Studies* 26, pp. 509–31.

Hay, C. (2002) *Political Analysis: A Critical Introduction* (Basingstoke: Palgrave).

Hay, C. (2004) 'Common Trajectories, Variable Paces, Divergent Outcomes: Models of European Capitalism under Conditions of Complex Economic Interdependence', *Review of International Political Economy* 11 (2), pp. 231–62.

Hay, C. & B. Rosamond (2002) 'Globalization, European Integration and the Discursive Construction of Economic Imperatives', *Journal of European Public Policy* 9 (2), pp. 147–67.

Hay, C. & D. Wincott (2012) *The Political Economy of European Welfare Capitalism* (Basingstoke: Palgrave Macmillan).

Healy, N.M. (1995) 'From the Treaty of Rome to Maastricht' in N.M. Healy (ed.) *The Economics of the New Europe* (London: Routledge), pp. 1–41.

Heidenreich, M. (2003) 'Regional Inequalities in the Enlarged Europe', *Journal of European Social Policy* 13 (4), pp. 313–333.

Heinrich, M. & E. Kutter (2014) 'A Critical Juncture in EU Integration? The Eurozone Crisis and its Management 2010-2012', in F. Panizza & G. Philip (eds) *Moments of Truth: The Politics of Financial Crises in Comparative Perspective* (London: Routledge), pp. 120–39.

Helleiner, E. (1994) *States and the Re-emergence of Global Finance* (Ithaca, NY: Cornell University Press).

Helleiner, E. (2008) 'Political Determinants of International Currencies: What Future for the US Dollar?', *Review of International Political Economy* 15 (3), pp. 354–78

Hellema, D. et al. (2004) *The Netherlands and the Oil Crisis: Business as Usual* (Amsterdam: Amsterdam University Press).

Hemerijck, A. (2002) 'The Self-transformation of the European Social Model(s)', *International Politics and Society* 4/2002, pp. 39–66.

Henning, R. (1998) 'Systemic Conflict and Regional Monetary Integration: The Case of Europe', *International Organization* 52 (3), pp. 537–74.

Henning, R. (2006) 'The Exchange Rate Weapon and Macroeconomic Conflict' in D. Andrews (ed.) *International Monetary Power* (Ithaca, NY: Cornell University Press), pp. 117–38.

Herrhausen, A. (1989) *New Horizons in Europe: Dritte Arthur Burns Memorial Lecture*, (Hamburg: Atlantik-Brücke e.V).

Heyes, J. & P. Lewis (2014) 'Employment Protection under Fire: Labour Market Deregulation and Employment in the European Union', *Economic and Industrial Democracy* 35 (4), pp. 587–607.

Hicks, J.R. (1937) 'Mr. Keynes and the "Classics": A Suggested Interpretation', *Econometrica* 5 (2), pp. 147–59.

Hilferding, R. (1910 [2005]) *Finance Capital: A Study in the Latest Phase of Capitalist Development* (London: Routledge).

Hirschfeld, G. (1989) *Collaboration in France: Politics and Culture During the Nazi Occupation, 1940–44* (New York: Berg).

Hix, S. (1994) 'The Study of the European Community: The Challenge to Comparative Politics', *West European Politics* 17 (1), pp. 1–30.

Hix, S. (1999) *The Political System of the European Union* (Basingstoke: Palgrave Macmillan).

Hix, S. (2005) *The Political System of the European Union*, 2nd edition (Basingstoke: Palgrave Macmillan).

Hobbes, T. (1651 [1962]) *Leviathan: Or the Matter, Forme, and Power of A Commonwealth Ecclesiaticall and Civil* (London: Collier Macmillan).

Hodgson, G. (1996) 'Variety of Capitalism, Variety of Economic Theory', *Review of International Political Economy* 3 (3), pp. 380–433.

Hoffman, S. (1966) 'Obstinate or Obsolete? The Fate of the Nation-State and the Case of Western Europe', *Daedalus* 95 (3), pp. 862–915.

Holland, S. (1980) *Uncommon Market: Capital, Class and Power in the European Community* (London: Macmillan).

Holloway, J. & S. Picciotto (eds) (1978) *State and Capital: A Marxist Debate* (London: Edward Arnold).

Holman, O. (1992) 'European Unification in the 1990s: Myth and Reality', *International Journal of Political Economy* 22 (1), pp. 1–22.

Holman, O. (1993) Integrating Southern Europe: EC Expansion and the Transnationalisation of Spain, PhD Thesis, Department of International Relations, University of Amsterdam.

Holman, O. (2004) 'Asymmetrical Regulation and Multidimensional Governance in the European Union', *Review of International Political Economy* 11 (4), pp. 714–35.

Hooghe, L. (ed.) (1996) *Cohesion Policy and European Integration: Building Multilevel Governance* (Oxford: Clarendon Press).

Höpner, M. & A. Schäfer (2010) 'Polanyi in Brussels? Embeddedness and the Three Dimensions of European Economic Integration', *MPIfG Discussion Paper* 10/8.

Horkheimer, M. (1937 [2002]) 'Traditional and Critical Theory' in *Critical Theory: Selected Essays* (New York: Continuum), pp. 188–243.

Horn, L. (2012) *Regulating Corporate Governance in the EU: Towards A Marketization of Corporate Control* (Basingstoke: Palgrave Macmillan).

Hout, W. (2010) 'Governance and Development: Changing EU Policies', *Third World Quarterly* 31 (1), pp. 1–12.

Hurt, S.R. (2003) 'Cooperation and Coercion: The Cotonou Agreement between the European Union and ACP States and the End of the Lomé Convention', *Third World Quarterly* 24 (1), pp. 161–76.

Hurt, S.R. (2012) 'The EU-SADC Economic Partnership Agreement Negotiations: "Locking In" the Neoliberal Development Model in Southern Africa', *Third World Quarterly* 33 (3), pp. 495–510.

Hurt, S., K. Knio, & M. Ryner (2009) 'Social Forces and the Effect of (Post-) Washington Consensus Policy in Africa: Comparing Tunisia and South Africa', *The Round Table: The Commonwealth Journal of International Affairs* 98 (402), pp. 301–17.

IFO (2015) *IFO Institute Estimates of Refugee Costs to 21.1 Billion Euros for 2015 Alone*, accessed at http://www.cesifo-group.de/ifoHome/presse/Pressemitteilungen/Pressemitteilungen-Archiv/2015/Q4/press_20151110_fluechtlinge.html, accessed on 30.04.2016.

Ignatius, D. (2012) 'A Free Trade Agreement with Europe?', *Washington Post*, 6 December.

Ikenberry, J. (2001) *After Victory: Institutions, Strategic Restraint, and the Rebuilding of Order after Major Wars* (Princeton, NJ: Princeton University Press).

International Monetary Fund (2012) *Money and Banking Issues in European Transition Economies*, Tirana, Albania, 12 October, accessed at https://www.imf.org/external/region/BAL/rr/2012/102612.pdf, accessed on 30.04.2016.

International Monetary Fund (2013) *German-Central Europe Supply Chain— Cluster Report*, IMF Multi-Country Report No. 13/263, Washington, DC (August) http://www.imf.org/external/pubs/ft/scr/2013/cr13263.pdf, accessed on 30.04.2016.

International Monetary Fund (2014) *IMF Announces Staff Level Agreement with Ukraine on U.S. $14–18 billion Stand-by Arrangement*, International Monetary Fund, Washington, DC, accessed at https://www.imf.org/external/np/sec/pr/2014/pr14131.htm, accessed on 30.04.2016.

International Monetary Fund (2016) 'The Refugee Surge in Europe: Economic Challenges', *IMF Staff Discussion Note*, Washington, DC.

Ioannou, D., P. Leblond, and A. Niemann (2015) 'European Integration and the Crisis: Practice and Theory', *Journal of European Public Policy* 22 (2), pp. 155–76.

IPS (2011) "Libya: Broad German Consensus Against a 'Risky' War" (Berlin), 19 March, accessed at http://www.ipsnews.net/2011/03/libya-broad-german-consensus-against-a-risky-war/.

Issing, O. (2002) 'On Macroeconomic Policy Co-Ordination in EMU', *Journal of Common Market Studies* 40 (2) pp. 345–58.

Ivanova, M. (2007) 'Why There Was No Marshall Plan for Eastern Europe and Why This Still Matters', *Journal of Contemporary European Studies*, 15 (3) (December), pp. 349–380.

Ivanova, M. (2009) 'Growing through Debt and Inflation: an Inquiry into the Esoteric and Exoteric Aspects of Bulgaria's Currency Board', *Debatte: Journal of Contemporary Central and Eastern Europe* August, pp. 159–179.

Ivanova, M. (2013) 'The Crisis of Home-Centered Consumer Capitalism in the United States' in A. Cafruny and H. Schwartz (eds) *Exploring the Global Financial Crisis* (Boulder, CO: Lynne Rienner Publishers), pp. 165–78.

Iversen, T. & D. Soskice (2012) 'Modern Capitalism and the Advanced Nation State: Undestanding the Causes of the Crisis' in N. Bermeo and J. Pontusson (eds) *Coping with Crisis: Government Reactions to the Great Recession* (London: SAGE), pp. 35–64.

Iversen, T. & A. Wren (1998) 'Equality, Employment and Budgetary Restraint: The Trilemma of the Service Economy', *World Politics* 50 (4), pp. 507–46.

Jabko, N. (1999) 'In the Name of the Market: How the European Commission Paved the Way for Monetary Union', *Journal of European Public Policy* 6 (3), pp. 475–95.

Janssen, R. (2005) 'Policy Coordination in the Macroeconomic Dialogue of Cologne: Experiences from the ETUC' in E. Hein, N. Niechoj, T. Schulten and A. Truger (eds) *Macroeconomic Policy Coordination in Europe and the Role of Trade Unions* (Brussels: ETUI Press), pp. 213–36.

Jenson, J. & D. Saint-Martin (2005) 'Building Blocks for a New Social Architecture: The LEGO Paradigm of an Active Society', *Policy and Politics* 34 (3), pp. 429–51.

Jessop, B. (1990) *State Theory: Putting Capitalist States in their Place* (Cambridge: Polity Press).

Jessop, B. (1994) 'Changing Forms and Functions of the State in an Era of Globalization and Regionalization' in R. Delorme and K. Dopfer (eds) *The Political Economy of Diversity: Evolutionary Perspectives on Economic Order and Disorder* (Aldershot: Edward Elgar), pp. 102–25.

Jessop, B. (2012) 'The World Market, Variegated Capitalism and the Crisis of European Integration' in P. Nousios, H. Overbeek, and A. Tsolakis (eds) *Globalisation and European Integration* (London: Routledge), pp. 91–111.

Jessop, B. (2014) 'Variegated Capitalism, das Modell Deutschland, and the Eurozone Crisis', *Journal of Contemporary European Studies* 22 (3), pp. 248–60.

Jileva, E. (2004) 'Do Norms Matter? The Principle of Solidarity and the EU's Eastern Enlargement', *Journal of International Relations and Development* 7 (1), pp. 3–23.

Joerges, C. (2012) 'Europas Wirtschaftsverfassung in der Krise', *Der Staat* 51 (3), pp. 357–85.

Johnson, C. (2001) *Blowback: The Costs and Consequences of American Empire* (New York: Henry Holt).

Johnston, A., B. Hancké, & S. Pant (2013) 'Comparative Institutional Advantage in the European Sovereign debt Crisis', *LSE 'Europe in Question' Discussion Paper Series* 66.

Jones, E. (2003) 'Liberalized Capital Markets, State Autonomy and European Monetary Union', *European Journal of Political Research* 42 (2), pp. 197–222.

Jonung, L. & E. Drea (2009) 'The Euro: It Can't Happen. It's a Bad Idea. It Won't Last. U.S. Economists on the EMU, 1989–2002', *European Commission*, Economic and Financial Affairs, Brussels, November.

Junne, G. & R. van Tulder (1988) *European Multinationals in Core Technologies* (New York: John Wiley and Sons).

Jupille, J., J.A. Caporaso, & J.T. Checkel (2003) 'Integrating Institutions: Rationalism, Constructivism and the Study of the European Union', *Comparative Political Studies* 36 (1/2), pp. 7–40.

Kagan, R. (2003) *Americans Are From Mars, Europeans From Venus* (New York: Alfred Knopf).

Kaminski, B. (2001) 'How Accession to the European Union Has Affected External Trade and Foreign Direct Investment in Central European Economies', The World Bank Development Research Group Policy Research Working Paper 2578.

Kannankulam, J. & F. Georgi (2014) 'Varieties of Capitalism or Varieties of Relationships of Forces? Outlines of a Historical Materialist Policy Analysis', *Capital and Class* 38 (1), pp. 59–71.

Kant, I. (1795 [2010]) *Perpetual Peace* (New York: Cosimo Classics).

Kennedy, P. (1988) *The Rise and Fall of Great Powers* (New York: Vintage Press).

Keohane, R.O. (1984) *After Hegemony: Cooperation and Discord in the World Political Economy* (Princeton NJ: Princeton University Press).

Keukeleire, S. et al. (2011) 'The EU Foreign Policy towards the BRIC's and Other Emerging Powers: Objectives and Strategies', *AFET European Parliament*, October.

Keynes, J.M. (1936) *The General Theory of Employment, Interest and Money* (London: Macmillan).

Khandekar, G. (2013) 'Building a Sustainable EU-India Partnership', *European Strategic Partnership Observatory* Policy Brief 9.

Kinderman, D. (2005) 'Pressure from Without: Subversion from Within: The Two-Pronged German Employer Offensive', *Comparative European Politics* 3, pp. 432–63.

Kindleberger, C. (1973) *The World in Depression* (Berkeley, CA: University of California Press).

Kindleberger, C. (1978) *Manias, Panics and Crashes* (New York: Basic Books).

Kirshner, J. (2008) 'Dollar Primacy and American Power: What's at Stake?', *Review of International Political Economy* 15 (3), pp. 418–38.

Klinke, I. (2015) 'European Integration Studies and the European Union's Eastern Gaze', *Millennium: Journal of International Studies* 43 (2), pp. 567–83.

Kniou, K. (2013) *The European Union's Mediterranean Policy: Model or Muddle* (Basingstoke: Palgrave Macmillan).

Komarek, J. (2014) 'Waiting for the Existential Revolution in Europe', *International Journal of Constitutional Law* 12 (1), pp. 190–212.

Konings, M. (2008) 'European Finance in the American Mirror: Financial Change and the Reconfiguration of Competitiveness', *Contemporary Politics* 14 (3), pp. 253–75.

Konings, M. (2011) The *Development of American Finance* (Cambridge: Cambridge University Press).

Korpi, W. (2003) 'Welfare-State Regress in Western Europe: Politics, Institutions, Globalization and Europeanization', *Annual Review of Sociology* 29, pp. 589–609.

Korpi, W. & J. Palme (2003) 'New Politics and Class Politics in the Context of Austerity and Globalization: Welfare State Regress in 18 Countries 1975–1995', *American Political Science* 97 (3), pp. 425–46.

Krasner, S. (ed.) (1983) *International Regimes* (Ithaca, NY: Cornell University Press).

Kratochwil, F. & J.G. Ruggie (1986) 'International Organization: The State of the Art of the Art of the State', *International Organization* 40 (4), pp. 753–75.

Krauss, C. (2011) 'The Scramble for Access to Libya's Oil Wealth Now Begins', *New York Times*, 22 August.

Krotz, U. & J. Schild (2012) *Shaping Europe: France, Germany, and Embedded Bilateralism from the Elysee Treaty to 21st Century Politics* (Oxford: Oxford University Press).

Krugman, P. (1993) '8 Lessons from Massachusets for EMU' in F. Torres and F. Giavazzi (eds) *Adjustment and Growth in the European Monetary Union* (Cambridge: Cambridge University Press), pp. 241–61.

Krugman, P. & A. Venables (1990) 'Integration and the Competitiveness of Peripheral Industry', in C. Bliss and J. Braga de Macedo (eds) *Unity with Diversity in the European Economy: The Community's Southern Frontier* (Cambridge: Cambridge University Press), pp. 56–75.

Krzywdzinski, M. (2014) 'How the EU's Eastern Enlargement Changed the German Productive Model. The Case of the Automobile Industry', Revue de la Regulation, *Capitalisme, Institutions, Pouvoirs* 15, accessed at https://regulation.revues.org/10663, accessed on 03.05.2016.

Krzywdzinski, M. (2014) 'How the EU's Eastern Enlargement Changed the German Productive Model. The Case of the Automotive Industry', *Revue de la régulation - Capitalisme, institutions, pouvoirs* 15 (1), pp. 1–61.

Kuhn, T. (1962) *The Structure of Scientific Revolutions* (Chicago, IL: University of Chicago Press).

Kundnani, H. (2011) 'Germany as Geoeconomic Power', *Washington Quarterly* 34 (3) (Summer), pp. 1–15.

Kundnani, H. (2015a) 'Leaving the West Behind: Germany Looks East', *Foreign Affairs* 94 (1) (January–February), pp. 108–16.

Kundnani, H. (2015b) *The Paradox of German Power* (Oxford: Oxford University Press).

Kundnani, H. & J. Parello-Plesner (2012) *China and Germany: Why the Emerging Special Relationship Matters for Germany* (London: European Council on Foreign Relations).

Kupchan, C. (2002) *The End of the American Era: US Foreign Policy and the Geopolitics of the Twenty-First Century* (New York: Vintage).

Laïdi, Z. (2008) 'European Preferences and their Reception', in Laïdi, Z. (ed.) *ZEU Foreign Policy in a Globalised World: normative power and social preferences* (London: Routledge), pp. 1–20.

Lange, P. (1993) 'The Maastricht Social Protocol: Why Did They Do it?', *Politics and Society* 21, pp. 5–36.

Langley, P. (2008) *The Everyday Life of Global Finance: Saving and Borrowing in Anglo-America* (Oxford: Oxford University Press).

Lankowski, C. (1982) 'Modell Deutschland and the International Regionalization of the West German State' in A. Markovits (ed.) *The Political Economy of the German Model: Modell Deutschland* (New York: Praeger), pp. 90–115.

Lapavitsas, C. et al. (2012) *Crisis in the Eurozone* (London: Verso).

Lasswell, H. D (1936) *Politics: Who Gets What When How?* (New York: McGraw Hill).

Leborgne, D. & A. Lipietz (1988) 'New Technologies, New Modes of Regulation: Some Spatial Implications', *Environment and Planning D: Society and Space* 6 (3), pp. 263–80.

Leborgne, D. & A. Lipietz (1990) 'How to Avoid a Two-Tier Europe', *Labour and Society* 15 (2), pp. 177–200.

Lehmbruch, G. & P. Schmitter (eds) (1979) *Trends towards Corporatist Intermediation* (London: SAGE).

Lehndorff, S. (2015) 'Model or Liability? The New Career of the "German Model"' in S. Lehndorff (ed.) *Divisive Integration: The Triumph of Failed Ideas in Europe – Revisited* (Brussels: ETUI Press).

Leibfried, S. & P. Pierson (1995) 'Semi-sovereign Welfare States: Social Policy in a Multi-Tiered Europe' in S. Leibfried and P. Pierson (eds) *European Social Policy* (Washington, DC: Brookings Institution), pp. 43–77.

Leonard, E., R. Erne, P. Marginson, S. Smismans, and P. Tilly (2007) *New Structures, Forms, and Processes of Governance in European Industrial Relations* (Luxembourg: Office for Official Publications of the European Communities).

Leonard, M. (2005) *Why Europe Will Run the Twenty-First Century* (London: Fourth Estate).

Lepesant, G. (2014 [2004–2014]): 'Review of a Decade of Enlargements', *European Issues Policy Paper n. 311*, Robert Schuman Foundation, Brussels, 29 April.

Levi, P. (2015) The Economic and Security Benefits of a Successful TTIP are a Package Deal. Washington: Cato Institute. https://www.cato.org/publications/cato-online-forum/economics-security-benefits-successful-ttip-are-package-deal, accessed on 03.11.2016.

Lewis, J. & S. Giullari (2005) 'The Adult Worker Model, Family, Gender and Care: The Search for New Policy Principles and the Possibilities and Limits of a Capabilities Approach', *Economy and Society* 34 (1), pp. 76–104.

Lewis, J., T. Knijn, C. Martin, & I. Ostner (2008) 'Patterns of Development in Work/Family Reconciliation Policies for Parents in France, Germany and the Netherlands in the 2000s', *Social Politics* 15 (3), pp. 261–86.

Leys, C. (1983) *Politics in Britain* (London: Heinemann).

Lijphart, A. et al. (1988) 'A Mediterranean Model of Democracy? The Southern European Democracies in a Comparative Perspective', *West European Politics* 11 (1), pp. 7–25.

Lindberg, L., R. Alford, C. Crouch, & C. Offe (eds) (1975) *Stress and Contradiction in Modern Capitalism* (Lexington, MA: D.C. Heath).

Lindblom, C.E. (1977) *Politics and Markets: The World's Political-Economic Systems* (New York: Basic Books).

Lipietz, A. (1988) 'Reflections on a Tale: The Marxist Foundations of the Concepts of Accumulation and Regulation', *Studies in Political Economy* 26 (2), pp. 7–37.

Lipietz, A. (1989) 'The Debt Problem, European Integration and the New Phase of World Crisis', *New Left Review* 178 (old series), pp. 37–50.

Lipietz, A. (1987) 'Rebel Sons: The Regulation School', interview with Jane Jenson, *French Politics and Society* 5 (4), pp. 3–17.

List, F. (1856) *National System of Political Economy* (Philadelphia, PA: J.B. Lippincott).

Lister, M. (1988) *The European Community and the Developing World* (Aldershot: Avebury).

London Economics (2002) 'Quantification of the Macro-Economic Impact of Integration of EU Financial Markets', *Final Report by London Economics in association with Pricewaterhouse Coopers and Oxford Economic Forecasting to the European Commission*, November.

Love, K. (1969) *Suez: The Twice-Fought War* (New York: McGraw Hill).

Lowi, T. (1979) *The End of Liberalism* (New York: W.W. Norton).

Lowi, T. (1967) 'Making Democracy Safe for the World: National Politics and Foreign Policy' in James Rosenau (ed.) *Domestic Sources of Foreign Policy* (New York: Free Press), pp. 295–332.

Lundestad, G. (1991) 'Empire by Invitation? The United States and Western Europe, 1945–1952' in C. Maier (ed.) *The Cold War in Europe: Era of a Divided Continent* (New York: Markus Wiener Publishing), pp. 143–65.

Luttwak, E. (1990) 'From Geopolitics to Geo-economics', *The National Interest*, Summer.

Mabbett, D. & W. Schelkle (2007) 'Bringing Macroeconomics Back into the Political Economy of Reform: The Lisbon Agenda and the "Fiscal Philosophy" of EMU', *Journal of Common Market Studies* 45 (1), pp. 81–103

Macartney, H. (2011) *Variegated Neoliberalism: EU Varieties of Capitalism and International Political Economy* (London: Routledge).

MacKay, R.R. (1995) 'European Integration and Public Finance: The Political Economy of Regional Support' in S. Hardy et al. (eds) *An Enlarged Europe* (London: Jessica Kingsley), pp. 159–79.

Magdoff, H. (2003) *Imperialism without Colonies* (New York: Monthly Review Press).

Mahon, R. (1987) 'From Fordism to?: New Technology, Labour Markets and Unions', *Economic and Industrial Democracy* 8 (1), pp. 5–60.

Mahon, R. (2007) 'Swedish Model Dying of Baumols? Current Debates', *New Political Economy* 12 (1), pp. 79–85.

Maier, C. (1991) 'The Politics of Productivity: Foundations of American International Economic Power after World War II' in C. Maier (ed.) *The Cold War in Europe: Era of a Divided Continent* (New York: Markus Wiener Publishing), pp. 169–201.

Maier, C. (2012) 'Europe Needs a German Marshall Plan', *New York Times*, 13 June, p. 23.

Mair, P. (1990) *The West European Party System* (Oxford: Oxford University Press).

Mandel, E. (1967) 'International Capitalism and "Supra-Nationality"' in R. Miliband and J. Saville (eds) *The Socialist Register 1967* (London: Merlin Press), pp. 27–41.

Mandel, E. (1969) *Europe versus America? Contradictions of Imperialism* (London: New Left Books).

Mandelbaum, M. (1993) 'Introduction', in S. Islam and M. Mandelbaum (eds) *Making Markets: Economic Transformation in Eastern Europe and the Post-Soviet Council on Foreign Relations* (Council on Foreign Relations Press), pp. 1–15.

Manners, I. (2002) 'Normative Power Europe: A Contradiction in Terms?', *Journal of Common Market Studies* 40 (2), pp. 235–58.

Manners, I. (2008) 'The Normative Ethics of the European Union', *International Affairs* 83 (1), pp. 65–80.

Manners, I. (2008) 'The Normative Power of the European Union in a Globalised World', in Z. Laïdi (ed.) *EU Foreign Policy in a Globalised World: Normative Power and Social Preferences* (London: Routledge).

Manners, I. (2010) 'The European Union's Normative Power: Critical Perspectives on the Critical' in R. Whitman (ed.) *Normative Power Europe: Empirical and Theoretical Perspectives* (Basingstoke: Palgrave Macmillan), pp. 226–47.

March, J.G. & J.P. Olsen (1984) 'The New Institutionalism: Organizational Factors in Political Life', *American Political Science Review* 78 (3), pp. 734–49.

Marcuse, H. (1964 [1991]) *One-dimensional Man* (London: Routledge).

Marcussen, M. (1999) 'The Dynamics of EMU Ideas', *Cooperation and Conflict* 34 (4), pp. 383–411.

Marks, G., L. Hooghe, & K. Blank (1996) 'European Integration from the 1980s: State Centric v. Multilevel Governance', *Journal of Common Market Studies* 34 (3), pp. 341–78.

Marshall, T.H. (1950) *Citizenship and Social Class and other Essays* (Cambridge: Cambridge University Press).

Martin, M. & M. Kaldor (2012) *The European Union and Human Security* (London: Routledge).

Marx, K. ([1843] 1970) *The Critique of Hegel's Philosophy of Right* (Cambridge: Cambridge University Press).

Marx, K. (1867 [1977]) *Capital: A Critique of Political Economy Volume 1* (New York: Vintage Press).

Marx, K. (1893 [1967]) *Capital: The Process of Circulation of Capital, Volume 2*, edited by F. Engels (New York: International Publishers).

Marx, K. (1894 [1967]) *Capital: The Process of Capitalist Production as a Whole, Volume 3*, edited by F. Engels (New York: International Publishers).

Mattli, W. & A.-M. Slaughter (1995) 'Law and Politics in the European Union: A Reply to Garrett', *International Organization* 49 (1), pp. 183–90.

Mayhew, A. (1998) *Recreating Europe: The European Union's Policy Towards Central and Eastern Europe* (Cambridge: Cambridge University Press).

McCarthy, P. (1998) 'The Franco-German Axis from de Gaulle to Chirac' in D.P. Calleo and E.R. Staal (eds) *Europe's Franco-German Engine* (Washington, DC: Brookings Institution), pp. 101–36.

McCormick, J. & J. Olson (2014) *The European Union: Politics and Policies*, 5th edition (London: Palgrave MacMillan).

McMahon, S. (2015). 'Regional Integration and Migration in the European Union' in Leila Simona Talani and Simon McMahon (eds) *Handbook of the International Political Economy of Migration* (London: Palgrave), pp. 285–303.

McNamara, K. (1998) *The Currency of Ideas: Monetary Politics in the European Union* (Ithaca, NY: Cornell University Press).

McNamara, K. (2006) 'Economic Governance, Ideas and EMU: What Currency Does Policy Consensus Have Today', *Journal of Common Market Studies* 44 (4), pp. 803–21.

Menéndez, A.J. (2014) 'Editorial: A European Union in Constitutional Mutation?', *European Law Journal* 20 (2), pp. 127–41.

Migrants Files (2015) 'The Money Trail', *Migrants Research Network*, 18 June.

Mihut, A. (2012) 'Romanian Economy in the European Crisis', Studia Universitatis Vasile Goldis, *Arad Economics Series* 22 (3), pp. 116–21.

Milios, J. & D.P. Sotiropoulos (2010) 'Crisis of Greece or Crisis of the Euro? A View from the European "Periphery"', *Journal of Balkan and Near Eastern Studies* 12 (3), pp. 223–40.

Millberg, W.S. & D. Winkler (2013) *Outsourcing Economics: Global Value Chains in Capitalist Development* (Cambridge: Cambridge University Press).

Milward, A.S. (1984) *The Reconstruction of Western Europe 1945–51* (London: Routledge).

Milward, A.S. (1992) *The European Rescue of the Nation State* (London: Routledge).

Milward, A.S. & V. Sørensen (1993) 'Interdependence or Integration? A National Choice' in A.S Milward, F. Lynch, R. Ranieri, F. Romero, and V. Sørensen (eds) *The Frontier of National Sovereignty: History and Theory* (London: Routledge).

Minsky, H. (1986) *Stabilizing an Unstable Economy* (New Haven: Yale University Press).

Mitrany, D. (1943) *A Working Peace System: An Argument for the Functional Development of International Organization* (London: Royal Institute of International Affairs).

Monnet, J. (1976) *Memoirs* (New York: Doubleday).

Moravcsik, A. (1991) 'Negotiating the Single European Act: National Interests and Conventional Statecraft in the European Community', *International Organization* 45 (1), pp. 19–56.

Moravcsik, A. (1995) 'Liberal Intergovernmentalism and Integration: A Rejoinder', *Journal of Common Market Studies* 33 (4), pp. 611–28.

Moravcsik, A. (1998) *The Choice for Europe: Social Purpose and State Power from Messina to Maastricht* (London: UCL Press).

Moravcsik, A. & M. Vachudova (2003) '*National Interests, State Power, and Enlargement*', East European Politics and Societies 7 (1), pp. 42-57.

Moravcsik, A. (2006) 'What Can We Learn from the Collapse of the European Constitutional Project?', *Politische Vierteljahresschrift* 47 (2), pp. 219–41.

Mundell, R. (1961) 'A Theory of Optimal Currency Areas', *American Economic Review* 51, pp. 657–66.

Murphy, R. (2014) 'The Dollar and East Asia: The Endgame?' in A. Cafruny and H. Schwartz (eds) *Exploring the Global Financial Crisis* (Boulder, CO: Lynne Rienner Publishers), pp. 35–60.

Myers-Resende,M.(2013)'PreventingMoreHungarys:AStrongerHumanRights Architecture for the EU', *Open Democracy*, November, accessed at https://www.opendemocracy.net/can-europe-make-it/michael-meyer-resende/preventing-more-hungarys-%E2%80%93-stronger-human-rights-architectu.

Myrdal, G. (1954) *The Political Element in the Development of Economic Theory* (Cambridge, MA: Harvard University Press).

NATO (2010) *Lisbon Summit Declaration*, North Atlantic Treaty Organization, accessed at http://www.nato.int, 20 November, accessed on 30.04.2016.

NATO (2012) 'Deterrence and Defence Posture Review' (Brussels), 20 May, accessed at http://www.nato.int/cps/en/natohq/official_texts_87597.htm.

Neumann, F. (1937 [1958]) 'The Change in the Function of Law in Modern Society' in *The Democratic and Authoritarian State* (New York: The Free Press), pp. 22–68.

Niemann, A. & D. Iannou (2015) 'European Integration in Times of Crisis: A Case for Neofunctionalism?', *Journal of European Public Policy* 22 (2), pp. 196–218.

Nölke, A. (2010) 'A "BRIC" Variety of Capitalism and Social Inequality: The Case of Brazil', *Revista de Estudios e Pesquisas sobre as Américas* 7 (1), pp. 1–14.

Norloff, C. (2014) *America's Global Advantage: U.S. Hegemony and International Cooperation* (Cambridge: Cambridge University Press).

Novinite (2013) 'Bank Drain Ghosts to Haunt Bulgaria Again', 30 September, accessed at http://www.novinite.com/articles/154089/Bank+Drain+Ghosts+to+Haunt+Bulgaria+Again+-+Greek+Media, accessed on 30.04.2016.

Nye, J. (2004) *Soft Power: the Means to Success in World Politics* (Cambridge, MA: Public Affairs).

O'Donnell, T. (2015) 'Bypass Operation: A New Russian-Northern European Pipeline Raises Questions', *Berlin Policy Journal* (September–October), accessed at http://berlinpolicyjournal.com/bypass-operation/, accessed on 30.04.2016.

Oakland Institute (2014) '*The Corporate Takeover of Ukrainian* Agriculture: Country Fact Sheet' (Oakland, Calif.).

Oberndorfer, L. (2015) 'From New Constitutionalism to Authoritarian Constitutionalism: New European Governance and the State of European Democracy', in J. Jäger and E. Springler (eds) *Asymmetrical Regulation in Europe and Possible Futures* (London: Routledge), pp. 186–207.

OECD (2012) 'Structural Reforms in Times of Crisis', *Economic Policy Reforms: Going for Growth*, Chapter 1 (Paris: OECD).

OECD (2015a) 'Development Aid Stable But Flows to Poorest Countries Still Falling', Development Assistance Committee, Paris, 8 April, accessed at http://www.oecd.org/dac/stats/documentupload/ODA%202014%20Technical%20Note.pdf, accessed on 30.04.2016.

OECD (2015b) 'Is This Humanitarian Migration Crisis Different?' Migration Policy Debates, Number 7, Paris, September.

Onaran, Ö. and G. Galanis (2013) 'Is Aggregate Demand Wage-Led or Profit-Led?', International Labor Office, Conditions of Work and Employment Series, 40, Geneva, accessed at http://www.ilo.org/wcmsp5/groups/public/---ed_protect/---protrav/---travail/documents/publication/wcms_192121.pdf, accessed on 03.05.2016.

Otero-Iglesias, M. (2012) 'The (In-)tangible Euro Challenge to the Dollar: Insights from the Financial Elites in Brazil and China', *Cambridge Review of International Affairs* 25, pp. 1–20.

Otero-Iglesias, M. (2014) *The Euro, the Dollar and the Global Financial Crisis: Currency Challenges seen from Emerging Markets* (London: Routledge).

Overbeek, H. (ed.) (1993) *Restructuring Hegemony in the Global Political Economy: The Rise of Transnational Neoliberalism in the 1980s* (London: Routledge).

Overbeek, H. (2016) 'Globalizing China: A Critical Political Economy Perspective on China's Rise' in A. Cafruny, L. S. Talani, and G. Pozo (eds) *Handbook of Critical International Political Economy* (London: Palgrave), pp. 309–30.

Overbeek, H., B. van Apeldoorn, & A. Nölke (eds) (2007) *The Transnational Politics of Corporate Governance Regulation* (London: Routledge).

Padoa-Schioppa, T. (1994) *The Road to Monetary Union in Europe: The Emperor, the Kings and the Genies* (Oxford: Clarendon Press).

Padoa-Schioppa, T. et al. (1987) *Efficiency, Stability and Equity: A Strategy for the Evolution of the Economic System of the European Community* (Oxford: Oxford University Press).

Panitch, L. (1994) 'Globalisation and the State' in R. Miliband and L. Panitch (eds) *The Socialist Register 1994* (London: Merlin Press), pp. 60–93.

Panitch, L. & S. Gindin (2003) 'American Imperialism and Euro-Capitalism: The Making of Neoliberal Globalization', *Studies in Political Economy* 71/72, pp. 7–38.

Panitch, L. & S. Gindin (2012) *The Making of Global Capitalism: The Political Economy of American Empire* (London: Verso).

Parboni, R. (1982) *The Dollar and its Rivals* (London: Verso).

Peters, B.G. (2005) *Institutional Theory in Political Science* (London: Continuum).

Pierson, P. & S. Leibfried (1995) 'The Dynamics of Social Policy Integration' in S. Leibfried and P. Pierson (eds) *European Social Policy: Between Fragmentation and Integration* (Washington, DC: The Brookings Institution), pp. 432–65.

Pierson, P. (1996) 'The Path to European Integration: A Historical Institutionalist Analysis', *Comparative Political Studies* 29 (2), pp. 123–63.

Pisani-Ferry, J. & A. Posen (2009) 'Introduction: the euro at ten – successful but regional' in J. Pisani-Ferry and A. Posen (eds) *The Euro at Ten: The Next Global Currency?* (Washington, DC, and Brussels: The Peterson Institute of International Economics and Bruegel), pp. 1–15.

Pogatsa, Z. (2016) 'Hungary: From Star Transition Student to Backsliding Member State', *Journal of Contemporary European Research* 5 (4), pp. 597–613.

Pontusson, J. (1997) 'Between Neo-Liberalism and the German Model: Swedish Capitalism in Transition', in C. Crouch and W. Streeck (eds) *Political Economy of Modern Capitalism: Mapping Convergence and Diversity* (London: SAGE), pp. 55–70.

Poulantzas, N. (1969) 'The Problem of the Capitalist State', *New Left Review* 58 (old series), pp. 67–83.

Poulantzas, N. (1973) *Political Power and Social Classes* (London: New Left Books).

Poulantzas, N. (1974) 'Internationalisation of Capitalist Relations and the Nation State', *Economy and Society* 2 (1), pp. 145–79.

Poulantzas, N. (1975) 'The Capitalist State: A Reply to Miliband and Laclau', *New Left Review* 95 (old series), pp. 63–83.

Poulantzas, N. (1978) *State, Power, Socialism* (London: New Left Books).

Prebisch, R. (1950) 'The Economic Development of Latin America and Its Principal Problems', Economic Commission for Latin America (New York: United Nations Department of Economic Affairs).

President of Russia (2015) 'Meeting with Vice-Chancellor and Minister of Economic Affairs and Energy Sigmar Gabriel', Moscow, 28 October, accessed at http://en.kremlin.ru/events/president/news/50582, accessed on 30.04.2016.

Preston, C. (1997) *Enlargement and Integration in the European Union* (London: Routledge).

Putnam, R.D. (1988) 'Diplomacy and Domestic Politics', *International Organization* 42, pp. 427–61.

Radice, H. (2014) 'Enforcing Austerity in Europe: The Structural Deficit as a Policy Target', *Journal of Contemporary European Studies* 22 (3), pp. 318–28.

Rae, G. (2011) 'On the Periphery: the Uneven Development of the EU and the Effects of the Global Economic Crisis on Central-Eastern Europe', *Global Society* 25 (2), pp. 249–66.

Rae, G. (2016) 'Capitalism and the Dilemmas of the Polish Left', *Transform*, 8 February, Brussels www. Transform-network.net/

Ramsay, H. (1995) 'Le Défi Européen: Multinational Restructuring, Labour, and EU Policy', in A. Amin & J. Tomaney (eds) *Behind the Myth of the European Union* (London: Routledge), pp. 174–200.

Raviv, O. (2008) 'Chasing the Dragon East: Exploring the Frontiers of Western European Finance', *Contemporary Politics* 14 (3), pp. 297–314.

Raviv, O. (2011) 'Speculating on Convergence: The Western European Finance-led Growth Regime and the New European Periphery', PhD thesis, Department of International Relations, University of Sussex.

Reid, T. (2004) *The United States of Europe: The New Superpower and the End of American Supremacy* (New York: Penguin).

Rettman, A. (2011) 'France: Libya War Marks New Chapter in EU-US Relations', *Euobserver* 1 September, accessed at https://euobserver.com/defence/113486, accessed on 30.04.2016.

Rhodes, M. (1995) 'A Regulatory Conundrum: Industrial Relations and the Social Dimension' in S. Leibfried and P. Pierson (eds) *European Social Policy: Between Fragmentation and Integration* (Washington, DC: The Brookings Institution), pp. 78–122.

Rhodes, M. (2001) 'The Political Economy of Social Pacts: Competitive Corporatism and European Welfare Reform' in P. Pierson (ed.) *The New Politics of Welfare* (Oxford: Oxford University Press), pp. 165–94.

Rhodes, M. (2002) 'Why the EMU Is – or May Be – Good for the European Welfare States' in K. Dyson (ed.) *European States and the Euro: Europeanization, Variation and Convergence* (Oxford: Oxford University Press), pp. 305–34.

Rhodes, M. & B. van Apeldoorn (1998) 'Capital Unbound? The Transformation of European Corporate Governance', *Journal of European Public Policy* 5 (3), pp. 406–27.

Ricardo, D. (1817 [1997]) 'On Foreign Trade' in G.T. Crane and A. Amawi (eds) *The Evolution of International Political Economy: A Reader* (Oxford: Oxford University Press), pp. 72–82.

Risse-Kappen, T. (1996) 'Exploring the Nature of the Beast: International Relations Theory and Comparative Policy Analysis Meet the European Union', *Journal of Common Market Studies* 34 (1), pp. 53–80.

Risse, T. (2005) 'Neofunctionalism, European Identity, and the Puzzles of European Integration', *Journal of European Public Policy* 12 (2), pp. 291–309.

Risse, T., D. Engelmann-Martin, H.-J. Knope, & K. Roscher (1999) 'To Euro or Not to Euro? The EMU and Identity Politics in the European Union', *European Journal of International Relations* 5 (2), pp. 147–87.

Robinson, W. (2004) *A Theory of Global Capitalism* (Baltimore, MD: Johns Hopkins).

Roccu, R. (2013) *The Political Economy of the Egyptian Revolution: Mubarak, Economic Reforms, and Failed Hegemony* (Basingstoke: Palgrave Macmillan).

Rosamond, B. (1999) *Theories of European Integration* (Basingstoke: Palgrave Macmillan).

Rosamond, B. (2005) 'The Uniting of Europe and the Foundation of EU Studies: Revisiting the Neofunctionalism of Ernst B. Haas', *Journal of European Public Policy* 12 (2), pp. 237–54.

Rosamond, B. (2007) 'European Integration and the Social Science of EU Studies: The Disciplinary Politics of a Subfield', *International Affairs* 83 (1), pp. 231–52.

Rose, A.W. & E. van Wincoop (2001) 'National Money as a Barrier to Trade: The Real Case for Monetary Union', *American Economic Review* 91 (2), pp. 386–90.

Rosenberg, J. (1994) *The Empire of Civil Society: A Critique of Realist Theory of International Relations* (London: Verso).

Rosecrance, R. (2013) *The Resurgence of the West: How a Transatlantic Union Can Prevent War and Restore the United States and Europe* (New Haven, CT: Yale University Press).

Ruggie, J.G. (1982) 'International Regimes, Transaction and Change: Embedded Liberalism in the Postwar Economic Order', *International Organization* 36 (2), pp. 379–415.

Runciman, W.G. (1963) *Social Science and Political Theory* (Cambridge: Cambridge University Press).

Rupert, M. (1995) *Producing Hegemony: The Politics of Mass Production and American Global Power* (Cambridge: Cambridge University Press).

Ryner, M. (2009) 'European Monetary Union and the Politics of Welfare State Retrenchment: A Critique of the New Malthusians', in B. van Apeldoorn, J. Drahokoupil, and L. Horn (eds) *Contradictions and Limits of Neoliberal European Governance: From Lisbon to Lisbon* (Basingstoke: Palgrave Macmillan), pp. 44–63.

Ryner, M. (2012) 'Financial Crisis, Orthodoxy, Heterodoxy and the Production of Knowledge about the EU', *Millennium: Journal of International Studies* 40 (3), pp. 642–68.

Ryner, M. (2015) 'Europe's Ordo-liberal Iron Cage: Critical Political Economy and the Euro Area Crisis and Its Management', *Journal of European Public Policy* 22 (2), pp. 275–94.

Ryner, M. & T. Schulten (2003) 'The Political Economy of Labour Market Restructuring and Trade Union Responses in the Social Democratic Heartland', in H. Overbeek (ed.) *The Political Economy of European Employment: European Integration and the Transnationalization of the (Un)employment Question* (London: Routledge), pp. 176–98.

Sainsbury, D. (1996) *Gender Equality and Welfare States* (Cambridge: Cambridge University Press).

Salido, A., J. Carabana, and S. Torrejon (2012) 'Unemployment and poverty in Spain: a portrait of recent changes in the "welfare mix"', *Paper presented at the Interim Conference of the Disaster, Conflict and Social Crisis Research Network of the European Sociological Association*, University of the Aegean, Mytilene, Greece, 13–14 September.

Sandholtz, W. & J. Zysman (1989) '1992: Recasting the European Bargain', *World Politics* 42 (1), pp. 95–128.

Sapir, A. (2006) 'Globalization and the Reform of European Social Models', *Journal of Common Market Studies* 44 (2), pp. 369–90.

Sapir, A. (2007) 'European Strategies for Growth' in M. Artis and F. Nixson (eds) *The Economics of the European Union* (Oxford: Oxford University Press), pp. 402–15.

Sapir, A., P. Aghion, G. Bertola, M. Hellwig, J. Pisani-Ferri, D. Rosati, J. Viñals, H. Wallace, M. Buti, M. Nava, P.M. Smith (2003) *An Agenda for a Growing Europe: Making the EU Economic System Deliver (Report of an Independent High Level Study Group established on the initiative of the President of the European Commission)* (Brussels: European Commission).

Sarotte, M.E. (2014) 'A Broken Promise? What the West Really Told Moscow About NATO Expansion', *Foreign Affairs*, September/October.

Scharpf, F.W. (2002) 'The European Social Model: Coping with the Challenges of Diversity', *Journal of Common Market Studies* 40 (4), pp. 645–70.

Scharpf, F.W. (2011) 'Monetary Union, Fiscal Crisis and the Preemption of Democracy', MPIfG Discussion Paper 11/11.

Schelkle, W. (2013) 'Monetary Integration in Crisis: How Well Do Existing Theories Explain the Predicament of EMU', *Transfer: European Review of Labour and Research* 19 (1), pp. 37–48.

Schimmelfennig, F. (2001) 'The Community Trap: Liberal Norms, Rhetorical Action and Eastern Enlargement of the European Union', *International Organization* 55 (1), pp. 47–80.

Schimmelfennig, F. (2015) 'Liberal Intergovernmentalism and the Euro Area Crisis', *Journal of European Public Policy* 22 (2), pp. 177–95.

Schimmelfennig, F. & U. Sedermeier (2002) *'Theorizing EU Enlargement: 'Research Focus, Hypotheses, and the State of Research''*, *Journal of European Public Policy* 9 (4), pp. 500–528.

Schlapentokh, D. (2014) 'Russia and Germany and the Chance for a Menage à Trois', *Russia in Global Affairs*, 23 September.

Schmid, J. (1998) 'Wandel der Konsensstrukturen' in G. Simonis (ed.) *Deutschland nach der Wende: Neue Politikstrukturen* (Opladen: Leske and Budrich), pp. 87–140.

Schmitter, P. (1972) 'Autonomy of Dependence as Regional Integration Outcomes: Central America', *Institute of International Studies*, University of California, Berkeley, Research Series 17.

Schmitter, P. (1997) 'The Emerging Europolity and Its Impact on National Systems of Production' in R. Hollingsworth and R. Boyer (eds) *Contemporary Capitalism: The Embeddedness of Institutions* (Cambridge: Cambridge University Press), pp. 395–430.

Schmitter, P. (2003) 'Neo-neofunctionalism' in A. Wiener and T. Diez (eds) *European Integration Theory* (Oxford: Oxford University Press), pp. 45–74.

Schmitter, P. (2005) 'Ernst B. Haas and the Legacy of Neofunctionalism', *Journal of European Public Policy* 12 (2), pp. 255–72.

Scholl, C. & A. Freyberg-Inan (2012) 'Hegemony's Dirty Tricks: Explaining Counter-Globalization's Weakness in Times of Neoliberal Crisis', *Globalizations* 10 (4), pp. 1–20.

Schumpeter, J. (1942) *Capitalism, Socialism, and Democracy*, 3rd edition (New York: Harper Collins).

Schwartz, H. (1994) *States versus Markets* (New York: St. Martin's Press).

Schwartz, H. (2009) *Subprime Nation: American Power, Global Capital and the Housing Bubble* (Ithaca, NY: Cornell University Press).

Schwartz, H. (2014) 'China, the United States, and the Battle for Jobs and Growth', in A. Cafruny and H. Schwartz (eds) *Exploring the Global Financial Crisis* (Boulder, CO: Lynne Rienner Publishers), pp. 107–124.

Schwartz, H. & L. Seabrooke (2008) 'Varieties of Residential Capitalism in the International Political Economy', *Comparative European Politics* 6, pp. 237–61.

Servan-Shreiber, J.-J. (1969) *The American Challenge* (Harmondsworth: Pelican).

Seabrooke, L. (2001) *US Power in International Finance; The Victory of Dividends* (Basingstoke: Palgrave Macmillan).

Sharma, R. (2012) 'Broken BRICS: Why the Rest Stopped Rising', *Foreign Affairs*, November–December, pp. 2–7.

Shields, S. (2014) *The International Political Economy of Transition: Neoliberal Hegemony and Eastern Central Europe's Transformation* (London: Routledge).

Shifronson, J. (2014) 'Put It In Writing: How the West Broke its Promise to Moscow', *Foreign Affairs*, 29 October.

Siles-Brugge, G. (2014) *Constructing European Union Trade Policy* (Basingstoke: Palgrave Macmillan).

Simonazzi, A. (2016) *How to Make Europe Prosper Again: The Challenges of Unemployment and Economic Stagnation* (Berlin: Heinrich Böll Stiftung).

Smith, A. (1776 [2008]) *The Wealth of Nations* (New York: Bantam Classics).

Soederberg, S. (2014) *Debtfare States and the Poverty Industry: Money, Discipline and the Surplus Population* (London: Routledge).

Soete, L. (2009) 'Some Reflection on Innovation Policy' in M. J. Rodrigues (ed.) *Europe, Globalisation and the Lisbon Agenda* (Cheltenham: Edward Elgar), pp. 38–49.

Sonne, W. (2014) 'The Culture of Restraint is No More: Germany is Ready for a Larger Role in the World', *AIGS*, 3 February, accessed at http://www.aicgs.org/issue/the-culture-of-restraint-is-no-more-germany-is-ready-for-a-larger-role-in-the-world/, accessed on 30.04.2016.

Soros, G. (2012) 'The Tragedy of the EU and How to Resolve It', *The New York Review of Books*, 27 September 2012, accessed at http://www.nybooks.com/articles/2012/09/27/tragedy-european-union-and-how-resolve-it/, accessed on 03.05.2016.

Soskice, D. (2006) 'Macroeconomics and Varieties of Capitalism' in B. Hancké, M. Rhones, and M. Thatcher (eds) *Beyond Varieties of Capitalism: Conflict, Complementarities and Contradicitons in the European Economy* (Oxford: Oxford University Press), pp. 89–121.

Spiegel International Edition (2013) '"Brutal power politics": Merkel's banking union under fire', accessed at http://www.spiegel.de/international/europe/criticism-in-brussels-german-bankingunion-policy-under-fire-a-939314.html, accessed on 30.04.2016.

Starrs, S. (2013) 'American Economic Power', *International Studies Quarterly* 57 (April), pp. 817–830.

Starrs, S. (2014) 'The Chimera of Global Convergence', *New Left Review* 87 (April–May), pp. 81–96.

Steinbok, D. (2012) 'The Eurozone Debt Crisis: Prospects for Europe, China and the United States', *American Foreign Policy Interests* 34 (1), pp. 34–42.

Steingart, G. (2014) 'The West on the Wrong Path', *Handelsblatt*, 8 August.

Stevens, C. (2006) 'The EU, Africa and Economic Partnership Agreements: Unintended Consequences of Policy Leverage', *The Journal of Modern African Studies* 44 (3), pp. 441–58.

Stevenson, D. (2011) 'From Balkan Conflict to Global Conflict: The Spread of the First World War', *Foreign Policy Analysis* 7 (2) (April).

Stockhammer, E. (2008) 'Some Stylized Facts on the Finance-Dominated Accumulation Regime', *Competition and Change* 12 (2), pp. 184–202.

Stockhammer, E. (2016) 'Neoliberal Growth Models, Monetary Union, and the Euro Crisis: A Post-Keynesian Perspective', *New Political Economy* 21 (4), pp. 365–79

Stockhammer, E., O. Onaran, & S. Ederer (2009) 'Functional Income Distribution and Aggregate Demand in the Euro Area', *Cambridge Journal of Economics* 33, pp. 139–59.

Stockhammer, E. & D. Sotiropoulos (2014) 'Rebalancing the Euro Area: The Costs of Internal Devaluation', *Review of Political Economy* 26 (2), pp. 210–33

Stoffäes, C. (1978) *La grande menace industrielle* (Paris: Calmann-Levy).

Stone Sweet, A. & W. Sanholtz (1998) 'Integration, Supranational Governance and the Institutionalization of the European Polity' in W. Sandholtz and A. Stone Sweet (eds) *European Integration and Supranational Governance* (Oxford: Oxford University Press), pp. 1–26.

Strøby-Jensen, C. (2000) 'Neofunctionalist Theories and the Development of European Social and Labour Market Policies', *Journal of Common Market Studies* 38 (1), pp. 71–92.

Storm, S. & C. W. M. Naastepad (2014) 'Wage-led or Profit-led Supply: Wages, Productivity and Investment', in M. Lavoie & E. Stockhammer (eds) *Wage-led Growth: An Equitable Strategy for Economic Recovery* (Basingstoke: Palgrave Macmillan), pp. 100–24.

Story, J. & I. Walter (1997) *Political Economy of Financial Integration in Europe: The Battle of the Systems* (Cambridge, MA: The MIT Press).

Strange, S. (1986) *Casino Capitalism* (Oxford: Basil Blackwell).

Streeck, W. (1994) 'Pay Restraint without Incomes Policy: Institutionalized Monetarism and Industrial Unionism in Germany' in R. Boyer and R. Doré (eds) *The Return to Incomes Policy* (London: Pinter), pp. 118–40.

Streeck, W. (1995) 'From Market Making to State Building? Reflections on the Political Economy of European Social Policy' in S. Leibfried and P. Pierson (eds) *European Social Policy: Between Fragmentation and Integration* (Washington, DC: The Brookings Institution), pp. 389–431.

Streeck, W. & P. Schmitter (1991) 'From National Corporatism to Transnational Pluralism: Organized Interests in the Single European Market', *Politics and Society* 19 (2), pp. 133–64.

Sturn, S. & T. van Treeck (2014) 'The Role of Income Inequality as a Cause of the Great Recession and Global Imbalances' in M . Lavoie and E. Stockhammer (eds) *Wage Led Growth: An Equitable Strategy for Economic Recovery* (Basingstoke: Palgrave Macmillan), pp. 125–52.

Summers, L. (2015) 'Time U.S. Leadership Woke Up to New Economic Era', *Financial Times*, 5 April.

SWP-GMF (2014) 'New Power New Responsibility: Elements of a German Foreign and Security Policy for a Changing World' (Washington and Berlin), accessed at https://www.swpberlin.org/fileadmin/contents/products/projekt_papiere/GermanForeignSecurityPolicy_SWP_GMF_2013.pdf.

Tagesspiegel (2014a) 'Nicht in unserem Namen', 5 December.

Tagesspiegel (2014b) 'Osteuropa Experten sehen Russland als Aggressor', 11 December.

Talani, L.S. (2003) 'The Political Economy of Exchange Rate Commitments: Italy, the United Kingdom and the Process of European Monetary Integration' in A. Cafruny and M. Ryner (eds) *A Ruined Fortress? Neoliberal Hegemony and Transformation in Europe* (Lanham, MD: Rowman and Littlefield), pp. 123–46.

Talani, L. S. (2014) *The Arab Spring in the Global Political Economy* (London: Palgrave).

Tass (2014) *Russian News Agency*, 16 December, accessed at http://tass.ru/en/russia/767282, accessed on 30.04.2016.

Taylor, A.J.P. (1980) *The Struggle for Mastery in Europe 1848–1918* (Oxford: Oxford University Press).

Techau, J. (2014) 'Transformative Change From Within: What if the EU Had Acted Strategically to the Arab Spring?', *German Council on Foreign Relations*, 25 February, accessed at https://ip-journal.dgap.org/en/blog/eye-europe/transformative-change-within, accessed on 30.04.2016.

Teschke, B. (2003) *The Myth of 1648: Class, Geopolitics and the Making of Modern International Relations* (London: Verso).

Telis, A. (2014) 'The Geopolitics of the TTIP and the TPP', *Adelphi Series* 54 (450), pp. 93–120.

Thatcher, M. (1988) 'Speech at the College of Europe (The Bruges Speech)', Bruges, 20 September.

Therborn, G. (1995) *European Modernity and Beyond: The Trajectory of European Societies 1945–2000* (London: SAGE).

Thompson, G. (2012) The Constitutionalization of the Corporate Governance Sphere? (Oxford: Oxford University Press).

Tidow, S (2003) 'The Emergence of European Employment Policy as a Transnational Political Arena', in H. Overbeek (ed.) *The Political Economy of European Employment* (London: Routledge), pp. 77–98

Titmuss, R. (1974) *Social Policy* (London: Allen and Unwin).

Toynbee, A. (1957) *A Study of History, Volume 2* (Oxford: Oxford University Press).

Tranholm-Mikkelsen, J. (1991) 'Neofunctionalism: Obstinate or Obsolete? A Reappraisal in Light of the New Dynamism of the EC', *Millennium: Journal of International Studies* 20 (1), pp. 1–22.

Trommer, S. (2013) *Transformation in Trade Politics: Participatory Trade Politics in Western Africa* (London: Routledge).

Tsoukalis, L. (1997) *The New European Economy Revisited* (Oxford: Oxford University Press).

UNCTAD (2012) *The BRICS Report 2012* (Delhi: Oxford University Press).

Ungerer, H. et al. (1990) *The European Monetary System: Developments and Perspectives* (Washington, DC: IMF Occasional Paper 73).

United States Treasury (2013) 'Report to the Congress on International Economic and Exchange Rate Policies', Washington, DC, October.

Usheva, F. (2011) 'Emigration from Bulgaria: 1989 until Today', Aarhus School of Business and Social Science.

Vachudova, M. (2009) 'Corruption and Compliance in the EU's Post-Communist Members and Candidate', *Journal of Common Market Studies* 47, pp. 43–62.

Van Apeldoorn, B. (2002) *Transnational Capitalism and the Struggle over European Integration* (London: Routledge).

Van Apeldoorn, B. (2009) 'A National Case Study of Embedded Neoliberalism and Its Limits: The Dutch Political Economy and the "No" to the European Constitution' in B. van Apeldoorn, J. Drahokoupil, and L. Horn (eds) *Contradictions and Limits of Neoliberal European Governance: From Lisbon to Lisbon* (Basingstoke: Palgrave Macmillan), pp. 211–31.

Van Apeldoorn, B. (2014) 'The European Capitalist Class and the Crisis of its Hegemonic Project', in L. Panitch, G. Albo & V. Chibber (eds) *The Socialist Register 2014* (London: Merlin Press), pp. 189–206.

Van Apeldoorn, B. and S. Hager (2010) 'The Social Purpose of New Governance: Lisbon and the Limits to Legitimacy', *Journal of International Relations and Development* 13 (3), pp. 209–38.

Van der Pijl, K. (1978) *Een amerikaans plan voor Europa* (Amsterdam: SUA).

Van der Pijl, K. (1984) *The Making of an Atlantic Ruling Class* (London: Verso).

Van der Pijl, K. (1996) *Vordenker der Weltpolitik* (Opladen: Leske and Budrich)

Van der Pijl, K. (1997a) 'The History of Class Struggle from Original Accumulation to Neoliberalism', *Monthly Review* 49 (1), pp. 28–44.

Van der Pijl, K. (1997b) 'Atlantic Rivalries and the Collapse of the USSR', in S. Gill (ed.) *Globalization, Democratization and Multilateralism* (London: Macmillan), pp. 195–218.

Van der Pijl, K. (1998) *Transnational Classes and International Relations* (London: Routledge).

Van der Pijl, K. (2006) *Global Rivalries: From the Cold War to Iraq* (London: Pluto Press).

Van der Pijl, K., O. Holman, and O. Raviv (2011) 'The Resurgence of German Capital in Europe: EU Integration and the Restructuring of Atlantic Networks of Interlocking Directorates after 1991', *Review of International Political Economy* 18 (3), pp. 384–408.

Van Kersbergen, K. (1995) *Social Capitalism: Christian Democracy and the Welfare State in Europe* (London: Routledge).

Varble, D. (2003) *The Suez Crisis, 1956* (London: Osprey).

Varoufakis, Y. (2013) 'Europe Needs a Hegemonic Germany' Zed Books blog, accessed at http://zed-books.blogspot.com/2013/02/yanis-varoufakis-europe, accessed on 30.04.2016.

Varoufakis, Y., J. Halevi, and N. Theokarakis (2011) *Modern Political Economics: Making Sense of the Post-2008 World* (New York: Routledge).

Varoufakis, Y. (2011) *The Global Minotaur: America, Europe, and the Future of the Global Economy* (London: Zed Books).

Verdun, A. (2015) 'A Historical Institutionalist Explanation of the EU's Responses to the Euro Area Financial Crisis', *Journal of European Public Policy* 22 (2), pp. 219–37.

Viner, J. (1950 [1983]) *The Customs Union Issue* (New York: Garland).

Vitols, S. (2004) 'Negotiated Shareholder Value: The German Variant of an Anglo-American Practice', *Competition and Change* 8 (4), pp. 357–74.

Waever, O. (1997) 'Imperial Metaphors: Emerging Analogies to Pre-Nation-State Imperial systems' in O. Tunander, P. Baev, and V. I. Einagel (eds) *Geopolitics in Post-Wall Europe: Security, Territory, and Identity* (London: Sage), pp. 59–93.

Wallerstein, I. (2014) 'The Geopolitics of Ukraine's Schism: A Potential Alliance of France, Germany, and Russia Haunts U.S. Strategists', Aljazeera America, 15 February, accessed at http://america.aljazeera.com/opinions/2014/2/ukraine-nuland-europeyanukovychputin.html, accessed on 30.04.2016.

Walters, W. & J.E. Haahr (2005) *Governing Europe: Discourse, Governmentality and European Integration* (London: Routledge).

Waltz, K. (1979) *Theory of International Politics* (New York: McGraw Hill).

Watson, M. (2001) 'Embedding the 'New Economy' in Europe: A Study of the Institutional Specificities of Knowledge-Based Growth', *Economy and Society* 30 (4), pp. 504–23.

Weber, M. (1895 [1994]) 'The Nation State and Economic Policy' in P. Lassman and R. Speirs (eds) *Weber: Political Writings* (Cambridge: Cambridge University Press), pp. 1–28.

Weeks, J. (2014) 'Euro Crises and Euro Scams: Trade not Debt and Deficits Tell the Tale', *Review of Political Economy* 26 (2), pp. 171–89.

Welz, C. (2008) *The European Social Dialogue under Articles 138 and 139 of the EC Treaty: Actors, Processes, Outcomes* (Alphen aan den Rijn: Kluwer Law International).

Wiener, A. (2006) *'Soft Institutions' in von Bogdandy*, A. and J. Bast (eds) *Principles of European Constitutional Law*, Oxford: Hart Publishing, pp. 419-449.

Wilensky, H. (1974) *The Welfare State and Equality: Structural and Ideological Roots of Public Expenditure* (Berkeley, CA: University of California Press).

Williams, W.A. (2009) *The Tragedy of American Diplomacy, 50th anniversary edition* (New York: Norton).

Wincott, D. (1995) 'Institutional Interaction and European Integration: Towards an Everyday Critique of Liberal Intergovernmentalism', *Journal of Common Market Studies* 33 (4), pp. 597–609.

Wincott, D. (2003) 'Beyond Social Regulation? New Instruments and/or A New Agenda for Social Policy at Lisbon?', *Public Administration* 81 (3), pp. 533–53.

Wöhl, S. (2011) 'Gender Mainstreaming in European Employment Policies', *Critical Policy Studies* 5 (1), pp. 32–46.

Wood, E.M. (2002) 'Global Capital, National States' in M. Rupert and H.Smith (eds) *Historical Materialism and Globalization* (London: Routledge).

Wolf, M. (2014) 'Europe's Lonely and Reluctant Hegemon', *Financial Times*, 9 December.

Young, B. (2003) 'Economic and Monetary Union, Employment and Gender Politics: A Feminist Constructivist Analysis of Neo-liberal Labour Market Restructuring in Europe' in H. Overbeek (ed.) *The Political Economy of European Employment* (London: Routledge), pp. 99–112.

Young, B. (2011) 'Germany's Puzzling Response to the Eurozone Crisis: The Obstinate Defence of Ordnungspolitik', *EUSA Review* 24 (3), pp. 5–6

Yurchenko, Y. (2012) '"Black Holes" in the Political Economy of Ukraine: The Neoliberalization of Europe's "Wild East"', *Debatte: Journal of Contemporary Central and Eastern Europe* 20 (2), pp. 125–49.

Zeitonline (2012) 'Die Verschworung gegen Brandt' 49 (2 December).

Ziebura, G. (1982) 'Internationalization of Capital, International Division of Labour, and the Role of the European Community', *Journal of Common Market Studies* 21 (2), pp. 127–48.

Zielonka, J. (2006) *Europe as Empire: The Nature of the Enlarged European Union* (Oxford: Open University Press).

Zelikow, P. and Rice, C. (1995) *Germany Unified and Europe Transformed: A Study in Statecraft* (Cambridge: Harvard University Press).

Ziltener, P. (1999) *Strukturwander der europäischen Integration* (Münster: Westfälisches Dampfboot).

Zürn, M. & J. Checkel (2005) 'Getting Socialized to Build Bridges: Constructivism and Rationalism, Europe and the Nation State', *International Organization* 59 (4), pp. 1045–79.

Index

Printed in Great Britain
by Amazon

56827978R00163